MW00709687

Dirty Deals?

Dirty Deals?

An Encyclopedia of Lobbying, Political Influence, and Corruption

Volume 1: Essays

AMY HANDLIN, EDITOR

ABC-CLIO

Santa Barbara, California • Denver, Colorado • Oxford, England

Library of Congress Cataloging-in-Publication Data

Dirty deals? : an encyclopedia of lobbying, political influence, and corruption / Amy Handlin, editor.
   pages cm
   Includes index.
   ISBN 978-1-61069-245-8 (hardcopy : alk. paper) —
ISBN 978-1-61069-246-5 (ebook)
1. Lobbying—United States—Encyclopedias.   2. Pressure groups—
United States—Encyclopedias.   3. Political corruption—United States—
Encyclopedias.   I. Handlin, Amy H., 1956–, editor.
   JK1118.D64   2014
   324'.4097303—dc23   2014007976

ISBN: 978-1-61069-245-8
EISBN: 978-1-61069-246-5

18   17   16   15   14   1   2   3   4   5

This book is also available on the World Wide Web as an eBook.
Visit www.abc-clio.com for details.

ABC-CLIO, LLC
130 Cremona Drive, P.O. Box 1911
Santa Barbara, California 93116-1911

This book is printed on acid-free paper ∞

Manufactured in the United States of America

Contents

VOLUME 3: PRIMARY DOCUMENTS

Preface

Dirty Deals: An Encyclopedia of Lobbying, Political Influence, and Corruption has been designed as an integrated educational package, for students, researchers, and anyone interested in the topics of lobbying, political influence, and political corruption. However, each of the three volumes takes a distinctive approach and can stand alone as a source of information, insights, and resources.

Volume 1 begins with a brief introduction to lobbying, political influence, and corruption, with a focus on the issues and questions most important to citizens in the 21st century. At the core of this volume are essays written by scholars and lawyers, some offering well-informed opinion and others that are historical or factual in nature. The essays cover the following subtopics:

- The lobbying business and the world of citizen advocacy, including tools, techniques, and challenges.
- The major sources of political influence, especially the roles of money and media.
- The roots of corruption, and efforts to promote ethical choices in government.

Volume 2 is an A–Z compendium of entries offering essential background information on approximately 200 subjects, including people, events, laws, organizations, and more. There is also a timeline of key events, beginning in 1817. The entry subjects were chosen based on an extensive review of media, websites, textbooks, monographs, and government documents. The entries are cross-referenced and include a bibliography of additional print and electronic information resources.

Volume 3 is a collection of original resources. It has the following three parts:

- Part I: Key federal laws related to lobbying, political influence, and corruption.
- Part II: Major U.S. Supreme Court decisions related to lobbying, political influence, and corruption.
- Part III: Selected documents and data, including classic and modern texts in addition to sets of tables called "Lobbying by the Numbers" and "Corruption by the Numbers."

Each resource is preceded by an Overview, which places it in historical/political context and highlights its key contributions to the field. Except for a minority of documents brief enough to reproduce in full, excerpts are provided. Some laws and Supreme Court decisions are particularly lengthy and complex. These are accompanied by two types of excerpts: a Basic Excerpt captures those points best known or generally considered most influential, and a Supplemental Excerpt offers additional detail for the interested reader.

The volumes also include a general bibliography and a detailed subject index providing more detailed access to the information in the essays and short entries.

Introduction

The role of lobbying and the exercise of political influence in America have long been criticized by those who believe the voices of ordinary citizens are inevitably drowned out by special interests represented by hired advocates, or by their outsize campaign checks. Even before the founding of the Republic, James Madison expressed the concern that special interest influence could become "adverse to the rights of other citizens [as well as] the permanent and aggregate interests of the community" (Publius 1787). There is also a long, sordid history of lobbying scandals and of corruption associated with political campaign contributions. From the Credit Mobilier affair in the 19th century to the conviction of Jack Abramoff in 2006, bad actors have served to reinforce the public image of lobbyists and donors as greedy, unethical opportunists. But the system can and does further the larger goals of American democracy. Abuses and crimes notwithstanding, it has continually evolved to protect the public interest within a framework of free speech and private enterprise.

Suspicion of lobbying professionals is encouraged by the fact that their business is largely conducted behind closed doors, where neither the media nor the voters can witness what is actually said, done, exchanged, or promised. Likewise, the eye-popping amounts spent by corporate advocates underscore the potential to make big profits by influencing policy on Capitol Hill. For example, in 2010 the U.S. Chamber of Commerce's federal and state lobbying expenditures exceeded $130 million (OpenSecretblog 2011). Often described as the single most active advocacy group on Capitol Hill, the Chamber employs nearly 200 lobbyists (OpenSecretblog 2011).

The six- or seven-figure political contributions now made routinely by Wall Street titans have also become a popular target. These hefty checks may be written to Republicans, Democrats, or both, leading to accusations that both parties pander to the finance industry. In a typical case, prominent hedge fund manager Steven Cohen, together with his wife and employees, donated $1.5 million to Republicans during the congressional election of 2010—after giving over $500,000 to Democrat candidates and groups two years earlier. Another hedge fund chief, Robert Mercer, steered $527,000 to Democrats and $782,000 to Republicans in 2010 (Mullens et al. 2011).

But lobbying prowess is not limited to businesses or the super-rich. Thousands of organizations, often called Public Interest Groups (PIGs), advocate forcefully—and often successfully—on behalf of Americans with specific needs or beliefs. For example, various health-related advocacy groups maintain a significant presence in Washington. Taken together, the American Cancer Society, American Heart

Association, and American Diabetes Association spent over $5 million on federal lobbying in 2011. The American Association of Retired Persons spent nearly $12.5 million (OpenSecrets.org 2011). During the decade 1990–2010, campaign contributions made by the environmental protection groups Sierra Club and Natural Resources Defense Council dwarfed those of some of the their key corporate opponents, like the American Petroleum Institute (OpenSecrets.org, Lobbying Industry Profile 2011). Nor are business advocates always successful in the face of citizen pushback. On one particularly high-profile issue, grassroots support for clean, renewable energy helped ensure the passage of groundbreaking climate protection legislation in 2009, despite persistent and heavily funded corporate opposition.

So it would be overly simplistic—indeed, plain wrong—to portray lobbying and campaign contributions as necessarily corrupting or harmful to democracy. The First Amendment to the U.S. Constitution guarantees every American the right to free speech and "to petition the Government for redress of grievance." Restrictions placed on lobbying, and on other legal avenues of political influence, always have the potential to infringe on these fundamental rights, affecting not just wealthy corporate chieftains but Americans from all walks of life.

Moreover, the ebb and flow of politics means that over time, there are no guaranteed winners or losers in Washington. Instead, there are ever-changing challenges and opportunities that underscore the value of lobbying by those on different sides of virtually every contemporary debate.

A case in point is the battle over the Healthy, Hunger-Free Kids Act (HHFKA), passed by Congress and signed by President Obama in December 2010. The law gave the U.S. Department of Agriculture sweeping new powers to regulate the nutritional content of food available anywhere on the premises of a school, including vending machines and school stores. Promoted as a necessary response to rising childhood obesity, it was a culmination of years of lobbying by public health groups, nutrition experts, and advocates for low-income children whose main daily meal is an in-school, subsidized lunch. However, when the U.S. Department of Agriculture (USDA) issued its draft regulations in January 2011, opposition materialized from three main quarters. Makers of processed foods argued that the changes in fat and sodium content went too far too fast; farm interests took aim at proposed limits on starchy vegetables like potatoes; and advocates for large urban school districts worried about the added costs of preparing fresher meals. After months of debate, Congress directed the Agriculture Department to reconsider its rules and revise the timeframe for meeting them (Nixon 2011; HealthDay 2011).

Disappointed supporters of the HHFKA were quick to decry the lobbying expenditures of food companies, which spent over $5.6 million to defeat the USDA proposal. "It's unfortunate that the food industry is putting profits before the health of children," said one prominent nutritionist (quoted in Nixon 2011). Others attacked what they saw as shortsightedness on the part of poor cities with cash-strapped schools, or parochialism from farm-state lawmakers who pushed back against the potato limits.

But it is important to recognize this key point: after vigorous lobbying, both sides came away with more than they had at the start of the debate. Before 2010, there was little, if any, government oversight of food served in schools. The passage of HHFKA brought attention to long-neglected concerns of child nutritionists and public health officials and ensured some ongoing scrutiny of school meals. On the other side, the food industry got a reprieve from the requirement to immediately reformulate its products, as well as an opportunity to sell items tailored to the new standards. The farm lobby and urban school districts won adjustments that addressed their financial concerns. It is true that no one got exactly what they wanted. But on balance, the American public benefited from a policy change while the various economic interests were adequately protected.

Redeeming features notwithstanding, few would argue that lobbying and other forms of political influence should be entirely unfettered. History suggests that certain activities and expenditures need to be reined in, if only to reassure citizens that their government is not for sale and their representatives cannot be unduly pressured by slick operators. Such restrictions have always been controversial. But they seem, at least, to reflect a modern consensus around the value of transparency and of reasonable limits on the flow of money to political candidates. These principles have been built into the current system, albeit imperfectly, and offer a platform for continuous improvement.

Lobbying Restrictions

Lobbyists were required to register with the clerk of the U.S. House of Representatives as early as 1876. But neither registration nor reports of any kind were mandated by federal law until the 1930s, when a scandal erupted around a congressional proposal to break up public utility holding companies. The industry orchestrated a massive lobbying campaign against the bill—while hiding its role in the effort. Powerful lawmakers were angered not only by this deception but also by contemporaneous lobbying excesses of shipping firms seeking public funds. In response, Congress enacted two laws in 1935 and 1936 that forced lobbyists for those interests to file reports of their activities with the federal government (Katel 2005).

While limited to just two industries and lacking in strong enforcement provisions, this early legislation called attention to the absence of transparency and set a precedent for future lobbying restrictions. In 1938, the Foreign Agents Registration Act required registration by lobbyists representing other governments or overseas organizations. The far broader Federal Regulation of Lobbying Act of 1946 (FRLA) provided for financial reporting and registration by any individual or group hired to influence Congress.

However, the 1946 law did not apply to those who lobbied the executive branch, the courts, or federal regulatory agencies. Due to this and other shortcomings of the FRLA, only about 20 percent of all Washington lobbyists were actually registered in 1994, when an anti-incumbent tide swept many new, reform-minded legislators into office. In 1995, Congress took another stab at transparency: the Lobbying Disclosure Act provided for registration by anyone paid to lobby lawmakers, congressional staff, and policymakers in the executive branch. The law also set a new standard for lobbying reports, requiring semiannual disclosure of specific lobbyists' contacts and what issues they were paid to push. At the same time, the House and Senate enacted significant restrictions on lobbyist-funded gifts, meals, and trips (Hrebenar and Morgan 2009).

So the stage was set for congressional response to the lobbying scandals of 2005–2006. Among the highest-profile and most far-reaching in U.S. history, the cases ended in jail time for two House members and one of Washington's most prominent lobbyists, as well as significant embarrassment for congressional leadership and for the institution itself. Among the lowlights of the period, former representative Randy "Duke" Cunningham was convicted of accepting over $2.4 million in bribes from lobbyists in return for influencing defense contracts. His colleague, former representative William Jefferson, hid cash payoffs of $90,000 in his freezer. Star lobbyist Jack Abramoff was found to have padded bills, lied to clients, misrepresented expenditures, and engaged in shady tactics like inventing phony front groups. Around the same time, there were media revelations that 200 organizations had paid over $20 million for congressional trips without registering as lobbyists (Allen 2005; Robb 2003; Schmidt 2004; Smith 2005).

The most recent set of lobbying restrictions, codified in the Honest Leadership and Open Government Act of 2007, was clearly designed to prevent the crimes and abuses of 2005–2006. But it was very much in keeping with the general approach of earlier reforms, emphasizing increased transparency along with curtailment of questionable lobbying activities. For example, lobbyists must now file reports of their expenditures twice as often as in the past, and indicate when they have "bundled," or collected, numerous small political contributions. They are required to disclose donations to groups or causes only marginally associated with politics, like presidential libraries or inaugural committees. The law also took aim at the "revolving door" of former government officials who decide to sell their influence to the private sector, imposing waiting periods and bans on when and whom they can be hired to lobby.

Campaign Finance Restrictions

The 19th-century U.S. senator Marcus Hanna famously remarked, "There are two important things in politics. The first is money, and I can't remember what the second one is" (quoted in Crossen, 2004). His words have rung true throughout American history, which is replete with efforts to balance the right of private donors to support candidates of their choice against the public's right to unbiased representation.

Political campaigns have always cost money, and America has never instituted fully taxpayer-funded elections. So over the decades, politicians have devised various fund-raising vehicles in keeping with the norms and customs of their time. In the 18th century, for example, the practice of awarding government jobs in return for political support raised no eyebrows. It was generally accepted that public jobholders would pay a fixed portion of their salaries, called an assessment, to the political party that had sponsored their employment (Brickner and Mueller 2008).

But in 1883, assessments were prohibited in response to revelations of graft and diversion of tax revenue during the administration of Ulysses S. Grant. This change led politicians to turn for money to corporations and other interests with deep pockets (Ansolabehere et al. 2001). As corporate funds poured into the coffers of both major parties, campaign spending rapidly escalated and it became commonplace for businessmen to expect contracts and special treatment as a quid pro quo. By 1907, so many questions had been raised about favoritism and corruption that Congress was forced to restrain corporate campaign contributions (Corrado 2005). The Tillman Act forbade corporations from donating directly to candidates for federal office, though they could continue funding state and local campaigns.

In 1910, reformers began calling attention to the lack of transparency in the system; without disclosure, it was impossible to determine who was giving money to which party or candidate. The Federal Corrupt Practices Act (FCPA) established a new standard in campaign finance law by requiring all federal campaign committees to report their receipts and disbursements. While other parts of the FCPA were eventually invalidated by the Supreme Court, its transparency provisions stood—and became a cornerstone of future regulation (Brickner and Mueller 2008).

Modern times have seen the proliferation of campaign fund-raising vehicles, like political action committees, specifically designed to be exempt from most regulation (Corrado 2005). After the Watergate scandal, there were two more attempts to widen the scope of campaign finance rules; Congress passed the Federal Election Campaign Act in 1974 (FECA) and the Bipartisan Campaign Reform Act in 2002 (BCRA). While the primary targets and mechanisms of these laws were significantly different, they shared the goals of preventing corruption and boosting citizen confidence in the electoral system. FECA capped individual campaign contributions and expanded disclosure requirements. BCRA raised the ceiling on "hard money"—direct donations to candidates—while banning "soft money," funds contributed to political parties for activities like getting out the vote or staging nominating conventions. BCRA also clamped down on independent expenditures, like ads about specific issues or policies sponsored by corporations, unions, or wealthy individuals.

Recent court challenges upended the campaign finance laws yet again. In particular, BCRA's limits on independent expenditures were found unconstitutional in the 2011 *Citizens United v. Federal Election Commission* decision, opening a new door for virtually unlimited donations to so-called Super PACs (OpenSecrets.org, Super PACs 2012). These groups may advertise and otherwise support any federal candidate, as long as their donors are disclosed and their activities are not coordinated with the candidate's official campaign.

As Justices John Paul Stevens and Sandra Day O'Connor famously observed, "Money, like water, will always find an outlet." The same can be said for lobbying and other forms of political influence. Even as issues and advocates change, the American system continues to respond to them—perhaps not with uniform speed or effectiveness, but with the goal of achieving fairness and access for all.

Outlook for the Future

Time will tell whether or not the American public will demand another round of reforms to curtail the impact of Super PACs. In the meantime, it is important to note a newer arena of activity: state and local governments. Under the Constitution, federal officials have little jurisdiction over lobbying and elections outside of Washington. So, to reassure their own constituents, states have become increasingly aggressive in regulating lobbyists—in fact, all 50 states have lobbying registration and reporting requirements (National Conference of State Legislatures 2012c)—and mandating disclosure of receipts and expenditures from candidates, campaign committees, and political parties. Despite regional differences in specific oversight and enforcement mechanisms, 46 states now limit the amount and/or source of campaign contributions. It is likely that these efforts will continue, along with initiatives aimed at prohibiting lobbyist-funded gifts and slowing the "revolving door" at the state level (National Conference of State Legislatures 2011b).

However, 24 states have also been forced to come to grips with *Citizens United*. Before the decision, one of these states banned union political activity, 9 banned corporate political activity, and 14 banned political activity by both unions and corporations. Many legislatures must now consider repealing these bans; at a minimum, states will almost certainly abandon any serious attempt to enforce such restrictions.

Still, state reformers remain active. Since *Citizens United,* Arizona, South Dakota, Alaska, Colorado, Connecticut, Minnesota, North Carolina, and West Virginia have enacted laws that permit corporate and union independent expenditures but require the organizations to register before spending above a threshold amount. Massachusetts began to require a disclaimer statement on political advertisements paid for by corporations. In Iowa, the leadership body of a corporation must now approve political expenditures before they are made and on an annual basis thereafter (National Conference of State Legislatures 2011a). According to some experts, states have the latitude to adopt disclosure laws more far-reaching than federal statutes; for example, states could regulate electioneering communications that appear in print as well as in broadcast media (Torres-Spelliscy 2011).

Since the 2007 Honest Leadership and Open Government Act, no additional lobbying or ethics reforms have passed on Capitol Hill. But on this front too, states have been busy creating new oversight mechanisms and harsher punishments for those who cheat, deceive, or rob the taxpayers. In particular, many state laws have taken aim at conflicts of interest and at gift-giving by lobbyists.

For example, dual office-holding—the practice of holding two elected offices at the same time—is now recognized in most states as a wellspring of dubious decision making. Which master is being served at what time? When interests clash, whose win out? The vast majority of states now ban state lawmakers from holding other state offices; about half prohibit legislators from holding county or municipal offices, and from drawing two government paychecks. There are also limits on state officeholders seeking government contracts, lobbying on behalf of private interests, or representing private clients before public bodies (National Conference of State Legislatures 2012a).

While restrictions on gifts from lobbyists to state officials are highly inconsistent, there is a growing consensus on the need for rules to reassure the public that state government is not for sale. Most states with gift restrictions allow the giving of some items (or services) but limit them to a low threshold value; some legislatures have extended their lobbyist gift restrictions to all public officials, at every level and in every government sector in the state (National Conference of State Legislatures 2012b).

Another wild card is the future effect of social media on political influence. Most lobbyists have learned to harness the power of these tools in communicating with officials, while politicians now use them routinely to broaden their donor bases. More important, however, is the fact that Facebook, Twitter, and other interactive mechanisms are magnifying the lobbying power of groups and individuals who lack the resources to hire professional advocates or make significant campaign contributions.

Of course, the novelty of such tools will wear off. But the impact made by social media–driven movements like the Tea Party on the right or Occupy Wall Street on the left will not soon be forgotten. At a minimum, these grassroots efforts serve as proof that ordinary Americans intend to play a pivotal role in shaping the future of democracy.

References

Allen, Mike. (2005, May 5). "House GOP to Consider Tougher Lobbying Rules." *Washington Post*: A10.

Ansolabehere, Stephen, et al. (2001). Corruption and the Growth of Campaign Spending. In Gerald C. Lubenow, ed., *A User's Guide to Campaign Finance Reform*. Lanham, MD: Rowman and Littlefield, pp. 25–46.

Brickner, Benjamin, and Naomi Mueller. (2008). *Clean Elections: Public Financing in Six States*. New Brunswick, NJ: Eagleton Institute of Politics, Rutgers University.

Corrado, Anthony. (2005). Money and Politics: A History of Campaign Finance Law. In Anthony Corrado, et al. eds. *The New Campaign Finance Sourcebook*. Washington, DC: Brookings Institution Press.

Crossen, Cynthia. (2004, Sept.). "Dollar Mark": The Man Who Put the Money in Presidential Campaigns. *Wall Street Journal* Classroom Edition. Accessed July 27, 2013. http://www.wsjclassroomedition.com/archive/04sep/poli_politics.htm.

HealthDay, US News and World Report. (2011, May 13). "US Pushes School Cafeterias Toward Healthier Offerings." Accessed July 27, 2013. http://www.health.usnews.com/health-news/managing-your-healthcare/policy/articles/2011/05/.

Hrebenar, Ronald J., and Bryson B. Morgan. (2009). *Lobbying in America: A Reference Handbook*. Santa Barbara, CA: ABC-CLIO eBook Collection.

Katel, Peter. (2005, July 22). "Lobbying Boom." *The CQ Researcher* 15, no. 26: 613–636.

Mullins, Brody, Susan Pulliam, and Steve Eder. (2011, April 26). "Financiers Switch to GOP." *Wall Street Journal*. Accessed July 27, 2013. http://www.onlinewsj.com/article/SB10001424052748703461504576231121265117538.html.

National Conference of State Legislatures. (2011a, Jan. 4). "Life after *Citizens United*." Accessed July 27, 2013. http://www.ncsl.org/legislatures-elections/elections/citizens-united-and-the-states.aspx.

National Conference of State Legislatures. (2011b, Oct. 3). "Campaign Finance Reform: An Overview." Accessed July 27, 2013. http://www.ncsl.org/default/aspx?tabid=16603.

National Conference of State Legislatures. (2012a). "Conflict of Interest Overview." Accessed July 27, 2013. http://www.ncsl.org/legislatures-election/ethicshome/conflict-of-interest-overview.aspx.

National Conference of State Legislatures. (2012b). "Gifts." Accessed July 27, 2013. http://www.ncsl.org/legislatures-election/ethicshome/ethics-gifts.aspx.

National Conference of State Legislatures. (2012c). "Lobbyist Regulation." Accessed July 27, 2013. http://www.ncsl.org/legislatures-elections.aspx?tabs=1116,84,211.

Nixon, Ron. (2011, Nov. 1). "School Lunch Proposals Set Off a Dispute." *New York Times.* Accessed July 27, 2013. http://www.nytimes.com/2011/11/02/us/school-lunch-proposals-set-off-a-dispute.html?_r.

OpenSecretblog, Center for Responsive Politics (2011, Sept. 9). "The Politics of Ozone Regulation." Accessed July 27, 2013. http://www.opensecrets.org/news/2011/09/the-politics-of-ozone-regulation.html.

OpenSecrets.org. (2012). "Super PACs." Accessed July 27, 2013. http://www.opensecrets.org/pacs/superpacs/php?cycle=2012.

OpenSecrets.org, Lobbying Industry Profile. (2011). Accessed July 27, 2013. http://www.opensecrets.org/lobby/indusclient.php?id=Q09&year=2011.

Publius (James Madison). *The Federalist*, No. 10 (1787).

Robb, Julia. (2003, Sept. 21). "Millions Misspent?" *Daily Town Talk*: A15.

Schmidt, Susan. (2004, Feb. 22). "A Jackpot from Indian Gaming Tribes." *Washington Post*: A1.

Smith, Jeffrey (2005, April 24). "DeLay Airfare Was Charged to Lobbyist's Credit Card." *Washington Post*: A1.

Torres-Spelliscy, C. (2011, March 1). "Transparent Elections after Citizens United." Brennan Center for Justice at New York University School of Law. Accessed July 27, 2013. http://www.brennancenter.org/content/resource/transparent_elections_after_citizens_united/.

Chronology

1817: Bonus Bill vetoed

Proposed by Congressman John Calhoun of South Carolina, this bill would have used the earnings bonus from the Second Bank of the United States to fund construction of highways and canals across the nation. It was vetoed by President James Madison, who argued that Congress lacked constitutional authority to direct spending to specific, local "internal improvements." However, the Bonus Bill is seen as setting a precedent for earmarking in federal appropriation and budget bills.

1817: American Colonization Society founded

The founding of the American Colonization Society (ACS) marked the debut of the abolitionist movement as a national advocacy organization. Its cause—to free all slaves in the United States, compensate their owners, and transport the freed slaves to Africa—was later taken up by the American Anti-Slavery Society, founded by Lloyd Garrison in 1833. Abolitionism eventually became the most successful reform movement in American history.

1826: American Temperance Society established

Originally formed to promote "temperance," the American Temperance Society (ATS) grew quickly and soon set the more ambitious goal of prohibiting alcohol consumption. In 1893, the Anti-Saloon League became the lobbying arm for the movement; its efforts culminated in the passage of the Eighteenth Amendment to the Constitution, banning the manufacture, sale, import, and export of liquor in the United States. The failure of prohibition sparked a counter movement, resulting in repeal of the Eighteenth Amendment by the Twenty-First Amendment in 1933.

1838: New York Customs House scandal erupts

Until the adoption of a federal income tax in 1913, the federal government relied heavily on import duties to fund its operations. As this revenue stream steadily increased during the early 1800s, the job of chief customs collector—especially in the busy ports of New York, Boston, and Philadelphia—became a highly sought-after patronage position. In 1938, New York customs collector Samuel Swartwout fled to England with over $1 million in stolen funds. While it took several more decades for Congress to pass serious reforms of the patronage system, the Swartwout scandal succeeded in bringing this type of corruption into the open.

1847: American Medical Association founded

The American Medical Association was created to promote public health as well as to advance the interests of physicians and their patients. It has become the most influential health care lobbying group in the United States.

1852: Galphin Claim paid

After many years of seeking compensation for what they claimed had been illegal seizure of their land by two Native American tribes, the Galphin family hired attorney George Crawford to represent their interests before the U.S. Treasury Department. In 1849, Crawford became the secretary of war; he then intervened with the secretary of the treasury and attorney general to ensure payment for the Galphins. Critics of the $191,000 payment coined the term "Galphinism" to describe the improper involvement of federal officials in prosecuting a claim against the United States. A year later, Congress passed a law prohibiting officials from being paid for assisting private claimants, though they could still offer uncompensated help.

1860: Covode investigation begins

In the first half of the 19th century, most big city newspapers were openly aligned with political parties and candidates. When the Democrats controlled Congress during the Buchanan presidency in the 1850s, they frequently steered government printing contracts to friends and contributors to the Democratic Party. However, Republicans became the majority party after the 1858 midterm elections. Congressman John Covode of Pennsylvania then launched an investigation into political corruption within the Buchanan administration. He uncovered not only the trading of printing contracts for party contributions but also evidence that Buchanan's secretary of war improperly awarded military procurement contracts to political allies.

1862: Secretary of War Simon Cameron censured

Simon Cameron was appointed secretary of war by President Lincoln in 1861. By the end of the first year of the Civil War, it became clear that the Union Army's fighting ability was compromised by inferior supplies. After revelations that Cameron's War Department had vastly overpaid for spoiled food and defective equipment—and steered multiple procurement contracts to political supporters—Congress censured him and Lincoln removed him from office.

1867: National Grange founded

In the weak economy of the time, the Grange quickly became a strong advocacy group for farmers and the agricultural community. While its reach was national, most of its lobbying was focused on state governments.

1869: National Women's Suffrage Association formed

After the first women's rights convention was held in 1848 at Seneca Falls, New York, leaders formed the National Women's Suffrage Association and another organization, the American Woman Suffrage Association. The lobbying efforts of these groups culminated in the Nineteenth Amendment to the Constitution, which guaranteed women the right to vote after it was ratified in 1920.

1871: National Rifle Association founded

The National rifle Association (NRA) was established by Union Army veterans concerned about solders' poor shooting during the Civil War. Arguing that gun ownership is a civil right, it grew in part by emphasizing gun training and safety. Today the NRA is generally recognized as one of the most politically aggressive and potent lobbying groups on both the federal and state levels.

1872: Credit Mobilier controversy erupts

Credit Mobilier was a company established by the Union Pacific Railroad to construct part of its line originating in Omaha, Nebraska. Between 1867 and 1868, its stock was made available to members of Congress at prices far below those available to the public. Following a newspaper expose, some of the purchasers came under fire for alleged insider trading in these shares. Credit Mobilier was accused of facilitating the trades in order to head off a congressional investigation into construction costs for the transcontinental railroad. In 1873, Representatives Oakes Ames of Massachusetts and James Brooks of New York were censured for their roles in the scandal.

1876: Secretary of War William Belknap resigns

Belknap stood accused of accepting kickbacks in return for granting the rights to operate trading posts in the West. His resignation was accepted by President Ulysses S. Grant in anticipation of Congress beginning impeachment proceedings.

1881: American Federation of Labor established

The American Federation of Labor (AFL) brought together an array of previously unaffiliated unions, organizing them by crafts. To represent industrial workers, the Committee for Industrial Organizations (CIO) formed within the AFL but eventually left its parent group. In 1955, the AFL and CIO merged to become the premier labor lobbying organization in the United States.

1883: Pendleton Act signed into law

After years of ignoring the problem of corruption-ridden patronage appointments, Congress was finally persuaded to lay the foundations for a federal hiring system based on merit. The independent Civil Service Commission established under the Pendleton Act was empowered to administer open, competitive examinations for about 10 percent of the federal workforce. Later reforms would greatly expand the number of government employees protected from political pressures.

1892: Sierra Club formed

The first environmental advocacy organization in the United States, the Sierra Club was founded by San Francisco environmentalist John Muir. It originally came to prominence by urging protection of national forests, rivers, and parks.

1907: Tillman Act signed into law

This campaign finance reform measure was pushed by President Theodore Roosevelt in response to accusations that his 1904 campaign had accepted bribes from large corporations to withhold antitrust actions. The law prohibited corporations and interstate banks from making direct contributions to candidates for federal offices. While only marginally effective, it was the first step in a long process of restricting campaign funding from interest groups.

1909: National Association for the Advancement of Colored People formed

The National Association for the Advancement of Colored People (NAACP) started the modern American civil rights movement. Using a strategy of both lobbying and litigation, the NAACP targeted and eventually succeeded in eliminating all segregation laws in the South.

1912: U.S. Chamber of Commerce founded

The U.S. Chamber of Commerce was established to represent the interests of American business. Today it is the world's largest business federation and one of Washington's richest and most powerful lobbying groups.

1919: American Legion established

When it was formed after World War I, the American Legion expanded earlier veterans groups representing those who had fought in the Spanish-American War. Together with the Veterans of Foreign Wars, founded in 1914, the American Legion continues to advocate for education, health care, and other benefits for veterans.

1924: Teapot Dome scandal erupts

This Harding-era financial scandal revealed that Secretary of the Interior Albert Fall had been bribed by oil company executives seeking special access to U.S. Navy Oil Reserves in Teapot Dome, Wyoming. In return for leasing these reserves to the oil magnates, Fall took kickbacks equal to approximately $4 million in 21st-century dollars. He was convicted of bribery in 1929, becoming the first presidential cabinet member to go to prison for his actions in office. Teapot Dome is generally considered the first major government corruption scandal of the 20th century.

1935: Public Utilities Holding Company Act passed

The Public Utilities Holding Company Act (PUHCA) was the first federal law attempting to regulate lobbying by a specific industry—in this case, the electric power-generating companies. It was followed a year later by passage of the Merchant Marine Act, which restricted lobbying by the shipping industry.

1938: Foreign Agents Registration Act passed

On the eve of World War II, Congress passed this law to force agents of foreign governments operating in the United States to reveal themselves and their purposes by registering as lobbyists. While largely ineffective, the law gained attention many years later when it ensnared the brother of President Jimmy Carter.

1939: Hatch Act passed

In the 1930s, Congress became concerned about political pressures on—and partisan activities by—employees of various New Deal agencies. The Hatch Act prohibited career federal employees from engaging in most types of political activities, including running for elective office and soliciting campaign contributions.

1946: Federal Regulation of Lobbying Act passed

The precursor to the modern lobbying restrictions enacted in 1995 and 2007, this law was the first attempt to broadly regulate lobbying activities at the federal level.

1955: Dixon-Yates contract cancelled

This ethics controversy targeted a consultant used by the Bureau of the Budget to negotiate a power-generating contract for Memphis, Tennessee. The consultant, Adolphe Wenzell, was alleged to have a conflict of interest because his company was later hired to arrange financing for the new project. While Wenzell was found innocent of violating federal law, President Eisenhower cancelled the contract and refused to pay the multimillion dollar cancellation fee.

1962: Bribery and Conflict of Interest Act signed into law

This law revised most of the major federal bribery and conflict of interest statutes in existence at the time. It closed certain key loopholes, such as treating the financial interests of a federal employee's spouse as an interest of the employee, and banned all former federal employees from representing anyone in a federal proceeding with respect to matters they had handled while serving in government.

1965: Executive Order 11222 issued

President Lyndon Johnson issued this directive to update and tighten rules relating to acceptance of gifts, entertainment, and favors by federal employees. It also restricted outside employment, prohibited use of public information for private gain, directed all executive branch employees to take steps to avoid the appearance of impropriety, and established a confidential financial reporting system for high-level executive branch officials.

1966: Bobby Baker indicted

Bobby Baker served as secretary to two Senate Majority Leaders: Lyndon Johnson and Mike Mansfield. In 1963, a vending machine company filed suit against him, alleging that he had intervened to steer a contract to a firm in which he held a financial interest. Baker was ultimately indicted on nine counts of fraud, conspiracy, and tax evasion, unrelated to the vending company suit. He went to jail in 1970.

1970: Common Cause founded

Formed to push for campaign finance and lobbying reforms among others, Common Cause also opposed the Vietnam and Iraq wars. Today it remains a grassroots, nonpartisan government watchdog group focused on government transparency and accountability.

1971: Public Citizen founded

The organization Public Citizen was established by high-profile consumer advocate Ralph Nader. Its network of state-based public interest research groups have focused on ethics, citizen access to the courts, consumer protection, global trade, and a range of other policy concerns.

1971: Federal Election Campaign Act passed

This comprehensive campaign finance law addressed fund-raising in presidential and congressional races, enacting the first serious rules and restrictions and enabling the public to make small contributions to presidential candidates on their tax forms. Federal Election Campaign Act was modified several times in the 1970s and later by the Bipartisan Campaign Reform Act. Some of its key provisions were successfully challenged and overturned by the Supreme Court.

1974: President Richard Nixon resigns

Beginning with a Republican-planned break-in at the Watergate offices of the Democratic National Committee, the Watergate scandal revealed unprecedented abuses of power by an American president. It led to the criminal convictions of multiple top aides and Nixon campaign officials as well as the resignation of Nixon himself. In the post-Watergate era, a series of groundbreaking laws were enacted to restore trust in government. In addition, intense scrutiny of public officials became routine.

1976: *Buckley v. Valeo* ruling handed down

After hearing a challenge to the Federal Election Campaign Act, the Supreme Court upheld federal limits on campaign contributions and ruled that spending money to influence elections is a form of constitutionally protected free speech. The Court also ruled that candidates can give unlimited amounts of money to their own campaigns.

1976: Koreagate scandal investigated

Korean-born businessman Tongsun Park was charged with bribing members of Congress, using money from the Korean government, in an unsuccessful effort to convince the United States to keep troops in Vietnam. In 1977, he was convicted of bribery, illegal campaign contributions, mail fraud, racketeering, and failure to register as an agent of the Korean Central Intelligence Agency. Park avoided prison in exchange for immunity.

1978: Ethics in Government Act passed

The first major attempt to restore trust in government after Watergate, this law established financial disclosure requirements for federal officials and restrictions on lobbying by former government employees. It also provided for the appointment of special prosecutors, later called independent counsels, to investigate allegations of lawbreaking by high-level executive branch officials.

1980: ABSCAM investigation concluded

ABSCAM, the FBI's highest-profile early public corruption sting, began in 1978. Over a two-year period, undercover agents posing as representatives of wealthy Arabs offered bribes to members of Congress in return for various types of assistance. Representative Michael Myers of Pennsylvania was implicated in the scandal and became the first congressman expelled since the Civil War; the other members caught in ABSCAM resigned their seats.

1983: Lobby Restrictions Act passed

Intended to close some of the loopholes that had become evident in the 1946 Federal Regulation of Lobbying Act, this law redefined lobbying to mean more than just contact with members of Congress. It also required more extensive reporting on lobbying expenditures and clients, though it failed to address grassroots or religious lobbying campaigns.

1987: Michael Deaver convicted

Michael Deaver served as deputy chief of staff to President Ronald Reagan from 1981 to 1985. Soon after leaving the White House and starting a lobbying firm, he was charged with violating the ban on former high-level executive branch officials lobbying their former agencies for one year, the so-called revolving door prohibition. Ultimately convicted of lying to Congress and a federal grand jury about his lobbying activities, Deaver was sentenced to three years' probation, 1,500 hours of community service, and a $100,000 fine.

1989: Executive Order 12674 issued

This directive by President George H. W. Bush clarified various ethics rules relating to gifts, outside employment, conflicts of interest, misuse of public office for private gain, and other restrictions on federal employees. It also prohibited any full-time presidential appointee from accepting earned income from other sources.

1989: Iran-Contra investigation concludes

In the early 1980s, the U.S. Central Intelligence Agency (CIA) provided extensive support to Nicaraguan rebels, known as contras, who opposed the Sandinista regime. But in 1982, Congress prohibited the use of public funds for this purpose.

Over a four-year period, officials of the National Security Council (NSC) set up two covert operations to skirt the law by funneling money from private citizens and foreign governments to the contras.

The plan was exposed in 1986, resulting in the appointment of an independent counsel to investigate allegations of lawbreaking by various CIA and NSC officials. In 1989, NSC staffer Marine Colonel Oliver North became the first official convicted in connection with the affair; his conviction was later overturned.

1989: U.S. House Speaker Jim Wright resigns

Following a 10-month investigation of ethics abuse allegations filed by then-congressman Newt Gingrich, the House Committee on Standards of Official Conduct charged Speaker Wright with accepting improper gifts and violating restrictions on outside income. He resigned as Speaker and then left the House.

1995: Bipartisan Campaign Reform Act passed

Also known as McCain-Feingold, Bipartisan Campaign Reform Act (BCRA) attempted to restrict the use of soft money, limit the proliferation of issue ads, and otherwise regulate political contributions by interest groups. When first challenged in *McConnell v. FEC,* the U.S. Supreme Court upheld most of its provisions, but BCRA was seriously weakened by the Court's 2010 *Citizens United v. FEC* decision.

1997: U.S. House Speaker Newt Gingrich reprimanded

Accused of improperly using funds raised by a nonprofit organization to advocate the election of Republican congressional candidates, Speaker Gingrich was reprimanded by House vote and ordered to pay a $300,000 fine. Ironically, the charges were investigated by the same Committee on Standards of Official Conduct with which Gingrich had filed ethics complaints against his Democratic predecessor Jim Wright.

2000: Whitewater investigation concludes

In 1994, an independent counsel was appointed to investigate the involvement of President Bill Clinton and First Lady Hillary Clinton with the Arkansas-based Whitewater Development Corporation. The real estate company's failure was linked to the collapse of an Arkansas bank that cost taxpayers over $60 million. Fourteen convictions eventually resulted from the investigation, including two prominent officials: former associate attorney general Webster Hubbell and Arkansas governor Jim Guy Tucker. However, the Whitewater independent counsel announced that there was insufficient evidence to indict either of the Clintons.

2005: U.S. House Majority Leader Tom DeLay indicted

House Majority Leader Tom DeLay of Texas was the architect of the controversial "K Street Strategy" to extend Republican Party control into Washington's lobbying and interest group communities. Indicted for illegal campaign fund-raising in connection with his initiatives, DeLay was forced out of office.

2006: Jack Abramoff pleads guilty

Abramoff was one of Washington's most powerful lobbyists until he was caught overbilling Native American casino-gambling interests by approximately $85 million, among other fraudulent and unethical practices. Several influential officials were also convicted of lawbreaking because of their dealings with Abramoff, including Congressman Bob Ney of Ohio and former deputy interior secretary Steven Griles. The Abramoff scandal kicked off a wave of public anger and demands for tighter control of federal lobbying practices.

2006: Earmark reform begins

Following revelations of wasteful spending by some members of Congress on projects in their districts, reform of these "earmark" appropriations was initiated through House procedural rules. For the first time, earmarks were disclosed in public documents along with the names of the members requesting them. In addition, members were required to certify that neither they nor their spouses had any financial interest in the earmark. Similar rules were adopted by the Senate. In 2010, members were also required to post information on their websites explaining any earmark they requested.

2007: Honest Leadership and Open Government Act passed

New lobbying ethics rules and standards were passed in reaction to the Abramoff scandal. Honest Leadership and Open Government Act closed major loopholes in expenditures and reporting, and placed restrictions on the Washington lobbying social events that were common on the state level but previously unused on the federal level. It also incorporated the Senate version of new procedural rules related to earmarks.

2008: Countrywide Financial Corporation scandal revealed

Countrywide Financial Corporation financed approximately 20 percent of all mortgages in the United States when the firm was purchased by Bank of America in 2006. The operations of this heavyweight lender stood to benefit disproportionately from federal loan guarantees for distressed homeowners and other policies shaped to a significant degree by the Senate Banking Committee.

In 2008, media reports revealed that various powerful politicians had received preferential loans from Countrywide. Among them was Senator Christopher Dodd of Ohio, chairman of the Banking Committee. Dodd came under investigation by the Senate Committee on Ethics, which did not accuse him of wrongdoing but stated that he had erred by failing to question the favorable terms of his loan. Dodd chose not to run for reelection in 2010.

2010: *Citizens United v. Federal Election Commission* ruling handed down

In this case, the U.S. Supreme Court reconsidered the limits on campaign contributions imposed either explicitly or implicitly by the Bipartisan Campaign Reform

Act. It decided that a federal prohibition on independent contributions by corporations and unions was an unconstitutional ban on free speech.

Citizens United created the legal basis for the creation of Super PACs, federally registered political action committees able to raise and spend virtually unlimited amounts of money, as long as their expenditures are not coordinated with a candidate's campaign.

2012: Stop Trading in Congressional Knowledge (STOCK) Act passed

In 2011, CBS News exposed insider trading by various members of Congress who had obtained and acted on information related to companies and stocks that was unavailable to the public. Reacting to public outrage, Congress passed the Stop Trading in Congressional Knowledge Act in early 2012. The law required members to disclose their stock trades within 30 days, and prohibited the use of nonpublic information in making these transactions.

Sources

Morgan, Bryson B., and Ronald J. Hrebenar. "Chronology." In *Lobbying in America: A Reference Handbook*. Santa Barbara, CA: ABC-CLIO, 2009. ABC-CLIO eBook Collection.

Roberts, Robert North. *Ethics in U.S. Government*. Westport, CT: Greenwood Publishing Co., 2001.

Section A
Lobbying

Origins and Evolution of Lobbying in America

Ronald J. Hrebenar and Bryson B. Morgan

All political societies, ancient or modern, have had or currently have interest group politics and lobbying. Imagine being transported back to the earliest human societies that began to develop into specialized economic and political roles. Hunter-gatherers came to compete with warriors, agricultural workers, priests, governmental leaders, and bureaucrats for the scarce resources of the community. To paraphrase the definition of one famous political scientist, Thomas R. Dye, politics is the allocation of governmental resources; it is who gets what, when, where, why, and how (Dye 1995). Ancient Rome was famous for the various conflicts among the Roman Legions, aristocrats, and economic elites. Throughout history, even the powerless—the serfs and peasants—could participate in interest group politics by rioting, demonstrating, and even revolting. (They were not always successful in these tactics. Sometimes they paid with their lives for their decisions.) Politics in those times often was truly a "winner-take-all" game.

Starting with England, a more modern style of group politics began with the Magna Carta (1200s) and the expansion of participants to include more than the royal family; friends; and supporting economic, political, and military groups. As societies became more complex and economies more diverse, the interests that demanded a place at the decision-making tables greatly increased. With the enhanced role of Parliament in England, there was an arena for lobbying by the various interests

The most English of the British Empire's colonies were those in North America, and they inherited both the range of interests and the legislative arenas for the development of interest group politics. The 13 British colonies in what became the United States developed a lively style of politics by the mid-1700s, and various economic interests such as planters, importers, exporters, shipowners, small businessmen, farmers, and religious groups made demands on the colonial assemblies and British governors. The 13 colonies even developed a significant manufacturing base.

James Madison and the "Dangers of Factions"

Following the American War of Independence (1776–1783), the new American nation operated under a pre-Constitution document called the Articles of Confederation. Interest group politics among the 13 newly independent states (the former colonies) was mostly conducted on the state level because the structure of the national government prevented significant decision making. The Articles provided for an extremely weak national government with a largely symbolic president and a Congress that had no real taxing power and a need to have all decisions made by unanimous vote. By the mid-1780s, it had become clear to some national leaders, such as James Madison, that the key issues that faced the new national government could not be successfully addressed under the Articles. Among the challenges the new nation faced were economic, security, and political issues.

The economic position of the new states was precarious. The colonies' governing body during the Revolution, the Continental Congress, issued government bonds to cover the costs of the War of Independence against the British. The outstanding amount of these bonds was about $75 million, a very substantial amount of money—about one-seventh of the total property value of all 13 colonies. The revenue streams of the new national government consisted of customs taxes and revenue from postage stamps. Any additional funds had to be requested from the states, which were understandably resistant to the idea of such financial trans-

James Madison represented Virginia in the Second Continental Congress and is often called the "Father of the Constitution." (National Archives)

fers. Many of the bonds had been bought by "speculators," who went from house to house offering small amounts for bonds that many people had concluded were not worth much. These speculators represented an interest that demanded that the national government be reformed so it could raise tax money that could pay off, among other expenses, these war bonds. Several states, such as Rhode Island, were on the edge of fiscal bankruptcy. Their state-issued currencies were not accepted by citizens of other states. Some states had raised barriers around their borders, which prevented the development of national markets. Clearly, for these economic reasons, various business and financial interests supported a substantial revision to the Articles.

The security realm also experienced serious problems. The Peace Treaty of Paris that ended the War of Independence had given the new American nation the Northwest Territory—the region that is today's Midwestern states of Ohio, Michigan, Indiana, and Illinois. However, the region continued to be occupied by British troops in forts, and the American military had been disbanded. Besides issues of national honor, why was this occupation important? American investors and settlers were pushing west over the Appalachian Mountains, and profitable migration into the Ohio River Valley could not be accomplished so long as the region was occupied by the British. Additionally, and far more important, the world was aflame with war among the major superpowers of the 18th century: Great Britain, France, and Spain. One very important reason why the British gave up on their American colonies in 1783 was that more serious threats to British interests were posed by France (led by Napoleon), and other sites were compromised, such as those affected by the ongoing battle to control India and Asia. The 13 American colonies on the Atlantic coast of North America were a relatively minor irritant and distraction compared with the dangers in Europe

For these and other reasons, James Madison led a movement to call a convention in Philadelphia in the summer of 1787 to revise the Articles of Confederation. This action was highly irregular and not part of the written procedure for revising the Articles. In fact, the goal of revising the fundamental document of the American national government was quickly dropped during what is now called the Constitutional Convention. The Articles were too weak to use as a foundation for an effective national government. James Madison had spent the previous year researching various governments and constitutions and was prepared to help write a strong new constitution with sufficient limitations to protect liberty.

Madison's subsequent propaganda campaign in support of the proposed constitution marks the beginning of the discussion of interest group politics in the United States. Madison is considered the "father" of the American Constitution and, in reality, the father of interest group studies. The pro-Constitution propaganda campaign took many forms, but the most important was a series of 85 essays written by James Madison, Alexander Hamilton, and John Jay. (Madison later went on to become the nation's fourth president; Hamilton, the first secretary of the treasury; and John Jay, the first chief justice of the Supreme Court.)

The essays have come to be known as the Federalist Papers and are collectively now considered to be the finest piece of political writing in American political history (Wills 1982). They tried to defend the crucial elements of the proposed constitution. Of the 85 essays, the most famous is Madison's Federalist No. 10; it warns the nation of the dangers of "factions." Madison addressed No. 10 to the people of New York, one of the states that appeared to be most hostile to the proposed constitution. The opening sentence clearly describes the central point of his argument: "Among the numerous advantages promised by a well constructed Union, none deserves to be more accurately developed than its tendency to break and control the violence of faction" (Ketcham 2006, 84).

Madison's description of *faction* is basically what we will come to call "interests," or "interest group politics": "By a faction I understand a number of citizens, whether amounting to a majority or minority of the whole, who are united and actuated by some common impulse of passion, or of interest, adverse to the rights of other citizens, or to the permanent and aggregate interests of the community" (Ketcham 2006, 84).

Madison's significant contribution in No. 10 is his argument concerning the problems of trying to eliminate the negative outcomes of interest group politics. "There are two methods of curing the mischiefs of faction: the one, by removing its causes; the other, by controlling its effects" (Ketcham 2006, 85).

Again, two methods of removing the causes of faction exist:

> The one by destroying the liberty which is essential to its existence; the other, by giving to every citizen the same opinions, the same passions, and the same interests. It could never be more truly said, than of the first remedy, that it is worse than the disease. Liberty is to faction what air is to fire, an aliment with which it instantly expires. But it could not be a less folly to abolish liberty, which is essential to political life, because it nourishes faction, than it would be to wish the annihilation of air, which is essential to animal life, because it imparts to fire its destructive agency. (Ketcham 2006, 85)

In other words, the problems of factions (interests) can be avoided, but the method of avoidance could kill liberty and thus is completely unacceptable to the liberty-loving American citizenry. However, the second method he analyzes to control the "mischiefs" of factions is not acceptable either. "The second expedient is as impracticable, as the first would be unwise. As long as the reason of man continues to be fallible, and he is at liberty to exercise it, different opinions will be formed" (Ketcham 2006, 85).

Madison identifies the causes behind the formation of different opinions. It is property that ensures a division of the society into different issues and parties. So the causes of faction are based "in the nature of man" and the "most common and durable source of factions has been the various and unequal distribution of property" (Ketcham 2006, 85). Since property in a free society and economy will always be distributed in unequal amounts and types, factions will always be present.

Since, as Madison argued, no cure exists for the causes of faction, one must focus on methods for reducing the negative impacts of factions (or interests) on the political system. This philosophy is another of Madison's great contributions to the establishment of the American political system: the complex or large republic. "A Republic . . . promises the cure for which we are seeking." Madison designed a republic, not a democracy. Madison's republic is a representative government, not a government of direct citizen decision making. The representatives would use their wisdom to discover the true interest of their country. Madison suggested that his design was the best compromise: a large republic where the various interests could be countered in the national government and a series of state legislatures (small republics) where local and specific interests would be important (Ketcham 2006, 87–88).

So Madison argued that the advantage his republic had over a democracy was in controlling the effects of factions. He gives an example of a religious sect becoming a political faction in a given part of the republic, noting further that "a variety of sects dispersed over the entire face of it, must secure the national Councils against any danger from that source" (Wills 1982, 48).

Madison's Constitution of 1787 set the stage for what would become interest group politics in the new American government. This is not to say that such interest groups and their politics did not exist before 1787, but after 1787 the structure and rules of the new Constitution guided the development of American politics and government into a particular pattern much like a valley guides water into a riverbed. Before we move on to others who have commented on the historical development of American interest group politics, we would be remiss if we did not include the 1791 addition of the Bill of Rights and especially the First Amendment to the Constitution.

Madison, Hamilton, and Jay promoted the adoption of the proposed constitution in the Federalist Papers. Opponents to the adoption came to be called the anti-Federalists, and their collected propaganda efforts demanded that several fundamental problems existed in the Madisonian design. The anti-Federalists were especially concerned that the new national government had too much power or the potential to acquire too much power at the expense of the liberties of the American people. Why did the Constitution writers fail to include a "bill of rights" protecting the American people from abuses by the new national government? After all, they correctly noted that most of the 13 states had such protections. The anti-Federalists had other concerns as well, such as a president with the potential to have too much power, a judiciary appointed for life, and a federal government with areas of responsibility that were too vague. Actually, the two groups supporting and opposing the Constitution represented two collections of very different interests. The Federalists were mostly property owners, creditors, and merchants, while the anti-Federalists were mostly small farmers, debtors, and small shopkeepers (Ginsberg 2007, 53).

One of the arguments Madison and some of the Federalists (not including Hamilton, who, in Federalist No. 84, argued that a bill of rights was not needed) made to obtain final ratification for the Constitution was to address the need for a federal bill of rights to protect against federal government abuses. Madison led the fight for the Bill of Rights that was passed by Congress and adopted by the states by 1791. For the purposes of this analysis of the development of lobbying and interest group politics in the United States, we will examine only the First Amendment, which reads as follows:

Amendment I

(Freedom of Religion, of Speech and of the Press)

Congress shall make no law respecting an establishment of religion, or prohibiting the free exercise thereof; or abridging the freedom of speech, or of the press; or of the right of the people to peaceably assemble, and to petition the government for redress of grievances.

All of the First Amendment applies to our subject in various ways. By the 1790s, the diversity of religions in the 13 states was such that few people considered replicating the normal relationship between government and religion—the establishment of one religion as the official "state religion" of the nation. The United States had sizable Protestant communities, representing mainstream Protestant organizations as well as many of the smaller dissident groups such as Quakers and Puritans. Add the growing Catholic population centered in Maryland, Jews, and other groups, and the establishment of a national religion was a political impossibility in 1790. The "free exercise" clause tried to prevent any one religion from imposing its beliefs on others. Some of the battles regarding the relationship between government and religions and the issues of free exercise of religion continue to be very significant political concerns into the 21st century.

The next four clauses of the First Amendment all directly relate to how the U.S. government has come to view interest groups and lobbying. The "freedom of speech" clause has been interpreted by the U.S. Supreme Court to cover political speech (e.g., lobbying) and recently to protect the spending of money in attempts to influence political campaigns as well as lobbying. "Freedom of the press" also guarantees that interests (including the media as an interest itself) can make their political demands and communications without governmental obstruction. But it is the final two clauses, which protect the right of the people to assemble and petition government, that have enshrined the lobbying game as a fundamental part of American politics. The "assembly" clause has been read to mean that Americans have a right to join organizations that have political agendas, and the "petition" clause has been read as a prevention of almost all attempts to rein in the various strategies and tactics found in modern lobbying. We will discuss these aspects of the First Amendment in Chapter 2, where we consider the important issues regarding interest groups and lobbying in contemporary American politics and government

Evidence of the development of interest group politics in the new United States can be found in the writing of the French aristocrat Alexis de Tocqueville, who toured the young nation in 1831–1832 and later wrote the first great book about the nature of political life in the United States. His book *Democracy in America,* detailing his observations, was first published in 1835 and was re-published in 1840 and many times since then (Heffner 1956). Central to Tocqueville's concerns regarding the new nation were the American combination of the concepts of democracy and equality and, more specifically, the American thinking that equality means freedom and democracy means liberty. Additionally, Tocqueville viewed with some fear the dangers of the "tyranny of the majority." Had the United States so structured its politics and society to favor the masses to the detriment of important, but narrower, interests?

Tocqueville noted that the Americans used associations more than other major nations at that time. "Wherever, at the head of some new undertaking, you see the government in France, or a man of rank in England, in the United States you will be sure to find an association" (Heffner 1956, 198). In Tocqueville's section on political associations in the United States, he wrote one of his most famous and oft-quoted comments:

> In no country in the world has the principle of association been more successfully used, or applied to a greater multitude of objects, than in America. Besides the permanent associations, which are established by law, under the names of townships, cities and counties, a vast number of other are formed and maintained by the agency of private individuals. . . . If some public pleasure is concerned, an association is formed to give more splendor and regularity to the entertainment. Societies are formed to resist evils, which are exclusively of a moral nature, as to diminish the vice of intemperance. In the United States, associations are established to promote the public safety, commerce, industry, morality, and religion. There is no end which the human will despairs of attaining through the combined power of individuals united into a society. (Heffner 1956, 95)

What Are Interests, Interest Groups, Lobbies, and Lobbyists?

People participate in politics either as individuals or as formal or informal members of organizations. Individuals can have an impact on political decisions by the act of voting or can affect public opinion through such means as writing letters to the editors of newspapers or posting on political blogs. But the most effective way people can have a voice in politics is by joining a group of like-minded individuals and using the power of their group to magnify their political voices. Such organizations that have engaged in political activities to affect public policy decision making have been identified by many different names during the more than 200 years of U.S. history. Some of these names carry negative connotations because of their linkage to various lobbying scandals, including the terms *trust, vested interest, special interest,* and *pressure group.* Each of these terms comes with a public perception of unsavory tactics or a lack of concern for a broader public interest. Even the word *lobby* carries a bad image in many people's minds. The most neutral term, *interest group,* is defined by David Truman in his classic study *The Governmental Process* as "any group that is based on one or more shared attitudes and makes certain claims upon other groups or organizations in the society" (Truman 1971, 13). Two key ideas are derived from this definition. First, the organization is composed of individuals (or other organizations) who share some common characteristic or interest. For example, the American Federation of Labor and Congress of Industrial Organizations (AFL-CIO), a giant labor union confederation, shares the interests of its members on a wide range of economic, social, and political objectives that affect working people in the United States. Second, only those associations that engage the political system and seek to affect public policy are considered interest groups under this definition.

We must also differentiate among interest groups and lobbying and social and political movements (Meyer 2007). Movements or social movements are *emergent groups* that propose change and need to become political groups to effect change. Social movements have spontaneity and some structure. Sociologists tend to study social movement, and political scientists tend to study interest groups. Eventually, some social movements evolve into political interest groups with a well-defined membership, regular funding, a permanent staff, and knowledge on how to operate within the political system. Jo Freeman suggests that such types of social action can be seen as points along a continuum (Freeman 1983). At one end are those relatively unstructured social actions such as a riot; at the other end are the established, structured interest groups; and in the middle are the social movements having spontaneity and some structure, but not a well-defined formal organization. A social movement may have one or several core organizations within the larger movement. People who consider themselves part of a social movement often share identity as part of a group focusing on a particular concern. Social movement politics is often outside the mainstream of politics, and thus political movements are forced to rely on disruptive tactics to publicize their demands. If you cannot win in the legislatures or courts, you have to try to rally public opinion to your side by disruptive strategies and tactics.

In the 1960s and 1970s, most of the major political movements were found on the liberal or left end of the political spectrum and were associated with such causes as women's rights, sexual rights, civil rights for minorities, environmental rights, the antiwar movement, and animal rights. All of these are still in existence in the 21st century, with other national liberal movements crystallizing around gay rights and support for victims of AIDS. In 2011 Occupy Wall Street became the newest of many left-leaning groups formed to protest some facet of economic inequality. But the most significant change has been the rise of a number of major conservative, or right-wing, movements since the 1970s. The new conservative movements have focused on antiabortion law, antipornography, anti-gay marriage, and anti-immigrant (especially anti-illegal immigrant) stances. In 2009 the Tea Party mobilized hundreds of thousands of conservative voters in a bid to cut government spending and limit regulatory initiatives.

If a movement is successful in achieving its basic political goals, it will frequently evolve into one or more influential interest groups that have significant power to affect policy making in various governmental sites. On the other hand, unsuccessful movements tend to disappear as a result of cooptation, lack of interest, or even repression. Our primary focus is on the interest groups embedded within the broader movements. Some recent research has noted the difficulty in clearly separating interest groups from social movements. Costain and McFarland (1998) have argued that the two are really quite similar in many aspects and that they should be called "interest organizations." But they do argue that a very fundamental difference exists between interest organizations and political parties.

Interest groups are not usually political parties, and political parties are not usually interest groups. On rare occasions, interest groups and political parties do reflect the same organization. In the United States several interest groups have become political parties to use the political campaign opportunities in elections to further their goals. Among the examples of these merged organizations are the Socialist and Communist parties as well as the Libertarian and La Raza parties. These are really interest groups of an ideological bent presenting themselves as political parties to gain attention for their ideas.

Interest groups and political parties both serve as communications links between citizens and their government, but they are very different. Political parties have as their major reason for existence the objective of capturing control of the institutions of government. Parties want to occupy government physically, whereas interest groups want to influence some of the decisions made by government. In addition, parties focus their attention on elections and the selection of candidates to fill public offices. They are highly regulated by state laws and, in terms of membership, are usually broad-based coalitions of individuals who frequently share only one common objective, the capturing of government. Interest groups, in contrast, are almost totally free from legal restrictions on their activities and focus mainly on the public law-making phase of the governmental process.

Some nonpolitical interest groups serve important roles in the social system of the United States but very seldom get involved in politics, like the Boy Scouts, Girl Scouts, Masons, and Elks. In addition, thousands of groups exist that may on a very rare occasion come into contact with the political system on a very unusual issue. Our focus is on *political interest groups*. These are the groups that frequently participate in lobbying the government. This category can be conveniently divided into two subcategories: *self-oriented* and *public interest groups* (PIGs). Self-oriented groups seek to achieve some policy goal that will directly benefit their own membership. Usually these groups attempt to portray their political objectives as being in the interest of the general public and not just helpful to the

Evelyn Jackson, left, and director Steve McQueen, center, at the 2014 AARP's Movies for Grownups Gala in Beverly Hills, California. (Vince Bucci/Invision/AP)

group. PIGs seek benefits that will not advance their membership directly but will be enjoyed by the general public. The abolitionists of the 1850s sought an objective that would not directly benefit their membership, for none of them were slaves. Environmentalists seek clean air and water for all, not just their members. Many American groups claim to be PIGs because of the more favorable public image of such groups.

In recent decades, organizations have been formed to represent many previously unrepresented interests of society. Senior citizens have America's largest, and maybe most powerful, lobby in AARP (formerly the American Association of Retired Persons). The AARP grew from 1 million members in 1967 to more than 35 million members in 2010. A very large number of fundamentalist, evangelical, "born again" Christians organized into several formidable interest groups. The late Reverend Jerry Falwell founded the Moral Majority to act as the political agent for this previously unorganized interest and in 1980 the group claimed 400,000 members and a multimillion-dollar budget. Although the Moral Majority died as an organization in the late 1980s, it was successfully replaced by the Christian Coalition, which became a powerful force in conservative politics in the early 1990s and claimed more than 2 million members in 2005. In the 2012 Republican presidential primaries, Christian fundamentalist groups like the Family Research Council were extremely active in organizing debates, vetting candidates, and mobilizing voters.

Other ethnic and religious interests have also become organized in recent years. Asian Americans have been difficult to organize except for the Japanese, who organized under the Japanese American Citizens League. However, recent new Asian organizations, such as the Asian American Association and the Organization of Chinese Americans, have moved to represent the interests of their members. After 9/11, various groups of Islamic Americans felt the need to organize and protect their interests. Among these new American Muslim groups was the Free Muslim Coalition against Terrorism.

Thousands of American Interest Groups

No one really knows how many active interest groups are currently operating in the United States. However, of the three levels of American politics—national, state, and local—the best estimates regarding numbers of groups have been made on the national level. The *Encyclopedia of Associations* enumerates more than 24,000 nonprofit organizations with national reach or interests. More than 30,000 clients or interests have registered with the U.S. Congress under the provisions of the lobby registration requirements.

More and more groups are moving their headquarters to Washington, D.C. According to the National Trade and Professional Associations of the United States, 7,400 national associations were recently headquartered in Washington, D.C. The U.S. capital sometimes seems filled with lobbyists and lawyers—and these are not necessarily different professions. One street in the northwest quadrant of Washington, D.C., has come to symbolize the concentration of interest groups and lobbyists there—K Street. In fact, K Street was the focus of an HBO miniseries entitled *K Street: Politics from the Inside Out.*

On the state level, a clearer picture is emerging of the number of groups that are the result of lobby registration laws that have been enacted in various states. One interesting finding is the numerical domination of business, banks, and economic groups among the state-level registrants. The number of local-level groups (county and municipal) is impossible to determine because of their ephemeral nature; many deal with specific local problems and may be founded and dissolved within the same calendar year. Additionally, far fewer reporting requirements are in place for local groups in the United States. Despite these issues, estimates indicate that more than 200,000 different organizations exist at the state and local levels of American politics.

Patterns of Interest Group Proliferation

The interest group universe in the United States seems to expand in surges several decades apart. U.S. history has seen several periods of high group formation separated by longer periods of relatively small increases in the number of groups. Political scientist David Truman noted, "The formation of associations tends to occur in waves" (Truman 1971, 59). James Q. Wilson subsequently noted that three great waves of association formation occurred between 1800 and 1940 (Wilson 1995, 198). The first wave occurred between 1830 and 1860 and saw the establishment of the first national organizations in American history. The Young Men's Christian Association, the Grange, the Elks, and many abolitionist groups were formed during the three decades before the Civil War. Later, during the 1880s, a second wave was a result of the industrialization of the United States. Also at this time, economic associations were formed to represent the interests of both labor and business (AFL, Knights of Labor, and many manufacturing associations), and some of the most familiar present-day associations, such as the American Red Cross, were created in this era. The years between 1900 and 1920 can be seen as the period during which the greatest number of organizations was formed, including the U.S. Chamber of Commerce, National Association of Manufacturers, American Medical Association, National Association for the Advancement of Colored People, Urban League, American Farm Bureau Federation, Farm Union, American Cancer Society, and American Jewish Committee. Another increase in the number of groups occurred in the 1960s and 1970s, reflecting heightened social activism and increased governmental activity during that period.

What explains the increase in the number of political interest groups during the first several decades of the 20th century? A number of societal changes seem to have facilitated the association explosion (Wilson 1995). Nationwide organizations could be established because communications of nearly every sort became easier as radio, telephones, railroads, and national newspapers and magazines allowed people to participate in the new national organizations. As government escalated its regulation of the business world, the business world organized to deal with the governmental demands. Economic specialization resulted in the creation of many new economic associations. Additionally, new immigration contributed to the increased heterogeneity of the American population. "Organizations become more numerous when ideas become more important . . . widespread organizing seems always to be accompanied by numerous social movements" (Wilson 1995, 201). Each of these great organizing periods was simultaneously a period of great social unrest and social movement.

In the first decade of the 21st century, the advent of web-based communication and social media helped to spark another widespread burst in the creation of new political interest groups. Neither the Tea Party on the right nor Occupy Wall Street on the left could have mobilized as they did without free citizen access to tools like Facebook and Twitter.

Lobbying Power Is Built upon Interest Group Characteristics

A lobbying campaign's success or failure will be based upon the foundation of its interest group's organizational characteristics. What, then, is the basis of that foundation? Membership characteristics, the structure of the organization, and the quality of the leadership and staff are fundamental to a group's power.

The first place we should look for power potential is in the nature of its membership. Every group is advantaged and disadvantaged by its membership. A huge, powerful group such as the AARP has tremendous financial resources and the potential to convert its millions of members into a potent lobbying force; on the other hand, because it is so huge, it will have a difficult time developing a membership consensus to support a particular lobbying objective. Even a much smaller group, such as the American Civil Liberties Union (ACLU), with a membership that is highly educated and generally left of center, sometimes has to avoid certain issues because the membership is so divided on them.

Organizations with largely middle and upper social-economic class memberships seem to have additional resources associated with that income and social status that can be converted into lobbying resources. Common Cause, the largely middle-class political reform organization based in Washington, D.C., with state-level units in many states, has members who are willing and able to be activated into the political process. These characteristics tend to produce high degrees of personal efficacy and ego strength. The higher a person's education level and income, the more free time he or she has, and thus the greater his or her sense of obligation (or guilt) to participate. Often this equation can translate into more interest in politics and even past experience in politics. All of these factors tend to produce "the upper class bias of interest group participation" (Schattschneider 1960, 31–32).

The resources of interest groups are many and varied. No one group has all of them, and some groups have only one or two, but all groups have some resources available to support them. As noted, the most fundamental resource for any interest group is its membership. Rich or poor, active or passive, many or few, happy or unhappy, political or nonpolitical, interested or disinterested—all of these characteristics will either enhance or reduce the potential for converting the membership into a lobbying resource. Consider the following membership characteristics that may be enormously useful in lobbying. First, special knowledge or education may directly apply to a particular issue. For example, the American Medical Association, arguably the most important national organization of medical doctors, has dominated the political debates on health care in the United States for at least the past 50 years and, in reality, much earlier.

Another example is the small group of atomic scientists, producers of *The Bulletin of the Atomic Scientists* who have had a very powerful presence in the debates on nuclear weapons and the dangers of nuclear war.

Second, celebrities who join a group can greatly increase the potential of the group's ability to achieve its political goals. Robert Redford, the famous Hollywood actor and director, has brought enormous publicity and media attention to various issues related to the environmental movement. More recently, Angelina Jolie, the actress, has turned her attention to the plight of people in the underdeveloped world and has spent a great deal of time in Cambodia, Africa, and India. Everywhere she goes, Jolie garners media attention for her and her issues.

Third, the passion of members for the cause can be an enormously important resource. Even a small group with limited resources can have a significant impact on an issue—or at least force the public to take note of it—when members are willing to take extraordinary efforts to promote their cause. For example, the radical environmental group Earth Liberation Front set fire to a historic building on the campus of Michigan State University to protest biotechnology research taking place there. In 2008, members of the like-minded organization Earth First! used duct tape to link their arms and block access to a Florida power plant. In some respects, an organization with a few completely dedicated members may be more influential than a much larger organization with a largely apathetic membership.

Fourth, the geographical distribution of an organization's membership is important. For example, organized labor's membership is unevenly distributed across the United States. In states such as Michigan, Pennsylvania, New York, and Nevada, organized labor is a major political force, whereas in the Deep South and most of the Mountain West it exerts very little political influence. Another interest group whose influence is not consistent across the country is the ACLU; it is almost non-existent in conservative states such as Utah.

Some interest groups, such as those representing real estate brokers, bankers, and small businesspeople, are found in large numbers in every congressional district and legislative district in the United States. This type of widespread, visible presence is critical, for example, to public school teachers' unions. While the educators are represented on Capitol Hill by the National Education Association, their contracts and organizing rights often depend as heavily on effective state and local lobbying as on activity in Washington.

But sometimes, a concentration of members in a few places can be very useful. Muslim Americans have found that their relatively small numbers are more politically useful because of their concentration in a few places such as Michigan and California. Jews have long magnified their political power in American politics because of their heavy concentration in New York City, Los Angeles, and Miami.

What other resources are potentially important to interest groups seeking to play the lobbying game? Money, of course, comes to mind immediately. "Money is the mother's milk of politics" (Hoover Institution 2008). This comment, by Jesse Unruh, the former speaker of the California State Assembly, indicates the relationship between government and the lobbying world and the connection between the two: money. Of course, the bigger the group, the more likely it is to have money, such as the AARP, whose annual income from all of its activities is in the hundreds of millions of dollars. The AFL-CIO labor confederation is also in that financial category. Major business groups such as the Business Roundtable, the National Association of Manufacturers, and the Chamber of Commerce have large organization revenues for possible lobbying campaigns. Major trade associations that represent large business sectors such as oil, automobiles, computers, and airlines can tax their members for lobbying. The beneficial attribute of money is that it can be converted into almost every other resource useful for lobbying. With money, an organization can buy skilled leadership and professional staff, public opinion polling, scientific research, public relations campaigns, "volunteers," and media access. Clearly, money is the universal resource of interest group politics and campaigns. This is not to say that having large financial resources guarantees lobbying success; on occasion, a large bankroll does not result in a successful outcome. The failure of the very rich oil companies to open up the northern Alaska coast to oil exploration is one example of a situation in which money has not yet

President Barack Obama with AFL-CIO president Richard Trumka after he spoke about jobs and the economy at the AFL-CIO Executive Council in Washington on August 4, 2010. (AP Photo/Charles Dharapak)

produced political victory. But money wins much more often than it loses, and therefore, it is always advantageous to have money to launch a lobbying campaign

The large size of an organization does not automatically convert into lobbying power. Two of the two largest interest groups in the United States, the AARP and the AFL-CIO, have had unexpectedly poor lobbying records in recent years. The lobbying problems of the AFL-CIO reflect a general decline in organized labor in the past 50 years, and are also a function of its dependence on one political party (the Democrats). With Republicans in control of Congress, labor is no longer on the offensive, trying to get new benefits, but desperately on the defensive, trying to keep its enemies from passing more laws that will further weaken its power.

The AARP does not engage in partisan political battles in Washington, D.C., very often because, at 35 million members (both Republicans and Democrats, liberals and conservatives), getting the membership to support a controversial lobbying position is very difficult. But when it chooses to lobby, the AARP is not wedded to either side of the aisle. In 2004, it threw its support behind the Bush administration's proposal to extend Medicare to include prescription drugs. Six years later, the AARP lobbied hard for passage of the Obama administration's national health insurance plan, the Patient Protection and Affordable Care Act.

What Kinds of Groups Do Americans Join?

Americans are joiners. Most belong to a church, temple, or mosque. Millions belong to labor unions. Additional millions belong to thousands of trade and business associations related to their place of employment. A political science professor at a major university may carry up to 10 memberships related to his or her teaching or research specializations. But the single most frequently joined organization is a church. Churches usually do not participate directly in the lobbying process, but when they do decide to lobby, usually on so-called moral issues, they encourage their membership to establish new political action groups that frequently enjoy church support. Churches have been involved in the American political process throughout the nation's history, participating in such religious lobbying efforts as abolition, women's voting rights, Prohibition, gambling, civil rights, anti–Vietnam War, busing, gay rights, pornography, and abortion campaigns. Clearly, since the 1960s, churches have become more active in the lobbying process and consequently more significant as a type of political organization. As mentioned previously, conservative Christian groups emerged as formidable political actors by 1980, and have remained extremely active within the Republican Party.

Millions of Americans belong to sports associations and school service groups, and although the sports associations do not normally participate in lobbying, school groups have been increasingly active as the education process has become a central part of the so-called culture wars between liberals and conservatives. Most of the remaining association categories, such as hobby, literary, fraternal, youth, and service groups, participate very infrequently in politics. That leaves the heavyweights of the lobbying game: business, labor unions and professional, veterans, political, farm, and ethnic groups. These are the 800-pound gorillas of the lobbying game.

One membership characteristic that may be either positive or negative to building a lobbying campaign is *overlapping memberships*. Americans have multiple identities and multiple interest group memberships that may come into conflict with one another and result in *cross-pressuring* of an individual.

Take the hypothetical case of a university professor—a political scientist. A contentious congressional election is being held in the professor's home district between a Democratic candidate who supports women's rights, especially abortion rights, and a Republican candidate who argues that abortions are wrong. Since the majority of political scientists tend to vote for Democratic candidates, one would expect the academic to support the Democrat, but multiple identities have brought cross-pressures into the decision. Our academic is also a practicing Catholic and comes from a labor union family. The professor's church is urging a vote for the pro-life Republican candidate; the professor's father and mother are urging support for the union-endorsed Democrat. What to do? Our academic can select among several choices. If the identity or associational pressures are relatively equal and cannot be resolved in terms of one coming to be the dominant pressure, our cross-pressured academic may just decide not to vote in that particular contest. Or the professor may decide to emphasize one of the memberships over the other and reduce commitment to the less significant membership.

If the stress levels rise to crucial levels on additional issues, our academic may have to make a decision about the multiple identities and membership because they are in conflict. Cross-pressuring is thus another characteristic of interest groups that may be a problem or an advantage for an organization. Its effect depends on the number of individuals exposed to cross-pressuring in an organization, their commitment to the organization, and how leadership deals with the problem. Internal group cohesion is very important to a group's survival (Truman 1971). Sometimes, a group must accept a split on an important issue that is central to the group's mission. In the 1970s, the ACLU lost thousands of members when it decided to defend a Nazi group that wanted to parade in a largely Jewish suburb of Chicago. In 2010, the American Medical Association endured bitter internal divisions caused by its support of national health care. Yet, on other less central issues, such a cross-pressured organization may decide to drop the issue or perhaps redefine it in such a way that it reduces the cross-pressures. Often, multiple memberships have a reinforcing impact on the political commitment of individuals or organizations. A person with multiple memberships will usually belong to various organizations that hold the same policy positions. In such situations, the individual willingness to participate in political activities is enhanced.

Today's Lobbyists: Who They Are and What They Do

Interest groups have, generally speaking, two broad strategies at their disposal when attempting to influence the formation of public policy: direct and indirect lobbying. Direct lobbying is the strategy preferred by the vast majority of interest groups because it is simpler, less dangerous, and less subject to misinterpretation than indirect lobbying. By *lobbying*, we mean the communication of data or opinion by someone other than a citizen acting on his or her own behalf to a governmental decision maker in an effort to influence a specific decision. Direct lobbying usually uses the organization's designated agent in the lobbying process, a lobbyist who may be a staff member, an elected leader, a member, or a hired professional.

Direct Lobbying: Categories of Lobbyists

There is no "typical lobbyist." Lobbyists come from a wide variety of backgrounds and professions. Some people think former politicians make the best lobbyists; others believe lawyers or former bureaucrats make better lobbyists; some argue that a good lobbyist comes from within the interest group. In terms of conventional wisdom, general agreement has been reached on what skills the ideal lobbyist should have. The "ideal lobbyist" should have knowledge of four subjects: the legislative and political process, the law and legal process, the subject matter of concern to the lobbying organization, and public relations techniques (Milbrath 1963, 61). Most organizations seeking a lobbyist tend to look at persons who are or were in government, at lawyers, or at lobbyists in other organizations.

The following are some, but certainly not all, of the major categories of lobbyists: former politicians and bureaucrats, lawyers, public relations persons, accountants, and association personnel. One of the most visible categories of lobbyist both in Washington and in the various state capitals are former elected politicians. After retirement or electoral defeat, they decide to stay in Washington or their state capitals and work the political process from the lobbying position, which is considered the more lucrative end of the process. The numbers are significant—several hundred former congresspersons and senators serve as lobbyists in Washington—but tend to appear rather small compared with the city's total of more than 30,000 lobbyists. What these former official-lobbyists lack in numbers they make up for in clout, or influence. Major lobbying firms and political law firms in Washington pay top dollar for the services of those recently holding significant positions of political power. Salaries for those in this category have been running in the "mid-six figures" to highs of several million dollars a year. These former politician-lobbyists are expected to deliver inside knowledge, exceptional access, and subject matter expertise in such a quality to make these salaries a good investment for the groups or associations.

The recent big turnover years in the U.S. Congress (such as 2006, and 2010) saw a significant increase in the number of former members of Congress and senators seeking and gaining employment on K Street. If the former official also happens to be a lawyer, he or she is even more highly coveted because he or she adds a marketable skill to the other aspects brought to the position. Foreign economic and security interests seem to automatically assume that former elected officials retain their clout and can get things done for their country. After all, that is the way it is done back home in their own countries. U.S. senators seem to do quite well in this category because of their very high name visibility.

Within this category of elected officials working as lobbyists, an often overlooked collection of lobbyists are those we call "inside lobbyists." An *inside lobbyist* is a supporter of an interest who also happens to hold a congressional seat. Some legislators naturally represent with great vigor the dominant interests of their states or districts. One might expect the senators from Michigan, for example, to be on the side of the automobile manufacturers, just as one might expect the senators from Utah to represent the interests of the Mormon Church. This natural representation phenomenon is the reason Congress has had difficulty reducing various subsidies and price supports for farmers, for example; senators and congressmen from states like Iowa and Nebraska strongly oppose such bills. Other interests seek representation by inside lobbyists because of the personal characteristics of the members themselves. Israel's interests have long been watched over carefully by Connecticut's once Democratic, later Independent Senator Joseph Lieberman, who retired in 2013. Certain occupations and their interests are also represented by members in the legislature who come from those occupations. Military veterans were once well represented in Congress in the 50 years following World War II, but lately their inside numbers have been significantly reduced, and some say that veterans affairs and concerns have suffered as a result of the reduction of the size of the veterans' inside lobby. It is difficult to determine whether such a large inside lobby makes a great deal of difference on veterans' bills, however, for such bills normally receive near-unanimous congressional approval, especially in time of war.

Since the Reagan administration, inside lobbyists have also frequently been hired by the White House and executive branch's various departments. This situation is called by many in the reform community "putting the fox in charge of the chickens." Every president has about 4,000 appointments to fill positions within his or her administration. Interestingly, the United States is the only advanced democracy to allow such political appointments for policymaking and leadership positions as well as ambassadorships and judgeships. That is, the interest that is supposed to be regulated by government now runs the governmental office that is supposed to regulate it.

One of the clearest examples of such an appointment was Ron Brown early in the Clinton administration. Brown managed to span nearly every power position in the lobbying world in Washington. He held the chairmanship of the Democratic National Committee and was a lobbyist and advisor to the Clinton campaign all at the same time in 1992. He was then appointed by President Clinton as secretary of Commerce, where he could make many decisions affecting his former clients. Among President George W. Bush's numerous appointments in this mold was Gail Norton, who became secretary of the Interior after a long career as a lobbyist for various businesses seeking to reduce or eliminate regulation of their industries. Most of the hires in her department came from the energy industries, and many were top lobbyists for coal, mining, and oil interests.

In keeping with its support of curbs on the power of registered lobbyists, the Obama administration has, for the most part, avoided lobbyist appointments. But there has still been controversy. President Obama's first pick as secretary of Health and Human Services was former senator Tom Daschle of South Dakota, identified as a "strategic advisor" to clients looking to influence government policy but not actually registered as a lobbyist. After much criticism, the Daschle nomination was withdrawn.

In terms of actual numbers, however, many of the lobbyists in Washington and state capitals such as Sacramento, California, and Austin, Texas, are increasingly the former bureaucrats who work for the legislatures and executive branches. As far back as the late 1950s, former executive branch officials represented about 40 percent of lobbyists in Washington (Milbrath 1963). These former bureaucrats and politicians frequently were lobbyists themselves before they entered government. Additionally, they retain their contacts and knowledge of the governmental decision-making process. Thousands of lobbyists fit this pattern of working some years in government and then moving to the lobbying world. Some move back and forth several times, and this "revolving door" tends to produce huge salary jumps every time they return to the world of lobbying. The bigger the reputation or name of the appointed government official, the more money he or she can claim as a lobbyist. Perhaps the king of the lucrative revolving door was former secretary of state Henry Kissinger, who advised former president Richard Nixon on the opening of China in 1973 and then moved on to become one of the most successful advocates for the Chinese government at the time.

Since lawmaking in Congress is so complicated and largely mysterious to many outsiders, former legislative staff members are highly prized as lobbyists by many interest groups. They bring legislative and political skills, contacts, and subject matter expertise. A glance at the lobbying pages of the *National Journal* or *Congressional Quarterly Weekly Report,* two of the U.S. capital's weekly magazines of record, would give one a sense of the number of former legislative and executive branch staff members who have decided to become lobbyists.

The White House has a huge lobbying corps, carefully shrouded under the label Office of Congressional Relations. White House lobbyists are relatively new, a phenomenon of the last quarter century. In addition to the president's direct lobbying team, all of the departments and agencies of government have their own lobbyists on Capitol Hill, known as liaison staff. Many of these high-profile government lobbyists then move on to become richer private lobbyists. In some administrations, a trend appears to be emerging that the eagerly sought-after lobbying jobs inside the White House and the various departments require about two years of credential building before the "big move" to a more lucrative private lobbying position. Turnover is quite high in these jobs, but even for those who stay to the end of a presidential term or even two, the outside jobs as lobbyists are still available for most.

Private-Sector Lobbyists

Let us now turn to the more private-sector supply of lobbyists, the major law firms and public relations firms that fill the city of Washington, D.C. The "top dogs" of Washington lobbyists are a very special band of lawyer-lobbyists who function as the "lobbyist's lobbyists." Affiliated with the most prestigious Washington law firms, these men seldom participate in the direct contacts other lobbyists perform daily. Historically, they have been unwilling to even register as "mere" lobbyists. The role of one of the most famous lawyer-lobbyists of modern times, Clark Clifford, was described as follows:

Under law, anyone who seeks to influence the passage or defeat of any Federal legislation must register with the Clerk of the House of Representatives and the Secretary of the Senate. He must file quarterly reports detailing the interest represented and the amount of money spent. Clifford and other lawyers avoid registration in a perfectly legal manner: they sit in their offices two miles from Congress and tell the client what sort of legislation is needed, and exactly how he should go about obtaining it. Then they shake his hand at the door and send him a bill. Clifford was careful never to approach a Congressman face-to-face on behalf of a specific client. (Goulden 1972, 259)

The number of lawyers admitted to practice before the federal courts of the District of Columbia increased from just under 1,000 in 1950 to approximately 100,000 today (2014). Many of these are lawyer-lobbyists. Often, successful lawyer-lobbyists deny that they ever practice their lobbyist skills. For example, Robert Strauss, former chairman of the Democratic National Committee and former trade representative and ambassador to Russia, argues that he is not a lobbyist, although many would label him one of the best lobbyists in the history of the city.

Many of these super-lawyer lobbyists have served as cabinet-level officials in a variety of administrations and offer their clients a wealth of political wisdom. Some earn unbelievably high hourly rates for their lobbying advice, while others charge flat fees. Lobbyists in Washington often earn annual salaries of $1 million or higher. Some can command huge yearly retainers from foreign and domestic interests that run into the hundreds of thousands of dollars.

One Washington lawyer-lobbyist argues that these practitioners are far more useful than nonlawyer lobbyists. This is because they are trained to provide legal analysis and to gather and interpret facts. They can draft bills, be convincing witnesses at hearings, and even help write a bill's report at the end (Ablard 1970, 641–651). The increased role of Washington's lawyer-lobbyists can also be seen by the large number of non-Washington law firms that have opened up branch offices in the city in recent years.

Specialists in image building have also entered the world of lobbying in the United States. These *public relations (PR) lobbyists* usually work out of the largest public relations or advertising agencies on Madison Avenue in New York City and are frequently in the employ of foreign governments. But many of America's top corporations and interest groups will add a PR team to their lobbying operations if necessary. These PR firms offer a set of lobbying skills that most traditional lobbying shops cannot begin to envision. Public relations lobbying is heavily focused on mass media and, increasingly, social media. The PR lobbyists often come out of journalism and advertising backgrounds. The PR targets may be either governmental decision makers or general public opinion, or both.

One of the most important PR firms is Burson-Marsteller, a large New York PR firm that performed PR and lobbying tasks for the Argentine government. Many of the PR-challenged regimes in Africa, Asia, and South and Central America have spent millions of dollars hiring Burson-Marsteller or another of the famous PR lobbying firms. The award-winning political comic strip *Doonesbury* featured one of its most interesting recurring characters, Duke, in an August 2007 series titled "Duke, the Washington Super Lobbyist." His specialty? Representing the world's tyrants; as Duke put it, "Who knew I'd be so good at re-framing evil?" (Trudeau 2007).

One of the great Washington, D.C., PR stories involves a major PR triumph during the Gulf War in 1990–1991. After the Iraqi invasion of Kuwait in 1990, the Kuwaiti government-in-exile contracted with Hill and Knowlton to develop a PR campaign to increase support in the United States for the liberation of Kuwait. A front group was formed, Citizens for a Free Kuwait, financed almost entirely by the Kuwaiti government. Hill and Knowlton was paid $11.5 million for its PR lobbying. On October 10, 1990, a 15-year-old Kuwaiti girl testified to Congress that she witnessed Iraqi soldiers removing Kuwaiti babies from incubators and leaving them to die on a hospital floor. The story became a major part in the rising American support for the liberation of Kuwait. The girl turned out to be the daughter of the Kuwaiti ambassador to the United States, and no direct evidence was found to support the charges (Center for Media and Democracy 2007).

These elite PR firms tend to get hired by the traditional lobbying shops that need expertise beyond their abilities. However, a growing number of full-service lobbying firms have within their own ranks a wide range of lobbying skills and resources. They may provide a wide range of services, including campaign management, lobbying, polling, marketing, fund-raising, advertising, and public relations. Typically, these firms are nonpartisan, meaning their partners and staff have high-level contacts on both sides of the aisle.

Many of Washington's most successful lobbyists belong to small firms offering one or two lobbyists. Since more than 90 percent of Washington lobbyists work for law firms, trade associations, or corporations, the "boutique lobbying firms" often specialize in a particular issue or in a particular industry. They spend a large part of their time monitoring the actions of Congress or the departments that could affect their clients. Others write speeches or editorial page articles for their clients. The boutique firms' clients have much closer working relations with the small firms than with the full-service firms. Since these smaller boutique firms have one or only a very few clients, they can work full time on a client's issue if necessary.

In-House Lobbyists

The majority of association lobbyists who work in Washington and the state capitals across the country are *in-house lobbyists*. Larger and richer organizations have lobbying departments or legislature liaison staffs that work full or part time as lobbyists for their organizations. Smaller organizations usually have association managers or executive directors who can take the job of lobbyist when needed. These in-house lobbyists bring their knowledge of the interest area of the organization. Some groups, usually the more political and ad hoc ones, use volunteer lobbyists, drawn from their active memberships. Many groups dealing with moral, religious, women's, and environmental issues have used amateur lobbyists either by choice or because they lack finances to pay for professional, full-time lobbyists.

Sometimes *amateur lobbyists* can be effective if they possess special talents or resources. The top 180 American corporate executives who are members of the Business Roundtable can access the Washington, D.C., power elite because of the prestige of their positions. When these chief executive officers call on politicians, the latter group listens.

This summary of lobbyist categories is not exhaustive. Lobbyists working in Washington come from almost every possible background and have a variety of college degrees, ranging from English literature and microbiology to political science and law.

New Trends in Lobbyist Training and Makeup

A significant professionalization of the lobbying business has taken place in recent decades. Master's degree programs in lobbying have been established in a number of universities in the eastern part of the United States, including one in Washington, D.C., at George Washington University's Graduate Program in political management. Many of the students who enroll in these programs are already working in the policymaking process in one capacity or another but seek the professional credentials to move up to higher-level positions and responsibilities.

In addition, the American League of Lobbyists (ALL) has been created, which is dedicated to improving the image of lobbying as a profession. Hrebenar and Thomas have found that lobbying on the state level has become more professional in recent years as better-trained, better-educated, and higher-paid lobbyists have become more common in many states, and the contract professional, multiclient lobbyist has emerged in almost all the larger states and in many of the smaller states as well (Hrebenar and Thomas 2004). Although lobbying has long been dominated by males, a significant increase has been seen in the number of female lobbyists in Washington and in the state capitals. This increase is partly related to the increased status of lobbyists, the decline in unsavory lobbying techniques, and the increased expectations regarding special skills to be an effective lobbyist. The growing corps of female lobbyists has generally excellent political and educational backgrounds.

The Lobbyist's Role

What do lobbyists do? In fact, lobbyists may assume only a few major roles. Some are *contact persons,* who offer access to significant government decision makers. The quality of the person-to-person relationship is the important aspect here. A much smaller number of lobbyists serve as *strategists,* who plan lobbying campaigns. Far more common are the *liaison* lobbyists. In their *watch-dog* subrole, the liaison lobbyists listen and collect information about what is occurring in their assigned territory—be it Congress, the regulatory agencies, or the White House. Their job is to alert their clients to potential dangers or opportunities. The other major subrole of the liaison is that of *advocate.* Advocates perform as the popular stereotype pictures them: visiting politicians and bureaucrats, presenting data, and testifying at committee hearings.

The primary job for most lobbyists is to persuade policymakers to support their organization's policy objectives. So getting access to these decision makers is one of the keys to successful lobbying. Whether it is true or not, most legislators and bureaucrats think of themselves as extremely busy people, and with tens of thousands of lobbyists prowling the corridors of Washington, getting access can be very difficult.

Historically, bribes and parties were common ways to gain access not only in Washington but in many of the state capitals as well. Although these practices have not completely disappeared, they have certainly become much less common and important than in the past. The new lobbying laws and occasional increased media focus on lobbying have made direct bribery rare (but recent congressional scandals indicate that it still exists) and placed all sorts of restrictions on entertainment as a lobbying technique. Reflecting on what lobbying was like in the late 1800s, George Thayer described the half century following the 1876 election as America's Golden Age of Boodle. "Never has the American political process been so corrupt. No office was too high to purchase, no man too pure to bribe, no principle too sacred to destroy, no law too fundamental to break" (Thayer 1973, 37). But lobbying style in Washington has changed over the past 100 years. Milbrath concluded that by the 1960s, "bribes, broads, and booze" are near zero in influence effectiveness (Milbrath 1963, 274–276).

Certainly, money has not disappeared as an access-creating tool. A much more subtle and legal form of "indirect bribery" has evolved, and it is almost as effective as the older, coarser forms of blatant direct cash bribes it has replaced. Indirect bribery is most often found in the campaign contribution. Both sides of the exchange claim no direct relationship exists between the money the official receives and the decisions he or she makes as an official. As Hillary Rodham Clinton (D-NY) said during one of the Democratic Party presidential debates in 2007, she can take the money from the special interests such as insurance companies and it does not affect

A photographic exhibit that was introduced at the trial of David Safavian shows, from left, Jack Abramoff, an unidentified man, Ralph Reed, David Safavian, and Rep. Bob Ney, R-OH, during an August 2002 trip to Scotland. (AP Photo/U.S. District Court)

her votes in the Senate. Various political science studies have found some relationship, a mixed pattern, and even no relationship between campaign contributions and official votes (Maisel and Brewer 2008, 181). In reality, it is almost impossible to prove a quid pro quo exchange unless the lobbyist or official is incredibly careless or stupid, but almost everyone believes the money buys extraordinary access for the interest to the official and perhaps some special attention to the requests for assistance. If you listen to the politicians and the lobbyists, they almost always talk about the money creating access and not buying votes.

The Abramoff lobbying scandals of 2005–2006 involved free golfing trips to Scotland for high-level congressional leaders and selected lobbyists as well as free air travel on corporate jets in addition to tens of millions of dollars paid to several lobbyists in exchange for getting special policy favors from government officials. The reforms that were enacted in 2006–2007 have, at least for the moment, ended those types of trips and severely cut back on golf trips as an access-creating tactic.

The newer forms of access creation now center around low-cost social events and information-providing seminars. More and more, the lobbyists seek to provide help to legislators such as useful information and data on key issues and even help to write legislation for the legislators to introduce. Information and research have increased in value as money (outside of campaign contributions) has decreased in value. Information and person-to-person persuasion are at the core of direct lobbying.

Indirect Lobbying

The core element of indirect lobbying involves stimulating the grassroots or third parties into the lobbying game. It is used by lobbies to supplement their direct lobbying. Indirect lobbying takes many forms. Here we mention such tactics as using coalitions, initiatives and referendums, boycotts, demonstrations, and media lobbying because they are important parts of contemporary lobbying.

Media lobbying campaigns come in a variety of specialized forms. They try to generate positive feelings toward the group or conduct defensive or offensive campaigns to support a given policy objective. These campaigns can be seen on broadcast television and national cable television, in major newspapers and magazines, on the Internet, and even in handouts or fliers placed on the windshield of your car. Both electronic and print versions of these communications can be very expensive and thus are largely the tactics of the larger, richer associations. Small or poorer associations rely more heavily on social media and lower-cost outlets like regional cable TV. Free media can be sought by many groups that are small, politically impotent, or on the fringe of the mainstream political process where the use of normal paid media is out of the question. How does a group get free media attention? Demonstrations, protests, boycotts, and even forms of "cause terrorism" can and often do get the free media's attention. The big drawback is that the group cannot control the message found in such free media coverage. For example, Occupy Wall Street's encampments in major cities originally got sympathetic coverage in most mainstream newspapers and online reports; but after violent confrontations with police and weeks of unruly, disruptive behavior, much of the media coverage turned sour. In general, during the history of the United States, interest groups that are the victims of violence tend to fare better in the long-term achievement of their policy goals than those groups that commit the violence.

Interest groups will often band together in coalitions to multiply their lobbying resources to achieve a policy goal. Many of these coalitions will have dozens of informal members, and several are ad hoc, lasting only for the duration of the campaign and sometimes ending in failure. Coalitions offer an interest group several clear advantages. One is an efficient division of lobbying resources. Some organizations have special ties with one political party or congressional caucus and can use these resources to influence their special target. Labor unions can always have special access to the Democratic Party caucuses, while the business and fundamentalist religious groups have excellent access to the Republican Party caucuses. Groups with mass memberships can conduct more effective grassroots lobbying; groups with substantial research departments can collect data and publish information necessary to support a campaign. Coalitions can spread the risks and costs among the members. By sharing costs, a given group can participate in more campaigns or participate more powerfully in fewer efforts.

Most interest groups have to decide whether joining or even creating a coalition is worth the effort. A group may be able to achieve its goals by participating in a coalition of like-minded organizations or those that have similar goals. For some groups, joining a coalition may reveal to other groups some of a group's secrets and lobbying strategies and tactics. This approach also makes a group vulnerable to being identified with other groups that may have less than sterling reputations or leadership. Guilt by association is a danger in some coalitions. Finally, coalitions often cannot effectively control all of their members and the tactics they choose to use to further their objectives.

Coalitions are often brokered by a lobbyist who may specialize in putting together those kinds of legislative coalitions. Often front groups are used to hide the real membership of a coalition. Groups that may have PR problems (e.g., the tobacco industry) try to create coalition names that have a good or nice feel to them, such as the Calorie Control Council, a coalition in which the soft drink industry participates.

Boycotts are very popular tactics for interest groups in conflict with other powerful organizations in American society. Most boycotts fail to achieve their political objectives. One of the biggest boycotts in American history was the Equal Rights Amendment supporters' boycott in the 1970s of the states that did not support the amendment. The boycott failed to win approval of the amendment but helped create an environment in which many of the new laws passed by states following the boycott helped to move society closer to the political goals of the movement.

More demonstrations and protests are held in Washington, D.C., than in any other American city, and perhaps any other city in the world. Every day, an average of three demonstrations take place outside of the White House and at other sites in the city. Some of them (especially the civil rights marches of the 1960s and 1970s) have involved more than a million people.

Lobbying in the United States has become a huge business involving battles over governmental public policies, and trillions of dollars in appropriations, contracts, and profits are up for grabs. Lobbying expenditures by groups seeking to influence the federal government totaled $3.27 billion in 2011—up from $1.45 billion in 1998. The number of registered lobbyists in Washington during the same period grew from 10,400 to 12,600. Several billions more were also spent on lobbying at the state level (Center for Responsive Politics 2012). These lobbying expenditure totals represent the huge role played by lobbyists and lobbies in the United States, and they indicate the challenges such expenditures create for American democratic politics and responsible, honest government.

References

Ablard, Charles D. (1970). "The Washington Lawyer-Lobbyist." *George Washington Law Review* 38, no. 2: 641–651.

Bentley, Arthur F. (1949). *The Process of Government.* Bloomington, IN: Principia Press.

Center for Media and Democracy. (2007). "How PR Sold the War in the Persian Gulf." Accessed October 9, 2012. http://www.prwatch.org/books/tsigfy10.html.

Center for Responsive Politics. (2012). "Lobbying Database." Accessed October 9, 2012. http://opensecrets.org/lobbyists/index.asp.

Costain, Anne E., and Andrew S. McFarland. (1998). *Social Movements and American Political Institutions.* Lanham, MD: Rowman & Littlefield.

Dye, Thomas. (1995). *Politics in America.* Englewood Cliffs, NJ: Prentice Hall.

Freeman, Jo. (1983). *Social Movements in the Sixties and Seventies.* New York: Longman.

Garson, G. David. (1978). *Group Theories of Politics.* Beverly Hills, CA: Sage.

Ginsberg, Benjamin. (2007). *We the People.* New York: W. W. Norton.

Goulden, Joseph C. (1972). *The Super Lawyers.* New York: Dell.

Heffner, Richard D. (1956). *Alexis de Tocqueville: Democracy in America.* New York: Mentor.

Hoover Institution. (2008). "Jesse Unruh, Coming to Terms: A Money in Politics Glossary." Accessed October 9, 2012. http://www.campaignfinancesite.org/structure/terms/m.html.

Hrebenar, Ronald J., and Clive S. Thomas. (2004). Interest Groups in the States. In Virginia Gray and Russell L. Hanson, eds. *Politics in the American States.* Washington, DC: CQ Press, pp. 100–128.

Hunt, Kimberly N. (2004). *Encyclopedia of Associations.* Farmington Hills, MI: Gale-Thomson.

Ketcham, Ralph. (2006). *Selected Writings of James Madison.* Indianapolis, IN: Hackett.

Maisel, Sandy, and Mark D. Brewer. (2008). *Parties and Elections in America.* Boulder, CO: Rowman & Littlefield.

Meyer, David S. (2007). *The Politics of Protest: Social Movements in America.* New York: Oxford University Press.

Milbrath, Lester. (1963). *The Washington Lobbyists.* Chicago: Rand McNally.

Schattschneider, E.E. (1960). *The Semi-Sovereign People: A Realist's View of Democracy in America.* New York: Holt, Rinehart and Winston.

Thayer, George. (1973). *Who Shakes the Money Tree?* New York: Simon & Schuster.

Thomas, Clive S. (2004). *Research Guide to U.S. and International Interest Groups.* Westport, CT: Praeger.

Trudeau, Gary. (2007, Aug. 6). "Doonesbury." Accessed August 16, 2007. http://www.doonesbury.com/strip/dailydose/index.html?uc.fulldate=20070806/.

Truman, David. (1971). *The Governmental Process.* New York: Alfred A. Knopf.

Wills, Garry. (1982). *The Federalist Papers by Alexander Hamilton, James Madison and John Jay.* New York: Bantam.

Wilson, James Q. (1995). *Political Organizations.* Princeton, NJ: Princeton University Press.

History and Evolution
of Lobbying Regulation

Gregory Bordelon

Introduction

Our representative democracy vests the right to govern in a group of people selected by the voters to represent our interests in how the government should operate. These representatives form the law-making branch of government, our legislature. Inherit in this dynamic is that voters directly affect the work of representatives by virtue of the vote, by even giving representatives a job. However, to what degree are voters allowed to *influence* the work of these representatives, or have others engage in this *influence* on their behalf? What level of *access* should they have, and *who* should have this power of access in their place? Finally, should we allow the paid business of influence and access, and if so, what rules should be in place to sustain the representative-voter dynamic?

It is within this framework that the regulation of lobbying has developed. The phenomenon of influence and access on behalf of voters has been around since the country's founding and has been subject to varying levels of regulation since that time. Regulation has developed on several fronts: the type of individual or entity that is lobbying (lobbying by paid lobbyists, whether individually or in "firms," by interest groups), to whom lobbying efforts are targeted (legislatures, most notably, the Congress or directly to the people, so-called grassroots lobbying), the type of activity lobbyists can perform (advocacy versus gifts, dinner, etc.—how far can the idea of *access* go?), and what information lobbyists have to provide in the process of engaging in their craft (reporting and disclosure requirements). All of these points will be addressed in turn here, after reviewing the history of lobbying in the United States, focusing throughout on the constitutional elements and laws that have been enacted affecting the role of lobbyists.

History of Lobbying in the United States

18th-Century Notions of Lobbying—The Founding, Factions, and the First Amendment

In establishing a new government immediately after independence from Great Britain, the political leaders of the United States were charged with justifying the choice of a democratic form of government. James Madison, known as "father of the Constitution," was one of our most notable forefathers, particularly in explaining the structures of the new government. One of his pieces in *the Federalist Papers*, No. 10, would serve as the framework not only for basic governing principles like federalism and separation of powers but also for the idea of how to appease any group (or "faction," as he called it) in their involvement with the political process. "By a faction, I understand a number of citizens, whether amounting to a majority or a minority of the whole, who are united and actuated by some common impulse of passion, or of interest, adverse to the rights of other citizens, or to the permanent and aggregate interests of the community" (Madison 1787). These factions would later become known as interest groups and have a critical historical symbolism for the idea of lobbying. Madison stressed, however, the importance of not letting any one faction overpower the will of the voters, and from that idea, his idea of separating the branches of government into three co-equal but independent entities arose. It would be the law-making branch, the Congress, that Madison foreshadowed would be the focus of the pressure of these interest groups or "factions." Nicholas Allard writes:

> [T]he Framers created a layered and intricate system of government whereby the separation of powers and the system of federalism would provide multiple opportunities for organized groups to influence the workings of government, but also multiple forums for "ambition . . . to counteract ambition." . . . If, in drafting the Constitution, James Madison had consciously sought to create a governmental system that would encourage—indeed dictate—that lobbying would become central to policymaking, he could have scarcely done a better job. (Allard at pp. 37–38, 2008, quoting Burdett A. Loomis in *From the Framing to the Fifties: Lobbying in Historical and Constitutional Contexts* in Extensions, Fall 2006 at p. 1 in the latter section of the previous quote).

Madison may not have anticipated the increasing complexity of the federal government, where the growth of Congress into a large bureaucratic institution would necessitate the regulation of interactions with aides and advisors as well as with legislators. "Issues are too complex, the public too dispersed, and competing voices too cacophonous to rely exclusively on town hall meetings and citizen action to keep elected officials informed of constituent interests. . . . James Madison recognized the inevitability that factions or special interests, as we know them, would organize to influence government decisions" (Susman 2008).

The passage of the Bill of Rights in late 1791 provided an additional layer of protection for those seeking to advocate causes before Congress. In addition to the guarantees of free speech and free press that we are familiar with, lobbying is protected by the "right to petition" clause of the First Amendment. "Congress shall make no law . . . abridging . . . the right . . . to petition the Government for a redress of grievances" (U.S. Constitution). This right, along with free speech and the right to associate, was the basis for judicial action in the area of lobbying, discussed later on in this chapter. Although far less common than cases involving First Amendment rights, lobbying cases have set clear standards as to what should be the intersection between the government's interest in regulating lobbying and the right of someone to address concerns and advocate for reform. Were the anti-Federalists who succeeded in getting the Bill of Rights enacted thinking about the rights of what we know as lobbyists today? Likely not, but the language of the "right to peti-tion" clause is clear and direct. This may be one reason the U.S. Supreme Court has not heard a major case on lobbying since 1954 with *United States v. Harriss*.

19th-Century Lobbying

The word "lobbying" came into vogue during the 1800s as a colloquialism to refer to certain groups pressing their interests on those in power. It caught on when reporters in Washington, D.C., remarked how some would wait in the lobby of the Willard Hotel to "smoke a cigar with President Ulysses S. Grant or to meet Congressmen" (Allard 2008). President Grant's popularity as a Civil War–era hero won him the White House, but his presidential legacy was "forever marred" by the Credit Mobilier scandal in the 1870s (Glaeser and Goldin 2004). This controversy, involving revelations that congressmen took bribes and other improper payments related to Union Pacific Railroad contracts, motivated Congress to begin periodic investigations into lobbying practices; Crédit Mobilier also influenced several of the states to begin regulating the lobbying of their own state legislative bodies (Hasen 2012). For example, Georgia outlawed lobbying of state legislators in 1877; Massachusetts, in 1890, imposed a requirement that lobbyists report and disclose any expenses (Hasen 2012). Toward the end of the century, in 1893, California passed a law called "Purity of Elections" based on previous English statutes; this served as an innovative precursor to lobbying reform in the state in the 1940s (California Secretary of State 2012).

The U.S. Supreme Court had an early occasion to address the concept of lob-bying in *Trist v. Child*. Mr. Trist had hired the services of Mr. Child to recoup pay-ment against the United States for services rendered in 1848 and had hired Child as his attorney to pursue the matter before Congress. It was found that Mr. Child "had been to see various members of Congress, soliciting their influence in behalf of a bill introduced for the benefit of Mr. Trist, and in several instances obtaining a promise of it" (*Trist v. Child* at pp. 2–3, 1875). While the Supreme Court did not find evidence of bribery, it held that the payment in this case should not be allowed because

> A contract to take charge of claim before Congress, and prosecute it as an agent and attorney for the claimant (the same amounting to contract to procure by "lobby services"—that is to say, by personal participation by the agent, and others supported to have personal influence in any way with members of Congress—the passage of a bill [here, Mr. Trist's law authorizing payment of his 1848 claim] providing for the payment of the claim), is void. (*Trist v. Child* at p. 5, 1875)

This early judicial pronouncement is notable for the fact that it branded lobby-ing as de facto corruption. However, it left the door open for contracts of "purely professional services . . . [including] . . . attending to the taking of testimony, col-lecting facts, preparing arguments, and submitting them either orally or in writing to a committee . . . with other services of like character intended to reach only the understanding of the persons sought to be influenced" (*Trist v. Child* at p. 5, 1875). The struggle to discern the line between these two activities set the stage for regulation in the 20th century. Acknowledging the possibility of corruption inherent in lobbying but recognizing the constitutional element, the Court noted that it didn't want to:

> [O]pen the door to corrupt influence upon Congress, or to give aid to that which is popularly known as "lobbying," and is properly denounced as dishonorable. But we are asking that by giving the sanction of the law to an open and honorable advocacy by counsel of private rights before legislative bodies, the court shall aid in doing away with the employment of agencies which work secretly and dishonorably. (*Trist v. Child* at p. 8, 1875)

The disclosure and reporting requirements to come in the 1900s were clearly presaged by this opinion.

Lobbying in the Last One Hundred Years—Definitional and Regulatory Patchwork

Early Part of the 20th Century

In 1906, the Supreme Court decided (again on contract law grounds like in the *Trist* case) whether procuring legislation in favor of getting Congress to acquire property for public projects would be allowed. The Court, in *Hazelton v. Sheckells*, said no, and such an agreement is "void as against public policy" (*Hazelton v. Sheckells* at p. 1, 1906). Here, the Court introduced various issues that were the subject of future lobbying regulation, both the difference between lobbyists and contractors and the government institutions with which those parties engage, either in the legislative branch or in the executive branch. The Court said, "There is no real difference in principle between agreements to procure favors from legislative bodies, and agreements to procure favors in the shape of contracts from the heads of departments" (*Hazelton v. Sheckells* at pp. 15–16, 1906). It also mentioned that contingency contract arrangements in lobbying, where the lobbyist would receive a percentage-based fee based on the likelihood of obtaining a particular legislative outcome, were void (*Hazelton v. Sheckells* at p. 16, 1906). Both of these areas—who would be considered a "covered" official for purposes of lobbying regulation, and the legality of contingency arrangements in lobbying—are addressed later in this chapter.

Despite these intermittent court battles against a rising tide of lobbying, the pressure exerted by large industries on Congress was mounting. As author Robert Kaiser writes, "The ability of the railroads and the gigantic trusts that controlled entire sectors of the economy—including wool, sugar, tobacco, steel, and oil—to work their will in Washington was . . . eye-opening" (Kaiser 2009, 90). At the time, U.S. senators were selected by state legislatures, so industry leaders got extra "bang for the buck" by bankrolling state legislative campaigns. They also worked to influence U.S. senators directly, brazenly seeking deals for lucrative state contracts; nine U.S. senators were convicted of bribery between 1866 and 1905 (Kaiser 2009, 91). Even after the passage of the Seventeenth Amendment, which called for direct election of U.S. senators, controversy about the effect of monied interests on Congress did not abate (Kaiser 2009, 91). Eventually President Woodrow

Wilson's frustration with these entrenched "interests," coupled with the United States' involvement in World War I, resulted in Congress' first major piece of legislation covering lobbying activities—the Foreign Agents Registration Act of 1938.

Foreign Agents Registration Act of 1938

In the wake of increasing corruption earlier in the century and the growing concern over foreign government influence in the United States, Congress passed the Foreign Agents Registration Act in 1938. In particular, Nazi and Communist propaganda caused Congress to worry about "[t]hese foreign bodies . . . attempting to alter U.S. policy through subversive propaganda disseminated in this country by their agents" (Spak 1990, 242–243). The act did not attempt to block all foreign agents or limit the dissemination of information from foreign sources. However, it did require the agent to *disclose* its source as well as the agent himself. In one of the very few court challenges to the act, the federal district court in D.C. reasoned that the disclosure provisions were valid because if Americans knew the identity of foreign agents, then they could evaluate their statements accordingly (*United States v. Auhagen* 1941). Foreign agents were required to register with the secretary of State, who was also given authority to impose criminal penalties for those foreign agents not complying with the law (Spak 1990, 244). Four years later, the act was amended to transfer administrative authority to the attorney general and also to exempt certain foreign nations "declared vital to U.S. interests by the President" (Spak 1990, 245). The act was amended again multiple times and was ultimately overhauled in 1963 to move its focus "from controlling the dissemination of foreign propaganda to controlling the sophisticated activities of agents acting as paid lobbyists for foreign principals" (Spak 1990, 246).

The Foreign Agents Registration Act has now been effective—alongside strong domestic lobbying regulations—for decades, with enforcement still being pursued by the Justice Department and the attorney general. Most recently, in 2011, two individuals (acting as "agents of a foreign principal") were charged with failing to register their political and public relations activities on behalf of the Pakistani government. It was alleged that one of the individuals used an international advocacy group, the Kashmiri American Council (KAC), to covertly funnel money from the Pakistani government to U.S. officials (Pickard and Capeloto 2011).

Federal Regulation of Lobbying Act of 1946, the Rumely Case and the Seminal Case of United States v. Harriss

The first comprehensive piece of federal legislation covering domestic lobbying was the Federal Regulation of Lobbying Act (FRLA) of 1946. Considered the predecessor to the current lobbying governing framework, the Lobbying Disclosure Act, FRLA's passage was predicated on very clear concerns expressed by Congress at the time. As Professor Lloyd Hitoshi Mayer writes concerning the Senate Report that accompanied the passage of FRLA:

> Too often . . . the true attitude of public opinion is distorted and obscured by the pressures of special-interest groups. Beset by swarms of lobbyists seeking to protect

this or that small segment of the economy or to advance this or that narrow interest, legislators find it difficult to discover the real majority will and to legislate in the public interest. As Government control of economic life and its use as an instrument of popular welfare have increased, the activities of these powerful groups have multiplied. . . . Full information regarding the membership, source of contributions, and expenditures of organized groups would prove helpful to Congress in evaluating their representations and weighing their worth. Publicity is a mild step forward in protecting government under pressure and in promoting the democratization of pressure groups. (Mayer 2008, 503)

The law, passed as part of a larger measure, established registration requirements for those who lobbied Congress, as well as a quarterly reports of money spent and received for lobbying activities (Hasen 2012, 201). Although the intent of the statute was noble, many critics argued that it was drafted too vaguely and lacked an adequate enforcement mechanism for violations. While the goal of the FRLA was to regulate both direct and indirect communication with Congress by pressure groups and lobbyists, the ambiguous language in the law (with attendant criminal penalties as sanctions) almost guaranteed constitutional attacks in the courts (Zeller 1958, 94). The first attack came in 1953, arguing that the definition of lobbying in the FRLA was too vague for constitutional scrutiny. The second, still considered the most important Supreme Court case analyzing the constitutional strictures of lobbying regulation, was decided in 1954 and was the last time the U.S. Supreme Court directly addressed the limits on government's power to regulate lobbying.

In *United States v. Rumely*, the secretary of an organization that sold books of an extreme political nature was asked to disclose the list of those who purchased the organization's writings. The disclosure demand was made by the Select Committee on Lobbying Activities; this special, ad hoc body was established to study and investigate "(1) all lobbying activities intended to influence, encourage, promote, or retard legislation; and (2) all activities of agencies of the Federal Government intended to influence, encourage, promote, or retard legislation" (U.S. House of Representatives 1949). When Mr. Rumely refused to provide that list to Congress, he was criminally convicted of violating a federal statute, being held in contempt of a request of Congress. The government argued that the Select Committee was acting under the authority of the FRLA, but the Court pointed out that the FRLA did not explicitly define either "lobbying" or "lobbying activities." Moreover, the justices raised First Amendment concerns:

Surely it cannot be denied that giving the scope to the resolution for which the Government contends, that is, deriving from it the power to inquire into all efforts of private individuals to influence public opinion through books and periodicals, however remote the radiations of influence which they may exert upon the ultimate legislative process, raises doubts of constitutionality in view of the prohibition of the First Amendment. (*United States v. Rumely* at p. 46, 1953)

While declining to rule on the First Amendment issue, the Court held that the resolution creating the Select Committee only authorized the investigation of lobbying activity. Its opinion further held that the common definition of lobbying only included attempts to influence Congress, not the general population. Since the selling of the book did not constitute a direct appeal to Congress (though it involved indirect appeals, which became known as "grassroots" lobbying), there was no "lobbying" as defined by the FRLA. This meant the contempt proceeding was outside the scope of the committee's authority, and therefore invalid as applied to Rumely (whose conviction was overturned).

But the *Rumely* decision helped to advance the cause of federal lobbying regulation in three ways: (1) it avoided striking down the FRLA on constitutional grounds; (2) it affirmed the authority of Congress to investigate lobbying activities; and (3) it gave implicit suggestions as to what could define "lobbying" and "lobbying activity" to stave off a future constitutional challenge to the FRLA.

This frontal challenge was posed the next year in *United States v. Harriss*. The defendants were criminally charged with violations of the FRLA for failing to report the activities of "every person 'receiving any contributions or expending any money' for the purpose of influencing the passage or defeat of any legislation by Congress" (*United States v. Harriss* at p. 614, 1954). (Specifically, a Texas corporation called the National Farm Committee and Harris—among other individuals— were engaged in attempting to influence legislation related to the market prices and futures trading of certain agricultural commodities.) The actions alleged by the criminal charge included payment for face-to-face communication with members of Congress, at public functions and committee hearings as well as expenditures associated with "induc[ing] various interested groups and individuals to communicate by letter with members of Congress on such legislation" (*United States v. Harriss* at p. 615, 1954). The district court dismissed the criminal charges and ruled the relevant provisions of the FRLA unconstitutional.

On direct appeal, the U.S. Supreme Court was faced with several constitutional questions, including (1) whether the reporting provisions of the FRLA were too vague under due process standards and (2) whether the law violated defendants' First Amendment rights of free speech, free press and right to petition the government for redress of grievances.

The Court found that the statute was not too vague as to be enforced but warned Congress as follows:

> The constitutional requirement of definiteness is violated by a criminal statute that fails to give a person of ordinary intelligence fair notice that his contemplated conduct is forbidden by the statute. The underlying principle is that no man shall be held criminally responsible for conduct which he could not reasonably understand to be proscribed. . . . And if this general class of offenses can be made constitutionally definite by a reasonable construction of the statute, this Court is under a duty to give the statute that construction. (*United States v. Harriss* at pp. 617–618, 1954)

Furthermore, the justices ruled that the construction of the statute could apply only to "'lobbying in its commonly accepted sense'—to direct communication with members of Congress on pending or proposed federal legislation" (*United States v. Harriss* at p. 620, 1954). Although the charges were upheld, *Harriss*, in effect, "significantly rewrote and narrowed the [FRLA] statute to avoid the vagueness problem, holding the rewritten statute acceptable under the First Amendment" (Hasen 2012, 201). In its attempt to save the statute but recognizing the constitutional concerns inherit in it, the *Harriss* Court effectively "opened more loopholes in the already porous statute . . . decid[ing] that the law did not require all interests that spent money on lobbying to register—only those that solicited and collected money specifically with lobbying in mind, . . . as their 'principal purpose' when they collected the funds" (Birnbaum 1992, 14). As many scholars of lobbying regulation point out, the decision "all but ended" federal prosecutions under the FRLA.

Lobbying Disclosure Act of 1995

Regulation through Definitions

Harriss was the last case to come before the U.S. Supreme Court dealing with the direct issue of lobbying regulation. It became clear after the *Harriss* opinion that prosecutions under the FRLA were not an easy path, and lobbying went mostly unchecked for 50 years; requirements for disclosure of represented interests could not be even-handedly enforced in the face of a questionable constitutional framework for regulation. For this reason, lobbying law at the federal law remained virtually unchanged until the mid-1990s. The only minor change to federal lobbying laws in this time period came in 1989 with an amendment to a Department of Interior appropriations bill by Senator Robert Byrd from West Virginia, which prohibited the expenditure of appropriated funds to influence the award of a federal contract, grant, or loan. In those circumstances, the recipient was required to disclose the name and address of each person paid to influence the award (U.S. House of Representatives 1995).

Calls to tighten disclosure requirements were renewed in the 1992 presidential campaign, following media coverage of questionable awarding of federal contracts at the behest of lobbyists in the late 1980s. In 1995, Congress finally enacted sweeping reform (Luneberg 2008, 86) based on three principal findings:

(1) Responsible representative Government requires public awareness of the efforts of paid lobbyists to influence the public decision-making process in both the legislative and executive branches of the Federal Government;

(2) Existing lobbying disclosure statutes [the FRLA] have been ineffective because of unclear statutory language, weak administrative and enforcement provisions, and an absence of clear guidance as to who is required to register and what they are required to disclose;

(3) The effective public disclosure of the identity and extent of the efforts of paid lobbyists to influence Federal officials in the conduct of Government actions will increase public confidence in the integrity of Government. (2 U.S.C. § 1601; Luneberg 2008, 89–90)

The hope was "to strengthen public confidence in government by replacing the existing patchwork of lobbying disclosure laws with a single, uniform statute which covers the activities of all professional lobbyists" (Mayer 2008).

The Lobbying Disclosure Act of 1995 (LDA) sought to create a unified statutory scheme defining the actors involved and explicitly spelling out the requirements for registration and reporting of lobbying activity. Passed by unanimous vote in both the House of Representatives and the Senate, the LDA remains the principal regulatory framework of lobbying at the federal level, significantly amended only once (in 2007, as explained later). To better understand this "current" regulatory framework for lobbying, it is best to look at how the LDA is laid out and what (and whom) it seeks to regulate.

The provisions of the FRLA, previously in Chapters 8 and 8A of Title 2 of the U.S. Code, were repealed and superseded completely by the provisions of the LDA. Section 1602 of the LDA, while seemingly an innocuous set of definitions, actually has great importance because it clarifies the parameters of regulation. "Clients" of lobbyists include any person or entity that employs or retains another person for financial or other compensation to conduct lobbying activities on behalf of that person or entity (2 U.S.C. § 1602(2)). When an organization employs lobbyists who engage in lobbying on behalf of the employer, then the employer is considered a client for those purposes.

Interestingly, the LDA seeks to regulate the practice of lobbying not so much by the practice itself but by defining who lobbyists target in the interest of regulation; as a result of this focus, both the legislative branch and the executive branch are covered. "Covered" executive branch officials include the president, vice president, any officer or employee in the Executive Office of the president, and any high-level ranking executives above civil service levels as well as "any member of the uniformed services whose pay grade is at or above O-7" (2 U.S.C. § 1602(3)). The law also applies to lobbying of directors of executive agencies who promulgate rules and regulations within their respective spheres. For "covered legislative branch officials," the LDA expands the scope of the FRLA by including not only members of Congress but also congressional staff, often the target of lobbyists hoping to influence advisors close to particular members (2 U.S.C. § 1602(4)). "Foreign entities" incorporates the definition used in the Foreign Agents Registration Act of 1938, still valid today (as discussed earlier). These entities mean foreign principals such as "foreign governments, foreign political parties, and foreign commercial entities" (Luneberg 2008, 104).

Four of the definitions of section 1602 touch on the term "lobbying" itself and define "lobbying activities," "lobbying contacts," "lobbying firms," and "lobbyists." A "lobbying firm" is a person or an entity with one or more employees who are lobbyists on behalf of a client and self-employed individuals who are lobbyists (2 U.S.C. § 1602(9)). A "lobbyist" is any individual who is employed or retained by a client for financial or other compensation for services that include more than one lobbying contact when those lobbying activities constitute at least 20% of the time engaged by the lobbyist to the client over a six-month period (2 U.S.C. § 1602(10)).

What exactly constitutes "lobby contacts" that would lead to "lobbying activities" is at the heart of LDA's definitions. "Lobbying activities" include contacts and efforts in support of such contacts, including preparation and planning activities, research and other background work that is intended for use in contact, and coordination with the lobbying activities of others (2 U.S.C. § 1602(7)). "Lobbying contacts"—defined in more detail than any other concept in the LDA—mean *only* oral, written, or electronic communication to a covered official made on behalf of a client with regard to four things: (1) the formulation, modification, or adoption of federal legislation; (2) the formulation, modification, or adoption of federal rules, executive orders, or any other program, policy, or position of the government; (3) the administration or execution of a federal program or policy; or (4) the nomination or confirmation of anyone subject to confirmation by the U.S. Senate (2 U.S.C. § 1602(8)(A)). Communications outside these categories do not trigger the reporting, disclosure, and registration requirements.

Unsurprisingly, much of the subsequent debate about LDA centers around the question of what should be considered "lobbying contacts." The House of Representatives' website on the LDA presents the following two examples to clarify:

> *Example 1:* Lobbyist "A," a former chief of staff in a congressional office, is now a partner in the law firm retained to lobby for Client "B." After waiting one year to comply with post-employment restrictions on lobbying, Lobbyist "A" telephones the Member on whose staff she served. She asks about the status of legislation affecting Client "B's" interests. Presumably "B" will expect the call to have been part of an effort to influence the Member, even though only routine matters were raised at that particular time. (U.S. House of Representatives Office of the Clerk 2012)

In the preceding example, the contact is not considered lobbying activity since it was merely done in furtherance of obtaining information or a "request for the status of an action . . . [and] the request [did] not include an attempt to *influence* [emphasis added] a . . . covered legislative branch official" (2 U.S.C. § 1602(8)(B)(v)). A more obvious example of a "contact" that would not be considered a "lobbying contact" would be:

> *Example 2:* Company "Z" offers temporary employment to recent college graduates. The graduates are hired to conduct surveys of congressional staff by reading prepared questions and recording the answers. The questions seek only information. These communications do not amount to lobbying contacts. (U.S. House of Representatives Office of the Clerk 2012)

Information obtained in response to government demand such as a subpoena, or provided in response to an informal request, or made in response to a notice for comment on a matter of public concern are also examples of contacts that do not fall within the purview of the LDA.

While the LDA made progress toward consolidating the patchwork of previous regulation, it still left many loose ends. As scholars have often pointed out, "[t]here are numerous ways to influence government actions, ranging from suing government agencies to commenting on executive branch rulemaking to urging legislators to propose legislation. Yet no single existing legal definition of lobbying encompasses the entire range of these activities, and each covers a different, although often overlapping, subset" (Mayer 2008, 487–488).

Three Main Duties—Registration, Reporting, and Disclosure

The three principal obligations imposed on lobbyists by the LDA are registration, reporting, and disclosure. As to initial *registration*, a lobbyist is to register no later than 45 days after first making a lobbying contact or being employed or retained for such purposes, whichever is earlier. Lobbyists are required to register with offices within respective houses of Congress, with the clerk of the House of Representatives and the secretary of the Senate (2 U.S.C. § 1603(a)(1)). Registration is not required if total income related to lobbying activities on behalf of one client does not exceed $5,000 or total expenses for all lobbying activities do not exceed $20,000 (2 U.S.C. § 1603(a)(3)(A)). Each registration is to contain detailed information (e.g., name, address, principal place of business) about the registering lobbyist, his or her client, and any other organization that contributes more than $10,000 toward the lobbying activities of the lobbyist and who plans or supervises, in whole or in major part, such lobbying activities related to that contribution (2 U.S.C. § 1603(b)(3)). Lobbying registrants are also required to register any foreign interest or affiliate holding more than 20 percent equitable ownership in a client firm(2 U.S.C. § 1603(b)(4)).

The lobbyist is also to register a statement of general issue areas in which he or she expects to engage in lobbying activities on behalf of the client and to the extent possible, specific issues that have already been addressed or are likely to be addressed in lobbying activities (2 U.S.C. § 1603(b)(5)). Finally, the lobbyist is to register the name of each of his or her employee who has acted or may expect to act also as a lobbyist on behalf of the client when he or she served previously as a "covered legislative branch official" or "covered executive branch official" in the previous two years before acting initially as a lobbyist on behalf of the client (2 U.S.C. § 1603(b)(6)). (This is a variation of the so-called revolving door provision, explained more fully later.) Initial lobbyist registration forms (under section 1603) are housed in what are known as "LD-1" databases in both houses of Congress, and subsequent required reports (under section 1604) are filed as "LD-2" documents.

In addition to this initial registration, under the original 1995 provisions of the LDA, lobbyists are required to file continuous, semi-annual *reports* with the House and the Senate on all of their lobbying activities (as defined in the statute) separately for each client they represent (2 U.S.C. § 1604(a)). The reports are to contain the name of the lobbyist, his or her client, and any changes or updates to this basic information provided in the initial registration. They also are to include a list of specific lobbying issues (2 U.S.C. § 1604(b)(2)(A)). The report also is to include a list of the houses of Congress and federal agencies contacted by lobbyists on behalf of a particular client, a list of all employees acting with the registering lobbyist on behalf of a particular client, and a description of the interest, if any, of any foreign entity identified in the initial registration (2 U.S.C. § 1604(b)(2)(B)-(D)). Lobbyists or lobbying firms are also required to make good faith estimates of the total amount of income from a particular client during the semi-annual reporting period (2 U.S.C. § 1604(b)(3), (c)).

Finally, lobbyists subject to the registration and reporting requirements of the LDA are put on notice that both the secretary of the Senate and the clerk of the

House are to develop a comprehensive *disclosure* system to collect and catalog lobbyist information. This includes a "publicly available list of all registered lobbyists, lobbying firms, and their clients; and computerized systems designed to minimize the burden of filing and maximize public access to materials " (2 U.S.C. § 1605(3)). The respective officer of each house also is vested with the authority to notify any lobbyist or lobbying firm in noncompliance as well as notify the U.S. attorney for the District of Columbia of such noncompliance after the lobbyist fails to give a reason within 60 days for noncompliance (2 U.S.C. § 1605(7) & (8)). Both houses of Congress have set up comprehensive systems for public dissemination of and access to this information, cross-referenced by registered lobbyists, clients, amounts of income received in lobbying activities and specific pieces of legislation/matters of targeted actions. Civil fines of up to $50,000 are possible for violations of any provision of the LDA (2 U.S.C. § 1606); the change to civil from criminal penalties in the FRLA was driven partially by a desire to increase enforcement. However, like its predecessor, "vigorous enforcement [of the LDA] has not been realized" (Luneburg and Susman 2006, 53).

The remaining sections of the LDA concern rules of interpretation. For example, to avoid challenges like those posed by *Harriss*, the LDA must be construed so as not to impinge upon the First Amendment rights of petitioning the government, association, and speech (2 U.S.C. § 1607). Another interpretative section addresses the issue of severability, meaning that if a court should strike down one part of the LDA, the rest of the law will stand even with the stricken part removed (2 U.S.C. § 1608).

The final three sections of the pre-2007 LDA concern certain sections of the tax code. Of particular importance, the LDA posits that since ordinary Americans cannot deduct expenses relating to communicating with their representatives in Congress, lobbying expenses should generally not be tax deductible as well (2 U.S.C. § 1612). This is the foundation for the current regulation in the Internal Revenue Code, which "preclude[es] the deductibility of lobbying costs as business expenses and limit[s] the ability of tax-exempt charities to lobby [and] may be seen as intended to maintain a level playing field among competing lobbyists" (Briffault 2008, 114).

Abramoff Scandal—Into the Modern Context of Lobbying

The 12 years between the enactment of the LDA and its most comprehensive amendments to date in 2007 were mired in controversy relating to lobbying activity. Because of the transparency created by the disclosure provisions of the LDA and the lack of substantive spending limits on lobbying expenses, a small group of influential lobbyists came to the attention of the media—one in particular by the name of Jack Abramoff. Abramoff was the central figure in what became "the biggest congressional corruption scandal in generations" (Schmidt and Grimaldi 2005).

A lawyer educated at Georgetown, Abramoff built a business empire in Washington. He owned two D.C. restaurants and leased four arenas and stadium skyboxes to entertain members of Congress and key policymakers (Schmidt and Grimaldi

2005). As a lobbyist, he came to prominence while promoting the interests of certain Native American tribes—and directing their political contributions. The Mississippi Band of Choctaw Indians, his largest client, donated over $250,000 to an outfit called the U.S. Family Network, a public advocacy group (Smith 2005); the U.S. Family Network was almost exclusively funded by corporations and other interests linked to Abramoff, and heavily lobbied influential members of Congress such as then-House Majority Speaker Republican Tom DeLay of Texas. According to media reports, DeLay's former chief of staff facilitated a donation of $1 million from Russian private energy executives to the USFN, covertly intended to influence DeLay's vote on legislation concerning a potential bailout for Russia's faltering economy (Smith 2005).

The U.S. Family Network arrangement was just one of Abramoff's shady influence tactics. In another example, he arranged "lavish trips to the United Kingdom and the South Pacific for DeLay; one such outing involve[ing] . . . $70,000 to pay for DeLay, his wife, and two aides to visit Scotland and play golf at the famous St. Andrews Links" (Hasen 2012). When the extent of Abramoff's involvement and influence with DeLay and others came to light, Congress called for hearings. Ultimately the lobbyist pled guilty to fraud, tax evasion, and conspiracy to bribe public officials (Koger and Victor 2009).

Ironically, Abramoff was never charged with direct violations of the LDA or congressional ethics rules (Potter and Birkenstock 2008). It was largely the negative public reaction to the case, not attempts to enforce then-existing lobbying laws, that spurred Congress to enact a new round of legislation.

Modern-Day Regulation of Lobbying—HLOGA and Patchwork of Other Governing Laws

Honest Leadership and Open Government Act of 2007 (HLOGA)—As It Amends the LDA

In 2007, Congress reacted to the Abramoff debacle by drastically modifying the LDA. Designed to make lobbying practices more transparent, the Honest Leadership and Open Government Act (HLOGA) also modified other federal lobbying laws. It sought generally to "regulate the actions of lobbyists, elected officials and their staffs, appointed office holders, and other government employees" by amending the LDA, changing internal Senate ethics rules on gifts, travel, and earmarked funds in legislation, and modifying post-employment restrictions for members of both the legislative and executive branches (Allard 2008). HLOGA redefined the term "lobbyist" as including all those persons engaging in, for compensation and on behalf of a client, more than one lobbying contact when those lobbying activities constitute at least 20 percent of the time engaged by the lobbyist to the client over a *three*-month period (2 U.S.C. § 1602(10)). Registration thresholds were significantly lowered; now a lobbyist would have to register if he or she received income of at least $2,500 (down from $5,000) from any one client and spent a total of at least $10,000 (down from $20,000) on lobbying activities (2 U.S.C. § 1603(a)(3)(A)). Disclosures of third-party contributions to clients or to the registering lobbyist/lobbying firm were lowered to $5,000 and the threshold level of involvement by third parties was lowered from participating "in whole or in major part" to "actively participating" in planning or supervision of lobbying activities (2 U.S.C. § 1603(b)(3)). The two-year rule to disclose when lobbying on behalf of a client who previously served as a "covered" legislative or executive official was extended to a period of 20 years (2 U.S.C. § 1603(b)(6)). Ongoing reports were now required quarterly instead of semiannually. A provision requiring that lobbyists disclose representation of state or local units of government was also added in the HLOGA amendments (2 U.S.C. § 1604(b)(5)). The required good faith estimates of total income from a particular client during the quarterly reporting period were triggered at lower amounts (2 U.S.C. § 1604(b)(3), (c)).

Explicitly acknowledging a connection between campaign donations and lobbying activity, the HLOGA creates a new and distinct reporting requirement. All lobbyists obligated to register under the law must now also disclose the names of all political committees established or controlled by the lobbyist as well as the name of each candidate for federal office, current officeholder, leadership PAC, or political party committee to whom contributions from the lobbyist exceed $200. This section also requires disclosure of funds used by lobbyists for: (1) an event honoring or recognizing a "covered" legislative or executive official under the LDA, (2) contributions to entities named for a covered official, or persons or entities recognized in honor of such official, (3) contributions to entities established, financed, or otherwise operated by covered officials, or (4) meetings, retreats, conferences, or other similar events held by or in the name of covered officials (2 U.S.C. § 1604(d)). These contribution reports are semiannual, and are referred to as LD-203 forms (U.S. House of Representatives 2009). Lobbyists filing an LD-203 must also certify that they have read and understood the Senate and House Rules relating to gifts and travel and attest that they have not provided any gifts, including travel, knowingly in violation of those bodies' rules. A glance at the home page of the House of Representatives' lobbying disclosure site reveals that a total of 2,055 noncompliant registrants have been referred to the U.S. attorney's D.C. office.

Lastly, procedures were enhanced to make disclosure and enforcement more transparent. HLOGA requires all databases to be accessible, intuitive and free (online) for the public, and linked to related matters within the jurisdiction of the Federal Election Commission. The number of noncomplying lobbyists must be disclosed. Civil penalties for HLOGA were increased to a ceiling of $200,000; more importantly, criminal sanctions were reinstated, calling for anyone who "knowingly and corruptly" fails to comply with the law to be imprisoned for up to five years.

Two new sections added to the LDA now expressly prohibit any registered lobbyist from making a gift or providing travel to a "covered legislative branch official" under House and Senate rules. Additionally, there is a new requirement for the Comptroller General in the Government Accountability Office to annually audit a random sample of lobbyists, lobbying firms, and LDA registrants. The findings of the audit are to be submitted to Congress.

A survey of the 2011 Lobbying Disclosure Report by the Comptroller General reveals that the vast majority of registered lobbyists are in compliance with the reporting requirements of the LDA as modified by the HLOGA (88% filing the required quarterly reports in the last half of 2010 and first half of 2011); only 4 percent of all semiannual reports omitted one or more reportable political contributions to candidates for the House and Senate (Government Accountability Office 2011). With respect to enforcement and penalties, the report reveals that November 2011 marked the first time since the enactment of the HLOGA that a lobbying firm settled with the Justice Department for noncompliance issues; the settlement was in the amount of $45,000 (Government Accountability Office 2011).

Although the U.S. Supreme Court has not ruled on the HLOGA, the U.S. Court of Appeals for the D.C. Circuit—often a barometer for controversial issues pipelining to the Supreme Court—did hear a case concerning the constitutionality of requiring disclosure of third-party contributions and the interpretation of the language "actively participates" as it concerns the relationship between lobbyists and third-party contributors to clients of lobbyists. In *National Association of Manufacturers v. Taylor*, an industry trade association challenged the provision as vague and a violation of the group's rights under the First Amendment. In upholding the law, even in the face of the highest level of constitutional scrutiny, the court stated that disclosure provisions under the LDA and HLOGA do not prevent speech, they simply require disclosing the source of that speech. The court cited the *Harriss* decision in ruling that disclosure "serve[s] a 'vital national interest' in a 'manner restricted to its appropriate end.' In so doing, the [Supreme] Court emphasized that Congress had 'not sought to prohibit [lobbying] pressures,' but had 'merely provided for a modicum of information'" (*National Ass'n of Mfrs. v. Taylor* at pp. 12–13, 2009). Notwithstanding the First Amendment rights addressed over 50 years earlier in *Harriss*, the appellate court reiterated the purpose of lobbying disclosure laws and the government's critical interest in such restrictions, stating: "[the] goal of providing Congress with information with which to evaluate the pressures that lobbyists bring to bear upon it, the [*Harriss*] Court concluded, is 'a vital national interest'" (*National Ass'n of Mfrs. v. Taylor* at p. 25, 2009). The term "actively participates" was found not to be impermissibly vague and the court ended with:

> For more than sixty years, Congress has sought to expose the lobbying of government officials to public scrutiny. Acronyms and intricacies aside, the progression from the FRLA to the LDA to the HLOGA marks the legislature's attempt to shine increasing light on the efforts of paid lobbyists to influence the public decision making process. We find nothing unconstitutional in the way Congress has gone about that task. Accordingly, the decision of the district court, rejecting the appellant's challenge to the constitutionality of section 207 [2 U.S.C. § 1603(b)(3)] of the Honest Leadership and Open Government Act of 2007, is affirmed. (*National Ass'n of Mfrs. v. Taylor* at p. 29, 2009)

The LDA provisions amended by the HLOGA have been in effect now for over four years, through two cycles of Congress. As noted in the GAO report mentioned earlier, compliance has not been a problem; almost all lobbyists and lobbying firms adhere, apparently without resistance, to the more onerous reporting requirements put in place by the HLOGA. Interestingly, however, the total number of lobbyists has declined, while the total amount spent on lobbying has not dropped dramatically from pre-HLOGA levels.

In addition to amending the LDA's reporting and disclosure requirements, the HLOGA changed other portions of the U.S. Code related to lobbying. For example, the 2007 law addressed the "revolving door" problem of former members of Congress and their high-level employees going to work for lobbying firms; changed internal House and Senate rules; and tightened rules for the campaign finance tactic known as "bundling." However, HLOGA did not address the tax code as it affects lobbyists, or issues surrounding "grassroots lobbying," the practice of lobbyists' targeting voters directly (as opposed to members of Congress or the executive).

With all of these enhanced restrictions, the question remains: Is lobbying akin to campaign finance regulation? Is it something that constantly evades regulation because of constitutional concerns? Before I address each of the specific modern-day reforms , note the point of one scholar:

> There were already enough provisions in the existing law to prosecute those who blatantly violated the bribery laws (*e.g.*, Abramoff, Cunningham, Ney[1]). The new rules went further down the regulatory path in the sense that they applied a conflict-of-interest framework to lobbying related activities by prohibiting or limiting actions that might induce corrupt actions or that might have the appearance of doing so. This is especially true of the gift bans, travel restrictions, and revolving door provisions. (Apollonio, Cain, and Drutman 2008, 17)

Revolving Door Provisions

Lobbying laws restrict what members of Congress and executive branch officials are allowed to do once they leave office. Specifically, they are "prohibited by statute from engaging in certain types of lobbying activities—typically, direct contact with their respective congressional chamber or government agency—within a certain period after ending their government employment" (Mayer 2008, 506). These laws are referred to as "revolving door" provisions because of the frequency with which people once moved between working as lobbyists and serving as high-level employees or as members of Congress. The problem was recognized as especially acute with respect to earmarks in appropriations legislation; lobbyists who had previously served on the staff of a particular member of Congress would advocate for the inclusion of money in a budget bill favorable to the lobbyist's client

There was a simple explanation for the pre-HLOGA revolving door: money. Salaries for former politicians in lobbying firms were much higher, easily double those for employees without such previous affiliations (Birnbaum 2004). In fact, a study done in 2006 revealed that 43 percent of people who left Congress since 1998 became lobbyists, including such famous former members as

Zell Miller, Dick Gephardt, Bob Dole, Tom Daschle, and John Breaux (Jowers and Peterson 2006). Lobbying firms recruited them because of their level of access to and understanding of the congressional process. In addition, there was a "gradual de-stigmatization" of this career move in the mid-2000s (Jowers and Peterson 2006). As with the other federal lobbying laws changed in the wake of the Abramoff scandal, "revolving door" provisions, too, were changed by HLOGA, mostly through the U.S. Code's criminal statutes.

Before HLOGA, federal law contained a provision dealing with the "revolving door" concerns. Generally speaking, certain members of the executive branch were restricted from engaging in lobbying activities for one year after leaving their position. The same general restriction attached

Representative Randy Duke Cunningham, R-CA, speaking during a news conference in San Diego in 2005. (AP Photo/Denis Poroy)

to covered members of Congress and certain legislative officials. What separates these provisions from others touching on lobbying is their placement in the U.S. Code. Restrictions attempting to "close the revolving door" appear in Title 18 of the U.S. Code concerning crimes and criminal procedure, in the chapter addressing bribery. By placing the revolving door restrictions here, Congress has shown an intent to seriously punish violations of "revolving door" provisions and a recognition of the dangers of unusually high-level access. In discerning the subtle distinction between protected advocacy and impermissible influence, lawyer and former lobbyist Alan Morrison helps to explain the "revolving door" provisions location in Title 18:

> [I]t is essential to separate the lobbying activity of directly influencing legislation through advocacy from the indirect means of influencing a member of Congress to be generally favorable to you and your clients by contributing to his campaign for reelection or providing other financial benefits to him. It has long been illegal to give a gift (including a campaign contribution) with the explicit or even implicit understanding that the recipient will take some specific action, such as a vote on a bill, in exchange for the gift—that is called bribery. (2008, 3–4)

With this balance in mind, and the Abramoff scandal fresh in the minds of members of Congress and the public, the revolving door provisions of Title 18 were amended by HLOGA to increase the one-year limitation to two years for covered executive members seeking to engage in lobbying activities (18 U.S.C. § 207(d) (1)). As to Congress, the one-year prohibition for former members of the House remained, but new, detailed rules concerning the Senate were enacted. The "revolving door" rule for former senators becoming lobbyists was increased from one year to two years (18 U.S.C. § 207(e)(1)). This was presumably because the level of access within the Senate was of greater concern based on its smaller size and more congenial, less partisan character. Employees and staff members in the Senate were not subject to the two-year ban as were members of the Senate; they were still prohibited under the one-year rule.

Many scholars and public policy analysts have debated the anticorruption value of increasing the revolving door provision. Richard Hibey (2006) argues that legislative reform will never curtail lobbying problems or end concerns about access of lobbyists to the legislative process; instead, he advocates for more aggressive prosecution of violations and thus a heightened regulatory role for the executive branch (through Justice Department action and enforcement). With respect to gifts from lobbyists to officials, he writes:

> The law of bribery . . . is straightforward. A person is prohibited from providing money or other things of value to a public official intending to influence that person who likewise intends to be influenced to perform future specific official conduct, or even not to take such action. . . . The difference appears to be in the intent factor. . . . The mere fact of its investigation will resonate in the fishbowl community in which these parties operate. The consequences will be great: publicity, evisceration of effectiveness in the public forum, destruction of a lobbying practice—all before there is even a criminal charge or a conviction. The predisposition will be toward prosecution. (2006, 1365, 1369)

Internal House and Senate Rules

The internal rules of both the House and the Senate were also changed to reflect HLOGA's call for increased transparency. In the House of Representatives, the rules now required a disclosure statement by members affirming that they would not directly negotiate for future employment after service in the House while serving as a member of Congress until a successor was selected. Furthermore, a member would be required to prohibit his or her employees from making "lobbying contacts" (as defined by the LDA) with that employee's spouse if the spouse would be classified as a lobbyist under the LDA. All travel disclosures would be made public as well as the source of funding for such travel, to ensure that no lobbyists improperly provided travel funding. Lastly, a member of the House would not be allowed to participate in an event honoring that member at a national party convention if the event was directly paid for by a registered lobbyist.

Senate rules were more heavily affected by HLOGA. Last-minute earmarks in appropriations bills that sometimes went unnoticed in floor votes were now more unlikely, because individual senators were given more time to examine late changes to a bill. Like House members, senators had to affirm that they would not negotiate for prospective employment, but so did Senate employees "earning in excess of 75 percent of the salary paid to a Senator." Floor privileges previously allowed to former senators such as using the Senate's athletic facilities or member-only parking spaces would be denied to any former senator who became a registered lobbyist (after the now two-year "revolving door" waiting period). The HLOGA prohibition on gifts was reiterated in the Senate rules along with prohibitions on other amenities received from lobbyists, including tickets to sporting or national party convention events. Even attendance at a constituent event in a senator's home state was addressed, to ensure the event was not indirectly funded by lobbyists. Travel disclosures and spousal restrictions similar to those imposed on House members were put in place. Finally, senators and their staff were required to attend ethics training and awareness programs (for new senators within 60 days of commencing service and for sitting senators within 165 days of HLOGA's enactment date).

Campaign Finance Regulation—Relationship with Lobbying and the Idea of "Bundling"

As one scholar observed, "Campaign finance and lobbying are natural counterparts, with campaign finance spending typically serving as a lever for access to lobby its beneficiaries once in office" (Kang 2012, 1166). While most lobbyists do not contribute to congressional campaigns, "the most active lobbyists are frequent and significant donors" (Briffault 2008, 111). In HLOGA, Congress signaled its intent to more closely scrutinize the interplay between campaign finances and lobbying.

The governing law of federal election campaigns is the Federal Election Campaign Act of 1971 (FECA) as amended, most notably by the Bipartisan Campaign Reform Act of 2002. Most of that law details who must report campaign finances to the Federal Election Commission. In recent years, lobbying laws have not faced public scrutiny equal to that of campaign finance laws. However, the FECA was amended by HLOGA to monitor "bundling" contributions to a candidate's campaign. Section 204 of the HLOGA requires FEC reports from political committees (PACs, party committees, etc.) to include any contributions exceeding $15,000 by persons subject to registration under the LDA. The overlap in reporting and disclosure requirements has presented some challenges to lobbyists, particularly to the few that are substantial contributors to congressional campaigns, as Richard Briffault explains:

> As BCRA and [the] McConnell [case from the U.S. Supreme Court, interpreting the constitutionality of the BCRA] demonstrate, campaign finance law now reflects a greater understanding of how campaign contributions and expenditures are used to open the door for and enhance lobbying efforts. By the same token, a growing focus of lobbying law is campaign finance. . . . Campaign finance practices are generally more tightly regulated than lobbying. Although both campaigns and lobbying are

subject to disclosure requirements, campaign finance disclosure is generally more penetrating. At the federal level, the threshold for reporting is lower for campaigns than for lobbying, more information is required about campaign donations and expenditures than about lobbying expenses, and campaign reports are required more frequently. (2008, 119, 109)

The Supreme Court has not directly addressed a federal lobbying law since the *Harriss* case almost 60 years ago. But disclosure requirements under both campaign finance and lobbying laws have been upheld repeatedly. In *Citizens United*, its most recent campaign finance decision, the Court stated that "[it] has explained that disclosure is a less restrictive alternative to more comprehensive regulation of speech. . . . And the Court has upheld registration and disclosure requirements on lobbyists, even though Congress has no power to ban lobbying itself" (*Citizens United v. FEC* at p. 915, 2010). On the other side of the coin, Justice Elena Kagan's 2011 dissent in *Arizona Free Enterprise v. Bennett* envisioned a system ripe for corrupt influences because of the proliferation of bundling. The case dealt with the constitutionality of a compelled matching public funds arrangement for candidates for office in Arizona; that statute was struck down for violating the free speech rights of the candidates and groups who did not wish to have matching funds. However, in the beginning of her dissent, Kagan wrote the following:

> Individuals who "bundle" campaign contributions become indispensable to candidates in need of money. Simple disclosure fails to prevent shady dealing. And candidates choose not to participate in the public financing system because the sums provided do not make them competitive with their privately financed opponents. So the State remains afflicted with corruption. (*Arizona Free Enterprise v. Bennett* at p. 2829, 2011)

Many observers point out that limits on lobbying can be tailored to strike an adequate balance between lobbyists' constitutional rights and the government's rights to make those lobbyists' actions transparent. Significantly, the LDA and HLOGA do not outright ban any type of lobbying, or any class of lobbyists (with the exception of special restrictions placed on spouses and former members of Congress). Comments one scholar: "Lobbying regulation has traditionally been much less ambitious [than campaign finance regulations]. . . . [L]obbying laws do not limit lobbying—*that is, the communication of information and arguments by lobbyists to public officials concerning subjects of legislative or administrative action*—at all" [emphasis added] (Briffault 2008, 110) Thus the comprehensive disclosure and reporting requirements continue to escape judicial scrutiny.

Finally, it is important to note that lobbying has no related independent monitoring agency like the FEC. This was consciously deliberated during the passage of the HLOGA and passed on; "[n]either house opted for an independent agency to monitor and enforce lobbying and ethics regulations . . . [aside from] the Senate provid[ing] for annual audits of the lobbyist reports by the Comptroller General" (explained earlier in this chapter) (Apollonio et al. 2008, 17). The only other provision of the FECA amended by the HLOGA concerns the use of campaign funds from lobbyists for private airline flights by members of Congress.

Taxing Regulations—Influencing Lobbying through the Internal Revenue Code: Charitable Groups and Lobbying

When the LDA was originally enacted, Congress included express provisions concerning taxing and lobbying activity. Specifically, entities classified as 501(c)(4) groups (social welfare organizations) would not be eligible for federal grants if they engage in lobbying. However, 501(c)(4) organizations may operate as "action" groups and can have as their primary purpose some goal that can be accomplished only by legislation; they may lobby without limits to accomplish such a goal (Hasen 2012, 203). Since the LDA expressly mentions 501(c)(4) but not 501(c)(3) groups (religious, charitable, and educational organizations), there has been much debate about the lobbying efforts of the latter—particularly because these groups seek to influence legislation in the public interest and are not boosting the profits of private clients. The Internal Revenue Code has held since 1934 that charitable organizations cannot deduct lobbying expenses. According to the IRS, no organization may qualify for section 501(c)(3) (nonprofit entities organized exclusively for religious, charitable, or educational purposes) status if a *substantial part* of its activities attempts to influence legislation (Internal Revenue Service 2012b). In this context, "influencing legislation" does not extend to lobbying efforts before the executive or judicial branches. To retain tax-exempt status, organizations are specifically not allowed to "contact or urge the public to contact, members or employees of a legislative body for the purpose of proposing, supporting, or opposing legislation, or if the organization advocates the adoption or rejection of legislation" (Internal Revenue Service 2012c). Organizations may, however, engage their members in issues of public policy through educational methods, such as conducting meetings, distributing educational materials, or considering public policy issues in "an educational manner."

The definition of "substantial part" in the Internal Revenue Code is vague; whether or not a group's activities meet the standard is based on:

> all the pertinent facts and circumstances in each case . . . consider[ing] a variety of factors, including the time devoted (by both compensated and volunteer workers) and the expenditures devoted by the organization to the activity. (Internal Revenue Service 2012b)

Because of the standard's ad hoc approach and difficulty in ascertaining when 501(c)(3) groups engage in lobbying to the extent of endangering their tax-exempt status, many argue that this creates an undue burden relative to those private, economic lobbying groups that engage in for-profit lobbying. "[T]he tax code's restrictions on the lobbying activities of not-for-profit organizations may also have the effect of limiting the ability of non-business groups to counter the lobbying influence of for-profit actors" (Briffault 2008, 114). In attempting to curtail these groups' lobbying activities but still allowing them to maintain their tax-exempt status, some argue that a "right to petition" First Amendment challenge may be more viable for these groups than private lobbying interests (Dryer 2007, 291). Other writers on the subject have advocated for less restrictive taxing regulations on the lobbying activities of these groups because of their public interest focus, one that many argue would avert corrupting practices and most financial abuses.

The need for clarity on the "substantial part" test was addressed by the Supreme Court in *Regan v. Taxation with Representation of Washington* in 1983. In *Regan*, a nonprofit corporation organized to promote certain interests in the field of federal taxation was denied application as a 501(c)(3) organization because it was found that a "substantial part" of its activities consisted of lobbying (*Regan* at p. 540, 1983). The corporation alleged that the denial violated both its rights under the First Amendment and equal protection under the Fifth Amendment. The district court ruled against the corporation on both claims, but the appeals court reversed the judgment on Fifth Amendment grounds, declaring the application of the "substantial part" test in this manner to be unconstitutional. But the Supreme Court unanimously reversed that decision, finding no violation of the Fifth Amendment; if the group wanted to engage in lobbying beyond the "substantial part" standard, said the justices, they had the right to create a separate 501(c)(4) group (*Regan* at p. 544, 1983). (The IRS permits 501(c)(3) charitable organizations to form separate 501(c)(4) affiliates, though they must avoid commingling funds between the two) (Hasen 2012, 204).

In contrast to static "no-deduction" rule for charitable organizations, policies have shifted somewhat on the deductibility of lobbying activity as a business expense (Mayer 2008, 499). This has been because of both a change in public perception of lobbying and Congress's concern with judicial interpretation of the regulations.

When the Supreme Court has considered the taxing of lobbying activity as a business deduction, it has generally sided with the government in its interpretation of whether and when to tax lobbying activities of otherwise tax-exempt organizations. As early as 1941, in *Textile Mills Securities Corp. v. Commissioner of Internal Revenue*, the Court refused to support an individual's claim that his earnings from a contingency fee arrangement for lobbying Congress were deductible as an "ordinary and necessary expense." The taxpayer was employed to represent German textile interests and to procure legislation from Congress that would permit recovery of property seized during the war. Citing its earlier decisions in *Trist v. Child* and *Hazelton v. Sheckells*, the Court held that the exclusion of lobbying as a deductible expense by Congress was valid "in drawing a line between legitimate business expenses and those arising from the family of contracts to which the law has given no sanction" (*Textile Mills Securities Corp. v. Commissioner of Internal Revenue* at p. 339, 1941). If Congress determined, as a matter of public policy, that lobbying expenses were not tax deductible, that was good enough for the Supreme Court.

The Court considered the issue of whether certain charitable donations would be deductible 18 years later in *Cammarano v. United States*. In that case, the Court unanimously affirmed the decision against deductibility for donations earmarked to defeat proposed ballot initiatives. The money was given to fund publicity programs supporting grassroots efforts in Washington and Arkansas to rally voters against initiatives that would have "seriously affected, if not wholly destroyed, the taxpayers' businesses" (*Cammarano v. United States* at p. 498, 1959). The Court held that regulations excluding lobbying as an "ordinary and necessary" business expense cover not only attempts to persuade legislatures but also appeals to citizens when they are faced with direct legislative initiative (i.e., a law being enacted through the ballot box or referendum procedure). "[I]nitiatives are plainly 'legislation' within the meaning of these Regulations" (*Cammarano v. United States* at p. 505, 1959). The taxpayers alleged that denying a deduction for constitutionally protected activities presented a constitutional flaw in and of itself. But the Court was unconvinced:

> Petitioners are not being denied a tax deduction because they engage in constitutionally protected activities, but are simply being required to pay for those activities entirely out of their own pockets, as everyone else engaging in similar activities is required to do under the provisions of the Internal Revenue Code. Nondiscriminatory denial of deduction from gross income to sums expended to promote or defeat legislation is plainly *not* [emphasis added] aimed at the suppression of dangerous ideas. (*Cammarano v. United States* at p. 513, 1959)

In his concurring opinion, Justice Douglas conceded that the public interest nature of Cammarano's advocacy should have an influence on deductibility. However, in exercising judicial restraint and acknowledging Congress's power to regulate taxing schemes, he stated:

> Deductions are a matter of grace, not of right. To hold that this item of expense must be allowed as a deduction would be to give impetus to the view favored in some quarters that First Amendment rights must be protected by tax exemptions. But that proposition savors of the notion that First Amendment rights are somehow not fully realized unless they are subsidized by the State. Such a notion runs counter to our decisions. (*Cammarano v. United States* at p. 515, 1959)

The line of reasoning in these two Supreme Court cases revealed an inherit flaw in the logic of deducting lobbying expenses as business expenses. Notwithstanding the for-profit versus nonprofit distinction, some argued after the *Cammarano* case that the blanket prohibition on the deductibility of lobbying expenses did not accurately take into account the nature of these organizations' businesses that could dangerously lead to "an inflated amount of income being subject to tax" (Mayer 2008, 498). Recognizing this, Congress passed an amendment to the Internal Revenue Code in 1962, allowing the deductibility of lobbying expenses when those expenses were of a "direct interest to the business" (Mayer 2008, 498). The deduction went to direct lobbying (of Congress and state legislatures, for example) and not to grassroots lobbying, nor did it allow deductions for contributions used for political campaigns. This remained the rule for almost 30 years, until President Bill Clinton persuaded Congress to remove the provision in the early 1990s, eliminating the deductibility of all lobbying activity (Mayer 2008, 499). This decision, later formalized as part of the Internal Revenue Code, remains the rule today.

Regulation of "Grassroots Lobbying"

As noted earlier, lobbying regulation in the United States has only addressed attempts to influence legislators directly. "Grassroots lobbying" has escaped restriction, thus allowing virtually unlimited activity aimed at ordinary voters "in order to convince them to participate in letter or telephone campaigns expressing their views, en masse, to elected officials" (Krishnakumar 2007, 549). Put another way, grassroots lobbying has been viewed as "simply the efforts of average Americans to share their viewpoints with their elected representatives and encourage other Americans to do the same" (Sekulow and Zimmerman 2008, 174). Although the Court in *Cammarano* considered funds spent to influence voting on a ballot referendum the same as direct lobbying for tax purposes, Congress chose *not* to include grassroots lobbying in either the LDA or the HLOGA amendments. Some argue that the heightened disclosure and reporting rules in the HLOGA should also apply to groups who engage in grassroots lobbying. For example, one proponent writes:

> Indeed, disclosure of grassroots lobbying efforts may in some ways be *more* important than disclosure of other lobbying activities. Because votes are the ultimate currency in politics and officials must win reelection in order to continue in their jobs, lobbyists' and interest groups' ability to demonstrate (or generate the appearance of) public support of their positions may be the most critical element in convincing elected officials to support their policy preferences . . . In addition, failure to include grassroots lobbying regulation in the LDA would exacerbate the unequal access problem by disproportionately shielding from disclosure the lobbying activities of those interest groups that have substantial resources to spend on advertising campaigns and other means of reaching constituents. (Krishnakumar 2007, 549)

One need only take notice of billboards in the Washington, D.C. metro system or turn on the television during a contentious political climate to see the prevalence of grassroots lobbying. While the disclosure requirements mandated by the LDA allow voters to see who lobbies Congress and to what extent, there is no rule to require the disclosure of those who (under the statute) "engage in paid communication campaigns to influence the general public to lobby Congress." However, efforts to reform the LDA so as to restrict grassroots lobbying are unlikely to advance in the near future. As Sekulow and Zimmerman explain:

> First, support for the grassroots lobbying bills within the 110th Congress decreased after public interest and civil liberties organizations explained that the bills were broad enough to cover a wide range of issue advocacy by non-profit organizations. Some early support for the bills may have been based upon the misunderstanding that they only covered activities by professional lobbyists. Second, supporters of the bills that understood how broad they were argued that they were necessary to prevent corruption but never presented a persuasive argument that they were narrowly tailored to achieve that end. (2008, 176)

More simply, many believe that the constitutional protections of the First Amendment support an unfettered right for any citizen or group to lobby at the grassroots level.

The relatively recent phenomenon of "crowd funding" has been adapted as a viable form of grassroots lobbying. Crowd funding is defined generally as the use of the Internet and social media to raise small amounts of money from a large number of contributors (Bradford 2012). The government has been minimally involved in the regulation of crowd funding, so far speaking only to the ability of interested persons to fund securities through the practice in the "Jumpstart Our Business Startups Act" or JOBS Act legislation signed by President Obama on April 5, 2012. How the phenomenon of funding through crowd sourcing can affect lobbying is started to be felt in the political process. Groups like "BlassRoots" facilitate user-driven political lobbying, and as the idea takes off in the public sector as it is in the funding of private nonprofit enterprises, legislation in the 113th Congress and beyond will likely be imminent.

The States' Lobbying Practices—Laboratories for the Federal Government?

Including the District of Columbia, Puerto Rico, and other U.S. territories, the United States is made up of more than 50 sovereign units. The U.S. Constitution lays out their rights and obligations, in addition to the exclusive powers of the federal government. Where rights are not expressly delegated to the federal government, the states retain them. It is instructive to look at how the states handle regulation of lobbying, as some believe the states offer blueprints for reform at the federal level. "[F]ederal lobbying regulation, centered around the LDA and specific House and Senate ethics rules, is fairly static. Recently the states (such as California) have been more experimental than the federal government in their attempts to regulate lobbying" (Dryer 2007, 285).

In addition to the guarantee in the First Amendment of the U.S. Constitution protecting the right "to petition the government for a redress of grievances," all states except two (Minnesota and New Mexico) enshrine a similar right in their respective state constitutions (Devlin 1990, 828). Thus, any state regulations bearing on lobbying will be subject not only to the constitutional ceiling of the First Amendment but also any related state constitutional rights that may grant more rights to engage in lobbying at the state level. States have many varied approaches to lobbying regulation. For example, approximately 38 states prohibit contingency fee lobbying contracts, where lobbyists are paid only if they are successful in achieving a particular outcome from a state legislature or other governmental body (Susman and Martin 2009, 670). This reflects concern that lobbyists are more likely to cross ethical boundaries "if they know during the course of their efforts that they will not earn a fee unless their efforts are successful" (Susman and Martin 2009, 679–680). Likewise, just over a dozen states prohibit lobbyists from making campaign contributions to state legislators while that particular state's legislature is in session (Briffault 2008, 120).

Also, studies have shown that states with "professional legislatures" (those with the longest terms, largest staff, and highest pay) tend to be less strongly influenced by lobbyists than those with part-time legislators who meet infrequently (Dryer

2007, 293). Trevor Dryer's extensive studying of lobbying laws in California reveals that disclosure is warranted to curb any undue influence or negative public perception around lobbying the state legislature. He explains:

> [M]eaningful public disclosure would curb the influence of registered lobbyists without overly restricting their clients' ability to have their voices heard in Sacramento. Lobbyists reported that legislators wanted to avoid having to disclose expenditures or activities. . . . The study implies that it is public scrutiny (rather than an aversion to paperwork) that causes lobbyists and legislators to attempt to avoid having to disclose certain activities. . . . The findings suggest that one might better regulate lobbying activity by focusing less on restriction and more on reporting of all lobbying activity. . . . Most of the lobbyists did not advocate for eliminating the reporting and disclosure requirements altogether, but simply suggested simplification that would provide the public with what they termed "useful" information and create an incentive for lobbyists to conduct themselves above board. (2007, 321, 327–328)

Dryer also found that (at least in the California legislature) term limits actually boost lobbyist influence over legislators, because the limits "creat[es] a world of candidates perpetually running for different offices and thus perpetually needing the donations that can be arranged by lobbyists" (2007, 319). The comprehensive regulation of both campaign finance and lobbying in California is reflected in the sweeping reforms enacted in that state (e.g., Political Reform Act of 1974 and subsequent amendments) and the often controversial interplay between the two arenas.

State courts and lower federal courts interpreting state lobbying laws in light of both state constitutional law and the First Amendment have produced a broad range of interpretations. A few examples include:

- In *Fair Political Practices Commission v. Superior Court of Los Angeles County*, the California Supreme Court struck down portions of the California Political Reform Act of 1974 (enacted as part of Proposition 9, overwhelmingly approved by California voters), ruling that specific sections prohibiting lobbyist contributions to state politicians' campaigns and the disclosure of private financial matters of lobbyists irrelevant to lobbying violated the First Amendment. However, the court upheld other reporting and registration requirements as well as limitations on gifts. Stricken provisions were later amended and approved by voters to clearly define and delineate the role of lobbyists as campaign contributors. These changes have yet to be addressed by the California Supreme Court.
- In *Montana Automobile Association v. Montana Chamber of Commerce* (1981), the Montana Supreme Court reversed a lower court judgment prohibiting enforcement of I-85, an initiative covering lobbying in the state. But the court acknowledged that a portion of I-85 could not be enforced, noting that a reference to "unprofessional conduct" was unconstitutionally vague and could possibly impinge upon any voter's right to engage his or her state representatives.
- In *Florida Association of Professional Lobbyists, Inc. v. Division of Legislative Information Services*, the challengers argued that lobbying was tantamount to the practice of law in the state and as such only the Florida Supreme Court, not the legislature, had the

right to regulate the profession. The Supreme Court of Florida upheld provisions of the Florida law, which regulated and disciplined lobbyists and found that the laws were validly enacted by the Florida state legislature and not a violation of separation of powers. Lobbying, as defined in the law, did not constitute the practice of law.

- In *Green Party of Connecticut v. Garfield*, a Connecticut state law that banned political campaign contributions by state contractors, lobbyists, and related individuals was challenged on First Amendment grounds in the wake of a state scandal involving state contractors' donations to political campaigns and corruption stemming from that arrangement. The court in this case upheld the law as it related to state contractors, but held that the portion prohibiting lobbyists from making campaign contributions was a violation of the First Amendment. In other words, an outright ban went too far beyond addressing the state's anticorruption interest.

- Lastly, a New York city ordinance limiting campaign contributions and lobbying activities by those having business dealings with the city was upheld in the face of a challenge under the First Amendment by a class of plaintiffs, including New York City voters, aspiring candidates for local office, lobbyists, and political parties among others. This was decided by a federal appellate court in *Ognibene v. Parkes* in 2011.

One similar thread running through these disparate state cases is that, as in the federal sphere, issues of state campaign finance and lobbying are often intertwined. Also, the general theme of the cases is that courts are motivated to uphold state regulation as fully as possible, including limits on lobbyists' contributions to political campaigns and reporting and disclosure requirements. As in the federal cases of *Harriss* and *National Association of Manufacturers*, we see in these state cases a judiciary keenly aware of the government's interest in preventing corruption in lobbying practices. The complete ban in the Connecticut case is an exception, but even here the legislature was afforded broad leeway to refine the law. It is clear that with the host of legislation and jurisprudence on campaign finance at both the state and federal level, a challenge to lobbying laws is likely to echo the analysis given to campaign finance, as both spheres touch on constitutional rights couched in the First Amendment. The other interesting point is from the Florida case, addressing the role of lawyers and lobbyists. Many large law firms have full-time lobbyists in house, but acknowledge (unlike in the Florida case discussed earlier) the different roles of the two professions. While lawyers seek to remedy clients' problems within the context of existing law, lobbyists advocate for changes in those laws. Similar rules of ethics govern each role, but they stem from different sources of law.

Future of Lobbying—Reforms, Looking Forward

Not surprisingly, calls for reform have resonated even after the passage of the HLOGA and the Abramoff scandal. To many, lobbying laws are akin to the regulation of money in campaign finance laws: money, like water, will always find its way in. Abramoff himself, now out of prison, advocates for strict reforms, including a complete wall between spending in the realms of political campaigns and lobbying, as well as term limits to prevent entrenched access. The following are some examples of post-HLOGA developments.

Post-HLOGA Scandals and Internal Congressional Pressures

Lobbying scandals were still in the news even after the reforms of the HLOGA. One of the biggest controversies involved ties of former Pennsylvania Congressman John Murtha to the lobbying firm known as the PMA Group. The PMA Group was started by a former congressional aide, Paul Magliochetti and "specialize[d] in winning earmarked taxpayer funds for its clients" (Emma and Rood 2009). PMA Group benefited heavily from Murtha's position as chair of the Defense Appropriations subcommittee, bringing in $299 million in earmarked funds for its clients in 2008 alone (Emma and Rood 2009). The FBI raided offices of the PMA Group, and it eventually discontinued its operations, but the House declined to conduct a full investigation. Despite the controversy surrounding the PMA Group scandal, Murtha continued his 35-plus year tenure in Congress until his death in February of 2010. At that time, the House Ethics Committee also dismissed all PMA-related charges against seven members of Congress, including Murtha.

The PMA scandal did, however, help convince Congress to create the Office of Congressional Ethics (OCE), an "independent, non-partisan entity charged with reviewing allegations of misconduct" against House of Representatives members, officers and staff (Office of Congressional Ethics 2012). The OCE conducts investigations into misconduct and then refers its findings to the House Ethics Committee. While regulation of lobbyists *per se* is outside the jurisdiction of the OCE, it has proven an inherently useful tool by "regulating from within," drawing the attention of members of Congress to potential problems with lobbying practices.

President Obama's Position on Lobbying

While seeking the Democratic Party's nomination for president, Barack Obama pledged to refuse campaign contributions from lobbyists (Briffault 2008, 120–121). This, in turn, caused him to focus on the role of lobbyists once he won the office of president, and one of his initial actions was an executive order banning members of his administration from lobbying the executive branch and requiring a two-year waiting period for former lobbyists in his administration to work in subject areas in which they lobbied (Wingfield 2009). "He also banned direct lobbying for funds and tax breaks from the Troubled Assets Relief Program (TARP) and the American Recovery and Reinvestment Act of 2009 (ARRA) economic stimulus package Bill" (Thurber 2011, 361). Beyond that, however, the dynamic of "K Street" in Washington did not change, as Obama's actions did not affect the lobbying of Congress, any previously registered lobbyist, or the scores of people who operate on the fringe of regulated lobbying such as advisors, analysts, and public relations executives for lobbying firms (Wingfield 2009). Overall, President Obama found it difficult to get any traction for lobbying reform based on the "size, adaptability, and . . . integral part [lobbying] plays in pluralist democracy" (Thurber 2011, 363). Juxtaposing the size of the lobbying industry, the restrictive nature of who has to register under the LDA, and the holding of *Citizens United* in the realm of campaign finance law, many of Obama's reform proposals have yet to achieve any degree of permanency.

The American Bar Association's Proposed Reforms Strengthening
LDA and HLOGA Disclosure and Reporting Requirements

Many advocates for reform argue that the definitions in the LDA are too narrow, and that compliance with the law is undercut because the House and Senate have only a tenuous relationship to real enforcement practices. The American Bar Association's (ABA's) Section of Administrative Law and Regulatory Practice convened a special task force on federal lobbying laws in 2009; the task force issued a report in January 2011 calling for numerous reform proposals. Among them:

(1) The 20%-of-time standard for categorizing lobbying activities for a particular client should be eliminated, as it doesn't adequately capture the amount of work on a particular project under that ceiling.
(2) Disclosure requirements should include the specific congressional office lobbied.
(3) The LDA should recognize the multi-faceted approach to lobbying in contemporary politics, where a client may employ several different firms with the intent of influencing legislation (e.g., public relations firm, polling firm, etc.) but only the "end" lobbying firm is subject to disclosure.

According to the ABA, these "gaps" in existing coverage have been exacerbated by the shortened reporting periods required by HLOGA.

Some reforms in this vein seek to discontinue the 20 percent threshold, while others broaden the definition of a lobbying firm to accommodate related professional services and cover organizations that do not directly employ lobbyists but make "lobbying contacts" as defined by the LDA. The second reform is especially interesting because it would require reporting the target of lobbying activity, specifically what congressional office, committee, or federal agency was lobbied. In addition, it would add a new layer of activity defined as "lobbying support"[2] to "respond to the modern reality that much of the effort in a lobbying campaign may be dispersed among multiple entities" (Fried et al. 2011, 13). Finally, the task force believed that a lobbying client should be required to disclose "support that it has procured or performed itself" (Fried et al. 2011, 16).

The ABA also recommended a complete break between campaign finance and lobbying. When faced with the constitutional challenge inherent in such an arrangement, the task force relied on the interpretation of "limits" in the *Green Party of Connecticut v. Garfield* case, focusing on the court's language "ban[ning] only large-scale efforts to solicit contributions" (*Green Party of Connecticut v. Garfield* at p. 209, 2010) and stressing the need to "separate, so far as constitutionally and practically possible, the roles of advocate [of a lobbyist] and fundraiser [of a campaign]" (Fried et al. 2011, vi). The task force also proposed several other reforms; these included a total ban on contingency fee lobbying contracts at the federal level, and restructuring enforcement mechanisms so as to house[3] them within the FEC or another executive branch agency.

Lobbying Reform Bills Proposed in the 111th (2009–2010)
Congress and 112th (2011–2012) Congress

Several bills related to lobbying regulation have been introduced in the two most recent sessions of Congress, but none have advanced out of committee. Some of the most notable proposals in the 111th Congress include:

- H.R. 5751—A bill to amend the LDA to require registrants to pay a $50 annual fee and to impose a $500 penalty for failure to timely file required reports
- H.R. 4511—The Pick Your Poison Act of 2010 which would amend the FECA to prohibit corporations from making any expenditures in conjunction with a political campaign if they employ or retain a registered lobbyist under the LDA

In the 112th Congress, a sampling of proposed bills includes:

- H.R. 138—The Ethics in Foreign Lobbying Act of 2011 would amend the Foreign Agents Registration Act of 1938 to revise foreign agents' reporting requirements and provide civil penalties for violations. The act would also establish within the Federal Election Commission a clearinghouse for public information regarding the political activities of foreign principals and agents of foreign principals [A similar bill was introduced in the 111th Congress]
- H.R. 2339—The Lobbyist Disclosure Enhancement Act of 2011 would move notification of noncompliance of LDA provisions from the U.S. Attorney for the District of Columbia to the Attorney General, and would eliminate the existing exemption from lobbyist registration for those who work for a client part-time. The act would also shorten the time to register as a lobbyist after initial contact from 45 days to 5 days
- H.R. 4030—The Stop the Revolving Door in Washington Act of 2012 would increase the HLOGA two-year ban on former senators making lobbying contacts after they leave office to five years and applies the same term to House members [A similar bill was introduced in the 111th Congress.] H.R. 4343, a similar bill, would increase to ten years the ban on lobbying contacts by former Presidents, Vice Presidents, Members of Congress and specific covered officials of both branches to represent, aid, or advise a foreign entity
- H.R. 4054—The Restore Public Trust Act would amend the LDA to apply existing disclosure and reporting requirements to those who engage in "political intelligence activities." The phrase would be used to broaden the scope of existing lobbying laws and accommodate the multifaceted nature of access to the legislative process, incorporating preparation and planning activities, research, and other background work that is intended for use in lobbying contacts. The bill would also dramatically expand the criminal definition of "bribery" in federal law.

As long as the president and House are of different political parties, it is unlikely that any of these bills will ultimately be signed into law. Since the courts have been more active in determining the constitutional parameters of campaign finance laws than lobbying restrictions, the only lobbying reform in the near future may be whatever is forced by changes to campaign finance regulation. Also, it should be noted that both the LDA and the HLOGA were passed in the wake of major lobbying scandals and a heightened concern with corruption. No comparable lobbying scandal has since surfaced, and no meaningful prosecutions have come to fruition.

Conclusion

Much of the debate about lobbying stems from public perception. An intrinsic component of democracy, lobbying remains the avenue by which constituents express concern over the actions of their representatives and the course of public policy. It is the paid representation of interests that do not necessarily align with the public good that raises the specter of corruption. In *The Federalist Papers*, James Madison wrote: "If men were angels, no government would be necessary" (Madison 1788). But there is a general, if unstable, consensus that regulation is needed, enforcement is required, and the interplay between financing American elections and lobbying lawmakers must be carefully scrutinized.

Only when self-interest overtakes the common good do the anchors come unmoored. To be fair, not all lobbyists have bad intentions; as Jack Abramoff himself was recently quoted saying, "There aren't 150,000 Jack Abramoffs walking around out there" (Fox 2012). In fact, one of today's leading lobbyists comments:

> [L]obbying is an honorable profession. For the most part, public policy advocacy is necessary, difficult work performed by law-abiding, highly skilled professionals who help government arrive at better-informed, and hopefully better, decisions. Good lobbyists can contribute a lot to good government. The practice is hardly perfect. There is plenty of room for improvement, especially concerning the public perception that the system is rotten, and by throwing the covers back on how lobbying and government decision making works, both curb abuses and afford the public a better understanding of the public policy process. (Allard 2008, 66)

Also, as another observer points out: "In a country as expansive and diverse as ours, where politicians are increasingly removed from their constituents, lobbyists can play a vital role in crafting legislation that is in the public interest" (Dryer 2007, 329).

The Center for Responsive Politics (2012) reports that the number of active lobbyists tallied 12,651 in 2011. Comparing this to the 2007 number of 14,847 (immediately before the effective date of the HLOGA provisions), one could say that reform legislation has succeeded—if reducing the number of lobbyists was the goal. However, total lobbying spending has not dropped, with the 2011 total of approximately $3.33 billion nearly the same amount spent in 2008. Lobbying remains the third largest enterprise in the nation's capital—behind only government and tourism (Thurber 2011, 363). Of course, that enterprise depends on access. Unless the Supreme Court chooses to redefine the constitutional basis of that access, its cost will continue to increase—and so will the calls for reform. The enduring question is whether the rules regulating access align with democratic ideals, prevent corruption, and effectively represent the concerns of the American people.

Notes

1. "Duke" Cunningham was a member of Congress who was criminally convicted for taking bribes for earmarks in appropriations legislation. Bob Ney was also convicted for accepting illegal gifts from lobbyists. The literature covers other politicians falling

from grace because of lobbying concerns. In addition to DeLay mentioned earlier, former Alaska senator Ted Stevens (initially convicted but later overturned) was accused of taking illegal gifts from lobbyists as well. More recently, New York Congressman Charles Rangel was asked to step down from his chair position of the powerful House Ways and Means Committee because of violations of internal House ethics rules on gifts and travel associated with lobbyists (Thurber 2011, 358). Note that within the sphere of lobbying regulation, often it is the public official more often than the lobbyist who is punished.

2. "Lobbying support," as explained by the task force's report, would include the following: (1) provision of strategic advice; (2) monitoring of legislative and administrative developments related to lobbying goals; (3) advice and assistance with earned media (press/communications) related to bills or topics disclosed by the registering lobbyist or lobbying firm on one or more lobbying reports; (4) polling related to lobbying goals; (5) expenditures for advice on or production of public communications; and (6) expenditures for coalition building (or payments provided for the purpose of encouraging organizations to support or oppose bills or to take action with regard to topics otherwise identified by the registering lobbyist or lobbying firm).

3. Currently, the Office of the Clerk of the House and the secretary of the Senate refer LDA noncompliance cases to the U.S. attorney for the District of Columbia. An entity, the task force argues, is not designed to effectively follow up with these cases. Hence the reason there have been no criminal actions prosecuted under the criminal enforcement procedures of the LDA and HLOGA, and only three cases since the LDA was enacted in 1995 have reached out of court settlements.

References

Allard, Nicholas. (2008). "The Law of Lobbying: Lobbying Is an Honorable Profession: The Right to Petition and the Competition to Be Right." *Stanford Law and Policy Review* 19: 23–68.

Apollino, Dorie, Bruce E. Cain, and Lee Drutman. (2008). "Access and Lobbying: Looking Beyond the Corruption Paradigm." *Hastings Constitutional Law Quarterly* 36, no. 1: 13–50.

Arizona Free Enterprise v. Bennett. 131 S.Ct. 2806 (Supreme Court of the United States, 2011).

Birnbaum, Jeffrey H. (1992). *The Lobbyists: How Influence Peddlers Get Their Way in Washington.* New York: Random House.

Birnbaum, Jeffrey H. (2004, June 20). "Lawmaker Turned Lobbyist a Growing Trend on the Hill." *Washington Post.* Accessed July 31, 2013. http://www.washingtonpost.com/wp-dyn/articles/A54703–2004Jun19.html.

Bradford, C. Stephen. (2012). "The New Federal Crowdfunding Exemption: Promise Unfulfilled." *Securities Regulation Law Journal* 40, no. 3: 195–249.

Briffault, Richard. (2008). "The Law of Lobbying: Lobbying and Campaign Finance: Separate and Together." *Stanford Law and Policy Review* 19: 105–129.

California Secretary of State. (2012). "History of the Political Reform Division." Accessed July 2, 2012. http://www.sos.ca.gov.

Cammarano et ux. v. United States. 358 U.S. 498 (Supreme Court of the United States, 1959).

Center for Responsive Politics. (2012). "Lobbying Database." Accessed August 5, 2012. http://www.opensecrets.org/lobby/.

Citizens United v. Federal Election Commission. 130 S.Ct. 876 (Supreme Court of the United States, 2010).

Devlin, John. (1990). "Constructing an Alternative to "State Action" as a Limit on State Constitutional Rights Guarantees: A Survey, Critique and Proposal." *Rutgers Law Journal* 21: 819–902.

Dryer, Trevor D. (2007). "Gaining Access: A State Lobbying Case Study." *The Journal of Law and Politics* 23: 283–329.

Fair Political Practices Commission v. Superior Court of Los Angeles. 599 P.2d 46 (Supreme Court of California, 1979).

Florida Association of Professional Lobbyists, Inc. v. Division of Legislative Information Services. 7 So.3d 511 (Supreme Court of Florida, 2009).

Fried, Charles, Rebecca Gordon, Trevor Potter, Joseph Sandler, and Ronald Levin. (2011). "Lobbying Law in the Spotlight: Challenges and Proposed Improvements: Report of the Task Force on Federal Lobbying Laws." *American Bar Association Section of Administrative Law and Regulatory Practice.* Accessed August 4, 2012. http://www.americanbar.org/content/dam/aba/migrated/2011_build/administrative_law/lobbying_task_force_report_010311.authcheckdam.pdf.

Fox, Lauren. (2012, Feb. 6). "Jack Abramoff Proposes Reforms for Corrupt Lobbying." *U.S. News and World Reports.* Accessed July 31, 2013. http://www.usnews.com/news/blogs/washington-whispers/2012/02/06/jack-abramoff-proposes-reforms-for-corrupt-lobbying-.

Glaeser, Edward L., and Claudia Goldin. (2004, Sept. 1). "Corruption and Reform: An Introduction, Working Paper 10775." *National Bureau of Economic Research: NBER Working Paper Series.*

Government Accountability Office. (2011). "2011 Lobbying Disclosure: Observations on Lobbyists' Compliance with Disclosure Requirements (Highlights of GAO 12–492, a report to Congressional Committees)." Accessed July 20, 2012. http://www.gao.gov/assets/590/589805.pdf.

Green Party of Connecticut v. Garfield. 616 F.3d 189 (United States Court of Appeals for the Second Circuit, 2010).

Hasen, Richard L. (2012). "Lobbying, Rent-Seeking, and the Constitution." *Stanford Law Review* 64:191–253.

Hazelton v. Sheckells. 202 U.S. 71 (Supreme Court of the United States, 1906).

Hibey, Richard A. (2006). "Remarks: The Impact of the Abramoff Scandal on Public Corruption Cases." *Wayne Law Review* 52: 1363–1369.

Honest Leadership and Open Government Act ("HLOGA") of 2007, Pub. L. No. 110–81, 121 Stat. 735.

Internal Revenue Service. (2012a). "Lobbying." Accessed July 7, 2012. http://www.irs.gov/Charities-&-Non-Profits/Lobbying.

Internal Revenue Service. (2012b). "Measuring Lobbying: Substantial Part Test." Accessed July 7, 2012. http://www.irs.gov/Charities-&-Non-Profits/Measuring-Lobbying:-Substantial-Part-Test.

Internal Revenue Service. (2012c). "Social Welfare Organizations." Accessed July 7, 2012. http://www.irs.gov/Charities-&-Non-Profits/Other-Non-Profits/Social-Welfare-Organizations.

Jowers, Kirk L., and Luke E. Peterson. (2006). "Case Study: Service Is Its Own Reward?—The Revolving Door from Lawmaker to Lobbyist." *Teaching Ethics* Spring: 65–72.

Jumpstart Our Business Startups Act ("JOBS") of 2012, Pub. L. No. 112–106, 126 Stat. 306.

Kaiser, Robert G. (2009). *So Damn Much Money: The Triumph of Lobbying and the Corrosion of American Government.* New York: Alfred A. Knopf.

Kang, Michael. (2012). "The Campaign Finance Debate after *Citizens United.*" *Georgia State University Law Review* 27, no. 4: 1161–1167.

Koger, Gregory, and Jennifer Nicoll Victor. (2009). "Polarized Agents: Campaign Contributions by Lobbyists." *Political Science & Politics* 42, no. 3: 485–488.

Krishnakumar, Anita S. (2007). "Towards a Madisonian, Interest-Group-Based, Approach to Lobbying Regulation." *Alabama Law Review* 58, no. 3: 513–573.

Library of Congress. (2012). "Search Bill Text 111th Congress." Accessed July 17, 2012. http://thomas.loc.gov.

Lobbying Disclosure Act ("LDA") of 1995, Pub. L. No. 104–65, 109 Stat. 691.

Luneberg, William V. (2008). "Anonymity and Its Dubious Relevance to the Constitutionality of Lobbying Disclosure Legislation." *Stanford Law and Policy Review* 19: 69–104.

Luneberg, William V. (2009). "The Evolution of Federal Lobbying Regulation: Where We Are Now and Where We Should Be Going." *McGeorge Law Review* 41: 85–130.

Luneberg, William V., and Thomas M. Susman. (2006). "Lobbying Disclosure: A Recipe for Reform." *Journal of Legislation* 33: 32–56.

Madison, James. (1787). "Federalist No. 10: The Same Subject Continued: The Union as a Safeguard against Domestic Faction and Insurrection." *New York Daily Advertiser.* Accessed July 3, 2012. www.constitution.org.

Madison, James. (1788). "Federalist No. 51: The Structure of the Government Must Furnish the Proper Checks and Balances between the Different Departments." *Independent Journal.* Accessed July 18, 2012. www.constitution.org.

Mayer, Lloyd Hitoshi. (2008). "What Is This Lobbying That We Are So Worried About?" *Yale Law and Policy Review* 26: 485–566.

Montana Automobile Association v. Greely. 632 P.2d 300 (Supreme Court of Montana, 1981).

National Association of Manufacturers v. Taylor. 582 F.3d 1 (United States Court of Appeals for the District of Columbia Circuit, 2009).

Ognibene v. Parkes. 671 F.3d 174 (United States Court of Appeals for the Second Circuit, 2011).

Pickard, Daniel B., and Tessa Capeloto. (2011). "Two Criminal Prosecutions under the Foreign Agents Registration Act." Wiley Rein, LLP: Newsletter/Industry Update. Accessed July 3, 2012. http://www.wileyrein.com/publications.cfm?sp=articles&id=7268.

Potter, Trevor, and Joseph M. Birkenstock. (2008). *Political Activity, Lobbying Laws, and Gift Rules Guide.* Eagan, MN: Thomson-West.

Regan, Secretary of the Treasury v. Taxation with Representation of Washington. 461 U.S. 540 (Supreme Court of the United States, 1983).

Schmidt, Susan, and James Grimaldi. (2005, Dec. 29). "The Fast Rise and Steep Fall of Jack Abramoff." *Washington Post.* Accessed July 31, 2013. http://www.washingtonpost.com/wp-dyn/content/article/2005/12/28/AR2005122801588.html.

Schwartz, Emma, and Justin Rood. (2009). "FBI Raided Lobbying Firm Connected to Murtha." *ABC News.* Accessed July 12, 2012. http://abcnews.go.com/Blotter/story?id=6840438&page=1.

Sekulow, Jay Alan, and Erik M. Zimmerman. (2008). "The Law of Lobbying: Weeding Them Out by the Roots: The Unconstitutionality of Regulating Grassroots Issue Advocacy." *Stanford Law and Policy Review* 19: 164–197.

Smith, Jeffrey R. (2005, Dec. 31). "The DeLay-Abramoff Money Trail." *Washington Post.* Accessed July 31, 2013. http://www.washingtonpost.com/wp-dyn/content/article/2005/12/30/AR2005123001480.html.

Spak, Michael I. (1990). "America for Sale: When Well-Connected Former Federal Officials Peddle Their Influence to the Highest Foreign Bidder—A Statutory Analysis and Proposals for Reform of the Foreign Agents Registration Act and the Ethics in Government Act." *Kentucky Law Journal* 78: 237–292.

Susman, Thomas M. (2008). "The Law of Lobbying: Private Ethics, Public Conduct: An Essay on Ethical Lobbying, Campaign Contributions, Reciprocity, and the Public Good." *Stanford Law and Policy Review* 19: 10–22.

Susman, Thomas M., and Margaret H. Martin. (2009). "Contingent-Fee Lobbying." Chapter 33 In William Luneburg, Thomas Susman, and Rebecca Gordon, eds. *The Lobbying Manual.* Chicago: American Bar Association, pp. 669–679.

Textile Mills Securities Corporation v. Commissioner of Internal Revenue. 314 U.S. 326 (Supreme Court of the United States, 1941).

Thurber, James A. (2011). "The Contemporary Presidency: Changing the Way Washington Works?—Assessing President Obama's Battle with Lobbyists." *Presidential Studies Quarterly* 41, no. 2: 358–374.

Trist v. Child. 88 U.S. 441 (Supreme Court of the United States, 1875).

United States House of Representatives. (1949, Aug. 12). Resolution 298. 81st Congress, 1st Session.

United States House of Representatives. (1995). "104th Congress, 1st Session. *Report 104–339: Accompanying H.R. 2564.*" Accessed July 5, 2012. http://lobbyingdisclosure.house.gov/HReport104–339.pdf.

United States House of Representatives. (2009, July 1). "Lobbying Disclosure Electronic Filing Contribution Reporting System." Accessed July 11, 2012. https://lda.congress.gov/lc/help/WordDocuments/LCUserManual.pdf.

United States House of Representatives, Office of the Clerk. (2012, June 15). "Guide to the Lobbying Disclosure Act." Accessed July 12, 2012. http://lobbydisclosure.house.gov.

United States House of Representatives, Office of Congressional Ethics. (2012 May 9). "About." Accessed August 3, 2012. http://oce.house.gov/about.html.

United States v. Auhagen. 39 F.Supp. 590 (Federal District Court for the District of Columbia, 1941).

United States v. Harriss. 347 U.S. 612 (Supreme Court of the United States, 1954).

United States v. Rumely. 345 U.S. 41 (Supreme Court of the United States, 1953).

Wingfield, Brian (2009, Jan. 21). "Obama's Lobbying Limits." *Forbes.* Accessed July 31, 2013. http://www.forbes.com/2009/01/21/washington-lobbying-obama-biz-cx_bw_0121lobby.html

Zeller, Belle. (1958). "Regulation of Pressure Groups and Lobbyists." *Annals of the American Academy of Political and Social Science* 319, no. 1: 94–103.

Social Media, Political Influence, and Lobbying

Mary C. Harris and Michael Phillips-Anderson

Social media provide a new way for people and organizations to communicate about political issues important to them. While platforms such as Facebook and Twitter can seem like open-access, free-wheeling conversations, social media still involve a kind of middleman, in the form of constraints and limitations created by the various technologies. But there is no question that these tools afford more access for more people than traditional broadcast communications ever did, or could. In this chapter we will discuss the brief but active history of social media, define key concepts, and identify differences among platforms, particularly concerning their utility as sites for political communication. We will then look at three specific groups and movements that have engaged social media as part of their persuasive and political strategies.

Traditionally, lobbyists of various political ideologies spread their agendas and missions through grassroots efforts, conventional media coverage, and conventional public relations. Since the early 1980s, technology has been swiftly transformed into a user-friendly series of communication channels, where the users range from businesses and corporations of all sizes to individual citizens of virtually all ages. In just a brief span of time, the way human beings communicate with one another has been drastically reworked, not least when the goal is political influence. With its ease of use, cost efficiency, and seemingly infinite outreach potential, social media have changed the nature of many lobbying efforts, by providing a new and convenient way for people and organizations to organize and strategize.

Between the time of this chapter's publication and the time it is read, whether it be five months or five years from now, there is no doubt that new social media platforms will have cropped up. So instead of focusing entirely on current platforms, this chapter approaches the subject by illuminating the overall relationship between social networking and lobbying, and providing a sample of real-world cases that merit further exploration.

Defining Social Media

Prior to describing the intersection between social media and lobbying, it is essential to explain how social media are defined. For starters, the term is relatively new and the definition is somewhat broad and in flux; in fact, the term is frequently misunderstood. Even the experts disagree. Kaplan and Haenlein define social media as "a group of Internet-based applications that build on the ideological and technological foundations of Web 2.0, and that allow the creation and exchange of User Generated Content" (2010, 61). To add to that, Boyd and Ellison define social networking sites as "web-based services that (1) construct a public or semi-public profile within a bounded system, (2) articulate a list of other users with whom they share a connection, and (3) view and traverse their list of connections and those made by others within the system" (2007, 211). A third description of the term provided by Scott states: "Social media provide the way people share ideas, content, thoughts, and relationships online. Social media differ from so-called mainstream media in that anyone can create, comment on, and add to social media content. Social media can take the form of text, audio, video, images, and communities" (Scott 2011, 38). Moreover, the terms social media, social network, social networking sites, and social sharing sites are often used interchangeably.

For the purpose of this chapter, we offer the following multifaceted definition of social media:

> Social media are user-centered Internet applications constructed on the foundations of Web 2.0 that allow members to generate and share a variety of content, either original or from secondary sources, including text, audio, video, and images, construct a profile, build relationships with other users, engage in two-way communication providing and receiving feedback either privately or through a channel that is open to the public, and engage in an exploration of other network connections through lists and groups based upon interests and commonalities.

So social media are more than just websites where original content is generated through a variety of participants. These channels lay claim to an efficient, easy-to-use, and cost-effective approach to two-way communication that can be utilized by practically anyone savvy enough to operate a computer and access the Internet.

Historical Perspectives on Social Media

Many of today's social media users may remember the frenzied rise and decline of websites like Friendster and the MySpace, but social networking software existed before the inception of these websites. There are some parallels between the history of this topic and the age-old question: Which came first—the chicken or the egg? Some of the developmental milestones of this technology occurred simultaneously. It is beyond our scope to piece together the history of every social networking website in existence from inception to demise. But we can identify some key historical landmarks on the road that led forward.

Historically, although the term "social media" had not yet been coined, online forms of social communication and networking started to appear around the same time as e-mail. As a point of reference, the first e-mail was sent in 1971. In 1979, Ward Christensen and Randy Seuss invented the first Computerized Bulletin Board System (CBBS), which provided users the ability to share data through bulletins or message boards, and even access to games. That same year, Tom Truscott and Jim

Ellis, two Duke University students, developed a message system similar to a BBS called Usenet (Kaplan and Haenlein 2010, 60).

Bulletin Board Systems (BBS) continued throughout the 1980s; however, not all users of this software utilized it in a principled way. Some people participated in unethical and illegal behavior through underground niches such as bomb-building and hacking (Borders 2009). Soon after the start of CBBS, corporations created the first commercial Internet service providers—Compuserve, Prodigy, AOL, and others—in an attempt to bring this type of software to the general public. One of the first online communities was "The Well" (Whole Earth 'Lectronic Link) started by Stewart Brand and Larry Brilliant in 1985. Their community was part of a progressive movement, and members frequently discussed political issues online. In 1985, a company called Quantum Computer Services emerged from a failed initiative called Control Video Corporation, and started a dial-up Internet service that was later named America Online in1989; however, the service name change was not fully completed until about 1992, as Quantum Computer Services was still the parent company (McCracken 2010). Through direct mail CDs and an aggressive product placement campaign in the 1998 blockbuster film *You've Got Mail*, AOL quickly became a household name and came to dominate its competition (Borders 2009).

In 1991, the World Wide Web became available to the public. During the late 1990s, BBS and Usenet were replaced with Internet forums (Borders 2009). Internet Relay Chat (IRC) was developed in the late 1980s, but this really took off in 1996 when instant messenger (IM) for desktops, known as ICQ, was invented by four Israeli technologists. AOL purchased this messaging system, and instant messaging soon became a popular trend for communicating (Borders 2009). In 1997, AOL Instant Messenger was released, which aided in the eventual shift toward online communities (Simon 2009, 7). In 1998, a community for online journaling, known as Open Diary, was developed by Bruce and Susan Abelson. This was considered an early form of social media, and soon after, the term "weblog" was first used and eventually shortened to "blog" (Kaplan and Haenlein 2010, 60). Blogs continued to grow in popularity with websites such as LiveJournal and Blogger following suit in 1999. Online media sharing soon followed instant messaging, with websites such as Napster and Limewire. Through this peer-to-peer (P2P) file-sharing software, users were able to identify and showcase their musical preferences (Borders 2009).

One of the first websites to pave the way for the more current social sites was SixDegrees, which was released in 1997. SixDegrees worked off the premise of building circles of friends and was one of the first websites of its kind to focus on indirect relationships. In 2002, programmer Jonathan Abrams launched the next social networking boom when he released Friendster, a website that also created circles of friends through virtual communities. Even after they are eclipsed by other platforms, these sites often remain and reinvent themselves. Following Friendster's eventual decline, it was relaunched in 2011 as a social gaming website (Friendster). Next came MySpace, the widely popular website that was founded by Chris DeWolf and Tom Anderson in 2003, growing to become the most popular social networking website internationally by 2006. In April of that year MySpace had over 70 million members (Hansell 2006). Perhaps crucial to MySpace's success was the site's offerings for members to customize the layout and appearance of their own "space" or page and provide access to users to post and view content through comments, private messages, and even blogs. Eventually, MySpace expanded to include services ranging from instant messaging to video sharing in an attempt to keep up with the new competition of Facebook (Simon 2009, 8). Over time, a shift occurred where MySpace was accessed less and less by individual users and instead became known as a site for musical artists and band pages. In 2010, MySpace's Chief Executive Mike Jones essentially surrendered to Facebook, issuing the following public statement: "MySpace is not a social network anymore. It is now a social entertainment destination" (Barnett 2010). This was a turning point in the history of the website's future.

Photobucket, the first website for photo sharing, was released in 2003. Its model quickly exploded in popularity and has continued to thrive on additional sites. Photobucket allows users to upload their photographs into password-protected albums that can be shared with friends free of charge (Chapman 2009). MySpace later bought Photobucket, and it was sold again a couple of years later (Suster 2010, 15). Similar websites such as Flickr were also introduced. In 2005, the first major video-sharing website—YouTube—was opened to the public. Some of the most popular social networking sites today provide photo- and video-sharing services as part of their membership offerings, hinting at a general shift in social networking preferences from text-laden to image-driven.

The year 2003 was a watershed year for social media development. First there was the founding of LinkedIn, a site devoted to networking business professionals (Chapman 2009). This was one of the first mainstream social networking sites to allow users to post a resume to their profile page and to encourage business networking and job searching.

Then in October 2003, Harvard student Mark Zuckerberg "hacked into some of his fellow compatriots' 'face books' and set up his own site, Facemash, to compare their less-pleasing attributes in a split-screen comparison" (Simon 2009, 9). The university soon caught wind of this and shut down the website. Undaunted, Zuckerberg then partnered with fellow students Chris Hughes, Dustin Moskovitz, and Eduardo Saverin to create a universal social networking website for students at Harvard. Their product TheFacebook.com was later released to other universities such as Stanford, Columbia, and Yale. TheFacebook.com eventually became Facebook.com, and in 2005 Zuckerberg made it available to all higher education students, soon followed by high school students, and in September 2006 to the general public (Simon 2009). In 2004, as Facebook was progressing on its journey, the term "Web 2.0" was first coined to explain the new way that "software developers and end-users started to utilize the World Wide Web; as a platform whereby content and applications are no longer created and published by individuals, but instead are continuously modified by all users in a participatory and collaborative fashion" (Kaplan and Haenlein 2010, 61). One of the greatest strengths of Facebook was its simple layout, which allowed users to post status updates that could be seen instantaneously.

In 2006, Twitter was founded. The site capitalized on the success of Facebook's status update and news feed features by allowing users to quickly post an update to share with followers; each post was limited to 140 characters so that the system would be compatible with most SMS (short message service) systems. That is, you could text your tweet. This constraint also encouraged brevity and access to rapid snippets of information. Another unique piece of the Twitter puzzle was that it had some famous users, providing the general public with what felt like an insider's cult-like viewpoint (Chapman 2009). Most recently at the time of writing this chapter, the social networking site, Pinterest, has grown popular among certain demographic groups and businesses. Pinterest, founded by Ben Silbermann, Paul Sciarra, and Evan Sharp, is a website boasting virtual pin boards or dream boards that feature images that link to websites. It has grown popular among women, and users have the capability to categorize the boards into groups or themes (Carlson 2012). Although the website started out by attracting new users through an invitation-only method, today Pinterest is attracting more diversified audiences, including businesses and political groups.

The "circle of friends" theme, similar to the SixDegrees and Friendster premises of the past, was revived by the launch of Google+ in June 2011 (Mashable.com 2012). Google+ transformed this feature into what it calls "Circles," which "are simply small groups of people that you can share to, each with names like friends, family, classmates and co-workers" (Mashable.com). Google+ is newer than Facebook and while some tech experts predict it will overtake Facebook, its current performance is far from that level. Google+ has attracted a small subculture who use it regularly, and apart from that "a well-circulated report from comScore in February showed users spent, on average, 3.3 minutes a month on the site in January vs. *seven hours* on Facebook" (Wasserman 2012). Time will tell whether this website and others like it have a profitable future.

Instagram took the social media world by storm in 2012. Developed in 2012 by two Stanford University graduates, Kevin Systrom and Mike Krieger, it is a free mobile photo-sharing application This means it is not available through a regular personal computer, but (currently) only obtainable through iPhone and Android mobile devices. Photos can be taken with these mobile phones and shared through Instagram with the option of choosing "a filter to transform the image into a memory to keep around forever" (Instagram 2012). This is just one of many examples of a mobile application, known as Web 3.0, which is considered "a brave new frontier in communications and fundraising" (Mansfield 2012, 178). Mobile versions of some of the aforementioned social media sites such as Facebook and Twitter have paved the way for applications such as Instagram. This portable access to social media has also created instant gratification for users who seek to communicate with their social networks virtually any time of the day. From a political standpoint, Instagram has changed the way that campaign photos are taken and shared, because it offers an insider's look at the campaign trails for virtually any citizen to follow (Warzel 2012).

A final historical landmark is the advent of social petitioning websites such as Change.org, which was developed in 2006 by two former classmates from Stanford

University, Ben Rattray and Mark Dimas, and is described as "a social action platform that empowers anyone, anywhere to start, join, and win campaigns to change the world" (Change.org 2012). As described by one observer: "Though originally conceived as a nonprofit, Change.org is now part of an emerging group of 'social benefit corporations,' such as Patagonia, that seek to both make money and do good" (Mui 2012). To date, Change.org covers causes ranging from economic justice to human rights and health issues.

Many other specialized social networking sites were developed throughout the years, including Delicious, Ning, Reddit, Digg, Meetup, and Tumblr. Importantly, the most enduring of the entrants shared the feature of free membership. The landscape of social media is likely to look very different in a month, a year, and certainly in a decade. Regardless, it is clear that social media are here to stay. With so many individuals, groups, and companies now employing this technology as a component of their daily routines, it makes sense that the political arena has made the same communication shift.

The Intersection: Social Media and Politics

In Willard C. Richan's book *Lobbying for Social Change*, he emphasizes practical standards for individuals and groups to take part in advocacy, and describes five different contexts for advocacy. One of the contexts includes "what is becoming increasingly important in all facets of political action, the mass media" (Richan 2006, 141). Although this text was published in 2006, his comment reinforces the essential cross-connectedness between politics and methods of mass communication such as the social networking sites of today. At first glance, some may consider social media's primary purpose to be largely entertainment. However, many citizens find much more than entertainment on these platforms and take part in political communication and debate. In summation, these websites are "spaces where individuals share political opinions and information" (Himelboim, Lariscy, Tinkham, and Sweetser 2012, 95). One other point to note about this intersection is that because some of the communities, forums, and blogs allow anonymity or the use of an alias, some individuals may feel they can be more honest and open about their political views online than when communicating in person. "If anonymity is selected in online discourse, openness and transparency are perhaps more easily achieved; there may be a more honest disclosure in political social media than face-to-face" (Himelboim et al. 2012, 98). So if lobbyists recruit online, this model of communication would potentially encourage more participation. Another benefit to advocacy groups is that an abundance of open and cost-free communication channels enables their supporters to spread information like wildfire.

Because of the relatively new connection between politics and social media, there are many legal questions related to the regulation of these websites. In one 2011 legal booklet, the organization Alliance for Justice contends that it is legal for a 501(c)(3) public charity or 501(c)(4) to use social media for lobbying: "Social media provide myriad inexpensive opportunities to influence legislation. Organizations may leverage the low cost of emails, web postings, Facebook, and other social media to maximize their lobbying influence" (15). But there are likely to be court challenges on the finer points of how these groups manage and/or pay for social media–based campaigns.

With the advent of social media, many wonder about the future of more traditional media such as television, radio, and print. Currently, there is a significant degree of collaboration and cross-fertilization among traditional and social media in providing political news. But traditional media have experienced a serious and accelerating decline in reach, as people tire of one-way communication and increasingly turn to social media spaces for two-way sharing of information and opinion.

Additionally, social networking has generated a new form of grassroots lobbying, perhaps more advanced and influential than traditional grassroots efforts of the past. According to the Alliance for Justice:

> Communications on Facebook or a publicly accessible website that ask people to contact their legislators to support or oppose a particular bill will be considered grassroots lobbying. Under tax law, communications to an organization's members are treated as direct lobbying, rather than as grassroots lobbying, meaning that organizations may engage their members in more lobbying activities. Posts on Facebook, Twitter, and the like, which are not limited to an organization's members, will be treated as grassroots lobbying even if the publicly accessible post encourages only the organization's members to engage in lobbying. Organizations that want to limit a lobbying communication to their own members, so the communication will be treated as direct lobbying, should use email, text messages, or password-protected websites, rather than a publicly accessible website. (Mattison 2011, 15–16)

Social websites such as Facebook, Twitter, Google+, and others also give users a myriad of opportunities to join political affinity groups, interact with political institutions and candidates, and discuss political information with other citizens (Himelboim et al. 2012, 92). In turn, citizens can create and share content as news through avenues such as blog articles, tweets, status updates, and image and video sharing.

Change.org offers one of the clearest examples of how politics and social media intersect. The mission of the website is to empower anyone, whether it be an individual citizen or group, to start an online public petition that can "mobilize support" and "win change" (Change.org 2012). Some of the successful outcomes of Change.org petitions have included Bank of America dropping a $5 debit card fee; the U.S. Department of Agriculture offering schools an option to reject the meat byproduct dubbed "pink slime"; and Apple announcing its commitment to protect workers in its Chinese factories. Social petitioning sites are another pathway through which social media are transforming the nature of political influence.

Strategic Differences among Platforms

We have shown that social media as a group share certain characteristics and benefits. But it is important to understand what the different platforms allow users to do, as each website has unique capabilities. Across all platforms, a key point is that while social media appear to be user-controlled, that is not entirely the case. While most platforms allow users to contribute nearly anything (with some limitations for illegal material), the way the information is distributed is largely controlled by the platform and hidden from public view. How is it that Google returns the search results from your query? It uses a highly complex algorithm that takes into account your previous searches, your physical location, the popularity of various websites, and a host of protected, proprietary factors. This section will focus on three of the most prominent sites of today, Facebook, Twitter, and Pinterest; it will also highlight the petition website Change.org and independent blogs. Facebook and Twitter were especially relevant in building the political influence of the Tea Party and Occupy Wall Street, and in fueling the Komen Foundation/Planned Parenthood controversy, which we discuss later in this chapter.

Facebook allows users to create a personal profile, highlighting such fields as name, birthday, employment and education history, political views, and religious beliefs. Once an account is created and the profile is filled out accordingly, members have the options of adding and categorizing connections by the type of relationship, making public status updates that are visible through a newsfeed, liking and sharing other pages either through the Facebook website or on other external websites. They may also share pictures and videos, send private messages to other members, and join various interest groups. One unique component of the site is that it provides different platforms for businesses, nonprofits, and even individuals to build a virtual presence called "pages." There are six categories of pages to choose from: local business or place; company, organization, or institution; brand or product; artist, band, or public figure; entertainment; and cause or community (Facebook 2012). Regular individual/member pages allow individuals to add "friends," whereas Facebook pages allow users to build a following by obtaining "likes" (formerly known as "fans"). The National Rifle Association (with over 1.5 million likes), Non-GMO (Genetically Modified Organisms) Project (71,437 likes), and the American Medical Association (18,548 likes) are all examples of lobbying groups that utilize Facebook to link their mission to their specific targeted audiences, the news media, and the general public. One way this is done is through Facebook's timeline cover photo, which is a large customized photo located at the top of each member's page (available for individual users and Facebook pages alike). The National Rifle Association currently uses a cover photo with a montage of photos of citizens with rifles (Facebook 2012). As political interest and lobbying groups conduct their campaigns, they may use Facebook to get information to their publics who can relay it throughout their networks.

Next is Twitter, a microblogging service (or microblog) that utilizes a similar status update feature to Facebook, except updates are known as "tweets" and are limited to 140 characters or fewer. "Micro-blogging allows you to write brief text updates about your life on the go, and send them to friends and interested observers via text messaging, instant messaging, email or the web," and Twitter is the most popular to date (Glaser 2007). Apart from being considered a microblog, Twitter also championed the innovation of "asymmetry," meaning that a two-way relationship was not necessary to connect with other users (Suster 2010, 16). The Twitter

Sarah Ryan, left, and Shelby Knox with Change.org arrive at the Apple store at Grand Central to deliver petitions asking Apple to change its manufacturing practices and to address criticism of worker conditions at manufacturing partners operating in China. (AP Photo/Mary Altaffer)

news feed only includes links to other media, and does not show the preview of photos and videos, as does Facebook. Twitter also pioneered the hashtag (#) feature, developed by users of the microblogging service rather than as an option imposed from the top down. Hashtags function to denote keywords in tweets to make it easy for members to find similar posts and trending topics. Clicking on a hashtag (e.g., "#politics") "will lead you to a search featuring Tweets with that same hashtag. Think of it like choosing what a Tweet is filed under. Hashtags were originally created by Twitter users and have become a way to participate in global conversations" (Twitter Media 2012).

The political campaign that succeeded in electing President Barack Obama harnessed the strengths of social media with an unprecedented degree of effectiveness. The Obama campaign tapped into social networking sites like Facebook, Twitter, and Meetup to mobilize supporters and generate funding and votes (Learmonth 2009, 85).

As mentioned earlier, Pinterest encourages users to create their pin boards, name them, and categorize them. The hashtag and commenting features are also available on Pinterest, which allow users to engage in conversation and create trends. The site also has a search feature, which gives pinners the opportunity to search pins from any user on their network. While Pinterest is best known for recipes, crafts, and shopping-related images, it has attracted a growing number of political messages. Because two-thirds of Pinterest users are women, it offers a big strategic opportunity to political campaigns seeking to attract female supporters. For example, both the Obama and Romney 2012 presidential campaigns have Pinterest boards, including recipes and other female-friendly pins. The purpose of utilizing this website is not just to attract new voters, but to stay connected with supporters in a highly personal way.

Unlike the other social networking sites, Change.org is considered a "social good site" that attracts those who wish to create a petition as well as people who offer support to specific issues (Mansfield 2012, 22). These petitions are shared through e-mail and other social networking sites like Facebook and Twitter. When individuals create a Change.org account, they have the option of signing and sharing any petition, or they can opt out of displaying their signature publicly. Usually, the petition generates an e-mail to a politician asking him or her to support a position on an issue or a piece of legislation. The site also offers paid partnership opportunities that enable "organizations to feature their campaigns to targeted users and grow their email membership" (Change.org 2012). One example of an ongoing petition is "Tell the EPA (Environmental Protection Agency): We want stronger rules to fight climate change," which was created by Greenpeace (Change.org 2012). With its ease of use and accessibility to anyone, Change.org is a useful new tool in the political sector.

Blogs offer a unique opportunity for political movements to communicate, because a blog allows users "to have a consistent stream of fresh, timely new content to tweet, share on Facebook, use in [an] e-newsletter, and so on" (Mansfield 2012, 157). Blog hosting sites such as Blogger, WordPress, and Typepad offer users options to moderate comments; add share functionality to other social networking websites; and customize the blog name, layout, and design. They also offer a great opportunity for bloggers to receive feedback and direction from readers. Allison Palmer, director of digital initiatives for the Gay & Lesbian Alliance against Defamation (GLAAD), touches on the personal component that their blog offers: "It provides us an easy way to tell our stories on Facebook and Twitter, and because our blog posts are more personal than press releases and Web page text, it really allows people to get a sense of who we are as people, and not just who we are as an organization" (Mansfield 2012, 155). Some other political organizations with regular blogs include The Weston A. Price Foundation, Mothers against Drunk Driving (MADD), and People for the Ethical Treatment of Animals.

Each social platform has some features that overlap, but different platforms coexist because they offer different components for users. One key factor when it comes to anchoring these technologies for political communication is knowing and understanding the audiences who use social media.

The Digital Divide

There is a perception that political groups utilize social media primarily to connect to younger audiences. However, according to the Pew Internet and American Life Project, "as of February 2012, 66% of online adults use social networking sites" (Brenner 2012). The average age of adult users was 33 in 2008, but jumped to 38 by 2010. In 2010, 16 percent of social media users were between the ages of 18 and 22; 32 percent were 23 and 35; 26 percent were 36 and 49; 20 percent were 50 and 65; and 6 percent were 65 and older (Hampton, Goulet, Rainie, and Purcell 2011, 9). These statistics demonstrate that people of all age groups are engaging in this means of communication. Thus politicians can make use of social media to deliver messages to a myriad of constituent groups and campaign targets.

Men and women are fairly close in their overall rate of social media usage (in May 2011, 69% of users were women, compared with 60% of men). However, there are some persistent gender divides. Men dominate LinkedIn, but all other forms of social media platforms have more female users than male users. LinkedIn focuses on professional networks, whereas other social media may provide a better forum for political discourse. Patterns of use also differ among men and women; 42 percent of men and 54 percent of women, respectively, use social media every day. Political groups can frame their social media messages in accordance with these findings, especially in cases where issues revolve around gender.

Social media users also differ based on race and ethnicity. A 2012 Pew Research study found that the sites were used by 64 percent of white non-Hispanics; 68 percent of black non-Hispanics; and 72 percent of English- and Spanish-speaking Hispanics (Brenner 2012). Social media's expansive and diverse outreach potential seems infinite, further enticing individuals, nonprofits, and political entities to incorporate it as an essential advocacy tool.

The pace of social networking is rapid, and it is constantly in flux. An issue that dominated these channels two weeks ago may be completely forgotten two weeks hence. Thus we offer three examples that may prove to have different shelf lives. As we write this text, the Tea Party as a social networking phenomenon has endured through two election cycles; Occupy Wall Street gained significant attention in 2011, but faded in 2012; and the Planned Parenthood/Komen Foundation episode came to an end. However, all of these social media–powered developments offer useful insights and lessons.

The Tea Party Movement

It is hard to say exactly what the Tea Party is. It is not a single group, nor is it a fully coordinated collection of groups. Ronald Formisano observed that "the Tea Party is an umbrella that covers a loose confederation of grassroots groups as well as the corporate-funded offices of dedicated organizers who provide important infrastructure and guidance to the grassroots" (2012, 2). But there is no doubt that the Tea Party has used social media more effectively than virtually any other political or social movement in history.

The Tea Party movement developed largely in reaction to a perceived overreach of power by both Democrats and Republicans in Washington, bank bailouts, the Troubled Asset Relief Program, Obama's election, the American Recovery and Reinvestment Act (Obama's stimulus bill), and health insurance reforms (so-called Obamacare). Members rejected the idea of Republicans compromising with Democrats and/or RINOs (Republicans in Name Only). Some of the group's top priority issues, such as corporate bailouts, spanned both the Bush and Obama administrations, leaving many members suspicious of all politicians regardless of party affiliation

The goals of the Tea Party, while not stated in a universally supported document, are primarily lower taxes, lower spending, smaller government, and debt reduction. Some members are also concerned about social issues such as marriage equality and abortion. Their political orientation runs largely conservative to libertarian. Tea Party members argue that government expansion hurts the economy, though there is no clear agreement among economists about the relationship between government size and economic well-being. As for the name of the movement, the word "Tea" has a double meaning. First, it refers to the Boston Tea Party of 1773, a protest against British taxes imposed on the American colonists who lacked political representation. It is also used as an acronym for "Taxed Enough Already." Even if not all Tea Party members agree on every issue, it helps their visibility to have the same name mentioned consistently in media coverage.

In August 2009, Tea Party activists attempted to disrupt local congressional townhall meetings to call attention to the Democrats' proposed health insurance legislation. The considerable mainstream media attention drove people to the Tea Party's social media sites. This helped the Tea Party recruit members and provide more information about the movement to those who were just learning about it.

While not an official third political party that poses a real challenge to Democrats or Republicans for legislative or executive control, "the Tea Party grassroots share some of the classic hallmarks of the third party/independent tradition: suspicion of professional politicians, frustration with the two-party system and politics as usual, and a hankering for simple solutions to complex problems. They claim to be above the nitty-gritty of politics and the established parties and probably declare their unwillingness to negotiate or compromise" (Formisano 2012, 17). But unlike previous third-party movements, the Tea Party acts as a pressure group only within one established party, the Republicans. Tea Party stakeholders include local networks, political action committees, corporations, Republican officeholders and candidates, and conservative media. There are divides within the Tea Party over Social Security and Medicare, among corporate moneymen and Republican operatives and the grassroots, and between libertarians and evangelicals. But in general, most people involved at the grassroots level of the Tea Party feel that they previously lacked a voice in politics. By using social media, these activists found their voices in the multidirectional communication of the Internet.

Social Media and the Tea Party

During the 2008 campaign season, Democrats were more successful pioneers than Republicans in using social media to connect with, organize, and energize their adherents. But the Tea Party helped to narrow that gap. Also dominant in talk radio, which allows some of the two-way communication that defines social media, the Tea Party has used online social media as its primary organizing tool. The most important platforms for the movement have been Facebook, Twitter, and blogs.

Early social media efforts during the Tea Party's formative period included *Smart Girl Politics* and *Redistributing Knowledge*. Activists used a Twitter hash tag (#tcot, an acronym for "Top Conservatives on Twitter") to help members identify other activists and connect with them. This led to the use of conference calls, Facebook pages, and wikis to collect and distribute information. These tools, along with attention and endorsements from some traditional media sources (particularly Fox News), allowed the movement to grow from protests attended by a few dozen people in February 2009 to more than 75,000 marchers in Washington, D.C., in September 2009. Many sources credit a February 19, 2009, statement by CNBC commentator Rick Santelli with launching the Tea Party movement. But as an example of the back and forth of media influence, the cable television "rant" by Santelli only became widely known after a video of the incident went viral online.

The importance of the Tea Party and its members' use of social media became clear with the 2010 congressional elections, when 22 percent of adults who were online used social networking sites to connect with campaigns (Smith 2011). The national conservative organization FreedomWorks began offering activists training in how to use social media to advance their agenda, conducting 105 social media "boot camps" in 2011 (Travis 2012). Social media were used to gather supporters, draw attention to political news, organize boycotts of companies the user disagrees with, and run get-out-the-vote operations

A form of social media not commonly included with Facebook and Twitter is a selection of tools on websites that allow users to rate the quality of a product. At a social media training for Tea Party activists, the Speaker encouraged members to rate conservative books on Amazon.com with five stars and liberal books with one star. These ratings can affect what recommendations Amazon.com makes to its

Dave Ulsh, 22, of Virginia Beach, Virginia, left, and Matt Matyjek, 20, of New York, both interns with the Tea Party training group FreedomWorks, sort boxes of campaign signage to be shipped to Tea Party supporters throughout the United States, at their office in Washington on October 26, 2010. (AP Photo/Jacquelyn Martin)

customers. This trainer said "We become digital activists. We identify the medium, we learn the medium, we manipulate the medium. It was printing presses then, it's the Internet now" (quoted in Hiar 2010). At first glance, rating a book or a movie with one to five stars may not seem like social media, but the purpose is really to share your opinion with a network of people. As one scholar noted "When Amazon, or YouTube, or Facebook, offer to algorithmically and in real time report on what is 'most popular' or 'liked' or 'most viewed' or 'best selling' or 'most commented' or 'highest rated,' it is curating a list whose legitimacy is based on the presumption that it has not been curated" (Gillespie 2011). It turns out that users aware of the general method of the algorithms can affect the process collectively and strategically.

Grassroots or Astroturf?

The extensive use of social media would seem to be evidence that the Tea Party is primarily an outsider movement challenging institutional power. But how authentically grassroots is the Tea Party? Opponents have dismissed the movement as Astroturf rather than grassroots: that is, a political movement that appears to come from the ground up but is really controlled by powerful institutional interests. The grassroots members of the movement portray themselves as independent of both political and corporate influence, but critical, early tactical support came from FreedomWorks and Americans for Prosperity, both well-funded political organizations that had used the term "Tea Party" for several years before the expansion of the movement. The two major groups that represent the different sides of the movement are the Tea Party Patriots (a network of independent groups operating across the country, relying primarily on social media to gather support) and the Tea Party Express (originally formed by political consultants who seek to elect conservative candidates). Their early development was certainly kicked off online, but it took traditional media like television and newspapers (albeit often the newspapers' online versions) to bring widespread attention and resources to the fledgling groups. Fox News commentators encouraged viewers to participate in tax day protests in 2009 and then, while covering the protests, observed repeatedly that a movement was sweeping the nation. Perhaps the most accurate characterization of the Tea Party movement is that it is simultaneously grassroots and Astroturf. While corporate and political interests have provided various types of infrastructure and other support, social media have given deinstitutionalized participants a voice.

The Tea Party found success in the 2010 congressional elections, moving the Republican Party further to the right and helping its candidates achieve a majority in the House of Representatives. While they had some effect on the 2012 Republican primaries, nominee Mitt Romney was not embraced as a natural Tea Party member. Time will tell if the Tea Party continues to move from being a social movement to an institutionalized political player. It is likely that the more it becomes institutionalized, the less influence the true grassroots will have on its political agenda—though social media will continue to be used as the communication tool of choice for both institutional organizers and individual members.

Occupy Wall Street

The mission of Occupy Wall Street, found on the group's 2012 website Occupy-WallStreet.org, is:

> Occupy Wall Street is a leaderless resistance movement with people of many colors, genders and political persuasions. The one thing we all have in common is that We Are The 99% that will no longer tolerate the greed and corruption of the 1%. We are using the revolutionary Arab Spring tactic to achieve our ends and encourage the use of nonviolence to maximize the safety of all participants. This #ows movement empowers real people to create real change from the bottom up. We want to see a general assembly in every backyard, on every street corner because we don't need Wall Street and we don't need politicians to build a better society.

This statement encapsulates several important features of the movement. First is the claim that it is leaderless, and that decisions are made collectively. The group describes itself with the slogan, "We Are the 99%," coined by anthropologist David Graeber and identifying the enemy as an economically exploitative "1%." The clear statement that they will use nonviolent means to bring about social change presents both an ideology and a persuasive appeal for legitimacy. Use of social media is embedded in the group's mission statement through the designation of the hash tag "#ows" and the call for "bottom up" change. Although OWS says that activists "don't need politicians to build a better society," there is an implicit recognition of the need to persuade those in positions of power to accept their proposals for reform.

It started with a hashtag. On July 13, 2011, the Adbusters blog posted a call to action that included the #OCCUPYWALLSTREET hashtag (the Adbusters Media Foundation is a Canadian-based anti-consumerist group founded in 1989). Inspired by the Arab spring, particularly the protests in Tahrir Square, Cairo, the blog post proposed the following plan for social protest that could lead to political change: "The beauty of this new formula, and what makes this novel tactic exciting, is its pragmatic simplicity: we talk to each other in various physical gatherings and virtual people's assemblies . . . we zero in on what our one demand will be, a demand that awakens the imagination and, if achieved, would propel us toward the radical democracy of the future . . . and then we go out and seize a square of singular symbolic significance and put our asses on the line to make it happen" (Culture Jammers HQ 2011). The bloggers asked people to gather in lower Manhattan on September 17, 2011, to talk about what change they would like to work for. They suggested that "Democracy not Corporatocracy" would be a good place to start. Word of the meeting spread almost exclusively through social media, primarily through Twitter and Facebook.

When September 17 arrived, demonstrators gathered near the New York Stock Exchange. Access to the NYSE had already been blocked, so the 1,000 protesters moved onto Zuccotti Park, chosen for its openness and proximity to the Financial District. Fewer than 200 activists stayed in the park the first night, but over the next few weeks thousands more joined in the occupation. In order to sustain the protest on the ground, OWS formed working groups (small groups of activists who were interested in particular aspects of the protest) to address concerns such as food, sanitation, communication, physical and mental health, and fundraising. Since the movement specifically rejected the idea of leaders and hierarchies, decisions about all aspects of the movement were made through discussion and consensus building. The formal mechanism for achieving this consensus was a meeting known as "the general assembly." Because they were denied a permit to use electronic amplification, OWS used the "Human PA." This worked by having the crowd closest to a speaker repeat each statement so that those farther away could hear. In addition to the meetings in the park, OWS used their website and e-mail lists to continue the conversations and planning online.

Two events helped move OWS from social media to traditional media coverage: the pepper spray video and the Brooklyn Bridge. During a September 24 protest near Union Square, police used orange netting to block activists from advancing. NYPD deputy inspector Anthony Bologna walked up to the protesters and doused them with pepper spray. A video of the altercation quickly spread throughout social media. The protesters gained considerable attention and sympathy since they appeared to be following police instructions before being sprayed. Then on October 1, 2011, New York City police arrested more than 700 OWS protesters on the Brooklyn Bridge for blocking traffic and for protesting without a permit. The police maintained that the protesters were arrested only after being given multiple warnings to move. OWS argued that they were not given any warnings and were actually directed on the roadway by the police (a contention later upheld by the federal courts). Again, amateur video of the event spread from social media to mainstream news coverage. Without social media's distribution of these videos, the traditional media may never have covered the OWS movement; at a minimum, it is unlikely that OWS would have been propelled so quickly onto the front pages of major newspapers throughout America. The combination of social and traditional media fueled rapid expansion of the movement to other cities and countries, where activists set up their own Occupy marches and encampments. By October 29 there were 2,300 Occupy sites in 2,000 cities (Barton 2011). OWS continued to attract traditional media attention. The number of news stories focused on income inequality—the major OWS battle cry—also increased significantly during the occupations (Knefel 2012). New York City allowed the protests to continue for a few more weeks until just after midnight on November 15, when the NYPD began to evict the protesters from Zuccotti Park.

Social Media and Occupy Wall Street

OWS made use of several social media platforms. Among the most significant were Facebook, Twitter, and LiveStream (which allows users to broadcast real-time streaming video). While the technological aspects of these platforms are important, what is most significant from a political influence perspective is how they are used to persuade audiences and change minds. Ben Rattray argued, "Social change is less about the tools and more about the applications of those tools. The best way to get people away from their computer is through the computer; you can't organize thousands of people in New York City [the way Occupy Wall Street has] without the web" (quoted in Kanalley 2011). Multiple Facebook pages allowed OWS to disseminate ideological and logistical information to current and prospective participants. Within a few days of the start of the protests, there was a Facebook page linked to YouTube videos of the protests.

It is important to note that the traditional media and government authorities also kept careful watch on OWS's social media operations. While some social media communication may be private, most, by design of the platforms, are open to the public. LiveStream enabled OWS to create what was, in effect, their own television station. This platform allows users with a webcam and an Internet connection to display live video directly to the web; it enabled OWS to provide a window into Zuccotti Park for viewing by the interested public and traditional media. One of the great challenges to social movements in the past was how to get their message out without the distortions of media filters. By broadcasting the protest live, 24 hours a day, OWS succeeded in making people all over the world feel like they were part of the occupation.

Of all the social media platforms, perhaps the most important for OWS was Twitter. The microblogging site enabled OWS to quickly organize actions and distribute information. The #OccupyWallStreet hashtag was shortened to #OWS to permit more content within the 140-character Twitter limit. Numerous websites were developed to create and spread the message, including We Are the 99 Percent, Parents for Occupy Wall Street, and Occupy Together.

One of the features of Twitter allowed users to view what topics were "trending." Though created with social media in mind, it took a while for the Occupy hashtag to achieve this status. During its first month, only a few people tweeted and then retweeted (i.e., forwarded on to their Twitter followers) Adbusters' call to action. The idea gained significant attention, enough to become a top trending topic, only hours before the proposed start of the occupation. Social activists discovered that it is not easy to launch and sustain a trending topic; in fact, some OWS activists were concerned in October 2011 that Twitter was censoring its hashtags from the trending list. There was no censorship; this concern was the result of misunderstanding the trending list. As explained by one expert,

> Trends has been designed (and re-designed) by Twitter not to simply measure popularity, i.e. the sheer quantity of posts using a certain word or hashtag. Instead, Twitter designed the Trends algorithm to capture topics that are enjoying a surge in popularity, rising distinctly above the normal level of chatter. To do this, their algorithm is designed to take into account not just the number of tweets, but factors such as: is the term accelerating in its use? Has it trended before? Is it being used across several networks of people, as opposed to a single, densely-interconnected cluster of users? Are the tweets different, or are they largely re-tweets of the same post? (Gillespie 2011)

It turns out that a topic is less likely to trend if it has trended before. So each time something new happened with OWS, the number of tweets in the breadth of the network of tweeters had to increase for the topic to trend. Trends privileges "terms that spike, terms that exceed single clusters of interconnected users, new content over retweets, new terms over already trending ones" (Gillespie 2011). This demonstrates that while the Internet and social media are clearly powerful tools for social activists, they are not fully open, and all forms or topics of communication are not equal.

Much like the Tea Party, the Occupy movement did not have a central leadership or unified statement of beliefs. Their main focus concerned economic inequality, corporate influence, and a belief that politicians pay insufficient attention to the working and middle classes in American society. Much like the Tea Party, the OWS movement identified itself as nonpartisan. While both groups attacked Republicans as well as Democrats, OWS tended to identify Republicans as the main cause of the nation's problems, whereas the Tea Party identified Democrats as more culpable.

Some Democratic politicians expressed support for the OWS movement, but their endorsements paled in comparison to the strong and vocal support for the Tea Party found in a broad swath of the Republican Party. Following the eviction of the protesters from Zuccotti Park (and sites in several other cities) on November 14, 2011, the movement found itself at a point of transition. Without the public occupation to capture the traditional media's attention, coverage diminished considerably. The movement stayed alive largely through Facebook and Twitter, as OWS activists attempted to influence the conversation surrounding the 2012 U.S. national elections.

Planned Parenthood versus Komen Foundation

In January 2012, the Susan G. Komen Breast Cancer Foundation changed its grant-making policy in such a way as to end its long-standing support of Planned Parenthood. The response from the public was swift and extremely negative; the new policy was rescinded within days. The Komen Foundation/Planned Parenthood controversy illustrates issues related to social media, traditional media, political influence, electoral politics, and fund-raising. It also demonstrates that social media can greatly speed up the process of political influence, forcing political leaders, lobbyists, and traditional media to adapt more quickly than ever.

Background: The Komen Foundation

The Komen Foundation is the largest breast cancer education, prevention, and research organization in the United States. It was founded by Nancy Goodman Brinker in 1982 in memory of her sister, Susan Goodman Komen, who died from breast cancer in 1980. The signature activities of the foundation are Race for the Cure and the pink ribbon campaign, which have raised awareness and more than $2 billion. It raises funds from private donations, mostly in the form of pledges for participants in the Race for the Cure, as well as from cause marketing agreements; participating companies pay the foundation in return for permission to advertise this connection to consumers by displaying the pink ribbon on their products. In addition to raising its own funds, the Komen Foundation engages in extensive lobbying for federal dollars to fight breast cancer. The organization relies on the support and goodwill of a large public constituency to bolster its claim that the

American people want more money for research into this disease. The foundation funds research grants, cancer screenings, public health education, and treatment.

The Komen Foundation had been criticized for some of its activities, including the use of the pink ribbon on products sometimes characterized as unhealthy or unsafe (e.g., KFC's fried chicken "Buckets for the Cure" and a Smith & Wesson 9 mm handgun with a pink grip and engraved ribbon). Some critics had questioned the foundation's expenditure priorities, given that research funding accounts for only 20 percent of its allocations. There had also been concern that some of the Komen Foundation's goals, including universal screenings, may lead to overtreatment and are insufficiently focused on finding the causes of breast cancer and encouraging preventive care. (Other organizations such as the National Breast Cancer Coalition and the Breast Cancer Fund focus more on these issues, but are far less visible and well funded.) But despite such issues, the Komen Foundation remained one of the most respected and enthusiastically supported cause organizations in the United States. No prior criticism had stung so deeply as the social media response to its decision to stop funding Planned Parenthood's breast cancer programs.

Background: Planned Parenthood

Planned Parenthood was founded in 1942. Today it is America's largest provider of women's reproductive health services, including contraception and abortion. It has a budget of more than $1 billion per year, including revenues from the federal government, private fund-raising, grants, and clinic payments. It offers the only source of health care for many women with low incomes. Planned Parenthood has faced criticism for providing abortion services, though the organization claims these services make up only about 3 percent of its activities. While federal law prohibits the use of federal dollars for abortion services, some critics argue that any funding for Planned Parenthood pays for abortions either directly or indirectly. Several states have sought to stop all public funding for Planned Parenthood, and similar attempts have been made in Congress. Among the grants that Planned Parenthood has received from the private sector are breast cancer screening grants from the Komen Foundation.

Timeline of Events

Beginning in 2005, the Komen Foundation provided grants to Planned Parenthood for breast cancer screening and education initiatives. By 2011, this funding—nearly $700,000 per year—went to 19 Planned Parenthood clinics, providing examinations, mammograms, and ultrasounds to more than 750,000 women, many of whom had no other access to health care. On January 31, 2012, Komen announced that it would stop providing funds to Planned Parenthood because of a new rule adopted by the foundation prohibiting grants to any organization that was being investigated by local state, or federal governments.

Planned Parenthood immediately responded that the foundation was capitulating to anti-abortion activists, a charge which it denied. At the time of the decision, Planned Parenthood was the subject of an inquiry by Representative Cliff

Stearns, a Republican from Florida and chairman of the Energy and Commerce Committee's Oversight and Investigations Subcommittee. Stearns was concerned that Planned Parenthood was using taxpayer money to pay for abortion services and had requested documentation from Planned Parenthood, but had not held hearings on the issue. Planned Parenthood received more than $350 million in federal funding each year, and House Republicans attempted, but failed, to cancel the appropriation in February 2011.

After the Komen decision became public, the foundation declined to make any staff members available for comment. But this did not stop the debate, which quickly spread through social media. On February 1, "Susan G. Komen" was the top search term on Google and was a trending topic on Twitter (Preston, 2012). Bloggers and lobbying groups on both sides of the issue asked their supporters to use social media to respond to the developments on the Facebook pages for Planned Parenthood and the Komen Foundation. Posters on Twitter included @PPact (Planned Parenthood Action Fund) and @komenforthecure (Susan G. Komen for the Cure) in their comments, which allowed readers to follow what was being said about the organizations. An analysis of the content of social media communication in the day following the announcement found a 75 percent to 25 percent split opposing the Komen Foundation's action (Preston, 2012). Within hours, Planned Parenthood placed an online letter and fund-raising appeal on its website and used the #komen hashtag on Twitter to seek support ("Please RT: Help us make sure that women continue to get the care they need. Donate to Planned Parenthood today: bit.ly/AAlipY #komen). This tweet employed three strategic social media features. "RT" stands for "ReTweet," a request that readers forward the message onto their social media networks. A link "bit.ly/AAlipY" was provided to a Planned Parenthood website that accepted donations. The tweet used a link shortening service called "bitly" which will provide a link of only 13 characters. (The full URL for the Planned Parenthood site was 85 characters, leaving little room for the rest of its message.) The final feature was the #komen hashtag, which allowed Twitter users to search for the term.

Within a day, Planned Parenthood had raised more than $1 million, including a $250,000 donation from New York City mayor Michael Bloomberg. Some local Komen organizations used Facebook to express their support for Planned Parenthood. Several anti-abortion groups, including the Alliance Defense Fund Americans United for Life, supported the Komen Foundation's decision to stop supporting a major abortion provider. The foundation defended its decision on its website: "We regret that these new policies have impacted some longstanding grantees, such as Planned Parenthood, but want to be absolutely clear that our grant-making decisions are not about politics" (Susan G. Komen for the Cure 2012, February 1). Despite the foundation's use of the plural "grantees," Planned Parenthood was the only organization affected by the new policy. In addition to the online press release, Nancy Brinker made a video statement supporting the policy change that was shown on both social and traditional media.

The focus of the social media (and traditional media) attention turned to the political connections of two key leaders of the Komen Foundation. CEO Nancy

Brinker served as the U.S. ambassador to Hungary and Chief of Protocol of the United States in the George W. Bush administration. She was also a significant campaign contributor and bundler for Bush's campaigns. In 2009 she was awarded the Presidential Medal of Freedom by President Obama.

While Brinker's political affiliations are largely Republican, much more social media interest swirled around Karen Handel, the Komen Foundation's senior vice president for Public Policy and leader of its political advocacy team. Handel had served as Georgia's secretary of state and ran for the Republican gubernatorial nomination in 2010. Part of her campaign called for eliminating funding to Planned Parenthood as she articulated strong pro-life positions.

The funding policy decision was made in December 2011 (though not announced publicly until January 31, 2012) and caused significant conflict within the Komen Foundation. Dr. Mollie Williams, Komen's top public health official, resigned in protest of the decision. Despite Brinker's claim that "Karen [Handel] did not have anything to do with this decision" (quoted in Mitchell 2012), *The Atlantic* magazine reported that three sources with direct knowledge of the process said the funding policy change originated with Handel, and that "the rule was adopted in order to create an excuse to cut off Planned Parenthood" (Goldberg 2012). The conflicting stories about the process only added to the criticism, both of Komen's policy change and of how it handled the announcement.

Brinker also made a video statement, released on the Komen website and subsequently picked up by national media, in which she defended the new granting policy and criticized those who claimed that the decision was political. But nearly all public activities are affected by politics or have political consequences. Since the Komen Foundation and Planned Parenthood both lobby the federal government for resources, their actions are inevitably political. On February 3, Brinker posted a statement on the Koman website on behalf of the Board of Directors denying political or punitive motivations, but altering the original decision. She wrote, "We will amend the criteria to make clear that disqualifying investigations must be criminal and conclusive in nature and not political. That is what is right and fair" (Brinker 2012). This time, the foundation made the announcement only online, with no accompanying video from Brinker. Four days later, Handel resigned from Komen.

The first global Race for the Cure following the controversy took place on June 2, 2012, in Washington, D.C. Participation in the race was down by nearly 40 percent from 2011 when more than $5 million was raised. While this story may have received national media attention in any event, it is very likely that the rapid and widespread social media response drove both the traditional media coverage and the Komen Foundation's quick policy reversal. As shown in the other examples, social media do not exist in a vacuum and do not precipitate change on their own; but it is clearly influencing the agendas of traditional media as well as the priorities of public debate.

Conclusions

The use of social media is an essential component of modern lobbying and political communication. It allows political actors to cultivate supporters and distribute information at relatively low cost. The reach of social media enables political groups to target a wide range of audiences.

However, social media have their own particular challenges. When political communication uses the same channels as personal status updates, there may be a tendency to treat it less seriously than it deserves. The language, the tone, and the argument of social media messaging should all be strategically consistent and flawlessly executed. It is easier to make a mistake on a tweet than on a television commercial, but the negative consequences can be just as significant.

With so many political organizations and causes adopting social media to advance their agendas, there is a risk of attention fatigue among their intended publics. On the other hand, since social media rely on networks built by users, not all political messages will reach all audiences. Networks tend to frame themselves around collective interests; if politics is not among those interests, lobbying messages may fail to resonate.

Social media do not exist separately from traditional media. Although the numbers of social media users and the time they spend online continue to grow, traditional media remain an essential part of any communication strategy. For lobbying organizations, the lesson is that social media can drive participation, but cannot replace conventional activism and outreach. The lesson for citizens is that it is as important as ever to view all political communication, regardless of source, with a careful and critical eye.

References

Amerland, David. (2011, December 30). "Google Plus Social Network Forecast to Hit the 400m Mark." *Technorati*. Accessed June 21, 2012. http://technorati.com/social-media /article/google-plus-social-network-forecast-to/.

Andreasen, Alan R. (1995). *Marketing Social Change: Changing Behavior to Promote Health, Social Development, and the Environment*. San Francisco: Jossey-Bass Publishers.

Barnett, Emma. (2010, November 14). "MySpace Surrenders to Facebook in Battle of Social Networks." *The Telegraph*. Accessed June 21, 2012. http://www.telegraph.co.uk /technology/myspace/8130097/MySpace-surrenders-to-Facebook-in-battle-of-social-networks.html.

Barton, Chris. (2011, October 29). "'Occupy Auckland' Protest Speaks with Many Voices." *New Zealand Herald*. Accessed June 17, 2012. http://www.nzherald.co.nz/nz/news/article .cfm?c_id=1&objectid=10762353.

Bennett, W. Lance, Chris Wells, and Deen Freelon. (2011). "Communication Civic Engagement: Contrasting Models of Citizenship in the Youth Web Sphere." *Journal of Communication* 61: 835–856.

Blackmon, Douglas A., Jennifer Levitz, Alexandra Berzon, and Lauren Etter. (2010, October 28). "Birth of the Movement." *Wall Street Journal*. Accessed June 15, 2012. http:// online.wsj.com/article/SB10001424052702304173704575578332725182228.html ?mod=djemTMB_t#articleTabs%3Darticle.

Borders, Brett. (2009, June 2). "A Brief History of Social Media." *Copy Brighter Marketing*. Accessed Aug. 1, 2012. http://copybrighter.com/history-of-social-media.

Boyd, Danah M., and Nicole B Ellison. (2007). "Social Network Sites: Definition, History and Scholarship." *Journal of Computer-Mediated Communication* 13, no. 1: 210–230.

Brenner, Joanna. (2012, March 29). "Pew Internet: Social Networking (full detail)." *Research Center's Internet & American Life Project*. Accessed August 1, 2012. http://pewinternet .org/Commentary/2012/March/Pew-Internet-Social-Networking-full-detail.aspx.

Brinker, Nancy. (2012, February 3). "Statement from Susan G. Komen Board of Directors and Founder and CEO Nancy G. Brinker." *Susan G. Komen for the Cure.* Accessed June 17, 2012. http://ww5.komen.org/KomenNewsArticle.aspx?id=19327354148.

Carlson, Nicholas. (2012, April 24). "Pinterest CEO: Here's How We Became the Web's Next Big Thing [deck]." *Business Insider.* Accessed June 19, 2012. http://www.business insider.com/pinterest-founding-story-2012-4.

Chandler, Stephanie. (2012, June 13). "Pinterest Power: How to Use the Third Largest Social Media Site to Promote Your Business." *Forbes.* Accessed June 18, 2012. http://www.forbes.com/sites/work-in-progress/2012/06/13/pinterest-power-how-to-use-the-third-largest-social-media-site-to-promote-your-business/.

Change.org. (2012). "Change.org: The World's Premier Platform for Change." Accessed Aug. 1, 2012. http://www.change.org/.

Chapman, Cameron. (2009, October 7). "The History and Evolution of Social Media." Accessed June 18, 2012. http://www.webdesignerdepot.com/2009/10/the-history-and-evolution-of-social-media.

Culture Jammers HQ. (2011, July 13). "#OCCUPYWALLSTREET: A Shift in Revolutionary Tactics." *Adbusters.* Accessed June 20, 2012. http://www.adbusters.org/blogs/adbusters-blog/occupywallstreet.html.

Facebook. (2012). Facebook.com. Accessed Aug. 1, 2012. https://www.facebook.com/.

Formisano, Ronald P. (2012). *The Tea Party: A Brief History.* Baltimore: Johns Hopkins University Press.

Gillespie, Tarleton. (2011, October 19). "Can an Algorithm Be Wrong? Twitter Trends, the Specter of Censorship, and Our Faith in the Algorithms around Us." *Culture Digitally.* Accessed August 1, 2012. http://culturedigitally.org/2011/10/can-an-algorithm-be-wrong/.

Glaser, Mark. (2007, May 15). "Your Guide to Micro-Blogging and Twitter." PBS. Accessed June 17, 2012. http://www.pbs.org/mediashift/2007/05/your-guide-to-micro-blogging-and-twitter135.html.

Goggin, Gerard. (2006). *Cell Phone Culture: Mobile Technology in Everyday Life.* London and New York: Routledge.

Goldberg, Jeffrey. (2012, February 2). "Top Susan G. Komen Official Resigned over Planned Parenthood Cave-In." *The Atlantic.* Accessed June 22, 2012. http://www.theatlantic.com/health/archive/2012/02/top-susan-g-komen-official-resigned-over-planned-parenthood-cave-in/252405/.

Gustafsson, Nils. (2010). "This Time It's Personal: Social Networks, Viral Politics and Identity Management." *At the Interface/Probing the Boundaries* 69: 3–23.

Hampton, Keith, Lauren Sessions Goulet, Lee Rainie, and Kristen Purcell. (2011). *Social Networking Sites and Our Lives: How People's Trust, Personal Relationships, and Civic and Political Involvement Are Connected to Their Use of Social Networking Sites and Other Technologies.* Washington, DC: Pew Research Center's Internet & American Life Project.

Hansell, Saul. (2006, April 23). "For MySpace, Making Friends Was Easy. Big Profit Is Tougher." *The New York Times.* Accessed June 20, 2012. http://www.nytimes.com/2006/04/23/business/yourmoney/23myspace.html.

Hiar, Corbin. (2010, October 28). "How the Tea Party Utilized Digital Media to Gain Power." *Media Shift.* Accessed June 15, 2012. http://www.pbs.org/mediashift/2010/10/how-the-tea-party-utilized-digital-media-to-gain-power301.html.

Himelboim, Itai, Ruthann Weaver Lariscy, Spencer F. Tinkham, and Kaye D Sweetser. (2012). "Social Media and Online Political Communication: The Roles of Interpersonal Informational Trust and Openness." *Journal of Broadcasting & Electronic Media* 56, no. 1: 92–115.

Howard, Philip N., and Steve Jones, eds. (2004). *Society Online: The Internet in Context.* Thousand Oaks, CA: Sage Publications.

Hubbard, Sarah. (2011–2012). "Where Lobbying and Social Media Meet." Accessed June 17, 2012. http://lobbytiger.blogspot.com.

Instagram.com. (2012). "Instagram: Fast Beautiful Photo Sharing." Accessed Aug. 1, 2012. http://instagram.com/.

Kanalley, Craig. (2011, October 6). "Occupy Wall Street: Social Media's Role in Social Change." *The Huffington Post.* Accessed June 17, 2012. http://www.huffingtonpost .com/2011/10/06/occupy-wall-street-social-media_n_999178.html.

Kaplan, Andreas M., and Michael Haenlein. (2010). "Users of the World, Unite! The Challenges and Opportunities of Social Media." *Business Horizons* 53: 59–68.

Knefel, John. (2012). "Bored with Occupy—and Inequality." *Fairness & Accuracy in Reporting.* Accessed June 15, 2012. http://www.fair.org/index.php?page=4533.

Learmonth, Michael. (2009). "Social Media Paves Obama's Way to the White House." In K. Patridge, ed. *The Reference Shelf: Social Networking.* New York: The H.W. Wilson Company.

Mansfield, Heather. (2012). *Social Media for Social Good: A How-To Guide for Nonprofits.* New York: McGraw-Hill.

Mashable.com. (2012). "Google+." Accessed Aug. 1, 2012. http://mashable.com/follow /topics/google-plus/.

Mattison, Allen. (2011). *Advocacy Resource: Influencing Public Policy in the Digital Age: The Law of Online Lobbying and Election-Related Activities.* Washington, DC: Alliance for Justice.

McCracken, Harry. (2010). "A History of AOL, as Told in Its Own Press Releases: Big Moments, Little Triumphs, and Odd Sidelights in the Life of a 25-Year-Old Online Service." Accessed Aug. 1, 2012. http://technologizer.com/2010/05/24/aol-anniversary.

Mitchell, Andrea. (2012, February 2). "Interview with Ambassador Nancy Brinker." *MSNBC Special.* Accessed Aug. 1, 2012. http://firstread.nbcnews.com/_news/2012/02/02/10303379-andrea-mitchell-interviews-susan-g-komens-nancy-brinker.

Moore, Martha T. (2012, June 6). "Political Groups Target Key Voting Demographic on Pinterest." *USA Today.* Accessed Aug. 1, 2012. http://www.usatoday.com/news/politics /story/ 2012–06–12/pinterest-politics-campaign/55556910/1.

Mui, Ylan Q. (2012, January 23). "Change.org Emerges as Influential Advocate on Issues from Bullying to Bank Fees." *The Washington Post.* Accessed Aug. 1, 2012. http:// www.washingtonpost.com/business/economy/changeorg-emerges-as-influential-advo cate/2012/01/09/gIQAoCJHLQ_story.html.

Pfister, Damien Smith. (2010). "Introduction to Special Issue: Public Argument/Digital Media." *Argumentation and Advocacy* 47, no. 2: 63–66.

Preston, Jennifer. (2012, February 1). "Komen Split with Planned Parenthood Draws Fire Online." *The New York Times.* Accessed June 26, 2012. http://thelede.blogs.nytimes .com/2012/02/01/komen-split-with-planned-parenthood-draws-uproar-online/.

Richan, Willard C. (2006). *Lobbying for Social Change.* 3rd ed. Binghamton, NY: The Haworth Press, Inc.

Scott, David Meerman. (2011). *The New Rules of Marketing & PR: How to Use Social Media, Online Video, Mobile Applications, Blogs, News Releases, and Viral Marketing to Reach Buyers Directly.* Hoboken, NJ. John Wiley & Sons.

Shah, Semil. (2012, January 20). "The Dawn of Social Lobbying." *AOL Tech.* Accessed June 26, 2012. http://techcrunch.com/2012/01/20/the-dawn-of-social-lobbying.

Simon, Michael. (2009). "The Complete History of Social Networking—CBBS to Twitter." In K. Patridge, ed. *The Reference Shelf: Social Networking.* New York: The H.W. Wilson Company.

Smith, Aaron. (2011, January 27). "22% of Online Americans Used Social Networking or Twitter For Politics in 2010 Campaign." *Pew Internet & American Life Project.* Accessed June 15, 2012. http://www.pewinternet.org/Reports/2011/Politics-and-social-media .aspx.

Susan G. Komen for the Cure. (2012, February 1). "Statement from Susan G. Komen for the Cure." Accessed June 26, 2012. http://ww5.komen.org/KomenNewsArticle .aspx?id=19327354133.

Suster, Mark. (2010). "What the Past Can Tell Us about the Future of Social Networking." In K. Patridge, ed. *The Reference Shelf: Social Networking*. New York: The H.W. Wilson Company.

Taylor, Astra. (2011). *Occupy!: Scenes from Occupied America*. London: Verso.

Travis, Shannon. (2012, April 27). "Tea Party 2.0: Upgraded for 2012." *CNN*. Accessed June 15, 2012. http://www.cnn.com/2012/04/27/politics/tea-party-upgraded/index .html.

Twitter Media. (2012). "Twitter Media: Bringing the Power of Twitter to TV, Music, Entertainment, Sports and News." *Twitter.com*. Accessed June 26, 2012. https://dev.twitter .com/media.

Warzel, Charlie. (2012, March 5). "Instagram Is Changing Campaign Photography." *In the Capital: The View from Inside DC*. Accessed June 26, 2012. http://inthecapital .com/2012/03/05/instagram-is-changing-campaign-photography/.

Wasserman, Todd. (2012, June 28). "Google+: A Year of Missed Opportunities." *Mashable*. Accessed June 26, 2012. http://mashable.com/2012/06/28/google-plus-one-year-later/.

Worldwide Perspective on Lobbying

Ronald J. Hrebenar and Bryson B. Morgan

When they discuss their politics and political institutions, Americans often seem to emphasize how different the American system is from those of the other nearly 200 nations in the world and how the other countries should be following the American example in developing their emerging democracies. In terms of interest group politics and lobbying, the American system is clearly on one end of the international continuum with its extreme pluralism and armies of lobbyists, lobbying firms, money politics, and the merger of interest group and electoral campaigning in recent years. But vibrant interest group politics does exist in many other nations. Lobbying is a significant part of the policymaking process in Europe and all of the advanced industrialized nations in one style or another, and it exists in more personalized and traditional forms in all of the emerging nations and in even the authoritarian states in a very undemocratic form. In this chapter, some of the other nations' lobbying patterns are examined. Special attention is paid to Canada because it offers an interesting combination of a growing American-style pluralist interest group politics within a parliamentary political system. Also, the Japanese lobbying system is profiled. Japan was the first Asian nation to industrialize, was the first Asian nation to become a "great power;" and today has the world's second-largest economy and a level of modernization that is incredible while still retaining an Asian cultural tradition and style of politics. Europe, with its dozens of nations, is examined from several perspectives.

The special style of European interest group politics is examined by looking at lobbying in two nations (Austria and Sweden) with a very different style of interest group system—they are known as "corporatist" nations. Then a brief look at the largest nations in Europe (the United Kingdom, France, and Germany) is followed by examining in more detail how the former Communist nations of Eastern and Central Europe have begun to develop their interest group systems during the nearly two decades of democratization since their emergence from the Soviet bloc in 1991. A discussion of the emerging European "super state," the European Union (EU), and its exploding lobbyist community in Brussels, which presents another style of lobbying in an industrialized community, is followed. Other forms of international lobbying and nongovernmental organizations are discussed, and finally, a brief tour of the less-developed world attempts to draw some conclusions about how lobbying is depicted in Asia, Africa, and South America. Let us begin our survey in Canada.

Lobbying in Canada

Canada makes for a very interesting contrast in terms of its interest groups and lobbying patterns compared with its close and often dominant neighbor, the United States. It shares the continent with the United States, and American politics, news, and culture wash over it daily, but despite this presence, Canada has developed a different lobbying system from that of the United States. Perhaps its British-style parliamentary system makes its lobbying system appear closer to that of London than of Washington, D.C., in political style. Canada has also developed a multi-party system, unlike its two-party American neighbor. It has no nationally elected head of government like the American president, and it has carefully established and maintained a set of election laws that have effectively kept Canadian politics inexpensive to conduct and have largely eliminated the problems associated with the role of interest groups as financial sources for individual campaigns. In fact, some argue the Canadians do almost everything "right," from a reasonable universal health care system to effective gun control and reduced societal violence, as well as a low-cost and low-corruption governmental and political system.

One analysis of Canadian interest group politics noted that until just recently, the topic was largely ignored in Canada. It concluded "in the last twenty years a vibrant, expanding and public pressure group system has taken hold in Canada. This has happened despite the persistence of cabinet-parliamentary institutions. Since the 1960s interest groups have so proliferated and have become so active in the policy process, they have aroused public concern" (Press 1993, 67).

Press also noted that the style of lobbying had changed as well. Before the 1960s, lobbying was done mostly behind closed doors with very few public tactics used, such as holding demonstrations, lobbying in the American style, and creating associations for lobbyists. Today, lobbying is open and often intense, and it has become an established industry. The forces that promoted these changes are not directly associated with the influence of its neighbor to the south but with the increased complexity of Canada's government and the decentralization of policymaking and new attitudes reflecting changes in political culture.

Although the Canadian civil service or bureaucracy still dominates the policy-making process, changes in the nature and role of the parliament have increased the political power of individual members to such a level as to make them important targets for lobbies. Much more lobbying has taken place in the various stages of the parliamentary decision-making processes than in the past, such as in drafting legislation, committee hearings, and question sessions. Some reforms, such as changing the committee system in the House of Commons rules, have added to the ability of individual members to influence the details of ongoing legislation. The bureaucracy has expanded in size and thus lost some focus in the policy formation process, and the process has become much more transparent, allowing fewer backroom deals and more access by a wider range of better-organized interests.

Canada's strong federal structure also provides many opportunities for interest groups to participate at the provincial level. Many of the powerful organizations not only have offices in Ottawa but in the provincial capitals as well. In recent years, many of the policy issues have devolved from the federal level to the provinces, and the lobbying has moved with them. Culturally, Canadians historically have had a much more deferential attitude toward government decision making than their American counterparts, but that sentiment has changed since the 1970s, when most Canadians seemed willing to accept as legitimate public challenges and demands to the political elites. In this respect, the everyday presence of American media reports on the American style of politics has certainly had some impact.

Also until recently, almost no governmental restrictions or regulations were placed on lobbying and lobbyists. Just as the Americans have become more concerned over the abuses in their lobbying system, so have the Canadians, and in the past 20 years, several relatively light lobbying laws have been enacted. The Lobbyist Registration Act was passed in 1988, and one of the interesting items revealed by the law is a view of the growth of the professional consulting firms engaged in lobbying. The professional lobbying firms moved from interest-specific small firms to a few full-service firms to firms that now offer international lobbying. The Canadian firms offer a variety of services similar to those offered in the United States but call them different names: mapping, dating, and representation. *Mapping* refers to gathering information and advising on a topic; *dating* involves setting up meetings between clients and governmental officials; and *representation* is what Americans would term the lobbyist representing the interest group's interests. The American perspective of representation is not generally accepted in Canada, where it is assumed that the interest's own leaders are the best communicators for the interest. One point seems to be quite clear: the Canadian interest group and lobbying system seems to be moving quickly in the American direction. Finally, the kind of "policy area systems" or "subgovernments" the American scholars such as Schattschneider and others have been describing seems to have also taken root in Canada. Now a policy area's members will include governmental agencies, interest groups, media, and interested citizens, and leadership is taken by the appropriate bureaucracy, the most powerful interest groups, and maybe some provincial governmental units. This usually takes place at the industry level but tends to be balanced by regional demands and intergovernmental conferences. All in all, the Canadian interest group system is open, competitive, and decentralized, and it is coming to look very much like the system of the United States.

An Overview of Lobbying in Europe

European Corporatism

The political institutions, both formal and informal, of Europe have produced different patterns of interest groups and lobbying. Perhaps most important is the prevalence of parliamentary forms of government featuring mass membership parties, with disciplined, strong party line voting parties in the legislatures. Such a system severely reduces the independence of individual members of parliament and therefore makes them infrequent targets of lobbying. Instead, interests tend to lobby the central policymaking organs of the political parties, and especially the bureaucracies of the government that have oversight over the interests.

Whereas the American system, discussed in Chapters 2 and 3, has been described as pluralist or neopluralist, the pluralist label can be applied to some of the European interest group systems to a certain degree, but the label "neocorporatist" seems to be the consensus choice of many of the political scientists who specialize in European politics.

"Corporatism" is a term that describes how interest groups, political parties, and bureaucracy interact to produce public policy; it has its roots in 19th-century European politics. Its most well-known form was found in the fascist politics of Nazi Germany and fascist Italy in the 1930s, but those states collapsed at the end of World War II. It was also present in some of the Latin American nations and Spain and Portugal. This authoritarian form of corporatism is sometimes called *state corporatism*. The most recent examples have been found in Taiwan.

The newest form of corporatism is now generally referred to as "neocorporatism," and it describes a policymaking process based on a cooperative agreement among various powerful interest groups and the government. This cooperative arrangement has as a primary objective the establishment of economic stability in the nation's economy. In other words, it seeks to create an economic political situation with very few, if any, domestic surprises. This goal can be achieved by making sure that the most important actors in the economic world, big business and labor, are deeply involved in the policymaking process with the government and any decisions thus made are consensual and are enforceable in the broad society. Schmitter (1974) is largely credited with making the concept of neocorporatism a popular description of these patterns of decision making. One of the characteristics of neocorporatism is the creation of peak associations to represent each of the major sectors of the tripartite model. Thus, a large labor confederation represents almost all, if not all, the major labor unions in the nation, and a major business confederation represents the business world in that nation. These groups then meet regularly with the governmental bureaucrats to hammer out policies such as wage settlements, inflation policies, and tax levels. Such peak associations are recognized by the government as legitimate representatives of their sector, and in exchange for admission to the decision-making process, the peak associations agree to cooperate in producing reasonable outcomes.

It is often noted that Austria and Sweden are the most purist examples of the modern neocorporative system, although they exemplify the system in different ways. So, we begin our discussion of the European interest group system with a brief example of these two models.

The Two Best Examples of Neocorporatism: Austria and Sweden

Most studies of neocorporatism in Europe point to Austria and Sweden as the two best, but somewhat competing, models. Some observers have called the two basic forms of European corporatism the Continental Europe and the Scandinavian models. The Continental group is usually considered to be Switzerland, Belgium, the Netherlands, Germany, and Austria. The Scandinavian model is best seen in Sweden, but also includes, to a greater or lesser degree, Norway and the other Scandinavian nations. What seems to separate the two models most has been the strong emphasis in the former on the use of social agreements to avoid economic and social conflict in their societies. In fragmented societies, the development of democratic governments could result in severe conflicts that might endanger the existence of the nation. The Swedish model was characterized by a coordinated set of policies to produce full employment, low levels of inflation, and a relatively equal distribution of national wealth. Sweden's long run of social democratic corporatism ran into the wall of globalization, domestic societal changes, and the entry into the European Union in the 1990s, the result of which was rising unemployment; higher levels of inflation; and severe strains on the ability of the corporatist model to keep business, labor, and the farming sector happy in a very internationalized environment.

The strength of the Austrian commitment to its so-called social partnership is what separates it from the other neocorporatist nations of Europe (Bischof and Pelinka 1996). The Austrian model goes far beyond the usual pattern of governmental bureaucracy, business, and labor consulting each other and cooperating on labor conditions or annual wage agreement. In Austria, such cooperative, institutionalized patterns of policymaking are extended to nearly every aspect of Austrian society. The pattern started in the immediate post–World War II period as the nation tried to deal with the impact of severe inflation with informal cooperation; later it was extended to a broad range of social and economic policymaking.

The Austrian Parity Commission for Wages and Prices is central to the establishment of an income policy in the nation. The commission's members are the Austrian Trade Union Federation; the Chambers of Commerce, Labor, and Agriculture; and the various appropriate ministers of the federal bureaucracy. The chancellor (prime minister) of Austria is the chairman, but the government officials have no vote in the decision making. Unanimous decision making is a requirement, and the commission has no powers to enforce its decisions, which are implemented by the government almost always without resistance. It has price and wage subcommittees as well as the Economic and Social Advisory Board, which has a wide-ranging policy focus. In addition to the Parity Commission are many more advisory boards and committees that deal with such policy areas as social security, banking, foreign labor, and immigration and industrial policy.

The neocorporatist system seems to work best in a nation such as Austria for several reasons. Austria is a small and relatively homogeneous nation with an integrated economy; its economic, social, and political leaders are accustomed to working together. It has a multiparty parliamentary system with frequent coalitions that require cooperation across a range of interests. Supporters of the social partnership argue that without it Austria could not have progressed from its status as a poor country in the prewar era to become one of the world's richest countries. Contributing to this success has been a consensus by all the key participants on the need to emphasize economic growth and full employment over other policies such as income redistribution.

When Communism lost its control over the nations of Eastern Europe in the early 1990s, the newly democratizing nations looked at the two competing models of Austrian and Swedish corporatism as possible paths to follow. Of course, the American pluralist model was also an option, and in the next section, we examine the development of Eastern European interest group systems since 1991.

Party Development and Weak Interest Group Lobbying Systems in the Transitioning Democracies of Eastern Europe

The collapse of the Soviet Union and its Eastern European client states in the early 1990s produced an opportunity for an examination of how nations build party and interest group/lobbying systems. These two systems of representative democracy in that region have had a very mixed record. First, both parties and interest group politics developed with difficulty in the parts of the old Soviet Union. Russia itself seemed to have slid back to its old authoritarian roots under President Vladimir Putin. The other parts of the Soviet Union have experienced little democratic development, with the possible exception of the Ukraine, in the past several years. In terms of political parties and democratic elections, the various states of the Baltics and central Eastern Europe have produced surprising patterns of elections and parties. From Lithuania, Latvia, Estonia, and Poland in the north to the Czech Republic, Slovakia, and Hungary in the south, parties and elections have been established and they seem to work quite well.

In a recent study of Lithuanian interest group politics and lobbying, Hrebenar, McBeth, and Morgan (2008) found the lobbying system to be quite primitive, with just a handful of lobbyists, a couple of small lobbying firms, and broad and strong rejection of lobbying and lobbyists as illegitimate parts of the political system. Part of the legacy from its Communist era was a rejection of labor unions as powerful political actors and direct lobbying by big business to the powerful political parties, largely skipping any interest group or lobbyist intermediaries. Although democracy within the institutions of parties and elections seems to be fairly well rooted in Lithuania, interest group politics' roots are very shallow.

Poland is the easiest interest group system in Eastern Europe to understand. Ost (2001) has described the complicated relationship among the political parties, interest groups, and social movements in Poland that has become a special type of interest articulation in which the traditional roles played by the three actors have been blurred, transformed, and institutionalized. The Polish movement Solidarity, which began as a social movement, evolved into a labor-oriented interest group, and then became a political party, demonstrates this merging of functions and roles. Movements and parties in today's Poland remain weak (Millard 1999). Recent presidential and parliamentary elections in Poland indicate that the strength of parties to dominate politics is still a reflection of the weak organizations of the parties and the need to find attractive candidates to win elections

The other major Eastern European nation (after Poland and the former East German state that merged with West Germany) is Czechoslovakia. It split into two nations, the Czech Republic and the Slovak Republic, in 1995. In the Czech Republic, the political parties have sought to monopolize the policymaking process and thus have limited the roles and influence of interest groups and lobbying (Evanson and Magstadt 2001, 206). Czech political culture and its preference for centralized governmental decision making support this pattern. Also a factor is the Eastern European suspicion of interest group politics and lobbying as well as a personalism of direct person-to-person style of everyday politics that leaves interest groups on the outside in Prague (the Czech Republic capital). Finally, the legacy

Lech Walesa, head of the striking workers delegation, smokes a cigarette as he gives autographs on leaflets for solidarity movement workers on August 28, 1980. (AP Photo/Peter Knopp/ Reportagebild)

of Communism still lingers, with its preference for state-party decision making and the disorganized, fragmented, and poorly funded private-sector interests. The Czech Republic is the larger and more industrialized of the two nations and, in many respects, the more Westernized. In the Czech Republic, the interest groups are definitely subordinated to the stronger political parties, and Western-style lobbying and lobbyists are not common. Many of the Czech elite continue to hold the party-state model of politics that tends to exclude interests that are not channeled through either of those institutions. Most interest groups are poorly organized and poorly financed and thus at a tremendous disadvantage when they try to compete with the major parties for influence. As in Poland, corruption and lobbying scandals seem to be the nature of the game in the Czech Republic, with under-the-table payoffs the preferred method of influence acquisition. The peak associations of a tripartite social partnership have been established in the Czech Republic but lack the independent power base and legitimacy to operate effectively. Labor has been particularly disadvantaged in this arrangement. Business seems to be rather disorganized and unconnected to the world of politics, as are the farmers.

Some observers, such as Birgitt Haller, saw the emerging democracies in Central and Eastern Europe as having a similar situation to that in which Austria found itself in the early 1950s as it moved to democratize (Haller 1996). The need was urgent not only to establish new market economies but also to establish institutions of democratic government. Austria tried to export its model to its immediate neighboring countries, such as Hungary, the Czech and Slovak republics, and

Slovenia. Austria met with varying degrees of success in its effort to transplant its version of corporatism. Although all four former Communist nations have developed different forms of institutional tripartite employer/labor/state interest mediation, the Slovenes and Hungarians have evolved closer to the Austrian model than have the Czechs and Slovaks.

One of the problems in these emerging countries was that capitalism had to be built without capital and without capitalists (Haller 1996, 148). All four of these nations placed a priority on social peace between labor and business, but in the economies of the 1990s, it had become much more difficult to do this in a post-industrial world economy. In fact, the centralized nature of both the Austrian political and economic systems made corporatism easy to implement, but the much more complicated (fragmented and heterogeneous) worlds of these four nations' political and economic systems have proven to be more resistant to such institutional harmony. Trade unions and employers' associations have not developed in the same way as those in Austria and thus are unable to enforce any consensual agreements to seek a social partnership.

The Lithuanian example discussed earlier and the failure to develop the necessary social partnership institutions in some of the Central European nations are evidence that the Western styles of interest group politics and lobbying simply do not exist in these developing democracies. Lobbyists in the Western sense do not operate with any significant degree of legitimacy, and they do not use the strategies and tactics found in Western Europe or North America. Interests are represented, of course. They deal directly with powerful politicians and party leaders, and much of this contact is made behind closed doors with significant exchanges of money to lubricate the decision-making processes. As noted early in this chapter, it is far easier to build a party system with free and democratic elections than it is to build an interest group and lobbying system with a low level of corruption and effective representation of interests in the democratic forums of politics. Eastern and Central Europe have made some inroads, but they have a long distance left to travel in this institution building, though their inclusion in the European Union and its exploding interest group politics and lobbying will teach them the game much quicker than if they were trying to learn it on their own.

Lobbying in Western Europe

The "Big Four" nations of Western Europe are Germany, France, the United Kingdom, and Italy. All four are long-standing parliamentary democracies but have very different political cultures and interest group systems and lobbying patterns. Here we summarize the broad patterns of interest group politics of these nations.

The United Kingdom is in many respects the mother of modern democracy, at least in the modern European context. The Magna Carta—in which the interests of the landed aristocracy and religious orders forced the English king to acknowledge that they and others in the realm had specific political rights that must be protected from the asserted absolute power of the monarch—serves as a reminder of its role in democracy. Until recently, the major economic interests of business and labor were clearly allied with one of the two major political parties in such a way that defied the continental European pattern of social partnership or corporatism. The Conservative Party represented big business in the form of the Confederation of British Industries, professions, agriculture, and the labor sector. The antiwar groups, environmentalists, and big labor were solidly in the camp of the Labour Party. Under the leadership of former prime minister Tony Blair, the Labour Party moved much closer to the center, and various Conservative Party leaders have moved that party to the center as well; thus, both are less closely tied to their traditional interest group supporters (Jordan and Maloney 2001). With a parliamentary political system, the style of lobbying is quite different from that found in the United States. Lobbying is focused on the governmental bureaucracy and the party in government rather than on any other institutions. Of these two, the bureaucracy is still the main site of access and interest influence. The United Kingdom has developed a complex system of consultation between the many interest groups and the governmental bureaucracy. The knowledge and expertise of the interest groups are made available to the bureaucrats to assist in the policymaking process. Indeed, lobbying in the United Kingdom can be characterized as truly insider lobbying using the bureaucracy.

In terms of its gross domestic product in 2007, Germany ranked first at $2.9 trillion; following were the United Kingdom at $2.3 trillion, France at $2.2 trillion, and Italy at $1.8 trillion. Germany has been and continues to be the dominant political and economic power of Western Europe. Germany remains a classic neocorporatist democracy largely governed by close relationships among several peak associations, the several large political parties, and the governmental bureaucracy (Gellner and Robertson 2001). The various new social movements representing environmentalists and antiwar and antinuclear groups are vibrant but clearly secondary to the major corporatist institutions. These institutions are the Federation of German Industry, the German Trade Union Federation, the German Farmers Association, and various other peak small business or professional associations. More than 1,000 interest groups lobby the German Parliament, and many members of Parliament have close ties to one or more interest groups, but most of the influential interests have established firm ties to the relevant governmental bureaucratic units most important for their interests. When looking at the two access points, it is estimated that more than 80 percent of the "lobbying" is bureaucracy directed and less than 10 percent is Parliament directed (Gellner and Robertson 2001).

France is often characterized as the ultimate bureaucratic political system, with the elite civil servants making all the decisions and the democratic institutions of government ratifying them and announcing the will of the bureaucrats to the public. Actually, there is a great deal of truth to this generalization. The French Republic seems to promote associational politics, and there are thousands of interest groups in France, but the culture and government of France seem to channel interest group participation through the governmental bureaucracy and not lobbying or other types of American-style interest group politics. Recently, many French interest groups have come to see the strong French government as a protection against the growing interventionist policies of the European Union. However, most French interest groups have not been closely allied with political parties or often participants in French electoral politics. The bureaucracy has tremendous power in French policymaking and a strong disdain for popular politics or interest groups seeking to influence the policymaking process outside normal channels. This is not a classic neocorporatist pattern because the ties between the state and interests are far more ambiguous in France than in Germany or Austria. Two elements of French political culture also work against a greater role of interest groups in policymaking: a deep distrust of intermediary organizations in the political process and the general public's preference for direct action (Appleton 2001). All of these factors have produced a public attitude that is decidedly anti-interest group and antilobbying.

French peak associations have been very difficult to construct, and as such, labor remains largely fragmented. Business peak associations have not been very effective lobbying organizations either. The interest group/political party system in France is one of "strong party group relations with limited policy impact" (Appleton 2001). The state or French governmental bureaucracy continues to dominate in France's unusual style of channeled corporatist politics.

If France's politics has been well channeled over the past several decades, Italian politics has been pluralist and chaotic. Italy formerly had a one-party state (Christian Democratic Party, or CDP) and close relationships between that party and major interests seeking governmental favors and policies. The Italian pattern has often been compared with that described for Japan (1955–1993) and for Mexico in the 20th century. In Italy, the pattern of *clientela* (clientelism) and corruption came crashing down in a corruption scandal during 1992–1993. Until then, the pattern of party-group relationship was one of dominant party with a collection of close interest groups seeking all types of government favors and in return providing the party with the money and other support to stay in office. Italy's extremely fragmented interest group system contributed to this pattern of corruption, and the interest groups themselves have been almost completely unable to get their desires on the political policymaking table without the support of the dominant political party.

The 1992–1993 scandal destroyed the CDP and its cozy relationships with Italian interests. What emerged was the aforementioned chaos of more corruption and ambiguous paths of influence creation, access buying, and frequent and periodic influence peddling scandals. Business, labor, and agriculture were so fragmented as to preclude effective representation of their sectors' policy preferences. When combined with the impact of Italy's membership in the European Union, the destruction of the CDP severely reduced the power of political parties to control access to Italian policymaking venues. All the old governmental parties have been destroyed, and the old opposition parties have had to cope with the rise of many new parties (Constantelos 2001). Interest groups are trying new lobbying techniques such as data and research provision to bureaucrats and new party elites. Italy has been in a period of profound political change for several decades, and it continues. Its system is neither a pluralist nor a corporatist interest group one. What seems to be emerging is some combination of these patterns, but it is still too early to make any definitive statement on contemporary interest group politics in Italy.

Non-European Patterns of Interest Group Politics

Let us now shift from Europe to Asia in the survey of how interest group politics operate in different parts of the world. Democracy came late to much of Asia compared with Europe. Almost every Asian nation except Japan can claim a pattern of democratic politics only since the 1950s, and many can claim only a few years of real democracy over that time frame. So, let us begin with the best example of democratic politics in Asia—Japan—as our frame of reference.

Japan: Pluralist or Corporatist Pattern?

Japan, the first Asian nation to modernize, Westernize, and become a great power, continues to be one of the most difficult nation-states to categorize in terms of its interest group and lobbying system. In many respects, it appears to be remarkably Americanized. The United States supervised the rebuilding of Japan's government, society, and economy after the end of World War II in 1945. The United States, under its supreme commander, General Douglas MacArthur, did not insist that the new Japanese government and so-called MacArthur Constitution of 1948 be modeled exactly on the American system. It was decided to reconstruct the parliamentary system existing before the war with a wide range of reforms to strengthen democracy and reduce authoritarian tendencies.

The American-imposed Constitution of 1948 produced a British-style parliamentary system with a bicameral diet and an emperor as head of state. Like other unitary states, the Japanese national bureaucracy is professional and dominant in its dealings with subordinate political units and various constituent groups.

Japan developed a multiparty system during the 1955–1993 era as a powerful conservative party, the Liberal Democratic Party (LDP), dominated a much smaller left wing consisting of the larger Socialist Party and the smaller, but aggressive, Communist Party. The medium-size Buddhist Party; the Clean Government Party, or Komei-to; and a Socialist splinter party, the Democratic-Socialist Party, completed the party system. The interest group ties for these parties were generally quite clear. The LDP had ties to Japanese big and small businesses. It also represented the conservative farmers of Japan's rural sector as well as many of the conservative religious organizations in Japan, except the Soka Gakkai, which is the primary support organization for the Komei-to. The three left-wing parties (Socialist, Communist, and Democratic-Socialist) were all very closely tied to various labor unions or labor confederations. The labor confederations almost completely committed to the opposition left-wing parties and thus were effectively marginalized. Because of this nearly permanent exclusion of organized labor from political power, some political scientists have called the Japanese interest group system one of corporatism without labor.

Organized labor in Japan, like many of the new Asian democracies, has been organized in such a manner as to make it much weaker than its European and even American counterparts. In the pre–World War II era and during the war years, labor was very leftist and was nearly destroyed by the militarist regime. During the American occupation in the latter half of the 1940s, labor was encouraged to organize and participate in politics as part of the effort to democratize Japan, but MacArthur and his staff were convinced by the conservative Japanese officials that the Socialist- and Communist-dominated labor organizations posed a threat to the Japanese government in the dangerous times of the Cold War. Japan's major corporations, often using gangster (*yakuza*) muscle, crushed the labor movement and created a system of company unions in the private sector. So Toyota and Nissan labor unions emerged, and they were often led by Toyota and Nissan officials who alternated between working as company managers and union officials, coining the phrase *company unions*. The private-sector unions joined together in a labor confederation, Domei, that served as the supporting organization for the very moderate and impotent socialist splinter party, the Democratic-Socialists. The much stronger, but still constantly out of power, Socialist Party was the party of the labor confederation, Sohyo, which was largely organized by Japan's public-sector labor unions. The conservatives (LDP) controlled Japanese national-level politics without losing control of the Diet from their formation to the late 1980s; finally, after so many defeats, the two rival labor confederations merged to form a new organization, Rengo, which was truly a "peak association" in the European style, representing nearly the entire Japanese organized labor world.

In 1993, the LDP suffered a split, and over a number of years in the following decade, the various splinter parties and the old leftist parties (except for the Communists) merged together under Rengo's encouragement to form a true opposition party, the Democratic Party (DP), seemingly capable of defeating the LDP and taking control of Japan's national government. The DP won the elections of the upper house of the Diet in 2007, but it has never been able to replace the LDP in the much more powerful House of Representatives. Until it does, organized labor and the old left wing of Japan will be on the outside of the real game of Japanese politics.

Japan is closer to the European style of interest group system and lobbying than to that of the United States. American-style hordes of lobbyists do not exist in Tokyo, nor do Japan's interest groups use the American-style tools of mass media communications to put pressure on the governmental decision makers. Almost all successful lobbying in Japan takes place out of the public's eye, in the teahouses of Akasaka in Tokyo among associational leaders, powerful political brokers of the ruling party, and high-level bureaucrats.

On the other hand, Japan is also a very pluralist society, with every conceivable interest being organized in the society. The farmers' cooperatives have been especially powerful in an economy that has heavily subsidized the very high cost of rice and other agricultural products. Various professional groups, such as the Japan Medical Association, have had powerful roles to play in administering their professions and the governmental services associated with them.

The conventional wisdom model of Japanese policymaking has been a tripod of the LDP, big business, and the bureaucracy. Each of the three institutions gave the others what they needed in terms of influencing the output of the Japanese government. The bureaucracy has dominated the policy process since the foundations of modern Japan in the 1860s under the Meiji oligarchs. But to keep its power in the postwar era, it allied itself with the conservatives and the LDP and then provided the bureaucratic leaders with entrance into high elected offices and high-prestige, postretirement jobs.

Given the powerful role of the bureaucracy in Japanese policymaking, it is not surprising to find frequent consultations between government bureaucrats and the interests they regulate or represent. The Ministry of Agriculture, for example, spends a great deal of time discussing many different issues with the farmers' cooperative leadership; likewise, the Ministry of Economy Trade and Industry spends its time interacting with Japan's corporations, large and small, which export so many products to the world.

Japan's business peak organization, Nippon Keidanren, has long represented the industrial sector of Japan in the policymaking discussions with the LDP and the bureaucracy. The organization recently became even more powerful with its 2002 merger with Nikkeiren (Japanese Federation of Employers' Associations). Keidanren now represents 1,268 corporations, 128 industrial associations, and 47 regional employers' associations. Representing Japan's large corporations and being the more conservative of the various business groups in the country, Keidanren worked well with the conservative LDP during the decades of incredible economic growth (1950s–1990s). The less conservative and less powerful Japanese business groups are the Japanese Chamber of Commerce and the Japan Committee for Economic Development.

Japan's model of interest group politics is the closest to the American and European models. Japan is a Westernized, industrial democracy with a very pluralist pattern of interest group representation and a very corporatist pattern of policymaking, with the huge exception of the European corporatist model of having a very weak and largely excluded organized labor sector. Japan is, as mentioned, "corporatism without labor."

Developing Democracies

Compared with the pluralist, corporatist, and mixed systems of developed democracies, almost no research has been conducted on interest groups, lobbying, and lobbyists in the developing democracies of Eastern Europe, Africa, South America, and Asia. The lack of research is not because interest group politics does not exist in those societies but because it is more a function of a "first things first" attitude held by most political scientists and democracy funding institutions. "First, we build a party system and hold democratic elections and then, later we will think about the other parts of a democratic political system such as a responsible media, interest group politics and civil society" (Hrebenar et al. 2008). Even when interest groups are included in a study of a developing democracy, the data or interpretation is usually based on studies of other parts of the nation's political system, such as parties.

Among the transitional democracies, one can find several common patterns that will help us better understand their development (Thomas 2004). These patterns or characteristics can be viewed as guiding a system's development down several broad channels, much like a riverbed guides a body of water flowing toward the ocean. They may strongly influence the level of development and history of democracy in the state, the degree of legitimization of interest group activity in the society, the types of interests that play the political game, and the strategies and tactics that are considered to be acceptable in politics.

Clive S. Thomas (2004) has described the five patterns that guide the development of interest group systems in transitional democracies. The first is the degree of autonomy allowed to interest groups in the political system, or conversely, the degree of restriction the nation-state places on interest group politics. The right of freedom of association, the existence of private voluntary interest groups, and particularly their role in lobbying government may be legally restricted, curtailed by the official ideology, and in some cases banned. A wide range of restrictions may be imposed by authoritarian regimes. Schmitter's (1974) state corporatism as found in World War II Germany, Vichy France, and pre–World War II Austria is where the state determines the role of groups. Communist countries set up various organizations such as youth and labor organizations that were controlled by the party (Best, Rai, and Walsh 1986).

How interest groups are viewed by governmental and political elites as well as the general public can also strongly affect democratic development. Even in long-standing and successful democracies such as the United States, interest groups, lobbying, and lobbyists are often viewed with great suspicion. "Essential, but suspicious," as the recent American lobbying scandals involving Jack Abramoff have confirmed in many people's minds, lobbying and corruption go hand in hand. In many transitional states, interest groups and lobbying are viewed as injurious to the democratic development and are seen by many as illegitimate actors or, at best, as actors whose roles should be restricted and limited. Why are they viewed so negatively? Usually, the perception arises from some combination of being selfish about personal economic and political interests over the public interest of the larger society. This pattern can easily be seen in the research conducted on Lithuania and the Czech Republic and perceived not only in the former Communist states of Eastern Europe but also found among the elite attitudes in other developing democracies around the world. The idea that interest groups and lobbying are as essential for democratic development as political parties and elections has not been generally accepted in many nations.

Second, in developed societies the major form of interest group is the associational group based on formal membership. In transitional democracies, the interests tend to be represented by informal groups, such as political and professional elites, and broad-based interests, such as the bureaucracy and the military. Thus, one can say the developing state has more of an "interest-based politics" and less of an "interest group politics." In less-Westernized societies, the major type of interest is the group based on kinship, tribe, lineage, neighborhood, religion, and so on. The difficulty of the American effort to build democratic institutions in Iraq can be seen as strong evidence to support this observation. One characteristic of successful transitional regimes is an increase in the number of associational groups.

Third, the weakly developed and numerically limited interest groups and associational system groups mean that group strategies and tactics are less formalized compared with those of advanced pluralist democracies. Informal contacts and personal relationships are important in all societies for interests to achieve their goal of influencing public policy, but they seem to be much more important in these transitional democracies. In the advanced pluralist societies, the freedom of the interest group system and the accepted roles of groups in the policymaking process have tended to produce regularized channels of lobbying for the interest groups. Interest group politics in these developed societies is found and accepted in the corridors of the government (legislative, executive, and judicial as well as regulatory agencies), the media, and political campaigns.

On the other hand, such interest group activities are seldom or never found in nonpluralist, transitional, and developing states. In these systems, personal relationships and power plays within and between government entities and other organizations, such as the ruling party or the senior officers of the military, are the most significant. It may seem impossible to many who follow politics in the mature, democratic nations, but even more politics is conducted behind closed doors in these transitional systems than in pluralist democracies.

Fourth, groups act as a major link between citizens and government by collecting numbers of people with similar views and speaking their views to government. This is particularly the case with mass membership organizations such as trade unions and public interest groups like environmental interests (Thomas 2001). Interest groups, political parties, and the media all tend to perform these functions in developed political systems. In contrast, and due to a combination of the four elements just explained, interest groups in developing societies rarely perform the role of mass representation, as they represent a very small segment of the population. Interest groups and interests in these societies perform other functions similar to those in advanced pluralist democracies—such as providing information, aiding in policy implementation, and providing political training—but this lack of a representational role gives them a much less significant place in the politics of their societies. This role absence includes the mass organizations in one-party and totalitarian regimes whose representative role is perfunctory and tightly controlled by the party and/or the regime.

Many also see issues of social class, religion, problems of economic development and poverty, the role of the military, ethnic and racial conflict, the aftermath of colonialism, and so on, as the forces driving the politics of these societies. In this environment, interest groups and interest activity of advanced countries seemed much less important.

Although the states of South Asia (India, Pakistan, Bangladesh, and Sri Lanka) have been influenced by the British pluralist tradition, interest groups in the region have not been considered very important for a number of reasons. South Asian elites tend to see interest groups as illegitimate, and scholars in the region have been obsessed with social class as the most powerful explanation of political outcomes. In addition to social class, family, caste, religion, tribal identities, and language have been considered more important than interest groups. Powerful families in Pakistan, India, and Bangladesh play a political role more important than interest groups. Political parties are also thought to be much more powerful than any interest groups or combinations of interest groups, with the very important exception of the army in all of the South Asian nations.

Given India's size and importance, interest groups in India have been better studied than in the region's other nations. The powerful Indian governmental bureaucracy effectively limits interest group politics. Business simply could not match the power of the government to control the economy. It will be interesting to see if India's recent policies of opening up its economy to less governmental control will significantly change this pattern. More important forms of interest in India have been the so-called demand groups based on movements and issues groups such as students, workers, and farmers. Labor unions clearly do not have much access or influence in India, probably as a result of the powerful political parties dominating India's politics.

With regard to the interest group politics of the other South Asian nations of Pakistan, Bangladesh, and Sri Lanka, very little is known. Politics there seems to be driven by the powerful pattern of personalized politics and the significance of family ties over organizational identities. Business, labor, and other organized interests have great problems in these highly personalized political systems.

Chinese politics has become a combination of the powerful Communist Party and a growing number of associations that have sprung into existence in the decades of economic liberalism since the 1970s. Most of the studies conducted on Chinese interest groups conclude that a real civil society has not been developed yet in China, but the economic reforms have resulted in growing pluralism (Ogden 2000). Certainly within the political sector, the Communist Party is still the strongest power and has little interest in any competitors. As in all authoritarian states, the army and security forces hold extraordinary influence within the governmental decision-making processes.

Turning to the Middle East, again, very little is known about interest group politics except for studies on two countries, Egypt and Turkey (Ahmida 1997). Since most Middle Eastern states are one-party dictatorships or authoritarian states, the interest in studying group politics is very limited. The work on Egypt and Turkey (Bianchi 1984, 1986) suggests that the forces that restrict interest groups in the Middle East include an emphasis on culture, religion, family, and other personal relationships. Egypt seems to be closest to developed nations in terms of its interest group politics. Bianchi concludes that in Egypt, at least, the style of politics seems to be somewhere on the continuum between pluralism and corporatism (Bianchi 1989, 1990). Despite the history of authoritarian rule in the region, a very gradual rise has been seen in various democratic institutions that support an emerging interest group style of politics.

With the exception of a handful of countries, political scientists know very little about interest groups in African states. Research is essentially limited to South
Africa and the patterns of interest groups before and after the apartheid regime
(Borer 1998; Deegan 1999). The paucity of real democracies in Sub-Saharan Africa
contributes to the dearth of studies of interest group politics. Without democracy,
the military has, in country after country, assumed the dominant power position
in almost all the countries, and business has had to deal with the military regime to
gain influence in any given country in the region. Otherwise, the politics of family,
clan, tribe, region, and religion overwhelm what Westerners think of as interest
group politics.

Latin America and Central America have had a longer experience with democratic governments than the countries of Africa, the Middle East, and much of Asia,
and therefore one should expect a higher level and more complex pattern of interest
group politics in the region. The problem of Latin American politics, however, is
the lack of continuity in democratic politics. Nations have moved toward democratic politics and then retreated back to military regimes and then moved back
to democracy again. As a result, militaries have long been studied, because coups
were so common in many Latin American states until just recently (Nun 1968).
Organized labor has been very important in a number of the region's nations, such
as Argentina and Chile, and has been a source of support for populism, revolution, and democracy (Collier and Collier 1991). The Catholic Church, religious
movements, and peasants have been analyzed as sources of both conservatism and
grassroots activism (Sharpe 1977). But by the early 1970s, corporatism, along with
Marxian theory, had been used to describe the region's pattern.

Of the various nations of Central and Latin America, scholars know the most
about interest groups in the largest, most democratic, and most industrialized
nations, such as Mexico and Argentina. In Mexico, for example, the domination of
the one-party state (Institutional Revolutionary Party, or PRI) for most of the 20th
century produced a type of corporatism in which all the major actors were orchestrated by the dominant party leaders and their governments. Mexico is called a
"party corporatist" state, or a unique form of neocorporatism. Most neocorporatist systems place relatively little emphasis on political parties as key actors in the
system. But, in Mexico, the PRI is *the* key actor in orchestrating the policymaking
system—at least until very recently. The PRI is really a collection of interest group
confederations that join together to form the party. Central parts of the PRI include
the Confederation of Mexican Workers and the National Peasant Confederation;
and the National Confederation of Popular Organizations accounts for most of
the rest of Mexican society. The outcome of the mediation of the various interests
in Mexican society was, until the late 1990s, relative "political stability and social
peace achieved through elite accommodation and governmental mediation of class
conflict" (Rosenberg 2001). Note that members of the business world, who are
prohibited from joining political parties, are free to negotiate directly with the government as outside actors.

Argentina, on the other hand, while having also had a history of strong parties,
adds a pattern of strong organized labor movements and military intervention

into its political system. One interesting Argentine characteristic is that the strong interest group system and the often strong political party system have not usually been tied too tightly together. They have often operated independently of each other (Johnson 2001). Frequently, the interest groups would target the government directly, rather than use the institutions of the party system; then, if all such direct lobbying failed, the military stood ready to intervene as a last resort.

What, then, does one make of the authoritarian or semiauthoritarian states scattered around the world in nations such as Russia, many of the former Soviet Union states in Central Asia, the military regimes in Myanmar, and remaining Communist states in Vietnam and Cuba? Each nation has a different history and different political patterns, but several generalizations can be made regarding interest group politics in such undemocratic states. First, all nations, no matter how undemocratic, have forms of interest group politics. In authoritarian states, the security forces usually hold enormous political power, including the military, the police, and any paramilitary associated with the ruling party or regime. Additionally, the ruling party (if there is one) and its supporting interest or interests usually have tremendous power as well and may dominate the security forces in terms of big political issues such as budgetary allocations or foreign policy. The governmental bureaucracy and the various "power ministries," such as industrialization, development, religion, agriculture, and revenue collection, all may function as lobbies for their own interests as well as any clientele. Interest group politics does not disappear in quasi-authoritarian or authoritarian states; it just tends to be more centralized and concentrated in the hands of relatively few organizations that are fundamental to the continuation of the regime in both a security and an economic manner. Furthermore, lobbying in this type of political system almost always takes place behind closed doors, and lobbyists are the powerful politicians who represent the key interests in the policy decision-making processes.

Lobbying in the International Community: The EU

With the rise of the European Union (EU) as a significant transnational governmental entity, it should come as no surprise that lobbying has become a major business in Brussels, Belgium, the EU headquarters, and Strasbourg, France, the seat of the EU Council of Europe. A number of excellent academic studies have been done on the nature of lobbying in Brussels, including works by Greenwood (2003), Schendelen (2005), and McGrath (2005). What started out as a very European style of bureaucratic politics evolved to add on an interesting layer of increasingly American-style lobbyists and interest group politics.

The first professional lobbyists to descend on Brussels in large numbers came from London; later, Americans came in large numbers as they began to understand that the new European government was making decisions that significantly affected American businesses, products, and marketing. French bureaucrats who filled many of the top posts in the growing EU bureaucracy saw the need and the potential of lobbying the bureaucracy, and many of the later lobbying firms were staffed by these former bureaucrats from France. With the growth in the EU in number of member nations from the original 12 to 25 and with potentially many more nations who seek entry or special relations, the necessity to represent these nations' interests effectively fueled the growth in the lobbying community of Brussels. Many of these newly admitted EU nations, such as the Baltic nations and the former Communist nations of Eastern and Central Europe, have little or no lobbying traditions or experience, not to mention few or no real domestic lobbyists. To lobby effectively in Brussels, they were forced to hire the Brussels lobbyists, and the lobbying business grew. Schendelen (2005) notes that thousands of interest groups are representing governments and nongovernmental bodies seeking to lobby in Brussels.

One of the academic debates regarding EU politics is whether its dominant style of interest group politics is pluralist as in the United States or corporatist as in many of its European member states. Greenwood and Young (2005) note that although one can find examples of cases where a specialized interest will triumph over the more bureaucratic policymaking process, a more corporatist pattern seems to dominate most issues. They do observe that Brussels is an "insider town," where effective interest representation requires a dense network of personal and organizational relationships, making it very difficult for outsiders to come in and be successful. In other words, it is a perfect environment for Brussels's lobbyists and lobbying firms.

In Brussels, as in much if not almost all of Europe, the terms "lobbyist" and "lobbying firm" are not commonly heard or seen. The preferred terms are "public affairs" and "interest representation." Public affairs firms will often be much broader than American-style lobbying firms in terms of services and resource allocations. They will frequently be more business and product oriented, with an emphasis on representing a client in many types of venues—often not political at all. Some will be "event managers," setting up press conferences and conferences for the clients, and will devote a small part of the firm to traditional lobbying.

Some of the lobbying in the EU fits the corporatist pattern well, where the EU bureaucrats and the various peak organizations representing European business, labor, and agriculture come together to hammer out a consensus on a certain policy. Of course, the various nations will also have a role to play in the process, but if a consensus can be reached first among the major economic peak associations, the later impact of national-level politics can be reduced. But almost all the EU experts emphasize that, depending on the issue area and the type of policy being discussed (e.g., regulatory, distributive), a wide range of variations in types of interest group representation can be seen in Brussels.

The EU also has a wide range of institutions that can be targeted by interests. The EU Parliament in Strasbourg features a political system similar to those seen in most European parliaments. Additional targets of lobbying are the European Commission, the European Court of Justice, the European Council, the Council of Ministers, a wide range of consultative institutions such as the Economic and Social Committee, and sectoral institutions dealing with particular sectors or issues, such as EURATOM (European Atomic Energy Community).

The European Commission, which drafts the regulations for EU member states' politicians to consider, has a small staff and a huge amount of work. Therefore, it usually relies on interest groups and lobbyists for the data and information it needs for its work. Its staff is only a small fraction of the similar staff operating in Washington, D.C. Thus, the commission is an ideal place for interest groups to operate to help frame issues and draft future regulations. Experienced lobbyists argue that lobbying such as this in the bureaucracy is where crucial decisions are made in the EU.

EU interest group diversity is impressive. In a 2002 listing on EU interest groups, formal interest groups registered with the EU totaled 1,450, as did 350 companies, 170 national interest groups, and 143 commercial public affairs consultant firms in Brussels. A total of 3,400 annual passes are issued for public affairs monitoring purposes, although some have estimated the total number of lobbyists in Brussels to be near the 30,000 figure often noted in Washington, D.C. As in the United States, businesses make up more than two-thirds of interests seeking to influence the EU (Greenwood 2003, 19).

The EU supports a wide range of nongovernmental organizations (NGOs), with more than 1 billion Euros in annual support. This tends to produce a healthy NGO representation in Brussels that seems to have more influence than similar interests have in Washington, D.C. On the other hand, labor organizations and professions seem to have less influence than the social partnerships pattern of many European nations would lead one to expect. Perhaps this is a result of the nature of policy-making in Brussels that has been focused on expanding the EU powers in a liberal fashion rather than protecting specific sectors or professions.

Transnational and International Lobbying

The difference between transnational lobbying and international lobbying is a combination of actors and their targets. International lobbying refers to the nation-states as the actors or the targets of lobbying campaigns, whereas transnational lobbying refers to interest group lobbying across national boundaries. Three kinds of transnational actors operate on this stage: private economic organizations, such as corporations, unions, and business associations; international NGOs; and other transnational organizations, such as churches (e.g., the Roman Catholic Church) and other cause organizations (Morss 1991).

A great deal is known about the transnational economic organizations. Especially considering the rise of globalization, the international corporations have been the objects of many research projects. As political science has expanded its theoretical focus beyond the traditional nation-state, much greater attention has been devoted to the NGOs. Many recent observers of international politics have tried to paint a picture of an ever more interrelated and increasingly complex collection of actors, including many of these NGOs. Recent Nobel Peace Prizes have been awarded to NGOs in a variety of areas, including the International Campaign to Ban Landmines, microbanking organizations in Africa and Asia, and Doctors without Borders.

Perhaps more than any other factor, the end of the Cold War brought many new issues and problems to the public's attention, and suddenly, the NGOs that had been laboring in relative obscurity now became the focus of media attention. Just as many domestic NGOs in the past two decades have become much more important in the domestic delivery of once exclusive governmental services, many now realize transnational NGOS are often the only effective actors in addressing problems that cross borders and even continents, such as the AIDS epidemic and environmental dangers.

As was noted, the EU has been particularly receptive to the roles played by NGOs in its various policymaking arenas. It subsidizes well over 1,000 such groups, thus making Brussels and Strasbourg "hotbeds" for NGO activity in Europe. Also noteworthy is the role the United Nations (UN) plays in nurturing and supporting the international NGOs. The UN's New York City headquarters and European satellite headquarters sites in Geneva and Vienna are also venues of great activity for transnational lobbying. Weiss and Gordenker (1996) report significant UN lobbying on HIV/AIDS, the environment, and women's and human rights issues. Some research on Southeast Asia and Central America also indicates a growth of NGO activities in the regional organizations of those areas.

Nobel Peace Prize winners Al Gore, left, and Rajendra Pachauri, the U.N. climate panel's chief scientist, hold their medals and diplomas at the Nobel Peace Prize ceremony at City Hall in Oslo on December 10, 2007. (AP Photo/John McConnico)

Many readers are familiar with the more famous transnational environmentalist interest groups such as Greenpeace and Earth First! Interest groups such as Greenpeace operate on the national level in many nations but also have transnational operations. Greenpeace's recent antinuclear tactics and environmental demonstrations have received enormous coverage in the world's mass media. These transnational environmentalist groups have probably had the most policy success in recent years of all the cause-oriented international groups because of the success of the Kyoto Treaty and the attention on the Nobel Peace Prize awarded to former U.S. vice president Al Gore and the UN climate panel in 2007.

Probably the second most active transnational cause-oriented interest group category involves a wide range of human rights issues. Amnesty International is perhaps the best known such organization in the world, but many other such organizations are working on all types of human rights causes. Many of them can be found in Latin America, where human rights abuses are still common and the political systems have opened up sufficiently to allow such organizations to operate more freely. Such may not be the case in many parts of Africa and Asia, and even Russia under Putin's increasingly repressive regime. One area that needs much more attention in research effort is that of the transnational religious and cultural organizations (especially Catholic, Evangelical Protestant, and Islamic organizations and movements) and to study their impact on various populations.

One can see from this survey of the world that many different types of interest group and lobbying systems are in operation. This diversity is now a key characteristic of our globalized political and business world. From American pluralism to European corporatism to personalized politics common to much of the developing world, interest group politics is everywhere, and everywhere it is different. It is impossible to understand politics anywhere in the world without an understanding of interest group politics and lobbying.

References

Ahmida, Ali Abdullatif. (1997). "Inventing or Recovering Civil Society in the Middle East." *Critique* 10 (Spring): 127–134.

Appleton, Andrew. (2001). "France: Party-Group Relations in the Shadow of the State." In Clive S. Thomas, ed. *Political Parties & Interest Groups: Shaping Democratic Governance.* Boulder, CO: Lynne Rienner, pp. 45–62.

Armingeon, Klaus. (1997, Oct.). Swiss Corporatism in Comparative Perspective. *West European Politics.*

Best, Paul J., Kul B. Rai, and David F. Walsh. (1986). *Politics in Three Worlds.* New York: John Wiley and Sons.

Bianchi, Robert. (1984). *Interest Groups and Political Development in Turkey.* Princeton, NJ: Princeton University Press.

Bianchi, Robert. (1986). "Interest Group Politics in the Third World." *Third World Quarterly* 8: 507–539.

Bianchi, Robert. (1989). *Unruly Corporatism: Associational Life in Twentieth-Century Egypt.* New York: Oxford University Press.

Bianchi, Robert. (1990). "Interest Groups and Politics in Mubarak's Egypt." In Ibrahim Owciss, ed. *The Political Economy of Contemporary Egypt.* Washington, DC: Georgetown University Press.

Bischof, Gunter, and Anton Pelinka. (1996). *Austro-Corporatism: Past, Present, Future.* London: Transaction.

Borer, Tristan. (1998). *Challenging the State: Churches as Political Actors in South Africa.* Notre Dame, IN: University of Notre Dame Press.

Collier, David, and Ruth Collier. (1991). *Shaping the Political Arena: Critical Junctures, the Labor Movement and Regime Dynamics in Latin America.* Princeton, NJ: Princeton University Press.

Constantelos, John. (2001). "Italy: The Erosion and Demise of Party Dominance." In Clive S. Thomas, ed. *Political Parties & Interest Groups: Shaping Democratic Governance.* Boulder, CO: Lynne Rienner, pp. 119–137.

Deegan, Heather. (1999). *South Africa Reborn: Building a New Democracy.* London: University College of London Press.

Evanson, Robert K., and Thomas M. Magstadt. (2001). "The Czech Republic: Party Dominance in a Transitional System." In Clive S. Thomas, ed. *Political Parties & Interest Groups: Shaping Democratic Governance.* Boulder, CO: Lynne Rienner, pp. 193–210.

Gellner, Winand, and John D. Robertson. (2001). "Germany: The Continued Dominance of Neocorporatism." In Clive S. Thomas, ed. *Political Parties & Interest Groups: Shaping Democratic Governance.* Boulder, CO: Lynne Rienner, pp. 101–118.

Greenwood, Justin. (2003). *Interest Representation in the European Union.* New York: Palgrave-MacMillan.

Greenwood, Justin, and A. Young. (2005). "EU Interest Representation or US Lobbying." In Nicholas Jabko and Craig Parsons, eds. *With US or against US? The State of the European Union.* Vol. 7. Oxford: Oxford University Press, pp. 275–298.

Haller, Birgitt. (1996). "Austrian Social Partnership—A Model for Central and Eastern Europe?" Introduction. In Gunter Bischof and Anton Pelinka, eds. *Austro-Corporatism: Past, Present, Future.* London: Transaction, pp. 147–150.

Hrebenar, Ronald. (2001). "Japan: Strong State, Spectator Democracy, and Modified Corporatism." In Clive S. Thomas, ed. *Political Parties & Interest Groups: Shaping Democratic Governance.* Boulder, CO: Lynne Rienner, pp. 155–174.

Hrebenar, Ronald J., and Akira Nakamura. (1993). "Japan: Associational Politics in a Group-Oriented Society." In Clive S. Thomas, ed. *First World Interest Groups.* Westport, CT: Greenwood Press, pp. 199–216.

Hrebenar, Ronald, Courtney McBeth, and Bryson Morgan. (2008). "Understanding InterestGroup Activity in the Emergent Democracies of Eastern Europe: The Case of Lithuania." *Journal of Public Affairs.* Special Issue: Interest Groups, Lobbying and Lobbyists in Developing Democracies 8 (1–2): 51–65.

Johnson, Diana E. (2001). "Argentina: Parties and Interests Operating Separately by Design and Practice." In Clive S. Thomas, ed. *Political Parties & Interest Groups: Shaping Democratic Governance.* Boulder, CO: Lynne Rienner, pp. 229–246.

Jordan, Grant, and William Maloney. (2001). "Britain: Change and Continuity within the New Realities of British Politics." In Clive S. Thomas, ed. *Political Parties & Interest Groups: Shaping Democratic Governance.* Boulder, CO: Lynne Rienner, pp. 27–44.

Kindley, Randall. (1996). "The Evolution of Austria's Neo-Corporatist Institutions." In Gunter Bischof and Anton Pelinka, eds. *Austro-Corporatism: Past, Present, Future.* London: Transaction, pp. 53–93.

Lewin, Leif. (1994). "The Rise and Decline of Corporatism: The Case of Sweden." *Journal of Political Research* 26: 59–79.

Markovits, Andrei S. (1996). "Austrian Corporatism in Comparative Perspective." In Gunter Bischof and Anton Pelinka, eds. *Austro-Corporatism: Past, Present, Future.* London: Transaction, pp. 5–20.

McGrath, Conor. (2005). *Lobbying in Washington, London and Brussels: The Persuasive Communication of Political Issues.* Lewiston, NY: Edwin Mellen Press.

Millard, Francis. (1999). *Polish Politics and Society.* New York: Routledge.

Morss, Elliott R. (1991). "The New Global Players: How They Compete and Collaborate." *World Development* 19: 55–64.

Nowotny, Ewald. (1993, Feb.). The Austrian Social Partnership and Democracy. Working Paper 93–1, Center for Austrian Studies.

Nun, Jose. (1968). "A Latin American Perspective: The Middle-Class Military Coup." In J. Petras and M. Zeitlin, eds. *Latin America: Reform or Revolution?* New York: Fawcett.

Ogden, Suzanne. (2000). "China's Developing Civil Society: Interest Groups. Trade Unions and Associational Pluralism." In Malcolm Warner, ed. *Changing Workplace Relations on the Chinese Economy.* New York: St. Martin's Press.

Ost, David. (2001). "Poland: Parties, Movements and Ambiguity." In Clive S. Thomas, ed. *Political Parties & Interest Groups: Shaping Democratic Governance.* Boulder, CO: Lynne Rienner, pp. 211–228.

Pross, A. Paul. (1993). "The Mirror of the State: Canada's Interest Group System." In Clive S. Thomas, ed. *First World Interest Groups: A Comparative Perspective* Westport, CT: Greenwood Press, pp. 67–80.

Richardson, J. J. (1993). "Government and Groups in Britain: Changing Styles." In Clive S. Thomas, ed. *First World Interest Groups: A Comparative Perspective.* Westport, CT: Greenwood Press, pp. 55–66.

Rosenberg, Jonathan. (2001). "Mexico: The End of Party Corporatism?" In Clive S. Thomas, ed. *Political Parties & Interest Groups: Shaping Democratic Governance.* Boulder, CO: Lynne Rienner, pp. 247–268.

Schendelen, Rinus van. (2005). *Machiavelli in Brussels: The Art of Lobbying in the E.U.* Amsterdam: Amsterdam University Press.

Schmitter, P. C. (1974). "Still a Century of Corporatism?" *The Review of Politics* 36, no. 1: 85–131.

Schmitter, P. C. (1989). "Corporatism Is Dead! Long Live Corporatism!" *Government and Opposition* 24: 54–73.

Sharpe, Kenneth. (1977). *Peasant Politics.* Baltimore: Johns Hopkins University Press.

Thomas, Clive S. (1993). *First World Interest Groups: A Comparative Perspective.* Westport, CT: Greenwood Press.

Thomas, Clive S. (2001). *Political Parties & Interest Groups: Shaping Democratic Governance.* Boulder, CO: Lynne Rienner.

Thomas, Clive S. (2004). *Research Guide to U.S. and International Interest Groups.* Westport, CT: Praeger.

Wallace, Helen, and Alasdair R. Young. (1997). *Participation and Policy-Making in the European Union.* Oxford: Clarendon Press, Oxford.

Wallace, Helen, and William Wallace. (2000). *Policy-Making in the European Union.* Oxford: Oxford University Press.

Weiss, Thomas G., and Leon Gordenker. (1996). *NGOs, the UN and Global Governance.* Boulder, CO: Lynne Rienner.

Wilson, Frank L. (1993). "France: Group Politics in a Strong State." In Clive S. Thomas, ed. *First World Interest Groups: A Comparative Perspective.* Westport, CT: Greenwood Press, pp. 113–126.

Woll, Cornealia. (2006, April). "Lobbying in the European Union: From *Sui Generis* to a Comparative Perspective." *Journal of European Public Policy* 13, no. 3: 456–469.

Zeigler, Harmon. (1993). "Switzerland: Democratic Corporatism." In Clive S. Thomas, ed. *First World Interest Groups: A Comparative Perspective.* Westport, CT: Greenwood Press, pp. 153–164.

Issues in Overseas Lobbying by U.S. Firms

Duane Windsor

Introduction

U.S. firms operating overseas exert political influence using the same basic techniques they apply domestically: direct lobbying, indirect lobbying, and, sometimes, bribery or other forms of corruption (Windsor 2007). Direct lobbying involves gaining access to government officials (including through agents or middlemen) in order to provide information and persuasion concerning a specific issue or interest. Indirect lobbying involves attempting to influence government officials through various forms of grassroots mobilization, legal campaign contributions, and corporate philanthropy to build reputation and constituency support (Shapiro and Dowson 2012). Bribery of government officials is generally illegal throughout the world.

Direct and indirect lobbying forms and bribery may sometimes function as complements and/or substitutes (Campos and Giovannoni 2007). A firm can comply with a regulation (or public policy), bribe officials to get around the regulation (or public policy), or lobby government to relax the regulation (or change public policy). Some researchers posit that when the level of a country's development is low, firms are more likely to practice (i.e., switch to) bribery; when the level of a country's development is high, firms are more likely to practice (i.e., switch to) lobbying. When bribery discourages firms from investing in lobbying in a particular country, that country may be stuck in a poverty trap with bribery forever. As a result, bribery may be more common in poor countries, while lobbying is more common in rich countries (Harstad and Svensson 2011); this theory corresponds broadly to the Corruption Perceptions Index (CPI) information reported annually by Transparency International (2011b).

The term "overseas" can refer to any non-U.S. jurisdiction, including international organizations as well as other countries and their political subdivisions and dependencies. There is thus both international and transnational lobbying, the latter meaning cross-border and the former aimed at international organizations such as the United Nations (UN), International Accounting Standards Board (IASB) (Hansen 2011), or the World Trade Organization (WTO) (Woll 2007; Woll 2008). The topic of overseas lobbying by U.S. firms is understudied relative to U.S. lobbying by American or foreign firms, or lobbying in the European Union (EU) by European firms. But cross-border corporate political activity, both into and out of the United States, is increasingly important in globalization of economic activities (Boddewyn 1993; Rodriguez, Siegel, Hillman, and Eden 2006).

It is useful to distinguish among three broad terms. The term "business-government relations" is the broadest, encompassing all interactions between businesses and governments (Hart 2010). Businesses seek to obtain benefits from and prevent costs imposed by governments, which enact laws, regulations, and public policies affecting markets (Baron 1999). "Corporate political activity" (CPA) is the narrower concept within business-government relations, used to refer to all approaches used by businesses to influence governments (Hillman, Keim, and Schuler 2004). CPA thus operates from businesses to governments.

The term "lobbying" means advocacy of an interest, typically on a specific issue, that can be affected by government decisions (executive, legislative, administrative, or regulatory). Lobbying can be roughly synonymous with CPA in this general sense. The distinction between direct lobbying (or direct influence) and indirect lobbying (or indirect influence) can be explained as follows: direct lobbying, on the U.S. and EU models, typically involves organized efforts at obtaining access to and influence with public officials, including through their staffs, primarily by providing information. Direct lobbying is conducted by many kinds of organizations, including labor unions and nongovernmental organizations (NGOs) representing environmental and consumer interests, for instance, as well as businesses (Frankel and Højbjerg 2012; Hansen 2011; Klüver 2011). Over 14,000 lobbyists are estimated to operate in Washington, D.C. Lobbying is a legitimate dimension of democratic government, specifically protected by the First Amendment to the U.S. Constitution. Indirect lobbying, aimed at bringing influence to bear on public officials, is more diffuse but just as important and widespread in practice. U.S. firms may lobby U.S. officials to influence foreign officials on their behalf, especially in countries such as China, India, or Russia. For example, when Intel faced antitrust regulatory actions in the EU in May 2009, the company's response was to increase its lobbying activities in Washington, D.C.

Various approaches can be used, singly or in combination, to influence governments. The most important approaches include direct lobbying of public officials on specific issues; indirect influence involving grassroots mobilization of other interests (Lord 2003); political campaign contributions, use of well-placed agents (or middlemen), and political free speech; use of philanthropy to build reputation and legitimacy with public officials and other interests; and bribery (i.e., corruption) of public or quasi-public officials whether directly by corporate employees or indirectly through agents. Political action committees (PACs) supporting specific election campaigns, Super PACs (for issue advertising, though usually in support of particular candidates), and interest group or industry associations are typical devices in the United States. But how political influence operates in the United States may be, for businesses, relatively unique.

The scholars Kaufmann and Vicente (2011) argue that the conventional definition of corruption is itself misleading. They distinguish between legal corruption and illegal corruption as channels for private sector influence with government. The difference is a function of cross-country variation in legal frameworks. The authors further differentiate among three conditions: (1) illegal corruption in which the political elite does not face binding incentives to attempt to limit corruption; (2) legal corruption in which the political elite incurs some cost to protect corruption through the legal framework; and (3) no corruption in which the general population can effectively react against corruption (thus influencing the conduct of the political elite).

The remainder of this chapter is organized as follows. The second section discusses what is generally known about effective direct lobbying, even if it takes the form of legal corruption. The third section reports examples of overseas lobbying by U.S. firms. The fourth section shifts to examples of overseas corruption by U.S. firms, as a key instance of illegal lobbying. This chapter concludes with a discussion of the bargaining power of multinational enterprises in business-government relations and their corporate social responsibilities in this area.

Effective Lobbying

Corporate political activity involves multiple channels for acquiring access and influence (Schuler, Rehbein, and Cramer 2002). The presumption is that businesses lobby for benefits and against costs (Hasen 2011), though much of what is known is based on domestic lobbying especially in the United States and the EU (Baumgartner, Berry, Hojnacki, and Kimball 2009; Thomas 2004). Issue context appears to be an important consideration in effective lobbying by all interest groups, including businesses (Sawant 2012; Scholzman 2010). According to a recent study of European Commission consultations across 2,696 interest groups and 56 policy issues, relative size of lobbying coalitions and salience of policy issues appear important, while individual characteristics do not. An instance is the effort of record label group Impala and the International Federation of Musicians to influence the Czech Republic to use its EU presidency prior to July 1, 2009, to extend the length of EU sound recording copyrights from 50 to 70 years for the benefit of artists (Paine 2009). The European Parliament had backed the extension in April 2009, but EU governments had to approve the change in the European Council. The EU presidency rotated on July 1 to Sweden, which opposed the extension. In September 2011, the EU Council of Ministers passed the extension. Fine-grained details may be very important in effective lobbying.

There is considerable disagreement over whether lobbying is beneficial for businesses. Some studies suggest that corporate political activity generally affects market value and shareholder returns positively. One researcher (Lux, Crook, and Woehr 2011), drawing on information from more than 7,000 firms over various time periods, concluded that firms engaging in legal corporate political activity (e.g., lobbying and campaign contributions) had about 20 percent higher economic performance. (The relationship between corporate political activity and economic performance is associational rather than necessarily cause-and-effect.) The larger the firm, the more likely it was to be politically active. The study also found that contributions tended to go to politicians with more policy influence and to incumbents.

Others argue that firms engage in corporate political activity largely because their executives decide to do so, in the process losing their strategic business focus. A study by Hadani and Schuler (2013) finds that corporate political activity is associated generally with worse market and accounting performance except in closely regulated industries, like banking, insurance, and utilities, where a long-term investment in lobbying may yield some benefit. The authors looked at 943 firms between 1998 and 2008. Those firms spent some $5 billion in lobbying, contributions, and related activities. The authors also examined 70 companies with politically connected directors, finding that the connections were not beneficial. The contradictory findings cited earlier are for the United States; and that setting may reflect a possibly unique set of conditions.

However, these findings apply only to domestic lobbying by U.S. firms. Another body of evidence suggests that politically connected firms in various other countries may show benefits as measured in market value (Chen, Ding, and Kim 2010; Goldman, Rocholl, and So 2009). Faccio (2006) found for firms in 47 countries a widespread overlap of controlling shareholders and top officers with government or parliament connections. This overlap was more pronounced in countries with higher levels of corruption, barriers to foreign investment, and more transparent systems. The connections were reduced by regulations limiting official behavior. The announcement of a new political connection increased value significantly. An analysis of a global sample of sudden deaths of politicians (i.e., a natural experiment) finds a market-adjusted 1.7 percent decline in value of companies headquartered in that politician's hometown (Faccio and Parsley 2009). A drop in rate of growth in sales and in access to credit follows this decline in value. Faccio and Parsley find that these effects are most marked for family firms, firms with high growth prospects, firms in industries over which the politician had jurisdiction, and firms headquartered in highly corrupt countries.

A possible explanation is that corporate political activity operates differently in various countries. Here is one illustration of the role of political connections: following the effective expropriation of a U.S. investor by a local minority partner, international pressure was brought to bear on the Czech government to repay the U.S. investor. The U.S. investor was a former U.S. ambassador (Desai and Moel 2008).

One study (Bennedsen, Feldmann, and Lassen 2011) used survey responses by firms to examine firm-level determinants and effects of political influence, perception of corruption, and prevalence of bribe paying. The data came from the World Bank's World Business Environment Survey, conducted in 80 countries with at least 100 firms in each country during 1998 to 2000 (Batra, Kaufmann, and Andrew 2003). The study found measures of political influence and corruption (i.e., bribes) to be uncorrelated at the firm level, suggesting that influence and bribery tend to occur in different firms rather than operating as complementary approaches in the same firms. Firms with certain characteristics (e.g., larger, older, exporting, government-owned, widely held, and in less competitive industries) tended to have more political influence, perceive corruption as less of a problem, and pay bribes less often. More influential firms tended to bend laws and regulations, while less influential firms were more prone to pay bribes to reduce costs of government intervention.

Lobbying Examples

In 2010, the United States exported about $1.3 trillion in merchandise trade and imported about $1.97 trillion (World Trade Organization 2011, Table 1.13). Commercial services exports amounted to about $518 million in 2010. About 32.3 percent of merchandise exports went to Canada and Mexico (i.e., North America); 28.5 percent to Asia; 21.6 percent to Europe; 10.7 percent to South and Central America; 3.8 percent to the Middle East; 2.2 percent to Africa; and 0.7 percent to the Commonwealth of Independent States (CIS). The main importers of U.S. merchandise were Canada, the EU, Mexico, China, and Japan in that order. About 38.8 percent of U.S. merchandise came from Asia; 26 percent from Canada and Mexico (i.e., North America); 18.2 percent from Europe; 6.9 percent from South and Central America; 4.4 percent from Africa; 3.9 percent from the Middle East; and 1.5 percent from the CIS. The main merchandise exporters to the United States were China, the EU, Canada, Mexico, and Japan in that order.

The available literature on cross-country lobbying by U.S. firms appears to focus on a few key instances (see Boddewyn 2008; Hillman 2003; Johnson, Mirchandani, and Mezner 2012; Murtha and Lenway 1994). One set of instances involves specific countries with strongly democratic institutions and advanced economies of significant interest to U.S. firms, such as Canada, Germany, Japan, and the United Kingdom. The chief trading partners of the United States are of particular importance. A second set of instances involves developing or emerging economies such as Brazil, China, India, Mexico, and Russia. A third set of instances involves important oil-producing countries such as Saudi Arabia and Venezuela, while a fourth set includes other developing and emerging economies of varying interest to U.S. firms (Schneider 2004).

The EU, presently a set of 27 countries in Western, Central, and Eastern Europe, has been seeing increased lobbying by EU and non-EU firms of the multiple EU institutions (Barron and Hultén 2011; Coen 2007; Hauser 2011; Karr 2007; Klüver 2011; McGrath 2009a). One study of the EU political activities of 2,000 firms showed that firms' size and exposure to EU policymaking were the main determinants of lobbying activity (Bernhagen and Mitchell 2006). Firms active in European markets but without a government patron at the supranational level were more likely to lobby. Corporate lobbying in Brussels and Strasbourg appeared to be different from national-level corporate political activity within the EU states.

The EU has a unique set of pan-European institutions. The European Council, comprised of all national and two EU-level leaders (the European Commission president and a Council president), sets broad priorities. The European Council is basically a political summit operating by consensus and without power to adopt legislation. The Council of the European Union (the "Council"), a different institution operating at the ministerial level, meets in 10 configurations (or committees) of national ministers by policy area, such as foreign affairs or security affairs. A

General Affairs Council, usually attended by foreign ministers or European affairs ministers, is in effect the secretariat. The Council of the European Union adopts legislative acts (e.g., regulations and directives), often in a "co-decision" process with the European Parliament. This council is responsible for coordination of national policies, concludes international agreements on behalf of the EU, and with the European Parliament adopts the EU budget. This council is basically a forum for representation of national interests by governments (with leaders summiting in the European Council). The European Parliament, meeting at Strasbourg, represents European citizens (the people) who directly elect Members of the European Parliament (MEPs) for five-year terms. The Parliament adopts laws, in "co-decision" with the council; practices oversight of other EU institutions, especially the European Commission; and adopts, with the council, the EU budget. The European Commission (the "Commission" or EC), meeting at Brussels, in constitutional theory represents the interests of the EU as a whole. There is one commissioner for each country, appointed by the national governments for five-year terms. The Commission president is nominated by the European Council, which appoints the other commissioners in agreement with the nominated president. These appointments are all subject to approval of the Parliament, to which the Commission is accountable and which has sole power to dismiss the Commission. The EC proposes new laws to Parliament and the council, manages the EU budget, enforces EU law in combination with the Court of Justice, and represents the EU internationally including negotiation of agreements with non-EU countries. The Court of Justice of the European Union (the "Court") meets at Luxembourg. There are other committees and agencies of the EU not summarized here.

The Council of Europe, at Strasbourg, is not an EU institution. It has 47 members (including all 27 members of the EU) and is concerned principally with human rights and democracy. In addition to a secretary general, a Committee of Ministers, and a Parliamentary Assembly, the Council of Europe comprises the European Court of Human Rights, the Commissioner for Human Rights, and the Congress of Local and Regional Authorities.

Rasmussen and Alexandrova (2012) studied data on contributions to EC online consultations during the years 2001–2010. The authors conclude that a specific country's volume of EU trade, level of development, and degree of democracy contribute to increasing participation rather than region of the country's location. Variation in national economic and political structures helps to explain the types of actors by which a country is represented before the EC.

There is mandatory impact assessment of all major EU policies. The form of such impact assessment is thus important. A case study of British American Tobacco (BAT) suggests effort by BAT and allies to promote successfully a business-oriented form favoring large corporations. This form emphasizes economic impacts relative to health impacts. The Treaty of Amsterdam (1997), amending the Treaty of Rome (1957), minimized burdens on businesses (Smith et al. 2010).

Business lobbying may thus have significant effects on broad policy choices as distinct from specific issues and interests. The Transatlantic Business Dialogue, in Washington, D.C., and Brussels, has a mandate from the U.S. Department of

Commerce and the European Commission and funding solely from participating companies. The TABD seeks transatlantic free trade and informs governments in North America and the European Union of its views on policy issues.

Lobbying activities may occur through international associations as well as by individual firms. The European Round Table of Industrialists is an association of chief executives of important European multinational enterprises in industrial and technological sectors. The Business Roundtable is a similar CEO association in the United States. BRT supports an Institute for Business Ethics housed at the Darden School of Business of the University of Virginia. BUSINESSEUROPE represents some 41 central industrial and employers' federations from 35 countries, representing small, medium, and large companies.

The American Chamber of Commerce to the European Union (AMCHAM EU) represents U.S. firms to the EU. Am Cham EU has published a "Guide to the European Parliament 2012–2014," as well as position papers and other documents. Its online description reads:

> AmCham EU is a unique organisation comprised of 140 companies from a broad range of sectors. It is membership-led and membership driven. The secretariat is comprised of about 20 professionals. The members work through a network of committees, four management groups and an Executive Council and offers expertise from over 650 professionals. The organisation has long been valued as an independent source of quality information and analysis. This reputation has helped to build and benefit from its close ties with EU officials. Through the committee structure members prioritise and advocate on about 100 issues annually, hold workshops, seminars and conferences which provide a platform for discussion and debate. (http://www.amchameu.eu/AboutUs/tabid/61/Default.aspx, accessed on June 9, 2012)

Less is known about lobbying in developing and emerging countries (McGrath 2009b). Three key instances about which there is some recent literature are India, China, and Russia. Outside such instances, the literature has tended to focus on a model called "obsolescing bargaining," which is discussed in the final section of this chapter. In developing countries, multinational enterprises have also tended to build alliance networks with nongovernmental organizations (Dahan, Doh, and Guay 2006; den Hond, de Bakker, and Doh 2012; Kolk and Lenfant 2012). In part, this tendency reflects weakness and incapacity of governmental institutions in developing countries (Scherer and Smid 2000). In these situations, research suggests that multinational enterprises seek to influence institutional development by creating or participating in transnational policy networks.

India is an important, growing emerging economy and the world's largest democracy in terms of population. On the 2011 Corruption Perceptions Index, compiled by Transparency International, India ranked about 91 of 183 countries (i.e., it ranked between 91 and 95, tied with four other countries for 91), at the 3.1 level. (The index ranges from 0 for perfectly corrupt to 10 for perfectly clean, there generally being no 0 or 10 countries reported.) There is resistance in India to open markets and foreign direct investment (FDI). There have been recent lobbying efforts by a number of U.S. multinationals in Washington, D.C., to get backing for influencing India to ease fairly stringent foreign investment rules. The firms reportedly include Wal-Mart, Intel, Dow Chemical, Pfizer, AT&T, Alcatel-Lucent, Boeing, Raytheon, Lockheed Martin, Starbucks, and Morgan Stanley. There has also been lobbying efforts by the Securities Industry and Financial Markets Association and the Aerospace Industries Association of America (*Hindustan Times* 2011). In January 2012, Starbucks announced it would begin operating in India, a tea country, via a 50–50 joint venture with Tata Global Beverages. Tata is the largest business group in India and adheres to a strong Tata Code of Conduct. At the end of 2011, the Indian government postponed a decision to allow foreign retailers to take a 51 percent stake in Indian retailing stores because of protests by opposition parties and small retailers and wholesalers.

China is a single-party, Communist state attempting to promote economic development through exports and attraction of FDI while retaining power (Kennedy 2011; Luo and Zhao 2013). China ranks 75 (tied with Romania), at 3.6, on the 2011 CPI. Corruption is reportedly widespread at provincial and local levels (see Luo 2011). The economy is being marketized, with stock exchanges operating, but even privately owned firms are frequently either controlled or influenced by the government behind the scenes.

It appears the government is encouraging industry associations, public hearings, and comment periods for draft laws and regulations. As reported by Kennedy (2009), lobbying and media manipulation are becoming more frequent practices; and the government has not determined what kind of regulatory regime to operate (Cha 2007). Joint ventures and political alliances are important (see Roy and Oliver 2009). A transnational political alliance is a cooperation arrangement between a multinational enterprise and a local company to influence host-country public policies. In China, the political environment is officially hostile toward such alliances, which are nevertheless reported to be quite common (Kennedy 2007). One researcher interviewed over 320 individuals (company executives, business association representatives, and government officials) during 1998 to 2003 to study the influence of domestic and foreign businesses on public policies in China. He found that neither a view of policymaking occurring entirely within the state apparatus nor a conventional view of business-government relations explains fully policy outcomes in China (Gunde 2005; Kennedy 2005, 2007). The research showed that business lobbying is widespread and regularly influential on policy and that the specific contexts of firms and industries affect how lobbying is conducted. There are tens of thousands of national and local business and trade associations and chambers of commerce that, while not autonomous with respect to government, are not necessarily without influence. It appears that zero-autonomy associations have no influence and full-autonomy associations have no access. The lobbying process lies in the middle, where some autonomy is sacrificed to gain some access.

In the late 1990s, a government effort to set price floors through some 20 or more cartels, approved by the State Economic and Trade Commission during a period of deflation, largely failed. More efficient firms resisted and lobbied other government agencies against the SETC decision. There is relatively low concentration in most industries. In 1993–1994, a Chinese company and a foreign partner invented a video compact disc (VCD) player. There was then a struggle over setting standards. Two coalitions formed over alternative standards, and each coalition had politically connected firms during the late 1990s. The result, in September 1998, was a compromise outcome that included standard preferences of both coalitions such that a new single standard simply masked the two competing standards.

Russia is reportedly more corrupt, and significantly so, than China. Russia ranks 143 (tied with seven other countries, including Nigeria and Belarus), at 2.4 on the 2011 Corruption Perceptions Index. There are organized criminal gangs, and police may be corrupt. While constitutionally a competitive democracy, Russia is dominated by the United Russia Party. The party leader is Medvedev, the former president and current and former prime minister. Putin is the current president, former prime minister under Medvedev, and former president. Although formally elected presidents, Putin and Medvedev essentially swapped offices over time. Putin was former leader of the United Russia Party. An emphasis in Russian policy is reassertion of control over natural resources such as oil and gas, reversing the earlier program of privatization. The regime has also waged a campaign of what could be described as criminal imprisonment against former business oligarchs (which is not to say that the specific charges brought are bogus).

A report by the Association of Accredited Lobbyists to the European Union summarizes the situation as follows: there is no legal framework regulating lobbying. Legislation for that purpose has been in the State Duma (the Russian legislature) for several years. Domestic firms interact with government directly or through business organizations and associations such as the Russian Union of Industrialists and Entrepreneurs and the Russian Chamber of Commerce and Industry. In addition to direct lobbying through meetings with government officials, reports, and appeals to the press, firms may help organize strikes, leak compromising information to the press, and complain up the government chain of command. AALEP predicts that increased professionalism in business-government relations and Russia's accession to the WTO will increase lobbying activity and standards. China's accession to the WTO might not have the same effects, or at least not on the same trajectory as predicted for Russia.

Recent Examples of Corruption

Illegal corruption, in the form of bribery of and extortion by government officials, is a serious tax on the activities of domestic and foreign enterprises in developing and emerging economies in particular. Bribery is initiated or paid by the business; extortion is initiated by a government official. One report noted that widespread fraud had a significant effect on the Global Fund to Fight AIDS, Tuberculosis and Malaria (Heilprin 2011). Of $21.7 billion pledged, about $10 billion had been spent since 2002 by the end of 2010. There was some evidence that some donated drugs were sold on black markets and as much as two-thirds of some grants misspent. In response, Sweden suspended its annual donation.

The causes and remedies for corruption are not fully established as yet (Treisman 2007). A recent study based on World Bank Enterprise Surveys of 2002–2005 finds that firms are more likely to engage in bribery when owner-managed and when the principal-owner is male, and that the equity share of the largest shareholder can decrease this bribery likelihood. The effect of the owner-manager is smaller as the equity share of the largest shareholder increases (Ramdani and van Witteloostuijn 2012).

There is however a formal consensus against corruption reflected in the UN Convention against Corruption (UNCAC), in force December 2005, Principle 10 of the UN Global Compact, and the 1997 OECD Convention on Combating Bribery of Foreign Public Officials in International Business Transactions, and various other international conventions (see lists provided at http://www.transparency .org and http://www.anticorruptionforum.org.uk/acf/fs/resources/instruments/). The World Bank and International Monetary Fund (IMF) also operate against corruption.

Enforcement of the U.S. Foreign Corrupt Practices Act of 1977 (FCPA; amended 1988 and 1998) has ramped up in recent years. As amended in 1988, the FCPA permits facilitating payments (or "grease") and use of agents. The distinction between a bribe and a facilitating payment is as follows: a bribe is paid secretly to a government official or intermediary for a policy decision or contract, while a facilitating payment is paid to a low-level government employee for carrying out a mandatory action speedily. Facilitating payments and funds provided to agents (middlemen) have to be properly recorded and accounted for. However, facilitating payments are typically illegal in the country where paid. The OECD has recommended against facilitating payments. Even those payments, apparently made to individuals, may simply be the foundation of corruption rings operated by higher-level officials who receive a cut. During 2005–2011, the U.S. government settled 57 company cases without trial obtaining $4.1 billion (Pettersson 2012). Charges against individuals had a very mixed record in comparison, potentially discouraging the kinds of settlements effected with companies (Pettersson 2012). U.S. Department of Justice enforcement actions were increased in 2009, when 43 individual charges were brought. A sting operation against more than 20 defendants who were accused of agreeing to bribe Gabon officials concerning military contract awards resulted in a mixed outcome. A U.S. district court granted the Department's motion to dismiss charges against all defendants who had not pleaded guilty; the initial two trials had not produced convictions. In December 2011, another U.S. district court threw out the jury conviction of Lindsey Manufacturing and two Lindsey executives on grounds of prosecutorial misconduct (Frankel 2012).

U.S. agencies involved with federal anticorruption efforts include the Department of Justice (DOJ), the Securities and Exchange Commission (SEC), the Departments of Commerce, State, and Treasury (which are concerned with trade issues), the Department of Defense (which is concerned with procurement), the U.S. Trade Representative (USTR), and the Agency for International Development (USAID).

The U.S. investigates both U.S. and non-U.S. firms; the latter are subject to the law through some form of participation in U.S. stock exchanges. The biggest recent case against a non-U.S. firm was the U.S. and German investigations of Siemens (Baron 2008; Schubert and Miller 2008). Until February 1999, bribes were deductible expenses under the German tax code, as in about 14 EU countries in total. This deductibility vanished with the OECD and EU anticorruption accords. A new management cooperated with the authorities, and reportedly agreed to pay about $1.6 billion in fines and fees to Germany and the United States and in excess of $1 billion for internal investigations and reforms. A German executive, sentenced to two years' probation and a $150,000 fine after cooperating with authorities, reportedly supervised an annual bribery budget (or slush fund) of some $40–50 million annually during 2002–2006 in the telecommunications unit. About $10–15 million was budgeted annually for Greece. Bribes were paid typically through consultants in various countries, including Argentina, Bangladesh, China, Iraq, Israel, Nigeria, Russia, and Venezuela. There were also apparently payments in Norway. Siemens maintained a system of more than 2,700 business consultant agreements. The spokesman for the association of federal criminal investigators in Germany was quoted as stating: "Bribery was Siemens's business model. Siemens had institutionalized corruption." Of some $1.4 billion in corrupt payments during 2001–2007, more than $800 million occurred in the telecommunications unit. False records were created to conceal this pattern of corruption. In 2007, a newly appointed CEO began a program of training and education concerning anticorruption practices, announced a month-long amnesty program excluding former directors (from whom damages were sought), and received information from some 40 whistle-blowers. TI co-founder Michael Hershman was appointed as an adviser.

Siemens supervisory board chairman Gerhard Cromme, right, and Peter Loescher, CEO of German industrial conglomerate Siemens, at a news conference in Munich, southern Germany on December 15, 2008. (AP Photo/Matthias Schrader)

The apparently systematic, concealed, and condoned approach at Siemens can be contrasted with the following report concerning Jack Welch, CEO of General Electric (GE). Bill Lytton was hired in 2002 as general counsel at Tyco International following the Kozlowski scandal. "He recalled that when he worked previously for General Electric, . . . Jack Welch publicly praised a manager who had failed to reach his sales targets because he refused to pay a bribe to win a contract to build engines for a foreign airline" (Parsons 2009). GE is an important aircraft jet engine manufacturer.

Another notable foreign prosecution concerned the Lesotho Highlands Water Project (LHWP), a combined water supply and hydropower project in which the governments of Lesotho and South Africa were partners. The High Court of Lesotho concluded that the CEO of the Lesotho Highlands Development Agency had accepted at least $2 million in bribes from agents for 12 multinational enterprises over a decade to secure tenders in the LHWP. The individual was sentenced in 2002 to 18 years in prison on 13 counts. Investigations were launched, and charges were reportedly brought against companies from Canada (Acres International), France (Bouygues Construction, Dumez International, Spie Batigonells/Schneider Electric), Germany (Hochtief, Lahmeyer International), Italy (Impregilo), South Africa (Concor Limited, Group Five), Switzerland and Sweden (Asea Brown Boveri [ABB]), and the UK (Keir International, Stirling International). Some convictions resulted.

In the United States, a prosecution of Panalpina (a Swiss freight forwarding firm) found that the company had operated as a corruption agent for a number of energy companies such as Shell, Transocean, GlobalSantaFe (merged with Transocean), Tidewater Marine, Pride, and Noble Corp. (of Switzerland). Panalpina paid a $236 million fine (Fowler 2010).

In April 2012, *The New York Times* (Barstow 2012) alleged that Wal-Mart had failed to report to law enforcement officials alleged bribery by senior executives of the subsidiary Wal-Mart de Mexico and closed an internal investigation. Reportedly Wal-Mart received detailed information about the bribery in 2005 from a former executive of the subsidiary. That executive had been the lawyer responsible for obtaining construction permits in Mexico for which bribes had been paid. One in five Wal-Mart stores is located in Mexico, with 209,000 employees; Wal-Mart is the largest private employer in the country. Wal-Mart has opened more than 2,100 stores and restaurants in Mexico beginning in 1991. Mexico ranks 100 (tied with 11 other countries), at 3.0, on the 2011 CPI; other countries at 3.0 include Argentina, Gabon, and Indonesia. Wal-Mart reported to the U.S. Department of Justice in December 2011 that it had begun an internal investigation by external attorneys and-accountants, after learning of the newspaper's investigation. The Department of Justice opened a criminal investigation of the allegations. The news report alleged suspect payments of more than $24 million uncovered by the first investigation in Mexico City. Reportedly, the CEO at the time rebuked internal investigators for overly aggressive effort. The investigation was then handed to the subsidiary's general counsel, alleged to have authorized bribes. Wal-Mart participated in a lobbying campaign by the U.S. Chamber of Commerce to amend the FCPA more favorably to business. Wal-Mart's corporate secretary and top ethics officer (until 2010) was on the board of the Institute of Legal Reform, the unit of the Chamber conducting the lobbying effort; and reportedly received information about the bribery in 2005. The vice chairman of Wal-Mart from 2008, scheduled to retire in summer 2012, reportedly played a key role in the alleged bribery

Wal-Mart's stock price fell some 7.5 percent, equivalent to $17 billion in value (Foroohar 2012). California State Teachers' Retirement System, a large public pension fund, filed suit against various Wal-Mart executives and board members. There were also allegations that Wal-

John B. Menzer, chief executive of Michaels Stores and a former Wal-Mart executive. (© Jay Mallin/ ZUMA Press/Corbis)

Mart had received 31 similar reports of corporate violations in various countries during 2006 (Foroohar 2012). Issues concerning apparently another $16 million in "contributions" and "donations" to local governments were not further reviewed, according to one report. One Mexican fund manager for a large U.S. financial institution stated anonymously that most retailers pay bribes in Mexico (Foroohar 2012). Mexico (7.5), Indonesia (7.5), China (6.7), and Russia (6.6) are the 4 worst of the 28 countries in the TI 2011 bribe payers index (Transparency International 2011a). (On this index, 0 means a country's enterprises always bribe; while 10 means a country's enterprises never bribe.) The Mexican government reportedly first decided it would not investigate and then two days later announced it would review permits and seek information from U.S. authorities.

In June 2012, following revelations concerning alleged bribery in Mexico, about 13 percent of votes opposed reelection of the CEO, the board chairman (the son of founder Sam Walton), and the chairman of the audit committee; and over 15 percent of votes opposed reelection of the former CEO. Excluding family and insider shares, about 31–32 percent of votes were negative and 38 percent of votes concerning the former CEO—according to one analysis. The previous year, the

Wal-Mart board had received an average 98.4 percent shareholder vote for reelection (AP 2012).

Wal-Mart has reportedly strengthened anticorruption practices in India, where it operates through a 50–50 wholesale retailing joint venture Bharti Walmart with Bharti Enterprises of New Delhi (Roy and Oliver 2009). Wal-Mart has engaged KPMG to conduct due diligence on existing and potential future vendors. Wal-Mart initiated in March 2011 a worldwide review of anticorruption efforts. The reported plan is for KPMG to classify vendors into three categories of red, amber, and green. Walmart will do business with "green" vendors, end business with "red" vendors, and leave judgments concerning "amber" vendors to Bharti Walmart (Bailay 2012).

Another major U.S. case concerned KBR Inc. (formerly Kellogg Brown & Root) in Nigeria. The firm apparently paid $180 million in bribes to Nigeria officials during 1994–2004 to obtain $6 billion in natural gas construction contracts (including for business partners) for the Bonny Island liquefied natural gas facility. In February 2012, Albert Stanley, the former CEO, received a sentence of 30 months in prison; pleading guilty in September 2008, he had agreed to restitution of $10.8 million. He had cooperated with federal prosecutors, resulting in eight felony guilty pleas, four deferred-prosecution agreements, and fines of $1.7 billion (Calkins 2012). Two former consultants for KBR also pleaded guilty to facilitating the scheme. A U.K. lawyer, holding dual U.K. and Israeli citizenship, was sentenced to 21 months prison, two years' supervised release, a fine of $25,000, and forfeiture of $149 million. Another consultant, a U.K. citizen, received one year of unsupervised probation and a fine of $20,000. Both these individuals had been extradited from the United Kingdom for trial. KBR was spun off in April 2007 from Halliburton Co. KBR agreed in February 2009 to pay $579 million to resolve charges and claims by the SEC.

The Bargaining Power and Corporate Social Responsibilities of Multinational Enterprises

This chapter concludes with an assessment of the relative bargaining power and corporate social responsibilities of U.S. multinational enterprises operating overseas. Milton Friedman (1970), winner of the 1976 Nobel Memorial Prize in economic sciences, accepted that there should be legal and moral "rules of the game." His conception was a minimalist set of market-supporting rules such as honesty and absence of fraud. He argued that if the rules included lobbying of government, then businesses should lobby legitimately for benefits and against costs. Friedman's argument involves two problems.

One problem is the relative balance of bargaining power between business and government in developing countries particularly. A conventional view in the 1970s was that these firms were more powerful than many governments, such that the former exploited the latter. A subsequent view was the "obsolescing bargaining model," in which whatever relative power possessed by multinational enterprises at the beginning of business-government interactions deteriorated thereafter (Eden, Lenway, and Schuler 2005; Gould and Winters 2007). The actual situation likely varies greatly by country and business. For example, Russia and Nigeria have the largest volume of natural gas flaring in the world, although arguably significant reductions have occurred; gas flaring generates serious environmental damages. Flaring has been illegal in Nigeria since the mid-1980s. Deadlines for cessation of flaring have passed without effective action. Whether the government and multinational enterprises in the oil industry are seriously committed to ceasing flaring and can in fact effectively do so, technologically and economically, is open to question.

The other problem concerns how businesses lobby governments in developing countries plagued with corruption and incapacity. Lobbying in a relatively clean context, such as Scandinavia, is a different situation. In developing countries, direct lobbying is likely to be ineffective and indirect lobbying is likely to degenerate into bribery and extortion. A number of authors have proposed, on various grounds, that multinational enterprises have a responsibility to help promote the kind of political and social institutions that will seek justice in host countries lacking such institutions. One argument is that the companies have a negative duty not to cause harm (Hsieh 2009)—and thus a duty to protect (Wettstein 2010). Lobbying and corruption of weak governmental institutions in developing countries may cause such harm. This argument is reinforced by the developing UN human rights regime. Businesses have negative duties not to harm human rights. Another argument is that multinational enterprises have a positive duty to promote democracy and to help provide public goods where governments lack the capacity to act effectively (Palazzo and Scherer 2008; Scherer and Smid 2000). Banking institutions have a special responsibility to combat money laundering (Maggetti 2012).

A good illustration of the potential conflict between business opportunity and CSR is Google's situation in China. The Chinese regime attempts to suppress prodemocracy efforts and restrict citizens' access to sensitive information. Google has tried to strike a balance between improving access within the controls imposed by the regime, and honoring its own commitment to prodemocracy values. Google co-founder Sergey Brin stated: "We felt that perhaps we could compromise our principles but provide ultimately more information for the Chinese and be a more effective service and perhaps make more of a difference." Google's approach at least tries to resist regime demands: "Brin said Google had agreed to the censorship demands only after Chinese authorities blocked its service in that country. Google's rivals accommodated the same demands . . . without international criticism, he said." Brin reflected that, "Perhaps now the principled approach makes more sense" (Bridis 2006).

Salter (2011) points out: "The gaming of society's rules by corporations contributes to the problem of institutional corruption in the world of business." By "gaming" Salter means the use of technically legal means to subvert the intent of society's rules for private gain. This "institutional corruption" then becomes company-sanctioned behavior which is lawful but harms the public interest or weakens institutional capacity. An effect of such institutional corruption is reduced public trust.

There is a strong argument for reforming lobbying regulations in both the United States and the EU for both domestic and foreign interests (Holman 2009).

Lobbying reform appears to be weak and ineffective. Mandatory lobbying registration and lobbying rules for the European Commission have been proposed (Chari and O'Donovan 2011), but the EU operates with a small budget and staff and is dependent on lobbyists for technical information (Hauser 2011). In the United States, the Foreign Agent Registration Act of 1938, the Lobbying Disclosure Act of 1995, and the Honest Leadership and Open Government Act of 1997 comprise the current lobbying regulations for foreign and U.S. firms, respectively. The Washington, D.C.,–based Organization for International Investment represents U.S. subsidiaries of foreign firms, advocating on behalf of foreign business interests to U.S. political institutions.

This chapter has covered a number of topics. First, it presented what is known about effective direct lobbying, which may be simply legal corruption. It provided recent examples of overseas lobbying by U.S. firms—corrupt as well as legal. Finally, it touched on the bargaining power and corporate social responsibilities (Porter and Kramer 2006) of multinational enterprises in business-government relations (Hillman and Wan 2005). Just as lobbying and political activities by these firms are never finished, the issues raised by their choices and contexts will continue to evolve and raise new questions.

References

American Chamber of Commerce to the European Union (AMCHAM EU). Accessed June 9, 2012. http://www.amchameu.eu/AboutUs/tabid/61/Default.aspx.

Associated Press (AP). (2012). "Dissent Surfaces in Wal-Mart Voting." *Houston Chronicle* 111, no. 235: B8 (Business/City&State).

Bailay, Rasul. (2012). "Beware! Walmart Will Not Do Business with Corrupt Businesses!!!" Accessed November 19, 2012. http://www.mxmindia.com/2012/06/beware-walmart-will-not-do-business-with-corrupt-businesses/.

Baron, David P. (1999). "Integrated Market and Nonmarket Strategy in Client and Interest Group Politics." *Business and Politics* 1: 3–34.

Baron, David P. (2008). "Siemens: Anatomy of Bribery." *Stanford Graduate School of Business*: Case P-68.

Barone, Michael. (2008). "In Defense of Lobbyists." *U.S. News & World Report* 144, no 18: 22.

Barron , Andrew, and Peter Hultén. (2011). "Corporate Political Strategizing in the European Union during the 2007–10 Recession: An Exploratory Study." *Environment & Planning C: Government & Policy* 29, no. 5: 783–801.

Barstow, David. (2012). "Vast Mexico Bribery Case Hushed Up by Wal-Mart after Top-Level Struggle." *New York Times*. Accessed November 19, 2012. http://www.nytimes.com/2012/04/22/business/at-wal-mart-in-mexico-a-bribe-inquiry-silenced.html?_r=1&nl=todaysheadlines&emc=edit_th_20120422.

Batra, Geeta, Daniel Kaufmann, and Andrew H. W. Stone. (2003). *Investment Climate Around the World: Voices of the Firms from the World Business Environment Survey (WBES)*. Washington, DC: The World Bank. Accessed November 19, 2012. http://siteresources.worldbank.org/INTWBIGOVANTCOR/Resources/1740479–1149112210081/2604389–1149699424544/wbes.pdf and http://books.google.com/books/about/Investment_Climate_Around_the_World.html?id=R2vmHLUuSq8C.

Baumgartner, Frank R., Jeffrey M. Berry, Marie Hojnacki, and David C. Kimball. (2009). *Lobbying and Policy Change: Who Wins, Who Loses, and Why*. Chicago: University of Chicago Press.

Bennedsen, Morten, Sven E. Feldmann, and David D. Lassen. (2011). "Lobbying and Bribes—A Survey-Based Analysis of the Demand for Influence and Corruption." *CESifo Working Paper Series:* No. 3496. Accessed November 9, 2012. http://ssrn.com/abstract=1873891.

Bernhagen, Patrick, and Neil J. Mitchell. (2006). "Global Corporations and Lobbying in the European Union." *Midwestern Political Science Association Annual Meeting.* Accessed November 19, 2012. http://www.abdn.ac.uk/~pol209/EUlobby_web.pdf.

Boddewyn, Jean J. (1993). "Political Resources and Markets in International Business: Beyond Porter's Generic Strategies." In Alan Rugman and Alain Verbeke, eds. *Research in Global Strategic Management.* Greenwich, CT: JAI Press, pp. 162–184.

Boddewyn, Jean J. (2008). "The Internationalization of the Public-Affairs Function in U.S. Multinational Enterprises." *Business & Society* 46, no. 2: 136–173.

Bridis, Ted (AP). (2006, June 6). "Google Compromised Its Principles in China, Founder Says." *USA Today.* Accessed April 17, 2014. http://usatoday30.usatoday.com/tech/news/2006-06-06-google-china_x.htm?POE=TECISVA.

Calkins, Laurel B. (2012, Feb. 24). "Ex-KBR CEO Stanley Gets 2 1/2 Years in Prison for Foreign Bribes." *Bloomberg.* Accessed November 19, 2012. http://www.bloomberg.com/news/2012-01-12/foreign-bribery-defendants-may-fight-more-as-prosecutors-falter.html.

Campos, Nauro F., and Francesco Giovannoni. (2007). "Lobbying, Corruption and Political Influence." *Public Choice* 131: 1–12.

Cha, Ariana E. (2007). "As China Opens, U.S. Lobbyists Get Ready to Move In." *The Washington Post Foreign Service.* http://www.washingtonpost.com/wp-dyn/content/article/2007/10/01/AR2007100101672.html.

Chari, Raj, and Daniel H. O'Donovan. (2011). "Lobbying the European Commission: Open or Secret?" *Socialism & Democracy* 25, no. 2: 104–124.

Chen, Charles J. P., Yuan Ding, and Chansog Kim. (2010). "High-Level Politically Connected Firms, Corruption, and Analyst Forecast Accuracy around the World." *Journal of International Business Studies* 41: 1505–1524.

Coen, David. (2007). "Empirical and Theoretical Studies in EU Lobbying." *Journal of European Public Policy* 14, no. 3: 333–345.

Dahan, Nicolas, Jonathan Doh, and Terrence Guay. (2006). "The Role of Multinational Corporations in Transnational Institution Building: A Policy Network Perspective." *Human Relations* 59, no. 11: 1571–1600.

Den Hond, Frank, Frank G. A. de Bakker, and Jonathan Doh. (2012, June 12). "What Prompts Companies to Collaboration with NGOs? Recent Evidence from the Netherlands." *Business & Society.* doi:10.1177/0007650312439549.

Desai, Mihir A., and Alberto Moel. (2008). "Czech Mate: Expropriation and Investor Protection in a Converging World." *Review of Finance* 12, no. 1: 221–251.

Eden, Lorraine, Stephanie Lenway, and Douglas A. Schuler. (2005). "Revisiting the Obsolescing Bargain Model." In R. Grosse, ed. *International Business-Government Relations in the 21st Century.* Cambridge: Cambridge University Press, pp. 251–272.

Faccio, Mara. (2006). "Politically Connected Firms." *American Economic Review* 96: 369–386.

Faccio, Mara, and David C. Parsley. (2009). "Sudden Deaths: Taking Stock of Geographic Ties." *Journal of Financial and Quantitative Analysis* 44, no. 3: 683–718.

Foroohar, Rana. (2012). "Walmart's Discounted Ethics: Its Mexican Bribery Scandal Shows the Perils of Bowing to Local 'Custom.'" *Time* 179, no. 18: 19.

Fowler, Tom. (2010). "Energy Companies to Pay over Bribery: Swiss Freight Forwarder at Heart of Case That's Netting $236 Million." *Houston Chronicle.* Accessed November 20, 2012. http://www.chron.com.

Frankel, Alison. (2012). "News Corp. and the FCPA Paradox." *Thomson Reuters News & Insight.* Accessed November 19, 2012. http://newsandinsight.thomsonreuters.com/Legal/News/2012/02_ _February/News_Corp__and_the_FCPA_paradox/.

Frankel, Christian, and Erik Højbjerg. (2012). "The Political Standardizer." *Business & Society* 51, no. 4:602–625.

Friedman, Milton. (1970). "The Social Responsibility of Business Is to Increase Its Profits." *New York Times Magazine*: 32–33, 122, 124, 126.

Goldman, Eitan, Jörg Rocholl, and Jongil So. (2009). "Do Politically Connected Boards Affect Firm Value?" *Review of Financial Studies* 22, no. 6: 2331–2360.

Gould, John A., and Matthew S. Winters. (2007). "An Obsolescing Bargain in Chad: Shifts in Leverage between the Government and the World Bank." *Business and Politics* 9, no. 2: Article 4. Accessed November 19, 2012. http://www.bepress.com/bap/vol9/iss2/art4.

Gunde, Richard. (2005). "The Business of Lobbying in China." *UCLA International Institute*, Asia Institute lecture by Scott Kennedy. Accessed November 19, 2012. http://www.international.ucla.edu/asia/article.asp?parentid=23249.

Hadani, Michael, and Douglas A. Schuler. (2013). "In Search of El Dorado: The Elusive Financial Returns on Corporate Political Investments." *Strategic Management Journal* 34, no. 2: 165–181.

Hansen, T. Bowe. (2011). "Lobbying of the International Accounting Standards Board: An Empirical Investigation." *Journal of International Accounting Research* 10, no. 2: 57–75.

Harstad, Bård, and Jakob Svensson. (2011). "Bribes, Lobbying and Development." *American Political Science Review* 105, no. 1: 46–63.

Hart, David M. (2010). "The Political Theory of the Firm." In David Coen, Wyn P. Grant, and Graham K. Wilson, eds. *The Oxford Handbook of Business and Government*. Oxford and New York: Oxford University Press, pp. 173–190.

Hasen, Richard L. (2011). "Lobbying, Rent-Seeking, and the Constitution." *Stanford Law Review* 64: 191–254.

Hauser, Henry. (2011). "European Union Lobbying Post-Lisbon: An Economic Analysis." *Berkeley Journal of International Law* 29, no. 2: 680–709.

Heilprin, John (AP). (2011). "Widespread Fraud Exacting a Toll on Global Health Fund: Two-Thirds of Some Grants Were Misspent." *Houston Chronicle* 110, no. 103: A10.

Hillman, Amy J. (2003). "Determinants of Political Strategies in US Multinationals." *Business & Society* 42, no. 4: 455–484.

Hillman, Amy J., and William P. Wan. (2005). "The Determinants of MNE Subsidiaries' Political Strategies: Evidence of Institutional Duality." *Journal of International Business Studies* 36, no. 3: 322–340.

Hillman, Amy J., Gerald D. Keim, and Douglas A. Schuler. (2004). "Corporate Political Activity: A Review and Research Agenda." *Journal of Management* 30, no. 6: 837–857.

Hindustan Times. (2011). "From Wal-Mart to Starbucks: All Lobbying Hard to Enter India." Accessed November 19, 2012. http://www.hindustantimes.com/business-news/CorporateNews/From-Wal-Mart-to-Starbucks-All-lobbying-hard-to-enter-India/Article1–757895.aspx.

Holman, Craig. (2009). "Lobbying Reform in the US and the EU: Progress on Two Continents." In Conor McGrath, ed. *Interest Groups and Lobbying in United States and Comparative Perspectives: Essays in Ethics, Institutional Pluralism, Regulation, and Management*. Lewiston, NY: Edwin Mellen Press. Accessed November 19, 2012. http://www.citizen.org/documents/Lobbying-Reform-in-the-US-EU.pdf.

Hsieh, Nien-hê. (2009). "Does Global Business Have a Responsibility to Promote Just Institutions?" *Business Ethics Quarterly* 19, no. 2: 251–273.

Johnson, Julius H., Jr., Dinesh A. Mirchandani, and Martin B. Meznar. (2012, April 1). "The Impact of Internationalization of U.S. Multinationals on Public Affairs Strategy and Performance: A Comparison at 1993 and 2003." *Business & Society*. doi:10.1177/0007650312438530.

Karr, Karolina. (2007). *Democracy and Lobbying in the European Union*. Chicago: University of Chicago Press, distributed for Campus Verlag.

Kaufmann, Daniel, and Pedro C. Vicente. (2011). "Legal Corruption." *Economics & Politics* 23, no. 2: 195–219.

Kennedy, Scott. (2005). *The Business of Lobbying in China*. Cambridge, MA: Harvard University Press.

Kennedy, Scott. (2007). "Transnational Political Alliances: An Exploration with Evidence from China." *Business & Society* 46, no. 2: 174–200.

Kennedy, Scott. (2009). "Comparing Formal and Informal Lobbying Practices in China: The Capital's Ambivalent Embrace of Capitalists." *China Information* 23, no.2: 195–222.

Kennedy, Scott. (2011). *Beyond the Middle Kingdom: Comparative Perspectives on China's Capitalist Transformation*. Stanford, CA: Stanford University Press.

Klüver, Heike. (2011). "The Contextual Nature of Lobbying: Explaining Lobbying Success in the European Union." *European Union Politics* 12, no. 4: 483–506.

Kolk, Ans, and François Lenfant. (2012). "Business–NGO Collaboration in a Conflict Setting: Partnership Activities in the Democratic Republic of Congo." *Business & Society* 51, no. 3:478–511.

Lord, Michael D. (2003). "Constituency Building as the Foundation for Corporate Political Strategy." *Academy of Management Executive* 17, no. 1: 112–124.

Luo, Yadong. (2011). "Strategic Responses to Perceived Corruption in an Emerging Market: Lessons from MNEs Investing in China." *Business & Society* 50, no. 2: 350–387.

Luo, Yadong, and Hongxin Zhao (2013). "Doing Business in a Transitional Society: Economic Environment and Relational Political Strategy for Multinationals." *Business & Society* 52, no. 3: 515–549.

Lux, Sean, T. Russell Crook, and David J. Woehr. (2011). "Mixing Business with Politics: A Meta-Analysis of the Antecedents and Outcomes of Corporate Political Activity." *Journal of Management* 37, no. 1: 223–247.

Maggetti, Martino. (2012, March 28). "Promoting Corporate Responsibility in Private Banking: Necessary and Sufficient Conditions for Joining the Wolfsberg Initiative against Money Laundering." *Business & Society*. doi:10.1177/0007650312439448.

McGrath, Conor, ed. (2009a). *Interest Groups and Lobbying in Europe*. Lewiston, NY: Edwin Mellen Press.

McGrath, Conor, ed. (2009b). *Interest Groups and Lobbying in Latin America, Africa, the Middle East, and Asia*. Lewiston, NY: Edwin Mellen Press.

Murtha, Thomas P., and Stefanie Ann Lenway. (1994). "Country Capabilities and the Strategic State: How National Political Institutions Affect Multinational Corporations' Strategies." *Strategic Management Journal* 15 (Supplement S2): 113–129.

Paine, Andre. (2009). "BIZ Urges EU Copyright Extension." *Billboard* 121, no. 25: 14.

Palazzo, Guido, and Andreas G. Scherer. (2008). "Corporate Social Responsibility, Democracy, and the Politicization of the Corporation." *Academy of Management Review* 33, no. 3: 773–775.

Parsons, Claudia. (2009, Feb. 9). "From Madoff to Merrill Lynch, 'Where Was Ethics Officer?'" *The New York Times*. http://www.nytimes.com/2009/01/29/business/worldbusiness/29iht-ethics.4.19786426.html.

Pettersson, Edvard. (2012). "Foreign Bribery Defendants May Fight More as Cases Falter." *Bloomberg*. Accessed November 19, 2012. http://www.bloomberg.com/news/2012–01–12/foreign-bribery-defendants-may-fight-more-as-prosecutors-falter.html.

Porter, Michael E., and Mark R. Kramer. (2006). "Strategy & Society: The Link between Competitive Advantage and Corporate Social Responsibility." *Harvard Business Review* 84, no. 12: 78–92, 163.

Ramdani, Dendi, and Arjen van Witteloostuijn. (2012). "The Shareholder-Manager Relationship and Its Impact on the Likelihood of Firm Bribery." *Journal of Business Ethics* 108, no. 4: 495–507.

Rasmussen, Anne, and Petya Alexandrova. (2012). "Foreign Interests Lobbying Brussels: Participation of Non-EU Members in Commission Consultations." *Journal of Common Market Studies* 50, no. 4: 614–631.

Rodriguez, Peter, Donald S. Siegel, Amy Hillman, and Lorraine Eden. (2006). "Three Lenses on the MNE: Politics, Corruption and Corporate Social Responsibility." *Journal of International Business Studies* 37, no. 6: 733–746.

Roy, Jean-Paul, and Christine Oliver. (2009). "International Joint Venture Partner Selection: The Role of the Host-Country Legal Environment." *Journal of International Business Studies* 48, no. 5: 779–801.

Salter, Malcolm S. (2011). "Lawful but Corrupt: Gaming and the Problem of Institutional Corruption in the Private Sector." Harvard Business School (HBS) Research Paper No. 11–060.

Sawant, Rajeev J. (2012). "Asset Specificity and Corporate Political Activity in Regulated Industries." *Academy of Management Review* 37, no. 2: 194–210.

Scherer, Andreas G., and Marc Smid. (2000). "The Downward Spiral and the US Model Business Principles—Why MNEs Should Take Responsibility for the Improvement of World-Wide Social and Environmental Conditions." *Management International Review* 40, no. 4: 351–371.

Schlozman, Kay Lehman. (2010). "Who Sings in the Heavenly Chorus? The Shape of the Organized Interest System." In L. Sandy Maisel and Jeffrey M. Berry, eds. *The Oxford Handbook of American Political Parties and Interest Groups*. New York: Oxford University Press.

Schneider, Ben Ross. (2004). *Business Politics and the State in Twentieth-Century Latin America*. Cambridge and New York: Cambridge University Press.

Schubert, Siri, and T. Christian Miller. (2008). "At Siemens, Bribery Was Just a Line Item." *New York Times*. Accessed November 19, 2012. http://www.nytimes.com/2008/12/21/business/worldbusiness/21siemens.html?pagewanted=all.

Schuler, Douglas A., Kathleen Rehbein, and Roxy D. Cramer. (2002). "Pursuing Strategic Advantage through Political Means: A Multivariate Approach." *Academy of Management Journal* 45, no. 4: 659–672.

Shapiro, Robert J., and Douglas Dowson. (2012). "Corporate Political Spending: Why the New Critics Are Wrong." *Manhattan Institute for Policy Research*, Legal Policy Report No. 15. Accessed November 19, 2012. http://www.manhattan-institute.org/html/lpr_15.htm.

Smith, Katherine E., Gary Fooks, Jeff Collin, Heide Weishaar, Sema Mandal, and Anna B. Gilmore. (2010). "'Working the System'—British American Tobacco's Influence on the European Union Treaty and Its Implications for Policy: An Analysis of Internal Tobacco Industry Documents." *PLoS Medicine* 7, no. 1: 1–17.

Thomas, Clive S., ed. (2004). *Research Guide to U.S. and International Interest Groups*. Westport, CT: Praeger.

Transparency International (TI). (2011a). *Bribe Payers Index 2011*. Berlin, Germany.

Transparency International (TI). (2011b). *Corruption Perceptions Index 2011*. Berlin, Germany.

Treisman, Daniel. (2007). "What Have We Learned about the Causes of Corruption from Ten Years of Cross-National Empirical Research?" *Annual Review of Political Science* 10: 211–244.

Wettstein, Florian. (2010). "The Duty to Protect: Corporate Complicity, Political Responsibility, and Human Rights Advocacy." *Journal of Business Ethics* 96, no. 1: 33–47.

Windsor, Duane. (2007). "Toward a Global Theory of Cross-Border and Multilevel Corporate Political Activity." *Business & Society* 46, no. 2: 253–278.

Woll, Cornelia. (2007). "From National Champions to Global Players? Lobbying by Network Operators during the WTO's Basic Telecommunication Negotiations." *Business & Society* 46, no. 2: 229–252.

Woll, Cornelia. (2008). *Firm Interests: How Governments Shape Business Lobbying on Global Trade.* Ithaca, NY: Cornell University Press.

World Trade Organization (WTO). (2011). *International Trade Statistics 2011.* Accessed November 19, 2012. http://www.wto.org/statistics.

A Citizen's Guide to Lobbying

Amy Handlin

The American system of government is designed to enable you to lobby your representatives at the federal, state, and local levels. You do not need a particular degree, political experience, or an "inside track." But you do need certain skills and information to maximize your effectiveness. As with any other worthwhile endeavor, advance preparation and careful thought will increase your chances of success. Don't get discouraged: while lobbying can be challenging, it will get easier every time you do it.

Citizen lobbying is based on three building blocks:

1. Research: identifying, analyzing, and connecting with the person or public body in the best position to help you.
2. Choosing Communication Tools: selecting and mastering the communication device most appropriate to the task.
3. Developing a Message: shaping a message that gets attention and serious consideration.

Building Block I: Research

Think of research as more than a way to educate yourself; it is also an advocacy tool. The most important key to influencing government is to give the right information to the right people at the right time. In fact, the majority of wrong-headed government decisions are made not because the decision makers are obtuse or ill-intentioned, but simply because the only data available to them when they need it is insufficient or incorrect.

Armed with information, you can identify opportunities, diagnose problems, and facilitate good decisions. More generally, you will be recognized as a knowledgeable, formidable advocate.

Where to Look

You won't be surprised to learn that official government websites are the best places to start your research. What you may not expect: these sites have important limitations, especially if your focus is on a county, city, or town. To maximize efficiency (and minimize frustration) it is helpful to understand upfront what these sites can deliver—and what they cannot.

As a general rule, federal websites provide considerably more information, in more sophisticated formats, than state or local sites. While there is significant variation among federal agencies, you can easily find overviews of each one's functions, processes, and leadership, along with links to related resources and support services. Expect a high degree of interactivity and a wide range of online research tools.

State sites, however, differ greatly both in substance and in ease of navigation. Unless you have some familiarity with state government, it is not unusual to be stumped by arcane lists or headings. If this happens, don't waste time clicking and scrolling through material that is far afield of your needs; instead, go directly to the home page search engine. Every state government is complicated both in structure and in terminology, and you might be pleasantly surprised to find the information you want pop up quickly in a place you didn't know to look.

Few county or municipal websites can rival the online resources provided by a state. However, the smaller scale of local sites can allow for significant depth of information and a high degree of interactivity. For example, the zoning code of a town is often available online in its entirety, complete with downloadable maps, photos, and illustrations. With increasing frequency, local sites are making it possible to complete forms, file applications, and pay fees online. You may be able to send questions not just indirectly (to a general e-mail box) but also directly to the mayor and each department head.

Watch out for a key pitfall of local websites: information may be labeled in such a way as to obscure its source or purpose. From a practical perspective, this means you can't be certain what you're looking at. A link to "recreation" could lump together both public and private programs. A budget line item called "general operations" could camouflage a slush fund. If there is no clear definition, request one.

A few jurisdictions still host very primitive websites, offering little more than a list of offices at town hall. If yours is among them, it may be hard to determine where your problem fits in. In this case, don't hesitate to e-mail or call whatever office seems to handle matters in the same ballpark. For example, it would be logical to pose your question about hazardous waste disposal to the environmental commission if there is no more appropriate link.

Unfortunately, even the most comprehensive, cutting-edge government website is not a one-stop shop for all the information you are likely to need to solve a problem. Here are five major shortcomings of these sites:

1. They are focused on what and how, not why. For example, the website of your state's public health agency may list regulations and describe inspections for food safety in certain types of restaurants, but won't explain why other outlets aren't subject to the rules.
2. Questions may be invited, but getting answers can take considerable time and several follow-up requests. Moreover, many officials will not be completely frank

in writing (for fear that their words could become part of a legal proceeding or otherwise used against them).

3. The sites are not always up to date, especially with pending legislation or regulatory action. In particular, the names and titles of agency personnel may not be current.

4. Like the vast majority of other government documents, official websites rarely acknowledge mistakes.

5. They are written in government-speak. There is no reason why you can't master this wordy, ponderous language—in fact, one good reason to peruse these websites is to get accustomed to the jargon. But you can waste time scratching your head over a directive like this: "Pursuant to State Law XQ746912:403, this jurisdiction has specified a processing period during which duly authorized persons may request documents or other materials including but not limited to those immediately available to applicants or credentialed representatives at this or other sites." In English, this means: Expect to be asked for more paperwork.

After doing as much as you can on official government sites, you can turn to these alternative online resources:

- Media archives

  In today's wired world, many people don't make the time to read a daily newspaper, or believe they can get the same information elsewhere. Sometimes, they can. But skilled journalists add value—context, background, and fact-checking. Thoughtful editorials challenge conventional assumptions, helping readers develop well-informed points of view.

  Whether or not you choose to be a regular reader, don't overlook the informational riches contained in newspaper or newsmagazine archives. While every media website is unique, it rarely takes more than a few keystrokes to access all recent reportage and commentary on any major topic. Some publications provide only abstracts (brief summaries) of stories more than a few weeks old, requiring payment to retrieve the full text. But that small fee may save you many hours of independent searching.

  Increasingly, radio and television stations also offer online archives. In broadcast media, these resources are commonly termed "on demand." A small local station may not routinely post this material, but often will provide it in some written form on request.

  What about blogs? It's fine to peruse their archives too, but keep in mind that there is no editorial filter. Blogs can run the gamut from rigorous journalism to personal vendettas. Many are blatantly partisan; some habitually disguise political attacks as hard data. Before making a judgment about an unfamiliar blog, take a close look at the nature and tone of the posts. It can also be helpful to check the quality of other blogs linked to the one you are searching.

- Reports and publications issued by academic institutions, government agencies, and public interest organizations

  A vast array of world-class scholarly investigations and analyses, once available only within the academic community, are now published online. They can originate with public and private universities, government research agencies, or public interest nonprofits. Some have a small cost, but many are free.

However, before using this material, you must try to make sure that the research was conducted or the analysis vetted by reputable groups. Remember that on the web, anyone can pose as an "expert." Here are a few indicators of quality:

A domain extension appropriate to the source. Check for .edu (an academic institution), .gov (a public agency) or .org (a registered nonprofit). Of course, you can't assume that a publication is flawless just because it has one of these imprimaturs; but at least you know that someone stands behind its basic veracity.

The author's credentials. Even if a report is issued by a respected institution, its writer may simply be musing on issues beyond his or her expertise. Alternatively, he or she may be known for an unconventional perspective that you don't share. Review his or her biography and note his or her other works.

Links, footnotes, and other documentation. What kinds of sites or other publications does this author refer to? Are they current? Reputable? Real? One-sided? If there are links, do they work? If there are footnotes, are they clear?

- Political literature

By its very nature, political literature (or broadcast material, like campaign commercials) is biased. Its assertions and denials can be over the top. But candidates craft this material to showcase what they see as their strongest positions. You should know if their beliefs align with yours.

YouTube and political blogs notwithstanding, political literature can be hard to find on the web after the election. If it's not available on the website of the candidate's political party, you will need to e-mail either a party official or the candidate.

Now it's time to get out from behind your computer. Even the highest-quality cyber-research can be vastly improved by a human touch. For example, you can:

Attend public meetings. Even streaming video can't fully capture the tone and temperature of a meeting, or the personalities of participants. Especially if you plan to speak at a town hall meeting or public hearing at some future date, the best way to educate yourself about this type of forum is to attend one (or more.)

Talk to knowledgeable people. Computers have not replaced human brains as repositories and processors of information. In many situations, the most important insights and advice are unpublished. They are, however, available for the asking from other citizens, government decision makers, or bureaucrats who deal with matters related to yours. Put the word out to your social media communities that you are seeking input. Don't hesitate to arrange fact-finding appointments with politicians or their staffs.

- Be sensitive to shifts in the political and economic climate.

It is well known that new presidents or leaders on Capitol Hill bring new priorities, appointments, and voting blocs. The same phenomenon occurs in your community and state; in fact, even small changes in the local political landscape can lead to seismic shifts in government. For example, if a governing body has a one-seat majority of Democrats, losing that single seat to a Republican will mean new priorities, appointments, and voting blocs. On the state level, the initiatives of a governor can be stymied by the opposition of just two or three leaders in the legislature.

You shouldn't depend exclusively on news reports or disinterested analysis to alert you to political or economic climate change. Instead, you must pay attention to word of mouth, the behavior of community leaders, and tips or insights from friends who share your beliefs.

- Go to the library.

At a minimum, almost all public libraries contain copies of municipal, county, and state "codes"—compilations of current laws and ordinances. More generally, an experienced librarian can be enormously valuable to a novice government researcher. He or she can steer you to emerging or little-known print and online resources; warn you about unreliable material; and help you wade through the dense terminology and complex indexing procedures common to the vast majority of official documents.

How and When to Look

Whatever the topic of your research, it should be guided by four principles:

Principle #1: Seek Clarity on the Parameters of Your Issue

There is no point to plunging blindly into the sea of government information until you know what you've diving for. In particular, you should know—or try to find out—who has authority in the matter that concerns you, and in what part of government.

Let's say you receive a citation from the municipal building department that says your garage is in violation of a fire code regulation you never heard of. According to the letter, you must pay a big fine, or invest thousands of dollars to reconfigure the space. Angered, you rush to your computer determined to identify someone—anyone—with an e-mail box at town hall. Without asking a single question about who is involved or why there is a problem, you pick the first name listed on the roster of the fire department, and shoot off a nasty note. Then you sit back, confident you'll get an explanation for what you're sure is a mistake.

But you're already off track, for two reasons. First, in your town, enforcement of the fire code is under the jurisdiction of the building department. Most of the staff at the fire department are part-time employees, so it could take weeks until your e-mail even gets forwarded to the right person. During that time, you could rack up additional penalties.

Second, in your state, the fire code itself is part of a set of uniform construction regulations stipulated by state law. Unbeknownst to you, the law was recently changed and your garage is, in fact, in violation of the new standards. This means you need to lobby your state legislator to repeal or modify the law; perhaps he could advocate for a grandfather clause or a gradual phase-in of the changes. (Of course, you could still challenge the building inspector's report. But even if he made some technical error this time, it won't be long until he returns to check for the same violation.)

Here is another example. For years, you have happily attended free cultural programs at Big Town Civic Center. Then you are turned away at the door because you didn't bring proof of local residency. Outraged at what seems like bureaucratic nonsense, you immediately call your congressman and the governor to complain.

While there is nothing wrong with making these calls, they are misdirected. Big Town Civic Center is heavily subsidized by the municipal government. To keep tuition low, the mayor has decided to limit free seats to local taxpayers—not an unreasonable policy. You would have realized this if you'd read the notice mailed to your home before the show.

Depending on your issue, it may not be easy to pinpoint the right people or level of government. But you can save a good deal of time by taking two steps:

1. If there is money involved, track where it goes. To whom are you expected to remit a payment? For what purpose? In the fire code scenario, your first clue might have been a statement that a fine has been incurred "pursuant to state law."
2. Scrutinize the documentation. Sometimes the most obvious clues to where or with whom an issue originates are the ones you are least likely to notice: letterhead, titles, addresses, or stamps.

Principle #2: Clarify the Goal of Your Research

Depending on what you need to learn or how you intend to use the information you gather, here are three examples of different directions your research could take:

1. Are you primarily concerned with a process, or with a person?

    Researching a process, like how to apply for a license or enroll in a program, is usually straightforward. If some aspect is not fully explained on the jurisdiction's website or if forms are not downloadable, you can readily identify whom to call or where to go for more information. Don't hesitate to request an informational meeting with officials who administer the process; often they will share tips and insights that no one has thought to publish.

    But researching a person is more complicated. On federal and state websites, how much you can learn about a key decision maker will depend on what office he or she holds. For the most part, profiles of top people in the executive branch (like the president or governor) and in the judicial branch (judges, prosecutors, and other key court officials) will be lengthy, often hyperbolic. But you may find next to nothing about the mid- or low-level staffers with whom you are likely to interact.

    However, if you are researching federal or state lawmakers, most sites contain a treasure trove of insights. There will be biographies, committee assignments, and partisan leadership positions; most revealing, you will find each legislator's voting record, what bills he or she has sponsored and how many of his or her bills have become law. From this information, you can easily get a sense of his or her interests, priorities, and overall effectiveness in representing your interests. By watching live-stream or archived webcasts of legislative sessions, you can watch your representatives in action and judge for yourself how passionate and well-informed they are about your issue.

    Getting to know a county or municipal decision maker online is a bigger challenge. Again, you should start with the jurisdiction's website. But because few local sites make it easy to learn more than an official wishes to tell you, it will be necessary to do some digging. While voting records will exist in some form, they may or may not be logically organized online. Importantly, you should also look for the minutes (or recordings) of public meetings to see what comments have been made about your issue. If this information is unavailable on the site, out of date, or not easily retrievable, a call to city hall should get you what you're missing.

You can fill in the blanks of any politician's background by turning to media archives. A skilled journalist is able to capture a subject's temperament as well as his or her actions. Pay particular attention to direct quotes: what an official says, asks, criticizes, and defends in public is a window onto both his or her opinions and his or her personality. If his or her campaign literature is accessible, it can be enlightening to read his or her own twist on your issue. Most elected officials (and certain appointed officials, depending on the state) are required to disclose lists of their political donors and expenditures; check with the board of elections to learn how to access this data. Some jurisdictions also require disclosure of personal financial records.

2. Are you seeking background data to incorporate into a document or public comment?

Perhaps you are preparing testimony for a public hearing, or writing a letter to the editor of a local newspaper. Instead of describing only your own problem, you will make a bigger impact by citing statistics or the experiences of others like you.

In this situation, you should search for reports and publications issued on your topic by academic institutions, government agencies, or public interest organizations. Let's say you want to address economic opportunities in Maryland: Johns Hopkins University's Institute for Policy Studies publishes papers on many aspects of the regional economy. Do you hope to make a case for job training in Arizona? A good place to start would be the Arizona Workforce Informer, a website produced by the state's Department of Commerce Research Administration.

3. Do you want to know the reason why a law was passed, or a regulation enacted?

You won't find this kind of information on a government website. Turn to media archives, political or government watchdog blogs, or the campaign literature of the officials who supported or opposed the law/regulation.

Of course, the best way to understand someone's thinking is to ask him. If you can identify the key sponsor of the law or supporter of the regulation, you shouldn't hesitate to call his office, or approach him at a meeting. He may be unwilling to speak frankly about his position—but that reaction, in itself, would be revealing.

Principle #3: Don't Give Up

Too many citizens are easily intimidated by public officials. When asking questions or looking for data, they allow themselves to be distracted, blown off, or simply ignored. Don't let this happen to you. Remember: as a taxpayer, you are the ultimate employer of everyone on the government payroll. From the loftiest to the lowliest, their work product belongs to you. It never helps to be nasty; if a staffer tells you that it will take a lot of time to fulfill your request, you won't get anything faster by yelling at him or her. But you shouldn't apologize for asking, or hesitate to follow up. (If there is a legitimate reason to withhold information, public officials are obligated to explain it to you.)

Principle #4: Timing Matters

Doing your research at the right time can be as important as doing it the right way. As a general rule, you should avoid much data-gathering just before or just after an election. Unless the outcome is certain—and it almost never is—a lot of basic information, like who is in charge of what, will be subject to change with a new administration. (This holds true on every level of government, from Washington to the tiniest town.)

If your topic is time-sensitive and you are using an unfamiliar website, be cautious about how (or whether) the information is dated. Some sites regularly change the date at the bottom of their home page, but this doesn't mean that all the data is current. Cached pages, in particular, can be tricky; try checking references or footnotes to get some sense of when the material was actually written.

Freedom of Information Requests

Let's say you're the manager of a college cafe, and you had an unpleasant run-in with the local health department inspector. He got angry when you challenged his claim that your food was improperly stored, cutting you off when you tried to respond and even accusing you of falsifying records. So it came as no surprise when his report was extremely unfavorable. Unless you contest the findings, your boss will face thousands of dollars in fines.

You've heard on the grapevine that this inspector is known for persecuting young restaurateurs, slamming them, on average, with twice as many violations as any other sanitarian. By documenting his bad behavior, you can bolster your case. All you need to do is compare a year's worth of his reports to those of other inspectors.

Then you learn that your town does not publish individual restaurant inspection reports, either by inspector or by establishment. The only information on the health department's website is a composite set of statistics. Have you reached a dead end?

You are not at an end, but at a beginning. It is time to learn how to exercise one of your lesser-known but critical rights as a citizen. Whether or not information is published by federal, state, or local government—if it pertains to public business, you are entitled to it.

From the earliest days of the Republic, American leaders have recognized that freedom of information is central to democracy. Throughout our history, officials in every city and state have reaffirmed the right of citizens to know where their money is spent; what decisions are made on their behalf; and how their government operates.

During a debate on the floor of the U.S. Senate in 1792, Elbridge Gerry of Massachusetts warned his colleagues that transparency is fundamental to democracy: "However firmly liberty may be established in any country, it cannot long subsist if the channels of information be stopped." At least one other senator needed no convincing. During the same debate, James Madison added: "In such [a government] as ours, where members are so far removed from the eye of their constituents, an easy and prompt circulation of public proceedings is peculiarly essential" (Blumenthal 2010).

But it is one thing to proclaim a principle, another to put it into practice. Information disclosure was spotty until 1966, when the Freedom of Information (FOI) law standardized the responsibilities and procedures of every federal agency. FOI

THE

FEDERALIST:

A COLLECTION OF

E S S A Y S,

WRITTEN IN FAVOUR OF THE

NEW CONSTITUTION,

AS AGREED·UPON BY THE

FEDERAL CONVENTION,

SEPTEMBER 17, 1787.

IN TWO VOLUMES.
VOL. I.

NEW-YORK:
PRINTED AND SOLD BY JOHN TIEBOUT,
No. 358 PEARL-STREET.
1799.

James Madison and his contemporaries, including Alexander Hamilton and John Jay, had a long history of bringing government proceedings into the public eye. *The Federalist* encouraged public debate regarding the proposed ratification of the Constitution. (Vol. 1. N.Y. John Tiebout, 1799. Library of Congress)

specified exactly what types of records must be made available as a matter of routine, either in print or (thanks to a 1996 amendment) online. The law also guaranteed every citizen's right to request copies of information not normally disseminated to the public. While FOI allowed agencies to withhold certain material from disclosure, such as medical records or military secrets, it provided a mechanism to appeal any denial.

Today, if you are seeking public records from Washington, the website of the U.S. Department of Justice is an excellent, citizen-friendly place to start. It offers not only a wide-ranging collection of FOI guidelines and recommendations, but referrals to a myriad of FOI resources elsewhere. Other federal agencies also maintain their own FOI websites, with agency-specific information. For example, the Securities and Exchange Commission explains that an FOI request is required to obtain the record of an investigation, but not to read the decision resulting from that investigation. If you are denied information for what you believe is an inappropriate reason, you may ask for your case to be reviewed by the FOI ombudsman, housed in the National Archives and Records Administration.

However, FOI does not apply to state and local governments. The good news is that all 50 states, and many counties and municipalities, have their own laws guaranteeing access to public documents and meetings. The bad news: these laws are not uniformly effective. Procedures are sometimes cumbersome or unclear. Compliance may be grudging: a 2008 audit by the Florida Society of Newspaper Editors, for instance, found a 43 percent noncompliance rate among local officials in 56 counties (Palm 2010). Worse, many citizens don't know the laws exist; when seeking information about government, they take no for an answer when they have every right to a yes.

If you have a need for hard-to-access government information, here are the steps to take—and the tripwires to prepare for.

Step 1: Learn Your Rights and Responsibilities under the Freedom of Information Laws in Your State or Local Government

Start by checking online resources; if there is no category called "freedom of information," search for terms like "open government" or "sunshine laws." Look for at least these four guidelines: who is entitled to what information, how requests should be made, how much time is allowed for a response to your request, and how to appeal if your request is denied. Download any sample text or formats (even if you don't use them, these materials will help you understand what officials want). Keep in mind that different levels of government may have different forms, fees, and transmittal instructions. For instance, your town may accept information requests by phone, while the county insists on written formats.

Some websites are highly interactive and easy to use. For example, New Jersey allows the public to submit FOI requests to different state agencies from a central portal. Some cities, like Seattle, also offer online public disclosure request forms. Web-based educational resources can be extensive: Oregon provides an especially comprehensive, downloadable "Citizens Guide to Public Records and Meetings."

But some local governments can make the process of requesting information more complicated than the information itself. The website may post little more than a cursory reference to the law, or nothing. Where instructions exist, they can be confusing. It may be hard to identify who, if anyone, is responsible for compliance within a particular agency or department. Officials may subtly communicate that they want you—and your request—to go away.

Don't get discouraged. Remember: just as taxpayers must comply with regulations whether they like them or not, so must the government. If you can't find what you need on a state website, call the office of the governor or the attorney general. While the implementation of FOI may fall under the auspices of another official—in Ohio, for instance, it is the auditor of state—ultimate responsibility for enforcing these laws rests with the top executives.

If you are stymied by a county or municipality, contact the chief administrator or clerk. Alternatively, you could reach out to the mayor or any other elected official. Such a call is always appropriate: Mayor Jones took an oath to uphold the law—including applicable disclosure regulations—whether he likes it or not.

Step 2: Determine What to Ask For

This is trickier than it sounds. As a general rule, while officials must provide information, they are not required to sort, compile, summarize, or analyze it. This means that you may need to request material in a form less convenient or comprehensive than you might have liked.

Let's say you hope to determine how many city contracts a certain political donor received after the last three elections. But the city organizes its contract award records by year instead of by name. Since officials are not obligated to extract data relating to an individual vendor, you would have to ask for the last three years' worth of contract records and comb through them yourself.

In another example, you want a record of all the building permits issued in a redevelopment district. However, many permits go to developers' post office boxes, so they can't be linked to a street. To achieve your goal, you would need to obtain the address of every new building in the district, determine the name of each developer, and then get the list of every permit issued to that name.

This illustrates another point: an FOI request can take much more of your time than you expected. So before going this route, make sure you have exhausted all other options. Did you try available search engines? Have you asked your neighbors? Did you check a wide array of newspaper archives? In many cases, even if something isn't posted on an official website, a polite phone call to the right person will get results (return to Building Block 1to learn how to identify that person).

Step 3: Determine How to Ask

This is another often-unforeseen FOI challenge. That's because of the language gap: you are likely to state the information you want in simple, colloquial terms that don't match how a government office describes or stores it. A request that seems straightforward to you can end up being ambiguous or vague to the person who, with the best of intentions, tries to fulfill it.

Here is what can happen. You want to review the prices paid by your town for computer monitors over the past five years. So in the "record description" space on the FOI form, you write "town computer bills—five years." After weeks of delay, you get hundreds of pages of invoices for hardware, software, supplies, service, and other expenditures related to computers but of no interest to you. Depending on how the FOI official interprets your request, you might get only those bills attached to five-year contracts—or even a huge pile of all the town's computer-generated bills.

This would be bad enough if the only result was wasted paper. But a poorly crafted FOI request can mean big, unanticipated copying costs—not to mention exasperation on both sides. In some states, the law also allows local jurisdictions to charge you for the labor involved in reproducing the material (and as a taxpayer you pay for it a second time, indirectly.)

How can you know the best way to phrase your request? In most cases, you can't. Instead of guessing, call the appropriate agency and explain the goal of your research. While not all FOI administrators are equally responsive, most realize that they help themselves by helping you. Government does not make money on this service: it is in everyone's interest to make the process as smooth as possible. In fact, there are many proactive officials who will take the initiative to reach out to you if they suspect your request needs clarification. Don't be defensive— be grateful.

Step #4: Follow Up

Most FOI laws stipulate a maximum response time, so the process can't drag on forever. But it can be significantly delayed by a time-intensive request, a backlog in the office, a copier breakdown, or for a myriad of other legitimate reasons.

In any case, it never hurts to be persistent—and it can help if your follow-up query alerts you to a problem like ambiguity or potentially exorbitant copying costs. If you suspect that someone mishandled or forgot your request, ask—politely—to talk with their supervisor. As with all other interactions with government, you will get further with courtesy than curtness.

In case you're wondering if FOI laws are taken seriously, be assured that they are vigorously enforced in the vast majority of state and local jurisdictions. While it is uncommon for disclosure disputes to go to court, this is a viable option—though obviously a last resort. Under normal circumstances, you don't need an attorney to file an information request.

A final note about research: don't waste money on commercial publications that are nothing but printouts of public information easily accessible for free. Also be wary of "consultants" who offer to expedite basic government processes. Few are worth their hefty fees.

Building Block II: Choosing Communication Tools

Reticence is never the best strategy when dealing with government. While speaking up doesn't ensure success, a lack of communication can guarantee failure. That's because the advocacy marketplace is extremely competitive: if you are absent from the marketplace of messages, someone else will take your place.

Moreover, if you make the effort to communicate, you will find that most public officials pay attention. When state legislators were asked in a survey about the origin of their policy ideas, the majority cited constituent input as extremely influential. One respondent commented: "The public underestimates what a difference one person can make in coming to their lawmaker with a problem. *A lot* of laws enacted begin with a constituent phone call or letter to a legislator. *A lot*" (Gray and Lowery 2000).

Several different communication tools are available to citizen lobbyists. All are potentially powerful, but not in every situation. The better you understand the alternatives, the more likely you'll select—and know how to use—precisely the right one.

Written Tools: E-Mail and Postal Letters, Testimony, Petitions, and Blogs

"Put it in writing" is a common admonition in business, and it is excellent advice when interacting with government. There are five reasons:

1. Multiple people are likely to be involved.
   Whatever your issue, chances are you'll need to reach out to more than one official. In turn, that person will likely involve his staff and some number of government bureaucrats. By documenting who is in the loop, you help to clarify the situation for everyone.

2. You may need to interact with overlapping jurisdictions.

   Again, bureaucratic complexity is a fact of government life. When there is a written record of who is responsible for what, there will be fewer people reinventing wheels or working at cross-purposes.

3. In government, nothing ever happens as fast as you hope.

   A written record will quickly bring everyone up to speed when the time lapses—between conversations and other interactions—become significant.

4. There can be legal ramifications of who says what.

   For the protection of everyone, it is always a good idea to have proof.

5. Certain processes require documentation.

   For example, most FOI requests must be made in writing. To comment on proposed regulations, you will need to submit written comments in the form and timeframe established by the agency. In some jurisdictions, a petition is not valid unless written in a required format and accompanied by a minimum number of signatures.

More generally, written words have staying power. They can be stored, shared, excerpted, reproduced, analyzed, and relied upon in ways that verbal communication cannot.

Let's say your state's environmental agency is crafting a new recycling regulation that you see as an environmental setback. During a meeting with your state legislator, you explain your concerns and ask him to pass them along to the agency. The conversation may well be very useful; for instance, it may deter this lawmaker from supporting future changes. But there is no guarantee that he will accurately convey your thoughts to the environmental officials. In fact, because he is busy and distracted by many other problems, he may not talk to them at all. By submitting written comments directly to the agency, you can't be assured of derailing the new rule—but at least you'll know your input was expressed correctly to the right people.

Another reason to put your case in writing: it is easier for opponents to misrepresent or challenge a verbal exchange than a document. This is especially important in a dispute that could end up in court, or if you are reporting suspected corruption.

Written tools are never quick fixes. No matter how brief your points, it takes time and thought to prepare them. You can, however, use that time efficiently by planning ways to adapt and reuse everything you write. A letter to an official can become a fact sheet for a personal meeting, or testimony for a public hearing. An e-mail can be the basis for a blog or Facebook post. Most importantly, every writing task you tackle will make you a better, faster writer.

E-Mail and Postal Letters

It is a mistake to view e-mail and postal letters as interchangeable. Even if both are appropriate in a given situation, one is likely to be more persuasive than the other, depending on the audience and what you need to communicate.

Obviously, e-mail maximizes the speed of communication and the ease of replication. Many people who feel daunted by old-fashioned composition are comfortable with e-mail. In fact, if you are addressing an issue that affects many people, like a state regulation, you don't even need to write your own text: the web sites of many public interest organizations offer standardized e-advocacy messages. With no more effort than a few clicks, you can customize the format or deliver it in the original format to a who's-who list of decision makers.

But this very simplicity can undermine an e-mail's persuasiveness. Think about it from an official's point of view: if you were deluged with hundreds, perhaps thousands of near-identical communications, how closely would you read any one of them?

Depending on the goal of your communication, this may not be a problem. Perhaps you simply want to join a collective advocacy movement on behalf of a large community—for example, an effort to show lawmakers that thousands of people are mobilizing for, or against, a new recycling regulation. In this case, it is enough to get counted.

But if you want to make a specific request or get a question answered via e-mail, it is critical to compose your own message. Write with care and precision; the informality of e-mail does not justify sloppiness. Be scrupulous about using correct names and titles and a professional, respectful tone. Also, provide offline contact information so your identity can be verified.

Odd though it seems in a wired world, postal mail can sometimes be a better choice than e-mail, especially on the local level. In general, your hard-copy missive will stand out from the pack—just because relatively few people still take the time to stuff and stamp an envelope. So much advocacy has shifted online that the average mayor who once received 50 constituent letters each week might now be surprised to see 5.

The more specific reason to go postal: if you need to supplement the text with other materials. For example, your complaint about a property maintenance code may not make sense without diagrams and photographs. By including them as part of a neat, well-organized physical package, you will maximize their impact. It may be possible to scan the same documents into an e-mail, but online attachments are easily overlooked, ignored, or deleted.

However, form letters have limited persuasiveness no matter how they are delivered. If you plan to make the extra effort to use postal mail, make it pay off by composing your own message. Keep it succinct, but use the opportunity to show how well you know your subject. Even an official who routinely ignores other types of communication will almost always respond to a thoughtful letter. It may not be the response you sought—but the door will be open for follow-up.

Importantly, you should stay away from colored, textured paper, decorated envelopes, or fancy boxes for your postal materials. It is a waste of money and a sign of inexperience. Never send breakable items or original documents unless there is some critical reason—such as a legal requirement—to do so. Also, be sure to include your name and (physical) address. In a government office, anonymous packages, no matter how compelling, will be ignored or discarded.

Testimony

The word itself sounds daunting: because "testimony" is best known as courtroom narrative, some people believe they need legal advice to write it. But as used in the normal course of interactions with government, testimony is nothing more than text you prepare to read, or "testify," at a public meeting. No one expects citizen testimony to be lawyerly; in fact, simple sincerity is more compelling than polished oratory.

Determining when and how you will be allowed to testify to a particular group of officials can be harder than writing the text itself. Every public body has its own rules: for instance, you cannot assume that a 10-minute narrative will be permitted by the city council just because you presented it to a committee of the state legislature.

At a minimum, expect restrictions on how long you can speak, at what point in the meeting, and on which topics. To participate in many public hearings, you must sign up in advance. Research these procedures well in advance (online or by phone) so you don't waste time preparing testimony that never gets heard—or worse, miss an opportunity to speak when your input would make the most difference.

Developing persuasive testimony is not easy. It requires careful research and clear (though not necessarily dramatic) expression. However, it can serve multiple purposes. After reading it as a speech, you can use it again as a background document for personal meetings, an op-ed in local newspapers, or a blog post. Unless it is highly specialized, you may be able to adapt the same testimony to several meetings on different topics. For example, if you testified to legislators that a new environmental regulation would encourage pollution of local lakes, you could make similar points to county commissioners against a new sewer line or to the mayor about an outsize housing development.

Whatever the subject of your testimony, remember that it will outlive the proceedings. Like testimony in a court of law, it becomes part of the official record: this means that what you say may be revisited many times and paraphrased in many ways—by officials, allies, opponents, other interested citizens, and the media.

You can boost the impact of your testimony by observing these dos and don'ts:

Do:

- Identify yourself and the group or institution you represent, if any. If you are speaking on behalf of a large number of people, say so.
- State precisely what you are supporting or opposing. For example, you may oppose restrictions on home-based businesses but support licensing some of them.
- Offer concrete, realistic illustrations. For example, how many jobs will your employer cut if a proposed tax increase goes into effect?
- Make your points in priority order. Chances are, not all of them will be noted or remembered; so try to leave enough time to repeat what you consider most significant.
- Focus on being audible, not on being theatrical.
- Bring enough copies of your testimony and business cards to distribute to every official (and to reporters, if you are seeking media attention).

Don't:

- Get testy if you are challenged, or asked for more information. View it as an opportunity to restate your facts and reemphasize your message.
- Guess the answer to a question. Offer to get back to the questioner (and don't forget!)

- Rely on rhetoric. Calling some policy a "death threat to the local economy" might get you a headline, but is not conducive to a productive exchange. You will accomplish more by calling the officials' attention to how many stores have closed since the policy began.
- Shout. Use the microphone even if you have a loud voice (some are just for recording, not for amplification).
- Ignore basic rules of courtesy and professionalism. For example, don't exceed the time limit; interrupt or disparage another speaker; tell silly jokes; make off color remarks; or neglect to thank the officials for their attention.

Petitions

Fundamentally, all petitions are alike: they are collective demands for action. Around the country, people are turning to them with increasing frequency as a means of getting attention or forcing change. However, the use of this tool can be complicated and challenging, depending on what you hope to accomplish.

In 24 states, citizens have the power to place their proposals on a statewide ballot, with or without the support of lawmakers. The two major types of proposals are initiatives (new laws) and referenda (repeal of existing laws). Many local governments offer some form of access to their own ballots, either for municipal initiatives and referenda or for "non-binding" questions (these express the sentiment of the community without affecting laws). But to get there, petitioners must clear some daunting hurdles. While rules differ by state and jurisdiction, the minimum number of signatures can range into seven figures. There are strict procedural requirements, like who is eligible to sign and how signatures must be authenticated. Large-scale petition drives are costly—and even if an initiative gets as far as the ballot, there is always the possibility that voters will reject it.

But you can wield a petition effectively, and with much less effort, to achieve goals unrelated to the ballot. Think of it as a marketing device: by circulating a petition, you can call attention to your issue, educate others, and mobilize support. When you deliver a petition to an official or governing body, it shows that your concerns are shared by the community—and that you are serious about getting them addressed. For example, it is one thing to tell the mayor that you are sick of red tape in city offices—and another to present a thousand signatures in support of a streamlined procedure.

How do you begin? For a statutory petition (to obtain ballot access), you must research applicable laws. These are available from the board of elections. Otherwise, you have the freedom to design any kind of document you wish, as long as it includes three elements: a heading ("A Petition to Mayor Brown"); a statement of what you support, oppose, or request ("We the undersigned demand a reduction in the driver's license fee"); and clearly defined spaces for signatures and contact information. As long as you are free of legal constraints, you can take advantage of many online petition templates like MyPetitionOnline.com or LobbyingForum.com.

Blogs

Blogs are not a means of communicating directly with an official, but this tool can be extremely effective in spreading the word about your issue and encouraging the involvement of others. You can get some attention by posting thoughtful comments on existing blogs. But if you hope to stand out in the marketplace of ideas and opinions, you should consider starting a blog of your own.

Getting a blog up and running is the easy part: any number of sites, like Blogger and WordPress, offer free, ready-to-use templates. But if you can't do blogging right, there is no reason to do it at all. The challenge is to decide if you have enough time, patience, and motivation to make it worth the effort. Unless you are a celebrity, no one will read your blog with any frequency unless it is interesting and well written. To keep it fresh, you need to commit to posting often and at some reasonable length.

Ask yourself: exactly how can blogging advance my interests? For example, it would be an excellent vehicle to call attention to a petition drive, or to educate your town about the impact of statewide policies. But you will accomplish nothing by simply railing against bureaucrats or politicians—except make enemies of the officials you complain about. A blog is not a problem-solving or relationship-building device; it is a megaphone.

Another question to consider is whether you are comfortable describing your problems, or even expressing your opinions, online. While you can password-protect your blog to limit the range of people allowed to comment, you can never erase what has been written. Think about how future coworkers or neighbors might interpret it.

Personal Contact: Phone Calls and In-Person Meetings

While written records have distinct advantages, direct human connections still make a difference. When time is of the essence, a phone call will convey urgency. A personal meeting can bring your issue to life in a way that no document can.

Phone Calls

Some situations demand immediate action. If a key vote on Capitol Hill is scheduled for this afternoon, you can't assume a congressman will read the e-mail you send this morning. Perhaps you need a fast answer to a question because you're up against a filing deadline. Times like these are when you should pick up a phone.

Don't kid yourself: a single call has limited persuasiveness, whatever the issue. Unless you are able to speak directly to the decision maker, the best you can do is leave a message—which may or may not be accurately conveyed. Still, responsible staff will recognize when the matter is exigent. Also, they keep track of how many calls come in on the same topic, from similar types of people, or requesting a particular response.

Unless you are calling just to ask a simple question or schedule an appointment, two steps will maximize your effectiveness:

1. Rehearse the call in your mind before you make it. Better yet, jot down some notes to make sure you don't forget anything: What is the nature of your problem? Are others involved? Do you need information, or intervention? Most importantly, be clear about what you want this official to do: Contact another department? Vote

a certain way? Give you guidance? The more explicit your request, the more constructive (and prompt) the response you're likely to get.

2. Follow up. While nagging never helps, it is reasonable to call back once a week until someone takes action. If appropriate, ask for the name of the staffperson working on your case, and confirm by e-mail your understanding of who is responsible for what. If you sense that you are being ignored or not taken seriously, don't waste time making accusations; simply call another official.

Personal Meetings

In some situations, a personal meeting is the best—or only—way to get results. For instance, a particular official may be unresponsive to phone calls or e-mails. To grasp a problem, he or she might need to see, hear, smell, or taste something. Perhaps you feel more confident in your face-to-face communication skills than in your writing. If the topic is potential corruption, you may not be ready to document your suspicions.

But whether or not it is necessary, a personal meeting is always desirable when it can establish a relationship, ferret out information, or ratchet up an official's level of involvement with your issue. However, the meeting won't be productive unless you prepare for it. Develop a plan of action: Which points do you intend to cover, and how? What documents and leave-behind materials will you bring? Who (if anyone) should accompany you? What outcome do you seek? In addition to its problem-solving potential, the meeting is an opportunity to impress a powerful person with your savvy, persuasiveness, and determination.

Especially if you have not met with government officials before, observe these key dos and don'ts:

Do:

- Avoid hubris. You will command respect from public officials by being professional and courteous—not by bragging about your own importance or expressing disdain for their work.
- Make sure you meet with someone who is in a position to help you. For example, there is no point in discussing a regulatory problem with a public affairs assistant.
- Bring one or two other people if they can add an extra dimension, like special expertise or personal experience.
- As soon as possible after the meeting, follow up with an e-mail that summarizes your understanding of what was discussed and/or agreed to.

Don't:

- Assume there will be a record of your meeting: while public meetings are routinely transcribed, personal meetings with public officials are not. It is always appropriate to take notes, or to ask if another person present in the room can do so. If you wish to record a private meeting, it is courteous to request permission.
- Squander valuable meeting time by provoking arguments, making baseless accusations, or endlessly repeating your complaints. State your case; provide background information; answer questions; sum up; and stop.

- Bring three or more extra people without asking permission.
- Forget to say thank you.

Communicating through the Media: Print and Talk Radio

Some problems, like unemployment or corruption, can be counted on to reso-nate with everyone. If your issue has an impact on many people outside your own circle, there is a potential opportunity to work with the media: specifically, to enlist the help of professional journalists in spreading the word.

Media coverage will give you a huge head start over any competing advocate. The disadvantage is that you cannot control how a third party interprets and explains—or fails to explain—your message. For example, if you are concerned about overbuilding in your town, you can use your own blog to slam a proposal to relax local zoning restrictions. But despite your best efforts to influence another blogger, he might tout the idea as an "economic stimulus." The potential upside may be worth the risk; but each situation (and media professional) is unique, and you must make a careful judgment.

Print

How do you get the attention of a reporter for a traditional or online publica-tion? It is a waste of time to randomly contact everyone listed on a homepage or masthead. Search archives to learn who has covered stories in your ballpark, then e-mail or call that person. (If there is no archive, or you can't identify a clear prospect, contact an editor.) A tip: every journalist has his or her own "voice," a characteristic style or perspective that colors how he or she writes. When reading archived articles, be alert to these nuances. Someone who tends to be hypercritical of your position—or simply nasty—wouldn't be your best target.

It is very hard to break into any vehicle with a statewide or national audience. There is no reason not to try, but it is more efficient to focus on regional or com-munity media. Also, keep in mind that any vehicle updated daily, online or in hard copy, has a much bigger appetite—and more space—for new information than a weekly or monthly publication.

Like any other cold call, your initial contact with a journalist may or may not produce results. Make your pitch by simply identifying yourself and stating what you have or can get, without a chatty, long-winded or jocular introduction. Media professionals work on tight deadlines; they appreciate leads but hate distractions. Also, keep in mind that reporters are trained to be skeptical: if your story isn't taken at face value, it isn't a personal slight but a professional precaution.

If you're uncomfortable cold-calling a journalist—or if that approach doesn't work—you can write a press release. This sounds more challenging than it is. You need no special training to prepare an effective release: just think of it as another way to organize and emphasize the same facts you would convey in a conversation. The same release can be sent to both print and broadcast media.

A press release need not be lengthy, eloquent, or complicated. But to be effective, it must include these elements: What is the news? Who is involved? Where and when is it happening? Why does it matter?

Let's say that for many years, weekend shoppers in your city have had to pay to park downtown. That may be a big issue for the community, but it isn't news. The news is that you have launched a petition drive calling on the mayor for free parking. Here is a sample release:

Petition Drive Off to Strong Start: Hundreds Want Free Parking

For immediate release:

A petition to provide free weekend parking downtown received 500 signatures in two days, announced Jane Jones, owner of Jane's Boutique and sponsor of the effort. "This shows that people value a vibrant local economy," Jones said. "Hundreds are calling on Mayor Smith to put out a welcome mat for weekend shoppers."

The petition is supported by every retailer on Main Street. It is available for signing at Jane's Boutique and at ten neighboring stores. It can also be accessed online at www.JanesBoutique.com.

Another avenue is to write a letter to the editor or an op-ed. A letter to the editor is a comment on a story, column, or previous letter. Depending on the publication, letters may be as brief as 50 words or as long as 250. Op-eds, essays featured in the opinions and editorials section of a publication, are typically 600–750 words. Many outlets have rigid length restrictions, so check the editorial page for guidelines.

The best letters are tightly focused on one or two points. It is important to state why you are writing: To refute an argument? To provide information? If relevant, the letter can be used to tell readers what you hope they will do or how they can learn more.

Because the average op-ed is three or four times the length of a letter, this format allows you to make a more detailed case. It is particularly effective when your issue is complicated or you are responding to multiple opponents. However, as with a letter, it is best to focus on a small number of key points, bolstered with specific examples. If you are refuting an argument, don't just assert that it is wrong; explain why.

Keep in mind that reputable media will not publish a letter to the editor or an op-ed if they cannot verify the identity of the author. Since an e-mail address is usually considered insufficient, don't send your submission without a phone number and postal address. If you have a good reason for wishing to remain anonymous, call the editor in advance to discuss it.

Why not bypass editorial control by commenting directly online, using the feedback mechanism on published articles or reporters' blogs? In fact, users of this approach—especially anonymous contributors—now far outnumber those who stick with traditional mechanisms. Unfortunately, these unfettered message boards have created a communications monster. As described by Wall Street columnist L. Gordon Crovitz: "The latest online reality [is] comment sections so uncivilized and uninformative that it's clear the free flow of anonymous comments has become way too much of a good thing. . . . The hope was that people would be civil. Instead, many comment areas have become wastelands of attacks and insults" (Crovitz 2010). In response, an increasing number of sites and blogs have begun to filter or edit online comments. Some allow only paying subscribers to comment; others give readers their own screening tool. However the changes evolve, the current free-for-all is unlikely to continue.

Talk Radio

There is a reason for the growing popularity of talk radio: in the universe of mass media, it is uniquely accessible to ordinary people. With the exception of a handful of celebrity-oriented shows, the format is driven by the interests and opinions of callers. If you are persistent—and well-spoken—you can realistically hope to get time on even a top-rated program.

The challenge of talk radio is not so much how to break in, but how to deal with the host once you are on the air. Remember: all talk show hosts are entertainers. They welcome interesting, well-informed guests, but won't hesitate to play devil's advocate—or worse. Some deliberately cultivate a prickly, combative manner. Unless you are prepared with facts and reasoned arguments, a few minutes on talk radio could hurt more than help.

If you choose this route, begin by checking station websites for call-in rules specific to each show. Also, take these precautions:

1. You will have very little time to communicate a message. From the moment you get on the air, stay focused on one or two key points.
2. Regardless of the host's demeanor, don't be defensive. Try not to waste time on jokes and pointless banter.
3. If possible, avoid calling from your car. Not only is it potentially dangerous, but a land connection is usually clearer and more stable.
4. Before you pick up the phone to call a show on a given day, listen to other live callers. The host might have chosen that day to showcase a particular issue. His choice could mean a stronger—or weaker—platform for you.

Communicating through Word of Mouth

If you find it hard to get media attention, turn to others who can spread the word through their own organizations, networks, and communities. Civic leaders—like PTA presidents or local business owners—can generate the most buzz, but you should encourage all your friends, neighbors, and colleagues to talk up your efforts. Disseminate information to your connections in sports, church, and social groups. Even if you've never discussed public issues on the basketball court or at the grocery stores, don't be shy; many of your acquaintances will take an interest simply because they know and respect you, and/or because their life circumstances are similar to yours.

Like media, word-of-mouth communication cannot be controlled. But that weakness is offset by two important strengths: credibility and relevance. If a newspaper reports that you are lobbying the mayor for streetlights to reduce neighborhood crime, readers may or may not take notice. But when your neighbors start telling each other to support your cause, their collective message will resonate—with each other and with City Hall.

Developing a Message

However you choose to speak up, your message is what you want officials to hear. It is more than a complaint or a demand. An effective message stands out from other communications because it is focused and purposeful. It gives the listener reasons why he or she should pay serious attention to you.

Let's say two people request meetings with their state legislator to advocate for lowering the sales tax. The official sees one of them in the morning, and the other in the afternoon. Mr. Morning vents about how the state is stealing all his money and threatens to make a big donation to the lawmaker's political opponent unless there is a change. Mr. Afternoon proposes a way to help state offices save money so they'll need less tax revenue. Which advocate is more likely to get results?

The daily environment of a government official is a cacophony of often-conflicting communications. The quality of your message will determine whether you break through—or just add to the noise.

Setting a Goal

An effective message always has a goal. It's as important as the destination for a trip: without one, the journey has no purpose. Your goal may be short- or long term; it may be process-oriented (like fighting red tape) or issue-based (like challenging the need for a law). It may be focused on achieving reform, or on maintaining the status quo. Whatever its object, as long as it is grounded in fact and conviction, your goal will give direction and clarity to your message.

Be careful to set a goal that is realistically related to what officials can do. Even the president of the United States has limited powers. No single official at any level can restructure government or change the constitution of the country or of his or her state.

However, every public official has influence within the sphere of his or her responsibilities and expertise. It is up to you to learn what a specific person (and public body) can and can't do, and to express your goal accordingly. For example, a congressman can't change a state regulation. A town council cannot build a county road. Of course, there is nothing wrong with presenting a wish list—but wishes rarely come true.

Realistically, some goals are harder to achieve than others. For example, you can aim at convincing a lawmaker to cast a particular vote. But it is impractical to try changing his or her overall ideology. By all means, be ambitious—but don't be naive.

Framing Your Message

When you frame a picture, you enhance its visual effect. When you frame a message, you enhance its meaning to your audience. More generally, a message frame is a context. It helps a listener understand how your goal aligns with his.

Of course, you may need to interact with many officials, and you can't know the personal goals of each one. But the vast majority share a broad, community service perspective. They hope to maximize the public good—or at least, to maximize the public's satisfaction with their performance.

Let's say you want to change an existing environmental regulation. Simply calling for "reform" won't get more than polite nods from regulators. A more compelling message would tap into the officials' own motivation: to get the best environmental results at the least cost. It would encourage them to see you more as an ally than an adversary. For example, you could frame your suggestions as ways to help the environmental agency:

- Clarify ambiguous language.
- Streamline compliance procedures.
- Eliminate redundant or counterproductive requirements.
- Reduce paperwork.
- Facilitate better environmental protection.

Whatever your issue, here is the key to persuasiveness: convince the decision maker that it will help him to help you.

The more you know about particular officials or public bodies, the easier it is to frame your message in accordance with their interests and priorities. For example, before presenting testimony to the environmental agency, revisit your research: Have these regulators been receptive to rule modifications in the past? For what reasons? Did you talk informally to agency staff about what ideas have the best chance to be considered?

Are you meeting with a lawmaker or mayor? Review her voting record and any public statements relevant to your topic. In particular, try to identify her "signature" issues, those she has worked hardest on and feels passionately about. Is she known as a corruption buster? Then she is an excellent choice to meet with to discuss your suspicions about shady development deals.

Sometimes you can choose whether to frame your message positively or negatively. A positive frame means describing what you seek as a gain; a negative frame depicts it as averting a loss. For example, expanding a state college could be positively framed as a boost to the local economy, or negatively framed as a means of slowing a brain drain.

Conventional wisdom suggests that it is always best to be upbeat, a belief bolstered by some consumer research. For instance, one study found that beef buyers were more likely to choose a product when it was labeled "75% lean" instead of "25% fat" (Levin and Gaeth 1988). But overall, the evidence is mixed. And every official, like every issue, is different. Try to get a sense of whether your target official is generally risk-averse (probably concerned with averting losses) or entrepreneurial (likely to champion bold, new initiatives).

Another facet of framing is to anticipate opposition. While you can't foresee every potential opponent, it is important to keep in mind that any government official—elected or not—is obligated to listen to both sides of every issue.

In some situations, like a public hearing, you can respond to critics directly. Look for opportunities to question their evidence, experience, inferences, or assumptions, such as:

- On what data are you basing that comment?
- How many times did you have that experience?
- Did you consider alternative plausible conclusions?
- Why did you make those assumptions?

If you can't respond in person, try to anticipate likely challenges. Provide officials with answers to the questions they are most likely to be asked, and make yourself readily available as a resource should they need additional information.

Message Comprehension and Tone

Even the most carefully framed message will not be persuasive unless it is comprehended, or understood, by the recipient. Government officials face a daily barrage of messages, often including information that is new and complex. To make sense of this bewildering overload, they try to categorize and evaluate it.

It is always easier to understand an unfamiliar concept if you can fit it into a familiar mental framework. That's why the first car was described as a "horseless carriage," and digital representations of text were introduced as "e-books." You can use the same technique to make your issue easier to comprehend. For example, instead of explaining all the onerous record-keeping you do to comply with a municipal regulation, you could say: "This regulation generates more paperwork than all the state rules combined." That description will get the attention of any experienced regulator.

You can also facilitate the evaluation of your issue by referring to simple benchmarks. A $100 fee may not sound like much to a listener who has no basis for comparison. But it takes on a different meaning if you can compare it to the $10 fee charged by a neighboring town for the same service.

Comprehension can be heightened—or undermined—by language. Just as you are stymied by government-speak, others can be confused by slang or techno-jargon. It takes more time to spell out words than to use abbreviations, and it might bolster your self-confidence to throw around technical terms. But you are hurting your case if your listener can't follow your argument. Also, keep in mind that complicated information may be better understood if conveyed in writing.

A message that is clearly understood can still be compromised by an inappropriate tone, or manner of expression. Remember: the way you come across is as crucial as what you say.

Here are dos and don'ts for setting the tone of your message.

Do:

- Be respectful toward government in general, regardless of how strongly you oppose a policy in particular. Trashing bureaucrats and politicians might make you feel good, but it is sure to alienate your listener. If you doubt the significance of civility, consider the view of Jim Leach, former congressman and chair of the National Endowment for the Humanities:

○ Little is more important . . . than establishing an ethos of thoughtfulness in the public square. Words . . . clarify—or cloud—thought and energize action. . . . The concept of civility implies politeness, but civil discourse is about more than good etiquette. At its core, civility requires respectful engagement: a willingness to consider other views and place them in the context of history. . . . If we can't respect our neighbors, how can we expect others to respect us, our values and way of life? (Leach 2010)

- In a personal interaction, build your case gradually and answer every question patiently. If you are in too much of a hurry, reschedule the meeting.
- In a written message, choose conciliatory language over inflammatory rhetoric. Putting an official on the defensive can be counterproductive—and once your attack is in writing, you can't take it back.

Don't:

- Be a show-off. It is fine to take pride in your accomplishments, but persistently blowing your own horn is obnoxious.
- Use sarcasm or jokes. Government is a serious enterprise; even if you have an established and comfortable relationship with an official, excessive humor is inappropriate.
- Exaggerate or distort information. Any kind of misrepresentation is sure to be exposed, and will permanently destroy your credibility.

Choosing Your Messenger

You can handle many government problems yourself. But sometimes it is necessary—and smart—to speak through or with others, both in personal meetings and for public communication efforts. In a face-to-face dialogue with an official, an ally can reinforce your comments by citing his or her own experience. If your issue has broad community implications, using multiple spokespeople is a concrete way to demonstrate that breadth.

But to further your effort, any messenger must have credibility—in itself a composite of other characteristics. A credible person is knowledgeable, trustworthy, and likeable. While he or she may not be equally strong on all three dimensions, he or she cannot be persuasive if entirely lacking on any of them.

A person's level of knowledge can be measured objectively. If it can't be established on the basis of a certification or degree, knowledge can be reasonably inferred from years of experience or success in a field.

But likeability and trustworthiness are subjective characteristics. This means they are subject to interpretation and can't be quantified. Psychologists have invented scales that purport to compare people on these dimensions; but for all practical purposes, the only meaningful gauges are your own judgment and a person's reputation.

If someone is widely respected in the community, does that automatically make him an ideal messenger? Unfortunately, no. He may be an excellent doctor, for example, but a poor communicator. A well-known local philanthropist may get an appointment with the mayor sooner than you could get one yourself, but if he is unfamiliar with or unenthusiastic about your issue, including him in the meeting won't help.

On the other hand, it can be extremely valuable to show support from some-one considered an "opinion leader" in a field related to your issue—an individual whose expertise and integrity are unassailable. For instance, a top hospital executive could speak very convincingly about a public health regulation. An professor of ethics would be effective in addressing corruption. Whomever you consider tapping to help deliver your message, be certain he or she understands your goal and is comfortable representing your interests.

When choosing a messenger, watch out for potential conflicts of interest. For example, you wouldn't want someone to speak before the city council on your behalf if that person is suing the municipality. Likewise, it wouldn't be smart to come to a meeting with a lawmaker accompanied by a political candidate who is running against him.

Recruiting people outside of your immediate circle to be part of public advocacy—a petition drive, a town meeting, a media push—is more challenging. The stakes can be higher, too: depending on the issue, your chances for success could hinge on demonstrating broad community support. So how do you go about this effort?

The easiest place to begin is with organizations you belong to. If they are not already involved with your issue, ask yourself why. Sometimes the reason will be obvious: a chamber of commerce cannot take a position that would benefit one category of members, like franchises, over another category, like independent stores. In other situations, it is a resource issue: a statewide group doesn't have the time or funds to get involved with local matters. There are also restrictions on what a nonprofit organization can do without jeopardizing its legal (and federal tax) status.

Whatever the obstacles, if your existing network can't help, you will need to create a coalition of new supporters. Here the steps to take:

1. Define your issue as broadly and inclusively as possible.
   Remember the old adage "Politics makes strange bedfellows"? So does advocacy: Some of the most unlikely coalitions can also be the most successful.
   Let's say you are fed up with red tape and bureaucratic snafus in your county's job training program. Looking at the problem narrowly, it only affects individuals looking for employment.
   But from a broader perspective, it could also be about top-heavy government (too many bureaucrats with redundant responsibilities), misdirected spending (multiple offices at different sites when one would do), or insufficient transparency (more information could be available online). Each of these issues has its own phalanx of interest groups and advocacy organizations whose efforts could complement yours.
   Opponents of public corruption, in particular, have a long history of working with other advocates who might otherwise be at odds over policy and politics. Their motives may be different: in a push to tighten campaign finance restrictions, for example, good government groups have long-term policy concerns while business groups want to stop the pressure on their members for big donations. But their goal—honesty in government—is the same.

Make a list of potential coalition partners. Do you have a relationship, or even a nodding acquaintanceship, with any of their leaders? If not, reach out to the president or chairperson and request an opportunity to address their membership.

2. Expect to do the lion's share of the work.

The priorities of another group are unlikely to mirror yours. Even if they are bursting with enthusiasm about your effort, don't expect them to divert significant resources from their own mission. Never pressure coalition partners for support they can't or won't provide. Instead, think about ways to help them help you. For example:

- Education about your issue: At a minimum, provide the results of your research and resources for more information.
- Readymade communications: Some organizations prefer to generate their own letters, testimony, and other material. But others will appreciate draft text or talking points.
- Publicity: Assuming they are interested, make sure your coalition partners have opportunities to share in your (positive) media exposure.
- Reciprocal support: It is simple courtesy to do your best to support the people who support you. Realistically, this won't always be possible. But even when you can't help them, you can usually refrain from hurting them.

3. Identify both existing and potential opponents.

The more you know about organizations likely to oppose you, the better you will be prepared to fight back. Using the same research techniques you have already learned, look for public statements, position papers, and media reports. Also educate yourself about their funding sources and membership base.

Because they are experienced in grassroots organizing, partisan political organizations can be valuable coalition partners. But be cautious. Depending on the political climate (and whether an election is imminent), you might risk alienating key officials or nonpartisan interest groups.

Conclusion: The Rewards of Citizen Lobbying

There are no guarantees in lobbying, no matter how skilled or savvy you become. Even the most experienced, highly paid professional lobbyists don't always get the decisions or votes they hope for.

Still, forceful advocacy offers its own rewards. Win or lose, you will develop important new relationships and insights. You'll learn how to get access and opportunities. You will educate others about issues important to you. More specifically, a citizen lobbyist is:

- Sophisticated about how government works. Your future lobbying targets are impossible to predict. But when you have learned to open doors at one level of government, it is infinitely easier to navigate another.
- On top of changing policies and laws. Now that you know how and where to find information, you can be vigilant in tracking and responding to changes that affect you.

- Unfazed by powerful officials. In lobbying, attitude matters. Timidity and insecurity show and can undermine the most polished presentation. But the more you interact with officials, the easier it is to stand up to them. You will get accustomed to striking just the right balance between respect for their positions and confidence in your own.

Finally, you'll know that you've made a difference by exercising your fundamental rights as an American citizen—the most important achievement of all.

References

Blumenthal, Paul. (2010). "The History of Transparency –Part 1." http://sunlightfoundation.com/blog/2010/03/23/the-history-of-transparency-part-1-opening-the-channels-of-information-to-the-people-in-the-18th-century/.

Crovitz, L. (2010, April 19). "Is Internet Civility an Oxymoron?" *Wall Street Journal*: A17.

Gray, V., and D. Lowery. (2000). "Where Do Policy Ideas Come From? A Study of Minnesota Legislators and Staffers." *Journal of Public Administration Research and Theory* 10, no. 3: 573–597.

Leach, J. (2010, Jan. 15). "Civil Discourse." *St. Petersburg Times*. Accessed Feb. 20, 2010. http://www.tampabay.com.

Levin, I., and G. Gaeth. (1988, Dec.). "How Consumers Are Affected by the Framing of Attribute Information before and after Consuming the Product." *Journal of Consumer Research* 15: 374–378.

Palm, A. (2010, March 15). "Want Public Records in Florida? Get Ready for a Hassle." *Palm Beach Post*. Accessed April 10, 2010. http://www.palmbeachpost.com.

Section B
Political Influence

All Politics Is Local

Amy Handlin

If you tell your neighbor that you hate local politics, you are making a harmless observation. But if you don't pay attention to local politics, you are making a serious mistake.

Too many people make that choice because they think of local politics as sleazy and inconsequential. The truth is while it can be unsavory, you cannot afford to ignore it. The political world at every level tends to attract larger-than-life personalities who can be abrasive and confrontational. But whether or not local policymakers are likeable, on your home turf you have easy access and a direct line of communication to them. More to the point, you can position yourself to influence how they allocate government resources and power.

What's at Stake?

The process labeled "local politics" actually has an impact well beyond a single locale. While it does produce hometown leaders, it is also an incubator for politicians at higher levels. Aspiring state lawmakers, in particular, commonly begin as mayors or county commissioners. Many top state agency officials began their careers running municipal boards or departments.

Beyond its role as a springboard for future policymakers, local politics can have an outsize influence on the implementation of state and federal laws. For example, notwithstanding pressure (and grants) from Washington to spend on social services like mental health and drug abuse programs, local governments differ widely in how—or even if—they use the funds. One town might create a full-blown treatment center; another could choose to refer its needy residents elsewhere. What accounts for the differences? As one county-based study explained: "We find that local policy outputs are influenced by counties' ideological dispositions where more liberal/conservative counties produce more liberal/conservative outputs across a wide range of policy areas including public health, educational services, and welfare" (Percival, Johnson, and Neiman 2009, 20). In other words, within the constraints of federal mandates, local officials are responsive to the political opinions of their constituents.

Many state laws are "permissive," meaning that it is up to local politicians to decide whether to enact them. Citizens—and especially small businesses—are extremely vulnerable when mayors or commissioners can choose whether to impose a fee, increase a tax, or enact a regulation.

For example, some states grant local governments the authority to slap builders with so-called impact fees on any new structure to defray the cost of roads, sewers, and other public improvements. These fees become particularly contentious during economic downturns, when towns are under pressure to expand infrastructure with shrinking budgets. Why are impact fees enacted regularly in parts of these states but never in others? Almost always, it comes down to the political visibility of local construction-related businesses. For instance, when the mayor argues that impact fees are the only source of funds for widening a bridge, builders can make the case that their projects will bring a new stream of tax revenues to replenish the town budget.

Virginia's battle over car taxes in the late 1990s showed how even a high-profile gubernatorial campaign can turn on local politics. Republican Jim Gilmore won election by promising to roll back an unpopular assessment on cars and trucks. But the tax was not collected by the state; it was based on the value of personal property and levied by each local government at a different rate. Because residents of property-rich communities in Northern Virginia stood to gain far more from the rollback than other voters, the statewide contest became a regional tussle, pitting town against town. At the polls, tax foes in the north overwhelmed other voters, sweeping in a new governor—and years of ongoing local debate. Town-by-town implementation of the rollback became so controversial and unwieldy that Gilmore's plan was suspended with barely a whimper just a few years after it started with a bang.

But local politics would be important even if its influence were confined to town hall. For better or worse, it is the system that gives rise to local regulation, taxation, and policy decisions. Political allies of elected officials end up on zoning boards, redevelopment authorities, and other bodies with influence over the quality of life for citizens and the opportunities for small businesses.

Given this impact, why do so many people shun local politics? Of course, it involves some time commitment; but citizens routinely accommodate other activities, like philanthropy, that have less impact on their daily lives.

One reason is its shady, ugly image. Unfortunately, politicians have brought this problem on themselves. The real harm caused by public corruption (discussed in Chapter 8) is compounded by perceptual damage done by the mudslinging and fear-mongering now routine in local campaigns. This is not to say that national races are free of acrimony—in fact, they have become increasingly bitter—but as one campaign expert points out: "I proposed a law of politics in the same vein of Parkinson's Law or Murphy's Law. My law read, 'The sleaziness in any political campaign is inversely proportional to the size of the election district'" (Grey 1999, 208).

Make no mistake: the goal of a local campaign can be considerably less than high-minded. Some people run for office to avenge personal grievances or pay back petty slights. Others just want attention. A handful of politicians are overtly racist or xenophobic. It is these kinds of candidates who engender public wariness—if not outright disgust.

Voters understand that tight races often turn negative. They accept the legitimacy of criticizing an opponent for committing a crime, lying to the media, or otherwise behaving irresponsibly. But they are not eager to sniff dirty laundry for its own sake.

The use of scare tactics is another visceral approach that alienates voters over the long term. Some local campaigns deliberately exploit people's common anxieties about environmental hazards like pollution, high-risk facilities like jails and power plants, or pocketbook threats like new taxes. Sounding an alarm may be warranted in extreme circumstances: for instance, a candidate who learns of an imminent bridge collapse would be justified in trying to scare travelers away from the bridge. But these situations are rare. Politicians are on shaky ethical ground when they deliberately frighten voters, spread unreliable information, or pit one group against another.

Often this approach will backfire, as it did for a Republican candidate running in Nassau County, New York. Aware that voters were extremely worried about reassessment of their properties, she ran on a single-issue anti-reassessment platform. Her campaign materials promised a vigorous fight to stop "the Democrats' tax reassessment scheme" (Cooper 2000).

But the reassessment had been approved months earlier by a bipartisan majority of the county legislature. When this fact was publicized, the candidate was widely criticized for fear-mongering. She lost the election.

Fortunately, most people who choose to take on the hard work of politics are responsible, realistic, and motivated by some genuine policy interest. It may be issue-specific: for example, Jane may run to reduce a local tax. It may be process-oriented: John might seek faster disclosure of budget documents. Either way, candidates focused on improving government tend to see more success than those with little more than animus—if only because, in marketing terms, they can build more appealing "brand identities" in the political marketplace.

Another major reason why people steer clear of local politics: to any novice, no matter how successful in other fields, the political landscape can be as murky and mysterious as the Amazon. The process of selecting candidates, developing platforms, and running campaigns is fairly orderly, but it is guided by norms and customs that vary widely across states, counties, and towns. The unwritten rules are fully comprehended only by insiders who learned by doing, by accident, or by mistake. It can take hours of hunting, online or on the phone, to find even the most basic facts—who's who, what matters, where to get help.

The problem is not that information is deliberately hidden from newcomers. While some insiders won't go out of their way to be helpful, most are eager to attract new blood. The stumbling block is what economists call "the curse of knowledge." People who have been part of a complex system for many years simply can't appreciate how confusing and intimidating it is to those who have not. As one writer put it: " Once you've become an expert in a particular subject, it's hard to imagine not knowing what you do. Your conversations with others in the field are peppered with catch phrases and jargon that are foreign to the uninitiated. When it's time to accomplish a task . . . those in the know get it done the way it has always been done, stifling innovation as they barrel along the well-worn path" (Rae-Dupree 2007).

In the face of so many disincentives, is it really worthwhile to get engaged with grassroots politics? What could you gain, for instance, by contributing time or money to a local campaign?

A later section of this chapter will discuss some specific benefits. But as a general rule, you will find that the payoffs of this investment—in relationships, insight, and access—are not only valuable, but unattainable in any other way. Some people mistakenly believe that by supporting a presidential candidate, for example, they will somehow win points with the town Democrats or county GOP. In fact—ideological parallels aside—local campaigns are, for all practical purposes, independent spheres of activity.

There are no roadmaps for the politically uninitiated. But there are landmarks: key players in the election process and basic features of a campaign.

The Most Important Politicians You've Never Heard Of

Political parties are the basic units of American democracy. In other countries, party money and power are concentrated at the national level. But the hearts of U.S. party organizations are their state and local participants. When it comes to electing candidates—the raison d'etre of any Democratic or Republican group—virtually all important decisions and activities bubble up from the grassroots.

A party is structured like a ladder. On the bottom rung are approximately 180,000 election precincts, each including up to a few hundred voters. Party members in each precinct (or group of precincts) elect representatives during primaries, who in turn choose party decision makers, called committeepersons, on the next two rungs: the municipality and county. In most regions, county committees wield the lion's share of influence in local party affairs: endorsing candidates, raising money, and recruiting campaign workers. There are state and national party committees higher up the ladder, but for the most part their role is to supplement, not supplant, the work of the counties.

So the members of a county committee are the most important politicians most people have never heard of. Few novices appreciate what they do, or how much they know. But it is not an exaggeration to say that the vast majority of America's elected officials owe their power to these low-profile volunteers.

The average county committeeperson has four main sources of influence. First, he or she is on a first-name basis with every official party leader and unofficial power broker. He or she knows who matters most in the local hierarchy, why, and to whom.

Second, he or she is likely to belong to other clubs and organizations. A national survey of local party leaders found majorities regularly engaged in community-building groups, events, and activities (Bearse 2004). This means he or she is in a position to identify issues, make introductions, and forge alliances.

Third, county committee members are committed to the political process and are aware of the importance of "retail," or grassroots, campaigns. While media-driven and web-based races are increasingly widespread, street smarts will always matter on a local level.

Finally, in states where candidates are nominated or endorsed in party conventions, county committeepersons serve as delegates. The votes they cast can make or break the future of aspiring governors, U.S. senators, and even presidential contenders.

However, anyone on the front lines of a political battle is likely to take some bullets, mostly rhetorical but still hurtful. The role of the unpaid foot soldier is not only time-consuming, but often thankless and unpleasant. In recent years, both major parties have begun to have trouble recruiting and retaining county committeepersons. One measure of the problem: in a 2006 survey conducted in New Jersey by the nonpartisan Citizens' Campaign, 40 percent of the state's 24,554 committee seats were found to be vacant (Walsh 2006).

While state parties cannot pay committeepersons, there are movements afoot to give them more autonomy and responsibility. New Jersey's Party Democracy Act is one: this 2009 law expands the role of the county committee in selecting legislative candidates. Elsewhere, party organizations are mounting newly aggressive outreach and training programs. One way or another, the clout of these grassroots activists is on the upswing. It is well worth cultivating and learning the ropes from them. You will find county committee members easily accessible: after all, they are your neighbors—and possibly your customers.

The local party chairman, selected by the committee, is often a forceful—some say domineering—presence. Many chairmen don't come up through the precinct ranks; often they are businesspeople with extensive political contacts. Their role is usually less potent in public than behind the scenes, where they spend enormous amounts of time raising money for campaigns and party-building efforts. At a minimum, chairmen can influence many other party players to support (or oppose) a candidacy. They are likely to be owed lots of favors, and unlikely to be shy about calling them in.

Most party chairman put in long hours for no more compensation than pride in a job well done. But others have been known to trade on their influence and connections for personal gain, sometimes illegally and often brazenly. For example, the political world of Brooklyn, New York, was riveted in 2007 by the corruption trial of Democratic party ex-chairman Clarence Norman. Formerly one of the country's most entrenched power-brokers, Norman stood accused of extorting over $20,000 from an aspiring judicial candidate. Allegedly, he routinely helped himself to campaign funds, using them as rewards for his friends and cronies. Norman was sentenced to three to nine years in jail but not before he made a statement to the press: "'The bottom line is I was convicted of asking candidates to pay their pro rata share of campaign expenses. . . . That's it. That's why I stand convicted of a felony. For helping people'" (Ginsberg 2007).

Former state Assemblyman Clarence Norman Jr. at the state Supreme Court in the Brooklyn borough of New York on June 5, 2007. (AP Photo/Mary Altaffer)

Since 2003, dozens of venal bosses (both Democrats and Republicans) have been prosecuted for egregious behaviors they once considered business as usual: bribery, extortion, bid-rigging, and tax fraud. On the heels of these scandals, legislators and courts, formerly loathe to intervene in partisan matters, have begun to step in. For example, a Michigan judge slapped down a power grab by party leaders in 2007: their attempt to get exclusive access to voter lists would have strangled the campaign of any candidate who tried to run without their support.

Like New Jersey's Party Democracy Act, these initiatives represent progress but cannot root out every abuse. However, the combination of increased media scrutiny and emboldened critics is likely to succeed, over the long term, in replacing many of the local parties' remaining tyrants and crooks.

What's at Stake II?

The ultimate goal of a political party is power. Whether the power in play in a given election is that of a small-town mayor or a big-state governor, partisan loyalists pursue it vigorously and single-mindedly. They know that today's local official could be tomorrow's national leader. And in the short term, they also know the basic calculus of politics: to the winner go the spoils. In government, this means appointments, jobs, contracts, and influence.

However, different elective officials have widely varying types and degrees of power, even on the same governing body. To better understand the local political scene, it is helpful to be familiar with the basic structures and policymakers in local and state government.

Municipal Governments

Your municipality may be known as a town, city, township, village, or borough. Whatever the name, it is the level of government closest and most responsive to citizens—at least, to those citizens who learn the system.

A council (sometimes called a board of aldermen, supervisors, or trustees) is the legislative body of municipal government, where local ordinances and regulations originate. There can be as few as three councilpersons, or dozens. Some are elected to represent just one district, or ward; others are chosen "at large," meaning they are supposed to represent the entire population. Council elections are nonpartisan in over half of U.S. municipalities—but local political organizations often align with candidates despite the absence of party labels on the ballot. In partisan council elections, candidates are nominated by their party's town or county committee, or by winning a party primary.

A mayor is the most visible elected official in city hall. Most people assume he or she is also the most important. However, how much power he or she actually wields is entirely dependent on the form of government. There are four common forms: strong mayor-council, weak mayor-council, council-manager, and municipal commission. (Certain regions and rural areas have distinctive variations. In particular, New England towns elect administrative boards called "selectmen," while legislative power is exercised by citizens themselves in periodic "town meetings.")

If Mayor Smith is elected in a strong mayor-council town, he is a chief executive officer with dominant administrative and policymaking authority. He appoints department heads and hires other key staff to advance his agenda; controls or heavily influences the budget; and can veto most actions of the council. Smith is probably a Democrat or Republican, though a strong mayor could be independent or nonpartisan.

Smith would experience culture shock if he moved to a weak mayor-council municipality. There, he could recommend policy to the council, but the members would have no obligation to listen. Important administrators, like the tax assessor and budget director, might be directly elected by the voters, meaning they wouldn't owe Smith their jobs. To a significant degree, Smith would be able to act only at the pleasure of other officials—who may or may not belong to the same political party or share his ideology.

In a council-manager government, the mayor's job is largely ceremonial. Limited mostly to cutting ribbons, proclaiming holidays, and the like, Smith would have far less authority than the city manager, a professional administrator. That official, accountable to the legislative body as a whole, would drive most day-to-day administrative, budgetary, personnel, and policy decisions.

Municipal commissions combine executive and legislative powers in one body. Each commissioner is chosen in a nonpartisan election to function as the head of one or more town departments or agencies. Collectively, with or without a mayor, the commissioners pass laws and set policy.

You will need to choose your approach to municipal government based on which of these forms it takes.

County Government
Counties may serve as few as 42 people (Loving County, Texas) or as many as 9.1 million (Los Angeles County, California). They may be compact and homogeneous, or sprawling and diverse. Some counties have responsibilities independent of other levels of government, and most levy their own property or sales tax. But

their autonomy is limited: counties exist largely for the purpose of allocating and coordinating state services among a designated group of cities and towns.

In most counties, a board of commissioners (often called supervisors) is elected to exercise both legislative and executive authority. A chair may be chosen either by the voters or by the commissioners themselves to run meetings and provide general oversight. Each commissioner takes responsibility for one or more areas of government, like land use planning, education, or transportation.

Certain functions are in the purview of other elected officials; for example, there may be a county sheriff to manage public safety, a prosecutor to enforce the law, a clerk to oversee records, and an assessor to administer the collection of taxes. In some regions, voters also elect a county executive to take on a mayor-like role. Typically, a professional county administrator is hired by the commission to fuse all these disparate pieces into a reasonably coherent whole.

The number of county chieftains can make for a fragmented, nebulous chain of command and a challenge for citizens who need to access the system. To add to the confusion, multiple types of judges and magistrates are also elected to preside in county and local courts.

State Government

Across the United States, state governments have a structure more consistent than counties or municipalities. Based on the federal model of separation of powers, there are distinct legislative, executive, and judicial branches designed to check and balance each other.

One or more state lawmakers, or legislators, are chosen in partisan elections to represent distinct, population-based legislative districts. They have the power to make laws and set policies. With the exception of Nebraska, all state legislatures are bicameral: this means citizens elect members of a lower house (generally called a house of representatives, house of delegates, or general assembly) and an upper house known as the state senate.

Many legislatures are part time, convening to vote on bills for only a few months each year. However, the business of state government must move forward whether or not the legislators are in session. For this reason, professional legislative staff play a major role. They provide continuity, stability, and expertise to lawmakers, and a critical point of access to constituents.

In the majority of states, voters also elect state judges, including supreme court justices. State trial and appellate judges hear both civil and criminal cases. The supreme court has the power of judicial review, meaning that it can invalidate laws determined to be inconsistent with the state constitution.

Executive authority rests with the governor and other key officials, including the lieutenant governor, attorney general, treasurer, and auditor. State departments and agencies are in charge of specialized functions like housing, education, labor, and commerce. The governor and lieutenant governor may be the sole executives directly elected by voters; at the other extreme, almost every key agency head may appear on a statewide ballot. Either way, because of the size of the population they serve and the vast scope of their responsibilities, state executive officials are far less accessible than lawmakers. However, their departments maintain staffs whose full-time jobs are to interact with the public. Like legislative staff, they offer wide-open doors onto the corridors of power.

This is the basic lay of the land from the perspective of a political activist, who might hope to snare one of the many public posts available in his or her state. In addition to elected offices and paid administrative jobs, there are hundreds of spots on volunteer advisory boards and influential policymaking bodies. For example, almost every city has its own land use boards, economic development committees, tourism commissions, and culture-oriented citizen panels.

The Workings of a Local Political Campaign

To the outside world, a campaign appears to hum smoothly like a well-oiled machine. But inside the headquarters (in a small-town race, this could mean the candidate's kitchen) it pulses wildly with frenetic, ever-changing activity. Before you consider getting involved in a local political campaign, you should be familiar with what makes it tick.

Whatever the office a candidate is seeking, he or she will have three primary needs: people, information, and money. And no matter how rich his or her campaign becomes in these resources, there is always room for more.

People

A political campaign is time-pressured, labor-intensive, and detail-oriented. In a hometown, low budget contest, most of the work involves scheduling the candidate's time and coordinating volunteers and vendors. In a large-scale, media-driven campaign, there must be staff to manage cash flow, advertising, press relations, and field operations. Just as in running a business, technology has helped speed up the daily grind; but when it comes to making strategic decisions, there is still no substitute for talent and judgment.

What kinds of people add value to a campaign? First, most should be willing—indeed, eager—to help without pay. Media and supply costs will quickly drain the bank book of even a wealthy candidate, leaving little for salaries. But within the pool of volunteers, those with business experience are especially sought after.

Unskilled supporters are always welcome in a campaign; they can take on important nuts-and-bolts tasks like distributing flyers, making phone calls, and erecting lawn signs. But people with knowledge of marketing and management are worth their weight in gold. For example, perhaps you are a small business owner who advertises your product on local radio. If so, you are in a position to recommend the best stations, a great help to a candidate with limited promotion funds. If you juggle schedules and delegate tasks among a dozen employees, you could readily manage campaign volunteers. Do you negotiate with vendors? That skill could bring down the cost of everything from paper to pizza.

Information

Every candidate needs a message. It is his or her brand identity—the way he or she positions himself or herself in the marketplace of competing candidates. Ideally, the message will be positive, distinctive, and memorable. It should also be simple enough to boil down to one catchy sentence.

No one has yet invented a message template that can guarantee success. But experienced politicians know what doesn't work: an empty, vapid collection of words unconnected to local issues. To develop a message that will resonate with voters, all campaigns need solid information about community concerns.

But no candidate can be everywhere, know everyone, or be aware of every problem. While polls can take the pulse of the public, they are unaffordable in many local races. So campaigns must rely on local supporters to be their eyes and ears in the neighborhoods—and to translate the information they gather into action, like writing a speech or arranging a public forum.

Money

Political campaigns cost money, no matter how small the district or how frugal the candidate. Every voter outreach tool has a price: advertising, signs, flyers, phone banks. From clipboards to coffee cups, dozens of incidental expenses add up. A big city or countywide campaign can easily raise and spend more money in six months than many small businesses handle in a year.

Covering the costs himself or herself is increasingly untenable for the average local candidate. Nor is the self-funding option necessarily desirable, as it fails to demonstrate community support. For better or worse, running for office means chasing donations. Every time someone comes through, even with a small amount, it counts as a step toward victory.

Getting Involved: Investors, Participants, and Civic Entrepreneurs

If a well-meaning neighbor claims there is only one effective type of political involvement in your community, he or she is wrong. In every campaign, each approach has pros and cons. Here are the three major options:

Investor

A campaign investor simply writes a check. He or she doesn't take time away from his or her job or risk unpleasant confrontations with supporters of opposing candidates. In fact, a citizen who can afford it will sometimes hedge his or her bets by investing in the campaigns of both sides.

Investor advantage:

- Donations in any amount will always be noticed and appreciated, even in a large-scale campaign.

Investor disadvantages:

- Every political donor becomes part of a mailing list used by other campaigns and partisan organizations.

- It is easy to run afoul of complicated campaign contribution laws.
- No matter how much you donate, a competitor could (and probably will) donate more.
- Under most circumstances, political donations are not tax-deductible.

Participants

Volunteering as an active campaign participant is, of course, more time-intensive than writing a check, but it is also more personal and distinctive. If you hope to be appointed to an advisory board, this is an excellent type of exposure.

Don't discount the fact that every political campaign is an exercise in marketing, management, and finance. Apart from these career-boosting advantages, you can also gain general practice in high-stakes decision making.

Participant advantages:

- You can build lasting relationships with candidates and party activists.
- You may make useful contacts among other participants—officeholders, opinion leaders, and businesspeople.
- You will learn what gets the attention of politicians.
- You will have an opportunity to shape policy debates.
- By helping to elect a good candidate, you will help to improve government.

Participant disadvantages:

- You will make enemies among the political opposition.
- You could be identified as a partisan loyalist, even if you're not.
- To make your participation worthwhile, you will need to commit considerable time to the campaign—probably more than you expect.

Civic Entrepreneur

Civic entrepreneurs differ from traditional political activists. In fact, the term was coined not by political scientists but by economic development experts. Typically, these are local business leaders who recognize a need to foster collaborations with government. When civic entrepreneurs get involved in politics, their primary goal is to win support for ideas that will, in their view, expand markets, jobs, and public-private partnerships. In particular, they welcome innovation, creativity, and risk.

Civic entrepreneur advantages:

- By bringing your ideas to the table, you could drive a new public discourse.
- You could forge new alliances and identify common interests among disparate groups.
- If you wish, you could avoid being identified with a political party.

Civic entrepreneur disadvantage:

- Your sphere of influence would be limited to those candidates and activists who share your perspective and take an interest in your issues.
- Politics isn't for everyone. A meaningful commitment to a local campaign requires an intensity of focus and level of energy you may not be able to spare. Also, political

involvement can damage the reputation of certain professionals, like journalists, scholars, or public opinion pollsters, who are expected to be scrupulously nonpartisan.

- If you are a high-profile decision maker for a hospital, foundation, university, or other nonprofit institution, your partisan alignment could compromise the legal or fundraising status of the organization. If you work in an industry like municipal finance or gambling, your state may prohibit a range of political activities. While state and local public employees are generally free to engage in campaigns (federal workers must comply with special restrictions), they can neither use government resources nor do any political work on government time.

Other reasons to steer clear: You are engaged in litigation with a public body (in this case, ask your attorney.) You fear publicity. Other people in your community have reported bad experiences with local politics. Or you simply find it distasteful.

There are plenty of legitimate concerns. But now you have enough knowledge of the system to make an informed judgment about what is right for you. If you decide to stay away from local politics, at least make a commitment to stay alert—to the issues, the players, and their potential impact on your quality of life.

Danger Signs

For as long as there have been political campaigns, there have been unethical candidates. In fact, ethicists observe that "in practice, political campaigns represent one of the circumstances most likely to bring out the worst in people. Many candidates seem to subscribe to the theory that almost anything is allowable to get elected, because once in office, they will be outstanding public servants" (Nadler and Schulman 2006). So you must protect yourself. As a general rule, you should always say no to a politician who makes you uneasy or a tactic that seems unsavory. More specifically, watch out for candidates who:

- Put the squeeze on you.

  If a candidate pressures you to hire one of his or her friends or steer business to his or her donors—don't. The kind of candidate who takes advantage of his or her supporters will make the kind of public official who looks out for his or her cronies instead of his or her constituents.

  The same goes for a candidate who threatens some kind of retribution, perhaps a boycott of your business, if you fail to donate. Ninety-nine percent of the time, his or her threat will be empty—but if something actually comes of it, you can respond by calling the press, the police, or the opposing candidate.

- Make light of, or ask you to circumvent campaign finance laws.

  Every state has its own raft of restrictions on how and in what amounts you may donate. The category of laws known as "pay-to-play" is designed to stop politicians from giving public jobs or contracts in return for contributions. But there are many other rules with equally important purposes. For example, to foster transparency, campaigns can be required to disclose the names and occupations of every contributor on a state database. This allows citizens, journalists, and other candidates to track who gets support from which interests.

Remember: In campaign finance law, "Everybody does it" or "No one cares" are not acceptable excuses. What seems a minor violation can be a serious offense, and donors may be as culpable as candidates. In general, alarm bells should ring anytime you are strong-armed to donate in cash, or to inappropriately alter a check.

- Expect you to enable dirty tricks.

  Publicly, no one endorses campaign tactics based on deception or misrepresentation. There is no guide to political dirty tricks. But behind closed doors, some candidates argue that the end (winning the election) justifies the means (dubious activities). They make a deliberate decision to jettison truthfulness and fairness.

  Don't enable them. If they tell you that their tactics are legal, they may be right: political advertising, for example, can make representations and promises that would never pass muster in ads for cereal or soap. But legal or not, shady tactics corrode the electoral process and undermine the public's faith in local politics.

The techniques devised by the political underworld are limited only by their imaginations (and budgets). Here are two of the more common types that you could be asked to fund or facilitate:

(1) Push polls

A political poll is a legitimate research tool. A push poll is a fraudulent form of telemarketing, designed to dish dirt on a candidate under the guise of research.

Unlike genuine voter surveys, push polls are typically very short (only one or two questions) and extremely negative toward a candidate or issue. The caller avoids naming the source of the call and will not explain how the information is being used or by whom. He asks questions like these: Would you vote for Betty Smith if you knew she abandoned her illegitimate child? Do you support Tom White even though he has been accused of extortion?

Even when there is a shred of truth to such slurs, the push poll is a deliberate attempt to distort and sensationalize them. For instance, Tom White may indeed have been accused of lawbreaking. But the criminal complaint could have been filed by his opponent, based on fabricated evidence. Bottom line: If a candidate tells you he or she needs a donation to pay for a poll, make sure it is a real one.

(2) Cyber-deception

Technology has enabled a new generation of tricksters. Do not allow your computers (or your funds) to be used for online shenanigans. These might include campaign e-mails disguised to look like they originated from a government office or a nonpartisan group; "phishing" messages that furtively obtain voters' personal data; and anonymous or fake-name blog posts.

- Encourage you to lie or coerce others.

  You could be asked to recruit supporters under false pretenses, lie to vendors, make dubious statements to the press, or coerce others to do so. Just say no.

- Have a bad reputation.

If a candidate has a good name in the community, it speaks well of his or her ethics. The opposite is also true: a candidate with a rascal's reputation probably has earned it.

References

Bearse, P. (2004). *We, the People*. Lafayette, LA: Alpha Publishers.

Cooper, M. (2000, May 1). "In Nassau County, a Small Election Will Settle the Political Balance." *New York Times*. www.nytimes.com. Accessed June 6, 2010.

Ginsberg, A. (2007, February 24). "3-Time Loser Norman Guilty." *New York Post*. www .nypost.com. Accessed July 13, 2010.

Grey, L. (1999). *How to Win a Local Election*. New York: M. Evans.

Nadler, J., and M. Schulman. (2006). "Campaign Ethics." Markkula Center for Applied Ethics at Santa Clara University. Accessed July 21, 2010. www.scu.edu/ethics.

Percival, G., M. Johnson, and M. Neiman. (2009). "Representation and Local Policy: Relating County-Level Public Opinion to Policy Outputs." *Political Research Quarterly* 62, no. 1: 20.

Rae-Dupree, J. (2007, December 30). "Innovative Minds Don't Think Alike." *New York Times Week in Review*. Accessed May 20, 2010. www.nytimes.com.

Walsh, D. (2006, April 9). "A Political Army in Need of a Few Good Soldiers." *Newark Star Ledger*. Accessed June 1, 2010. www.starledger.com.

The History of Campaign Finance Reform in the United States*

Benjamin T. Brickner

> There are two important things in politics. The first is money, and I can't remember what the second one is.
>
> —*Marcus Alonzo Hanna*

Introduction

For as long as there have been elections in the United States, there has been debate about how candidates should finance their campaigns. For as long as there have been campaigns to be financed, there has been debate about campaign finance reform. This issue is as old as the republic itself, predating such acronymous reform efforts as FECA and BCRA, the Watergate, Teapot Dome, and Whiskey Ring financing scandals, and even the steadily increasing amount of spending that has made campaign finance reform a mainstream topic of civic discourse today. At the heart of the debate lay tensions between economic inequality and the principle of one-person, one-vote; between political elitism and representative government; and between campaign finance and First Amendment protection of political speech. Running throughout the history of campaign finance reform is a struggle among these competing interests. It is an ongoing conversation about the nature of American democracy and the permissible means of obtaining elected office.

In America's third century, candidates for elected office require ever-increasing sums of money to wage competitive campaigns. For example, congressional candidates elected in 2010 raised $2.1 million on average (Center for Responsive Politics 2012c). Freshmen members of the House seeking reelection raised on average $2.0 million—$2,700 *every* day of their first term in office (Center for Responsive Politics 2012b). Unless independently wealthy, each of these elected officials relied upon private actors—individuals, political parties, and political action committees—for their campaign funding. A public official-private actor relationship, without something more, is not necessarily troubling. When a candidate becomes *dependent* upon this relationship to attain or keep his or her office, however, the potential

---

*This chapter was adapted from Brickner, B. T., with N. Mueller. (2008). *Clean Elections: Public Financing in Six States including New Jersey's Pilot Projects*. New Brunswick, NJ: Eagleton Institute of Politics.

for corruption is apparent. Private financing of public campaigns provides well-funded interests with potentially greater access and greater influence within our government. These special interests often diverge from the broader public interest all elected officials have sworn to uphold. Public officials who are beholden to private contributors must navigate a host of conflicts, and experience tells us these conflicts are not easily resolved. At very least, large amounts of private money in public campaigns create the appearance of impropriety, casting a shadow over public service and fueling skepticism of our government.

Even before the U.S. Constitution was ratified, founding father James Madison perceived special interest influence in democratic government as "adverse to the rights of other citizens [as well as] the permanent and aggregate interests of the community" (Madison 1787). Madison wrestled with this conflict, finally conceding that the same civic rights to be protected by the new government also would allow special interests to thrive. Eliminating the one would entail eliminating the other. The impracticality of Madison's fanciful alternative, "giving to every citizen the same opinions," anticipated the chronic tension between public and private interests. If the danger of special interest influence could not be eliminated without also imperiling core democratic principles, Madison concluded the danger could at best be contained.

Two centuries before the Watergate scandal inaugurated the modern era of campaign finance reform, the Framers already had identified the movement's competing concerns: personal liberty and integrity of the electoral process. Though the scope of government activity has changed dramatically since the nation's founding, the fundamental question remains unchanged: how can campaigns and elections be insulated from the corrupting influence of private interests without jeopardizing individual freedom? The history of campaign finance reform reflects an ongoing effort to reconcile these competing interests.

Article I, Section 4 of the U.S. Constitution assigns to individual states the responsibility for prescribing the "Times, Places and Manner of holding Elections for [U.S.] Senators and Representatives," while the Congress is permitted to "at any time by Law make or alter such Regulations." Reflecting 18th-century respect for state sovereignty and home rule, the Constitution is silent on nonfederal elections, which are administered primarily by the states. While this arrangement of shared responsibility has resulted in a patchwork of election law nationwide, it also has allowed each state to experiment with differing electoral methods and reform measures, creating what U.S. Supreme Court Justice Louis Brandeis described as a "laboratory" of reform (*New State Ice Co. v. Liebmann*, 1932, at 311). This characterization proved especially accurate during the 19th and early 20th centuries, when the nascent campaign finance reform movement was led by a handful of states undertaking progressive and, in some cases, quite radical reform.

It was not until passage of the Voting Rights Act of 1965 that the federal government began to overshadow states in the regulation of elections to public office. Watergate followed nine years later, sparking additional reform efforts, particularly in the Congress. Campaign finance reform has remained a national issue ever since, even while many states continued to enact measures limiting campaign contributions, requiring additional disclosure of campaign expenditures, and providing for public financing for political campaigns.

Reform has come slowly and incrementally as lawmakers and judges struggle to reconcile wealth inequality with political equality without undermining individual rights enshrined by the Constitution. Several recent U.S. Supreme Court decisions have emphasized a connection between campaign spending and constitutionally protected political speech (see, e.g., *McCutcheon v. Fed. Election Comm'n*, 2014; *Ariz. Free Enter. Club's Freedom Club PAC v. Bennett*, 2011; *Citizens United v. Fed. Election Comm'n*, 2010; and *Davis v. Fed. Election Comm'n*, 2008). Their effect has complicated current efforts at reform, which if not carefully targeted to deter actual corruption or the appearance thereof, risk being struck down as unconstitutional.

Given the length of its history, campaign finance reform may be seen as an endless, almost Sisyphean task. As one source of private funding is regulated or prohibited, a new source often quickly fills the vacuum, leading the Supreme Court in 2003 to quip that "[m]oney, like water, will always find an outlet" (*McConnell v. Fed. Election Comm'n*, 2003, at 224). Indeed, much of the history of campaign finance regulation has been reactionary, as reformers seek to plug the latest loopholes. But while campaign finance issues have enjoyed elevated prominence in the decades since Watergate, the reform movement began much earlier. The remainder of this chapter highlights federal and state campaign finance reform efforts from the 19th century to the present.

Early Federal Reform

Modern campaign practices scarcely resemble those that prevailed when the nation's first federal offices were established. In America's first century, it was accepted and generally understood that the political party in power would spoil its supporters with lucrative government contracts and official positions in the burgeoning federal bureaucracy.

Remnants of the spoils system exist today in the broad powers of executive appointment and legislative earmarking. Presidents and governors routinely appoint members of their political party to fill cabinets and executive agencies. The list of private firms awarded public contracts often resembles the list of contributors to successful campaigns for office. Modern patronage, however, lacks the overt corruption of extortion and bribery typical of old. In 18th-century America, appointed positions often were awarded to political loyalists, with only secondary regard for experience or competence. In return, these appointees were assessed fixed portions of their salaries, payable to the party responsible for their employment. These assessments, legal in their time, were the primary means of funding for political parties.

Organized resistance to this arrangement did not emerge until the 1830s, just as national political organizations and party nominating conventions were emerging. In 1837, Congressman John Bell, a member of the minority Whig Party, introduced a bill to prohibit assessments of patronage positions. This was among the earliest federal campaign finance reform measures (Mutch 2002 at 35). With opposition Democrats in control of Congress, the White House and most political patronage, Bell's bill was short-lived. In 1840, substantially similar legislation was introduced in the wake of scandal involving U.S. customs workers. That bill also went nowhere.

The first federal law to regulate assessments was enacted 27 years later as a last-minute amendment to a navy appropriations bill. Narrow in scope but bold in aspiration, the provision declared that "no officer or employee of the government shall require or request any workingman in any navy yard to contribute or pay any money for political purposes, nor shall any workingman be removed or discharged for political opinion" (Navy Appropriations Act of 1867). Widespread corruption during the Ulysses S. Grant administration, including graft (e.g., the Crédit Mobilier of America scandal of 1872) and diversion of tax revenue for political purposes (e.g., the Whiskey Ring of 1875), forced the issue of patronage again. Although the president never was implicated in any wrongdoing,

Ulysses S. Grant, as an acrobat, on trapeze third term, holding on to whiskey ring and Navy ring, with strap corruption in his mouth, and holding up other "acrobats." (Library of Congress)

his failure to denounce the malfeasance around him, combined with a legendary reputation for placing friends in high government office, further weakened Grant's tenuous political standing. To pacify critics within his own party, Grant agreed to prohibit assessment of all government officials, except those appointed by the president with the advice and consent of the Senate (Legislative, Executive, and Judicial Appropriations Act of 1876).

Grant's successor Rutherford B. Hayes took the additional step of issuing an executive order banning assessments altogether. In the same order, Hayes also eliminated political party affiliation requirements for government officials. Perhaps in deference to the Constitution's First Amendment, Hayes added, "[officers'] right to vote and to express their views on public questions . . . is not denied, provided it does not interfere with the discharge of their official duties" (Executive Order of June 22, 1877).

The terms of Hayes's executive order later were written into statutory law as the Pendleton Civil Service Act of 1883. Among the first comprehensive reform measures in political financing, Pendleton was in part a reaction to the 1881 assassination of President James A. Garfield by a disgruntled office-seeker who had been denied a government job. The act categorically prohibited assessments on the salaries of public servants, eliminating most political party funding and curtailing much of the associated corruption. The act also established the Civil Service Commission to administer competitive merit examinations and award employment based on professional ability, rather than political affiliation. Many government jobs were thereafter classified within the new civil service system and removed from the patronage system.

Ulysses Simpson Grant is best remembered for his military leadership during the Civil War and for the corruption that characterized his presidential administration during America's Gilded Age. (Library of Congress)

While assessments no longer were available as a source of political party funding, corporate contributions remained unregulated. Partisan fund-raisers wasted little time in adapting their strategies to take advantage of this omission. Shortly after Pendleton was enacted, political operatives turned to wealthy business owners, demanding a share of their corporate profits in return for preferential, or even just adequate, treatment by their government (Ansolabehere, Gerber, and Snyder 2001). These new assessments quickly became a principal source of funding for political parties, filling the patronage vacuum. In return, corporate contributors and their associates were awarded unclassified jobs, government business, or both. With the federal government's role in economic and trade policy expanding rapidly during the late-1800s, favorable consideration from the Congress and regulators was becoming increasingly profitable for business and industry. Political operatives were not shy in exploiting the new arrangement. In 1900, the chair of the Republican National Committee contacted several large corporations, suggesting that each "pay according to its stake in the general prosperity of the country and according to its special interest in a region in which a large amount of expensive canvassing had to be done" (Croly 1912, 325). Wealthy and generous interests enjoyed a closer, more productive relationship with their government, while shouldering the growing cost of political campaigns and party establishments. Such bold solicitations, however, only hastened the sentiment that this arrangement was corrupting the integrity of government.

In 1900, President William McKinley spent nearly $7 million, then a record-breaking amount, to defeat William Jennings Bryan, whom he outspent 10-to-1. This amount is equivalent to about $196 million in 2012 dollars, or about one-quarter of the amount spent by Barack Obama during his successful 2008 election campaign. Responding to the remarkable sums spent during the 1896 and 1900 presidential campaigns, as well as to growing appearances of impropriety, several states banned corporate contributions to political campaigns (Thayer 1974, 50). Congress did not consider doing the same until several years later when President Theodore Roosevelt, embarrassed by allegations of quid pro quo during his 1904 campaign, included the reform policy in his domestic agenda. Roosevelt's commitment to the issue was evidenced by its appearance in three consecutive State of the Union messages (Roosevelt 1904, 1905, 1906). In 1905, the president told Congress "[t]here is no enemy of free government more dangerous and none so insidious as the corruption of the electorate" and recommended "the enactment of a law directed against bribery and corruption in Federal elections" (Roosevelt 1905). Congress, however, remained unmoved. In 1906, Roosevelt took the additional step of calling for specific reform measures directed at elections for both federal and state office, proposing that "[a]ll contributions by corporations to any political committee or for any political purpose should be forbidden by law" (Roosevelt 1906). Again, Congress was unmoved. The following year, however, a coalition of public interest groups, newspaper editorial boards, and public officials joined in Roosevelt's call for reform (Corrado 2005, 12). Stirred to action by a corruption-weary public, Congress in 1907 adopted the Political Contributions by Corporations Act (also known as the Tillman Act) forbidding "any corporation organized by authority of any laws of Congress, to make a money contribution in connection with any election to any political office." Notwithstanding its broad language, Tillman was far from comprehensive. Most businesses then, as now, were formed under state law and thus were unregulated by Tillman. A second provision, though applicable to all corporations, was limited to campaigns for federal office. Most corporations still were able to contribute to state and local political party organizations and candidates, which then could transfer funds to their national counterparts. Nonetheless, the law marked a pivotal moment in the history of campaign finance reform. Just as Pendleton had done by creating the civil service system 24 years earlier, Tillman created new precedent by articulating a public interest in regulating corporate campaign contributions.

With yet another source of campaign funding checked by government regulation, reformers turned their attention to campaign finance disclosure. Until 1910, campaigns and political party committees were not compelled to reveal their financial transactions. Receipts and disbursements remained secret, and the public remained unaware of who was giving money to whom and for what activities those funds were used. Accordingly, political organizations and their benefactors operated with little oversight. This changed upon passage of the Publicity of Political

Contributions Act (also known as the Publicity Act) in 1910. As amended the following year (Publicity Act Amendments of 1911), the act required all federal campaign committees to report their finances both before and after primary and general elections. The act broke additional new ground by establishing spending limits on federal campaigns and allowing states discretion to set lower limits. Michigan, for example, established a primary election spending limit equal to one-quarter of the salary for the federal office sought (Corrupt Practice Act of 1913). In 1921, U.S. senator Truman Handy Newberry, a wealthy Michigan businessman and former secretary of the navy who had defeated automaker Henry Ford for the Senate in 1918, was convicted under the act for exceeding this limit by 25 fold. When the case reached the U.S. Supreme Court later that year, however, the law was invalidated on the ground that Congress did not have authority to regulate nominating contests and, by extension, primary election contests (*Newberry v. United States*, 1921). What remained of the federal Publicity Act included inadequate penalties for violations. Although Congress was entrusted with enforcing the act, thereafter it rarely did so. The *Newberry* decision was reinterpreted and effectively overturned in 1941 by *United States v. Classic*. Congress finally reasserted its authority to regulate primary contests in 1971 with its passage of the Federal Election Campaign Act.

By the 1920s, several factors led to a significant growth in campaign spending. In 1913, the Seventeenth Amendment established direct elections for U.S. senators, establishing an additional class of popular campaigns to be funded. In 1920, the Nineteenth Amendment granted women the right to vote, establishing an additional class of voters to be swayed. At the same time, primary elections began replacing elite conventions as the nominating tool of choice, establishing yet another class of popular campaigns.

In 1925, Congress amended and substantially strengthened the Publicity Act by requiring quarterly reports from all interstate campaign committees and establishing a reporting threshold of $100 (equivalent to about $1,300 in 2013 dollars) (Federal Corrupt Practices Act of 1925). Consistent with the Supreme Court's ruling four years earlier, the new regulation excluded primary election contests. Enforcement authority once again was entrusted to Congress, but because the act lacked an effective regulatory structure, its provisions went largely unenforced. No candidate for federal office was ever prosecuted under the Publicity Act after 1925, yet the act remained operative as the primary campaign finance law until the 1970s.

With the New Deal political realignment of 1932, Democrats found themselves in power following a 16-year hiatus. Republicans, on the other hand, were out of power and thus at a significant campaign finance disadvantage. Furthermore, with many of President Franklin Delano Roosevelt's New Deal policies being pro-worker, labor unions quickly developed into a potent political force that overwhelmingly supported the Democratic Party (see, e.g., the National Labor Relations Act of 1935, giving laborers the right to unionize). While the Tillman Act barred corporate campaign contributions, labor union contributions, the emerging Democratic Party lifeblood, remained unregulated. This was not the case for long, however. In response to unions' escalating political activity and a succession of labor strikes perceived as detrimental to World War II mobilization efforts, the Congress in 1943 enacted the War Labor Disputes Act, extending Tillman's provisions to organized labor (War Labor Disputes Act of 1943). Notably, the act was approved over President Roosevelt's veto and was designed by the Democratic Congress as a temporary measure that would expire shortly after the war's end. The Republican majority elected to Congress in 1946 revived the ban by enacting the Labor-Management Relations Act, this time over President Truman's veto (Labor-Management Relations Act of 1947). The renewed federal rules prohibited not only corporations but also labor unions from using any portion of their general funds for political purposes. Both direct contributions and indirect expenditures in support of a political party or campaign were restricted. While the Labor-Management Relations Act's regulation of direct contributions remains in place today, its restriction of independent expenditures was largely overturned by the Supreme Court in 2010 in its *Citizens United v. Federal Election Commission* decision.

Just as partisan fund-raisers had adjusted to the new reality created by Pendleton's civil service reform, organized labor quickly developed a new channel for their political activity during the wartime prohibition on union campaign contributions. In 1943, the Political Action Committee ("PAC") was conceived as a vehicle for campaign contributions outside the scope of the War Labor Disputes Act, and later the Labor-Management Relations Act. By soliciting funds independent of union dues, labor PACs were able to sidestep the spirit, if not the letter of the law, which had prohibited only the use of general treasury funds. Labor unions were the first to exploit this loophole and within a decade, more than a dozen PACs were active. Corporations followed suit in the early 1960s (Corrado 2005, 18).

The growing prominence of political action committees coincided with a broader shift in the nature of political campaigns. The increasing reach of radio and television media in the postwar era fueled dramatic growth in campaign spending. Aggregate campaign expenditures by congressional candidates nearly doubled between 1956 and 1968 with media expenditures accounting for much of the growth (Alexander 1976b, 78; Congressional Quarterly 1982, 8). In 1956, broadcast media expenses amounted to 6.3 percent of total campaign spending. By 1968, this figure was nearly 20 percent. As the cost of mounting viable and competitive campaigns continued to climb, members of Congress grew worried they soon would be unable to raise the funds necessary to wage multimedia reelection campaigns. This fear was amplified by the threat of a new class of candidates for public office: millionaires willing to part with substantial personal wealth to win elected office.

In the 13 decades since Congressman Bell first proposed legislation to regulate campaign financing, congressional action on the issue was almost exclusively reactionary. The Pendleton, Tillman, and Publicity Acts each were enacted in response to political scandal. Relevant provisions of the Labor-Management Relations and the War Labor Disputes Acts were drafted in response to political inequity and wartime necessity. With campaign costs rising and incumbents devoting increasing time and energy to the inelegant task of fund-raising, Congress in the 1970s turned to proactive measures.

The Federal Election Campaign Act ("FECA") of 1971, the foundation of modern campaign finance regulation, marked Congress's return to the issue after a 25-year hiatus. Motivated by a fear of self-financed candidates and a sense that media expenses were primarily to blame for rising campaign costs, Congress enacted FECA to cap media expenditures and limit the amount candidates could contribute to their own campaigns. FECA also imposed ceilings on individual contributions to candidates and party committees, and on monetary transfers between political committees. The act also strengthened reporting and disclosure requirements for all candidates and political committees, requiring itemization of all contributions greater than $100.

Despite its far-reaching provisions, FECA failed to achieve its principal goal of controlling campaign spending. While the upward trend in media expenditures briefly stabilized after FECA's passage, the rise in overall spending continued. Despite new contribution ceilings and self-financing limits, total campaign spending increased more than 40 percent between 1968 and 1972 (Alexander 1976b, 78). And although disclosure and reporting requirements were in place during the 1972 presidential campaign, enforcement was inconsistent at best. One explanation for FECA's failure was the absence of an oversight agency empowered to administer the act and enforce its provisions. This absence was short-lived.

Watergate-Era Reform

In June 1972, five men were caught attempting to wiretap the Democratic National Committee headquarters in Washington's Watergate Hotel. Several of the burglars later were discovered to have ties to the White House and in particular to Richard Nixon's Committee for the Re-Election of the President (better known by its unintended acronym, CREEP). The ensuing investigation spanned two years, culminating in the president's resignation in August 1974. As details of the break-in emerged, a vivid portrait of routine campaign finance abuse appeared, including corporate contributions laundered through foreign banks and used to finance clandestine campaign operations.

Richard Nixon says goodbye with a victorious salute to his staff members outside the White House as he boards a helicopter after resigning the presidency on August 9, 1974. (AP Photo)

Watergate revealed just how inadequate the existing campaign finance law was. Months before Nixon's resignation, the need for additional reform had become clear. In March 1974, Congress began work on what eventually would become an ambitious and comprehensive revision of FECA, which then was only three years old. Enacted days after Nixon's resignation, the Federal Election Campaign Act Amendments of 1974 included stricter disclosure rules, compelled additional reporting before and after Election Day, and restricted candidates to a single campaign committee for raising and spending campaign contributions. The 1974 amendments also capped individual campaign contributions, limits that would remain unchanged for almost 30 years. The original ceiling on media-related expenditures was abandoned in favor of a ceiling on total expenditures scaled by constituency size and the office sought. Political parties and their campaign committees also were subject to limits on independent expenditures that were coordinated with a particular candidate's campaign.

Perhaps most important, the 1974 amendments created an independent, bipartisan Federal Election Commission ("FEC") to administer the revised law and enforce its provisions. Correcting fundamental weaknesses in the original law, the FEC was empowered to collect financial disclosure reports, conduct investigations and audits, issue subpoenas, and assess civil penalties for noncompliance. Furthermore, the FEC's authority extended to both primary and general election cycles.

With the FECA amendments, the Congress finally implemented the nation's first federal public financing program. Initially proposed in 1962 by President John F. Kennedy's Commission on Campaign Costs (Executive Order of Nov. 10, 1963; President's Commission on Campaign Costs 1962), the idea had received little support from Congress. In 1966, Congress took a tentative first step by attaching a public financing rider to an unrelated bill. This Presidential Election Campaign Fund Act proposed to supplement traditional private funds with public dollars. Because the program did not also address private fund-raising, which was perceived by many to be the true source of public corruption, congressional opposition to the act was widespread. As a result, the program never was funded and implementation was delayed indefinitely.

The FECA amendments of 1974 ended the delay, combining public funding with other policies designed to address the corrosive effects of private fund-raising in presidential elections. During the primary election cycle, major party candidates first were required to cross a modest private fund-raising threshold in at least 20 states. The first $250 of each private contribution then would be matched by public funding once the candidate pledged to keep overall spending below a specified level. During the general election cycle, major party nominees were eligible to receive a $20 million grant upon pledging not to raise or solicit any additional funds from private sources. The Democratic and Republican national committees were eligible to receive $2 million for their nominating conventions. Third-party presidential candidates and their national committees also were eligible for public funding, though these amounts were smaller and in proportion to the party's vote-share during the previous presidential election cycle. The new law also authorized modest tax deductions and credits for individuals who made campaign contributions to political candidates. By easing the fund-raising burden on presidential candidates and their national party committees, the nation's first federal public funding program sought to address the concern that rising campaign costs had contributed to the corruption exposed by Watergate.

In addition to reforming the campaign finance system, the 1974 amendments sought to encourage wider social engagement in campaigns and elections. Despite the politically expansive Seventeenth and Nineteenth amendments, by the 1970s fewer than one in eight adults reported contributing any money to political candidates or parties (Alexander 1995, 8). The public financing funding mechanism, a voluntary federal income tax check-off, created a simple, cost-free means of taxpayer participation in the electoral process. New tax deductions and tax credits provided additional incentive for individuals to contribute to candidate campaigns. By increasing overall participation and interest in the political process, these initiatives were intended to increase candidate contact with voters, particularly with those who previously were isolated from national campaigns.

As controversial as it was comprehensive, several of FECA's provisions promptly were subjected to judicial scrutiny. These challenges resulted first in *Buckley v. Valeo*, a landmark U.S. Supreme Court decision in 1976 that rivals Watergate for its impact on modern campaign finance law. In *Buckley*, the Court concluded that campaign contributions and expenditures both were expressions of political speech protected by the First Amendment. FECA's expenditure limits were deemed to impose unjustifiably "direct and substantial restraints on the quantity of political speech" and were accordingly invalidated (*Buckley v. Valeo*, 1976, at 39). The Court struck down restrictions on candidate self-financing on similar grounds (*Buckley v. Valeo*, 1976, at 52). The Court also invalidated limits on independent expenditures, including those made by a political party, finding them impermissibly vague and unconnected to "the governmental interest in preventing corruption and the appearance of corruption" (*Buckley v. Valeo*, 1976, at 45). In particular, the Court noted that only those expenditures that "in express terms advocate the election or defeat of a clearly identified candidate" could be restricted (*Buckley v. Valeo*, 1976, at 44).

Upon balancing the competing interests, however, the Court upheld FECA's contribution limits, finding that they created only a "limited effect upon First Amendment freedoms" justified by a "basic governmental interest in safeguarding the integrity of the electoral process" (*Buckley v. Valeo*, 1976, at 29, 58). The Court also upheld FECA's provisions for public funding of primary elections, nominating conventions and general elections. Here, the Court found that elimination of "the improper influence of large private contributions [furthered] a significant governmental interest" to which public financing was well suited (*Buckley v. Valeo*, 1976, at 96). The Court stressed that acceptance of public funding and its associated restrictions was voluntary, noting that traditional avenues of campaign fund-raising remained open to all candidates (*Buckley v. Valeo*, 1976, at 95). Accordingly, the Court concluded that public financing was "an appropriate means of relieving major-party Presidential candidates from the rigors of soliciting private contributions" (*Buckley v. Valeo*, 1976, at 96).

Following *Buckley*, the growth of private money in political campaigns continued, checked only by FECA's ceiling on individual contributions and voluntary acceptance of fund-raising restrictions associated with public funding of presidential campaigns. The FECA provisions that survived *Buckley* have provided the foundation for most subsequent reform efforts at the federal and state levels.

Modern Federal Reform

Just as the Labor-Management Relations Act gave rise to the political action committee, *Buckley* encouraged new means of circumventing FECA's campaign finance regulations. *Buckley's* holding that only express political advocacy could be regulated created a legal loophole for *soft money*: funds that are not contributed directly to a candidate's campaign and technically are not used to advocate the election or defeat of a particular candidate. (By contrast, the term *hard money* is used to describe the strictly regulated individual contributions made directly to a candidate for elected office.)

The natural repositories of soft money were the national party committees and independent PACs. Wealthy donors could thus contribute vast amounts to these entities, legally independent of individual candidates, which then could spend these funds on such party-building activities as voter registration and get-out-the-vote drives. These largely unregulated contributions fueled much of the subsequent growth in campaign spending. Between 1992 and 2002, soft money expenditures rose nearly six-fold to a record $496 million, a trend that was not limited to national party organizations (U.S. Fed. Election Comm'n, Mar. 20, 2003). State parties reported an equally impressive increase in soft money expenditures during the same period (La Raja and Jarvis-Shean 2001, 6).

In a series of FEC rulings during the late-1970s, permissible uses of soft money were expanded to include *issue advertisements*: communications intended to comply with the unusually specific language of *Buckley*. In a footnote, the Court had explained that "express advocacy" included ads with such language as "vote for," "elect" and "support" (*Buckley v. Valeo*, 1976, at 44 n.52). The Court's precision here had the unintended effect of aiding party organizations and other interest groups in blurring the distinction between express advocacy and genuine issue advocacy. By avoiding the Supreme Court's buzz words, an ad that otherwise resembled express advocacy could plausibly be considered an unregulated issue advertisement under *Buckley*.

By the 1990s, rapid growth in soft money expenditures and proliferation of unregulated issue ads led some members of Congress to advocate a new attempt at campaign finance reform. These efforts culminated in 2002 with the Bipartisan Campaign Reform Act ("BCRA," also known as McCain-Feingold), which effectively abolished soft money. The legislation initially faced strong resistance in both Republican-led houses of Congress. Opposition to BCRA subsided in late

2001, however, after several members of Congress discovered their campaigns had accepted money from the Enron Corporation, which then was embroiled in a massive accounting scandal and teetering on the brink of the largest bankruptcy in American history.

BCRA was signed into law in March 2002 and became effective the following November, one day after the midterm elections, and included a complete ban on soft money contributions to party national committees. To compensate for the elimination of this pillar of political fund-raising, BCRA also increased limits on *hard money* contributions—those made to candidates directly—from $1,000 to $2,000 and indexed these to inflation. The act also narrowed the issue advocacy loophole by requiring that these ads be paid for with hard money contributions under the new limits. Anticipating a new regulatory loophole, BCRA further specified how state and local party organizations could use federally regulated funds that were transferred to them from national party organizations.

Like the FECA amendments before it, BCRA promptly was challenged in court. In *McConnell v. Federal Election Commission*, the Supreme Court in 2003 found that BCRA's key elements passed constitutional muster, leaving the law largely intact. The Court distinguished soft money contributions as less essential to protected political speech than hard money, which is contributed to a candidate directly. And since BCRA primarily regulated soft money, the act's cumulative restriction of political speech was deemed constitutionally acceptable. The regulatory scheme was upheld as being "closely drawn" to advance important governmental interests in preventing "the actual corruption threatened by large financial contributions and the eroding of public confidence in the electoral process through the appearance of corruption" (*McConnell v. Fed. Election Comm'n*, 2003, at 136). Responding to claims that BCRA was broader than necessary to protect these interests, the Court reflected upon the mixed record of campaign finance reform, observing that "money, like water, will always find an outlet" (*McConnell v. Fed. Election Comm'n*, 2003, at 224). The wide reach of BCRA, the Court concluded, was justified to prevent "circumvention of otherwise valid contribution limits" (*McConnell v. Fed. Election Comm'n*, 2003, at 185).

BCRA, like its predecessor FECA, did little to slow the growth of campaign fund-raising. Table 1 summarizes post-BCRA increases in campaign receipts by organization type.

By comparison, the Consumer Price Index, a common measure of price inflation, rose only 36 percent between 2000 and 2012 (U.S. Bureau of Labor Statistics).

BCRA also did not alter the presidential public financing system, which in 2000 already was losing appeal as nonparticipating candidates began raising private funds in excess of what the public system provided. In 2004, for the first time since FECA made public financing available three decades earlier, both major party presidential candidates opted not to participate during the primary election, choosing instead to raise and spend private funds. In 2012, also for the first time, both major party presidential candidates opted not to participate during either the primary or general election, thereby rendering the program completely unutilized by the major party nominees during that cycle.

Table 1

Committee Type	Last Pre-BCRA Election Cycle (in million) (1999–2000 or 2001–02)	2011–12 Election Cycle (in million)	Increase (in percentage)
Presidential Candidates	$579	$1,380	138
Congressional Candidates	$979	$1,879	192
Political Party Committees	$1,074	$1,618	51
Political Action Committees (PACs and Super PACs)	$714	$2,259	334

Source: U.S. Federal Election Commission, Apr. 19, 2013; U.S. Federal Election Commission, Campaign Finance Statistics.

BCRA also did not regulate so-called *527 Groups*, which preexisted BCRA but did not gain national attention until the 2004 election cycle when 527 Group *Swift Boat Veterans for Truth* aired provocative advertisements questioning presidential candidate John F. Kerry's Vietnam War service record. Named for the section of U.S. Tax Code under which they are organized, 527 Groups are largely unregulated by the FEC and state election commissions and are not subject to the same contribution limits as ordinary PACs. While these organizations cannot contribute directly to or in coordination with federal candidates, they still can advance a political agenda through issue advertisements and direct mail, operating outside many of BCRA's restrictions. In 2004, national 527 Groups raised $433 million, exceeding traditional PAC fund-raising for the first time (Center for Responsive Politics 2012a).

McConnell was not the last judicial review of BCRA. In June 2007, the Supreme Court reexamined several of its provisions, chipping away at *McConnell's* pro-BCRA ruling by creating a significant new exception for issue advertisements (*Fed. Election Comm'n v. Wis. Right to Life, Inc.*, 2007). Declaring, "enough is enough," the Court's then-newest members signaled that future campaign finance reform efforts would be examined with greater skepticism (*Fed. Election Comm'n v. Wis. Right to Life, Inc.*, 2007, at 464). Court watchers wondering what this would mean did not need to wait long. A June 2008 decision of the Supreme Court invalidated BCRA's provision increasing contribution limits on candidates who faced self-financed opponents (*Davis v. Fed. Election Comm'n*, 2008). The Court determined that variable fund-raising restrictions posed an impermissible burden on self-financed candidates' First Amendment right to robustly advocate their own election.

Citizens United and Beyond

Then in 2010 came the decision that still defines the contours of campaign finance today. The Supreme Court in *Citizens United v. Federal Election Commission* struck down limits on independent expenditures made by organizations that accept corporate and labor union contributions. So long as these organizations' advertisements avoided the *Buckley* buzz words ("vote for," "elect," "support," etc.), they

John Kerry with his crewmates during the Vietnam War. (AP Photo/Kerry-Edwards 2004, File)

remained outside the reach of existing campaign finance regulation. The Court concluded that independent expenditures, "including those made by corporations, do not give rise to corruption or the appearance of corruption" that would constitutionally permit their restriction (*Citizens United v. Fed. Election Comm'n*, 2010, at 909). On similar grounds, the Court weakened or overturned its own long-standing precedent to decide that corporations and labor unions also could make direct expenditures, so long as they were independent of a candidate's campaign (*Citizens United v. Fed. Election Comm'n*, 2010, at 913).

As of this writing, the impact of *Citizens United* has yet been fully realized, but it likely will be considerable. Shortly after *Citizens United*, a federal appeals court expanded the decision's reach by holding that organizations that make only independent expenditures also were not subject to the spending limits and reporting requirements imposed by campaign finance law (*SpeechNow.org v. Fed. Election Comm'n*, 2010). And in 2014, the Supreme Court struck down aggregate contribution limits (i.e., caps on total contributions made to all recipients in the same election cycle) as violating the First Amendment (*McCutcheon v. Fed. Election Comm'n, 2014*). Taken together, these decisions dramatically altered the regulatory landscape and gave rise to the latest campaign finance phenomenon: independent expenditure-only committees, more commonly known as *Super PACs*. These organizations can raise and spend unlimited funds from individuals or corporations, so long as their expenditures are uncoordinated with a candidate's campaign.

During the 2012 election cycle, more than 1,250 Super PACs collectively raised $824 million, of which $374 million was spent in connection with the presidential election (U.S. Fed. Election Comm'n, Campaign Finance Statistics, Political Action Committee (PAC); U.S. Fed. Election Comm'n, Apr. 19, 2013). By comparison, President Barack Obama and Republican nominee Mitt Romney raised $1.38 billion during the same period (U.S. Fed. Election Comm'n, Apr. 19, 2013). The Supreme Court's recent decision in *McCutcheon* likely will accelerate increases in spending among Super PACs, as well as national candidate and political party campaign committees.

The Court in *McConnell* may have stated the obvious when explaining it was "under no illusion that BCRA will be the last congressional statement on the matter [of campaign finance reform]" (*McConnell v. Fed. Election Comm'n*, 2003, at 224). The obsolescence of the presidential public financing program and the proliferation of unregulated 527 Groups and Super PACs virtually guarantee that Congress is not yet finished in this area. Notwithstanding recent landmark judicial decisions, what remains of BCRA represents the state of federal campaign finance regulation today, and it is within this framework that individual states continue to address the nature of campaign financing for state-elected office.

"Gentlemen, I cannot; my moral sense forbids!" An elderly man labeled Corporation Magnate is sandwiched between the Republican Elephant and the Democratic Donkey, each holding out cups, seeking campaign contributions. (Library of Congress)

Reform in the States

Article I of the U.S. Constitution assigns shared responsibility for administering elections for federal office. While the states are responsible for prescribing the "Times, Places and Manner of holding Elections for [U.S.] Senators and Representatives," Congress may "at any time by Law make or alter such Regulations" (U.S. Const. art. I, § 4). Though the states are charged with redrawing congressional district lines after each census, each house of Congress "shall be the Judge of the Elections, Returns and Qualifications of its own Members" (U.S. Const. art. I, § 5). The Congress, in short, has primary authority over campaigns and elections for federal office. The Constitution is silent, however, on the matter of campaigns and elections for local office. With a few exceptions, the states are free to organize their election laws however they choose. This arrangement has permitted considerable variability in state and local election law.

Most early attempts at campaign finance reform in the states amounted to courageous and novel experimentation, with mixed results to prove it. Many of these experiments were guided by the same macroeconomic trends and sensational scandals that were shaping the federal efforts discussed earlier. This shared experience has provided some consistency among the states' histories of reform, despite their independent lawmaking and regulatory agencies.

As the Congress began exercising broader regulatory authority over interstate commerce and the national economy during the late-19th century, favorable consideration from federal officials was becoming increasingly profitable for business and industry. As the cost of running for office increased, the regulators and those whom they regulated developed a mutually beneficial, wholly dependent, and mostly legal relationship. Congress, led by the majority political party, looked favorably upon businesses and industries that helped its members remain in power. One Republican fund-raiser in 1900 went so far as to contact several large corporations, suggesting that each "pay according to. . . . its special interest" (Croly 1912, 325).

At the dawn of the 20th century, such relationships were not unique to the national government. From their earliest days, state and colonial governments had been the center of regulatory authority. Colonial governors and assemblies were responsible for enforcing the common law within their territories. This continued with the Articles of Confederation, under which the states retained their sovereignty and were nominally united by a weak central government. While the U.S. Constitution stripped much sovereignty from the states upon their admission to the Union, the Constitution was notable for limiting the new federal government's powers to those enumerated by its text. The Tenth Amendment explicitly provides that "powers not delegated to the United States by the Constitution, nor prohibited by it to the States, are reserved to the States respectively, or to the people" (U.S. Const. amend. X).

Among its enumerated provisions, the Constitution also gave states broad authority over elections for federal office. The states' legislatures were to determine how electors for president and vice president would be chosen (U.S. Const. art. II, § 1) and until the Seventeenth Amendment was ratified, to select U.S. senators (U.S. Const. art. I, § 3). The states' executives were to fill vacancies arising in their congressional delegation (U.S. Const. art. I, § 2). These responsibilities, combined with near plenary power to regulate within their borders, ensured that the states also would attract official corruption and be targets for campaign finance reform. It has been said, for example, that "Standard Oil did everything to the Pennsylvania legislature except refine it" (Thayer 1974, 41).

Compared to today's closely monitored and extensively regulated campaigns for public office, those of the 19th century often were messy affairs. State political parties competed for newspaper editorial support with their money as often as their ideas. Political parties performed many of the same functions as today's nonpartisan boards of elections such as registering voters, printing ballots, and monitoring polling places. Accordingly, conflicts of interest and allegations of fraud were widespread. As the power of political bosses and their special interests grew during the late 1800s, states gradually began to assume greater oversight of campaign and electoral practices. Focusing initially on fraudulent voting and intimidation of voters by party operatives, this early wave of reform produced the secret ballot and nonpartisan voter registration. As late as 1890, however, most states did not require any disclosure of campaign receipts and expenditures and, in the few states that did, enforcement was lacking. During the 1890s, New York, Massachusetts, and California each adopted disclosure requirements. California's Purity of Elections Act of 1893 required detailed financial information to be filed with the secretary of state. The act also banned independent expenditures, capped campaign expenditures in proportion to the salary of the office sought, and prohibited wheeling: the practice of transferring money between political campaigns that can be used effectively to circumvent contribution limits. Unlike many other contemporaneous reform measures, California's law contained strict penalties for violators, including forfeiture of any public office won in violation of the act. As creative as it was far-reaching, the entire law was repealed by California's legislature in 1907 after it was rendered essentially unenforceable and inoperative by the state's supreme court (Purity of Elections Act Repeal of 1907; *see also Bradley v. Clark*, 1901 and *People v. Cavanaugh*, 1896).

Two years later, in 1909, Colorado combined new financial disclosure requirements with the nation's first system of public financing for political campaigns (State Payment of Campaign Expenses Act of 1909). As was the case in California, Colorado's law was struck down before it could be fully implemented (Bottomly 1986, 380). Nonetheless, other states establishing their own public financing programs nearly a century later embraced elements of the Colorado model. Specifically, Colorado's program would have provided public money to political parties, while preventing them from collecting additional contributions. The amount of funding each party received would have been determined by its performance during the previous election cycle. Candidates could raise their own money and accept public funds from their party organization, but were limited in the amount they could spend, based upon the salary of the office sought (*In re People* ex rel, *Galligan, State Treasurer*, et al. (unpublished opinion), 1910). According to one observer's account of *Galligan*, the court's "chief objections were to the unequal treatment of parties and the lack of provision for any new party" (Luce 2006, 432–33).

Perhaps chastened by these judicial defeats, reform efforts in the states stalled until the federal government enacted the Federal Election Campaign Act of 1971. Spurred to action by the rising costs of campaigns and then by the Watergate scandal, nearly every state enacted some form of campaign finance reform between 1972 and 1974. These reforms included tighter disclosure requirements and lower limits on campaign contributions and expenditures (Alexander 1976a, 1–2). As was also the case at the federal level, these regulatory changes did little to arrest the rising cost of state electoral campaigns, nor did they succeed in stemming the apparent influence of private dollars in campaigns for public office. In a study of post-Watergate campaign finance in 10 states, political scientist Herbert Alexander observed that "even the most stringent legislation will not wipe out corruption entirely. . . . The aim of reform must be to insulate the electoral system from abuses while assuring fairness and equity" (Alexander 1976a, 11–12). With hindsight, it appears the cascade of state reform in the 1970s failed even to achieve these modest goals. Alexander concluded, "[i]t is not clear . . . that legislation will greatly alter the traditional system of private giving . . . the traditional channels are still open and functioning" (Alexander 1976a, 12).

Public Financing in the States

Six decades after Colorado's failed experiment, the states refocused their attention on public financing of electoral campaigns. Following Watergate, more than 20 states adopted some form of public financing including Minnesota (1974), Idaho (1975), New Jersey (1975), Michigan (1976), and Hawaii (1979). The details of these programs varied widely. In New Jersey, for example, only gubernatorial candidates are eligible to receive public funding (N.J. Stat. Ann., § 19:44A-33). Until its law was repealed in 2010, Idaho disbursed to political parties funds raised from a voluntary tax return allocation, which could be earmarked to the political party of the taxpayer's choice (Idaho Code Ann. § 34–2503). Hawaii's program limits the amount of public money candidates receive to 10–15 percent of the spending limits established for the office sought (Haw. Rev. Stat. § 11–425). Additionally, in the decade after 1985, more than a dozen local governments enacted some form of public financing of elections within their jurisdictions. These programs also vary widely (*see* Levin 2006).

Until the 1990s, all of the state and local public financing programs provided only partial public financing. Full public financing, more commonly known as *Clean Elections*, was first enacted by popular initiative in Maine in 1996. Voters in Arizona adopted a similar program in 1998, also by popular initiative. Both states' programs were implemented for the 2000 election cycle. Various forms of Clean Elections programs also were adopted by popular initiative in Massachusetts, New Mexico, North Carolina, Vermont, and Wisconsin, by the legislature in Connecticut, and by the cities of Albuquerque, New Mexico and Portland, Oregon. New Jersey adopted limited Clean Elections pilot programs in 2005 and 2007 that were not renewed.

The essential feature of Clean Elections is that qualified candidates receive a public grant amounting to 100 percent of the authorized campaign spending limit for their race. Qualification standards vary, but generally require a candidate's demonstration of a threshold degree of support of eligible voters in the jurisdiction of the office sought. In Maine, for example, candidates for governor in 2010 needed to raise at least 3,250 five-dollar contributions from registered voters in the state (Maine Comm'n on Governmental Ethics and Election Practices, "Qualifying

Contributions"). In return for receiving public funds, participating candidates agree not to raise or spend any additional private funds.

The record of Clean Elections has been mixed. By certain measures, the amount of private money in campaigns has decreased, the competitiveness of elections has increased, and the public's opinion of the integrity of elections has improved (*see* Brickner 2008). The nonpartisan Government Accountability Office concluded in 2010, however, that many of the changes observed in Maine and Arizona could not be conclusively linked to those states' adoption of Clean Elections (U.S. Gov't Accountability Office 2010). And while several states' programs were adopted by popular initiative, their funding and implementation remained at the discretion of the states' legislatures, which did not always cooperate with the people's will. Massachusetts's program, for example, was never adequately funded and ultimately was repealed by the legislature before it could be fully implemented. Furthermore, as judicial interpretation of campaign finance law recently has tended to emphasize a connection between campaign spending and constitutionally protected political speech, Clean Elections in several states have encountered significant legal difficulties. Critical elements of Vermont's program were found unconstitutional in 2006, rendering Clean Elections there essentially defunct (*Randall v. Sorrell*, 2006). A 2011 U.S. Supreme Court decision struck down a common Clean Elections feature whereby participating candidates receive additional public funds when they are significantly outspent by nonparticipating opponents (*Ariz. Free Enter. Club's Freedom Club PAC v. Bennett*, 2011). Because a participating candidate cannot be certain whether her opponent also will participate, the absence of such additional funds increases the risk that the participating candidate could be significantly outspent and yet barred from soliciting private sources for additional funding.

In the states where Clean Elections was enacted by popular referendum, the reform effort typically began years before the ballot initiative ultimately was approved. Whether voters or legislators in those states will act quickly enough to salvage their programs in time for upcoming election cycles remains to be seen. Between the atrophy of presidential public financing, and the collapse of Clean Elections in some states, the immediate future of public campaign financing appears dim. But the successes enjoyed in other states strongly suggest a practical and constitutional model for such programs does exist. The challenge for advocates going forward will be to navigate the political and judicial obstacles in pursuit of a public financing program than effectively guards against undue influence of money in politics.

References

Alexander, H. E. (1976a). *Campaign Money: Reform and Reality in the States*. New York: The Free Press.

Alexander, H. E. (1976b). *Financing the 1972 Election*. Lexington, MA: Lexington Books.

Alexander, H. E. (1995). *Financing the 1992 Election*. Armonk, NY: M.E. Sharpe, Inc.

Ansolabehere, S., A. Gerber, and J. M. Snyder Jr. (2001). "Corruption and the Growth of Campaign Spending." In G. C. Lubenow, ed. *A User's Guide to Campaign Finance Reform*. Lanham, MD: Rowman & Littlefield Publishers, Inc., pp. 25–46.

Ariz. Free Enter. Club's Freedom Club PAC v. Bennett. 131 S. Ct. 2806 (Supreme Court of the United States, 2011).

Bipartisan Campaign Reform Act ("BCRA") of 2002, Pub. L. No. 107–155, 116 Stat. 81.

Bottomly, J.S. *Corrupt Practices in Political Campaigns*, 30 B.U. L. Rev. 331 (1950). Accessed May 20, 2013. http://heinonline.org/HOL/LandingPage?collection=journals&handle= hein.journals/bulr30&div=18.

Bradley v. Clark. 133 Cal. 196 (Supreme Court of California, 1901).

Brickner, B. T. with Mueller, N. (2008). *Clean Elections: Public Financing in Six States including New Jersey's Pilot Projects*. New Brunswick, NJ: Eagleton Institute of Politics. Accessed May 20, 2013. http://www.eagleton.rutgers.edu/research/newjersey/documents/CE-PublicFinancinginSixStates09-08.pdf.

Buckley v. Valeo. 424 U.S. 1 (Supreme Court of the United States, 1976).

Center for Responsive Politics. (2012a). "527s: Advocacy Group Spending." Accessed May 20, 2013. http://www.opensecrets.org/527s/index.php.

Center for Responsive Politics. (2012b). "The Big Picture: The Price of Admission—House Freshmen Only." Accessed May 20, 2013. http://www.opensecrets.org/bigpicture/stats .php?display=T&type=F&cycle=2010.

Center for Responsive Politics. (2012c). "The Big Picture: The Price of Admission—Winners." Accessed May 20, 2013. http://www.opensecrets.org/bigpicture/stats.php? display=T&type=W&cycle=2010.

Citizens United v. Fed. Election Comm'n. 558 U.S. 310 (Supreme Court of the United States, 2010).

Congressional Quarterly (1982). *Dollar Politics*. 3rd ed. Washington, DC: Congressional Quarterly, Inc.

Corrado, A. (2005). "Money and Politics: A History of Campaign Finance Law." In A. Corrado, T. E. Mann, D. Ortiz, and T. Potter, eds. *The New Campaign Finance Sourcebook*. Washington, DC: Brookings Institution Press, pp. 7–47.

Corrupt Practice Act of 1913, 1913 Mich. Pub. Acts 109.

Croly, H.D. (1912). *Marcus Alonzo Hanna: His Life and Work*. New York: The Macmillan Company.

Davis v. Fed. Election Comm'n. 554 U.S. 724 (Supreme Court of the United States, 2008).

Exec. Order of June 22, 1877 (Rutherford B. Hayes). Accessed May 20, 2013. http://www .presidency.ucsb.edu/ws/index.php?pid=68664.

Exec. Order No. 10974 (John F. Kennedy), 26 Fed. Reg. 10585 (Nov. 10, 1961). Accessed May 20, 2013. http://www.presidency.ucsb.edu/ws/index.php?pid=58912.

FECA Amendments of 1974, Pub. L. No. 93–443, 88 Stat. 1263.

Fed. Election Comm'n v. Wis. Right to Life, Inc. 551 U.S. 449 (Supreme Court of the United States, 2007).

Federal Corrupt Practices Act of 1925, 43 Stat. 1070.

Federal Election Campaign Act ("FECA") of 1971, Pub. L. No. 92–225, 86 Stat. 3.

Haw. Rev. Stat. § 11–425 (2011).

Idaho Code Ann. § 34–2503 (2008) (*repealed by* 2010 Idaho. Sess. Laws 4).

In re People ex rel, *Galligan, State Treasurer,* et al. (unpublished opinion) (Supreme Court of Colorado 1910).

Labor-Management Relations Act of 1947, Pub. L. No. 80–101, 61 Stat. 136.

La Raja, R., and Jarvis-Shean, E. (2001). *Assessing the Impact of a Ban on Soft Money: Party Soft Money Spending in the 2000 Elections*. Washington, DC: The Campaign Finance Institute. Accessed May 20, 2013. http://www.cfinst.org/parties/papers/laraja_softmoney .pdf.

Legislative, Executive, and Judicial Appropriations Act of 1876, 19 Stat. 169.

Levin, S. M. (2006). *Keeping It Clean: Public Financing in American Elections*. Los Angeles: Center for Government Studies. Accessed May 20, 2013. http://policyarchive.org /handle/10207/bitstreams/4523.pdf.

Luce, R. (2006). *Legislative Principles: The History and Theory of Lawmaking by Representative Government*. Clark, NJ: The Lawbook Exchange, Ltd.

Madison, J. (1787, November 22). "The Same Subject Continued: The Union as a Safeguard against Domestic Faction and Insurrection. [*The Federalist, No. 10*]." *New York Daily Advertiser*: p. 1.

Maine Comm'n on Governmental Ethics and Election Practices. "Qualifying Contributions." Accessed May 20, 2013. http://www.maine.gov/ethics/mcea/qualify.htm.

McConnell v. Fed. Election Comm'n. 540 U.S. 93 (Supreme Court of the United States, 2003).

McCutcheon v. Fed. Election Comm'n. No. 12-536 (Supreme Court of the United States, April 2, 2014).

Mutch, R.E. (2002). "The First Federal Campaign Finance Bills." In P. Baker, ed.*Money and Politic$*. University Park: Pennsylvania State University Press, pp. 30–48.

National Labor Relations Act of 1935, Pub. L. No. 74–198, 49 Stat. 449.

Navy Appropriations Act of 1867, 14 Stat. 489.

New State Ice Co. v. Liebmann. 285 U.S. 262 (Supreme Court of the United States 1932) (Brandeis, J., dissenting).

Newberry v. United States. 256 U.S. 232 (Supreme Court of the United States 1921), *rev'd United States v. Classic*. 313 U.S. 299 (Supreme Court of the United States 1941).

N.J. Stat. Ann. § 19:44A-33 (2012).

Pendleton Civil Service Act of 1883, 22 Stat. 403.

People v. Cavanaugh. 112 Cal. 647 (Supreme Court of California 1896).

Political Contributions by Corporations ("Tillman") Act of 1907, 34 Stat. 864.

Presidential Election Campaign Fund Act of 1966, Pub. L. No. 89–809, 80 Stat. 1587.

President's Comm'n on Campaign Costs, *Financing Presidential Campaigns* (1962).

Publicity Act Amendments of 1911, 37 Stat. 25.

Publicity of Political Contributions ("Publicity") Act of 1910, 36 Stat. 822.

Purity of Elections Act of 1893, 1893 Cal. Stat. 12.

Purity of Elections Act Repeal of 1907, 1907 Cal. Stat. 671.

Randall v. Sorrell. 548 U.S. 230 (Supreme Court of the United States 2006).

Roosevelt, T. (1904, December 6). [The President's Fourth Annual Message to Congress]. Message presented to the Senate and House of Representatives, Washington, DC.

Roosevelt, T. (1905, December 5). [The President's Fifth Annual Message to Congress]. Message presented to the Senate and House of Representatives, Washington, DC.

Roosevelt, T. (1906, December 3). [The President's Sixth Annual Message to Congress]. Message presented to the Senate and House of Representatives, Washington, DC.

SpeechNow.org v. Fed. Election Comm'n. 599 F.3d 686 (D.C. Circuit Court of Appeals 2010).

State Payment of Campaign Expenses Act of 1909, 1909 Colo. Sess. Laws 303.

Thayer, G. (1974). *Who Shakes the Money Tree? American Campaign Practices from 1789 to the Present*. New York: Simon and Schuster.

United States v. Classic. 313 U.S. 299 (Supreme Court of the United States, 1941).

U.S. Bureau of Labor Statistics, Consumer Price Index Archived News Releases. Accessed May 20, 2013. http://www.bls.gov/schedule/archives/cpi_nr.htm.

U.S. Fed. Election Comm'n, *Campaign Finance Statistics, 2001–2002, National Party Committee*. Accessed May 20, 2013. http://www.fec.gov/press/summaries/2002/ElectionCycle/24m_NatlParty.shtml.

U.S. Fed. Election Comm'n, *Campaign Finance Statistics, 2011–2012, Political Action Committee (PAC)*. Accessed May 20, 2013. http://www.fec.gov/press/summaries/2012/ElectionCycle/24m_PAC.shtml.

U.S. Fed. Election Comm'n, *FEC Summarizes Campaign Activity of the 2011–2012 Election Cycle* (Apr. 19, 2013). Accessed May 20, 2013. http://www.fec.gov/press/press2013/20130419_2012-24m-Summary_v2.shtml.

U.S. Fed. Election Comm'n, *Party Committees Raise More Than $1 Billion in 2001–2002* (Mar. 20, 2003). Accessed May 20, 2013. http://www.fec.gov/press/press2003/200303 20party/20030103party.html.

U.S. Gov't Accountability Office, *Campaign Finance Reform: Experiences of Two States that Offered Full Public Funding for Political Candidates* (2010). Accessed May 20, 2013. http://www.gao.gov/assets/310/305079.pdf.
Voting Rights Act of 1965, Pub. L. No. 89–110, 79 Stat. 437.
War Labor Disputes Act of 1943, Pub. L. No. 78–89, 57 Stat. 163.

The Future of Campaign Finance Regulation in a Post–*Citizens United* World

Gregory Bordelon

Introduction

Corruption and money have been connected controversies in American elections for quite some time. The attempt to prevent the former by limiting the amount of the latter has been the principal dilemma of regulation on campaign finance spending in this country. Although Congress has been the main actor in this regulation, the courts have been active as well. Our system as a constitutional democracy with certain guaranteed civil liberties in the Bill of Rights has spurned a continuous battle between the government's goal of preventing corruption and the individual's right to "speak freely" or "spend freely" in American electoral politics. That battle often takes place in our judicial system rather than the Congress, since the courts have the final say on "what the law is" when there is a conflict between the interest of the government and those of the individual (*Marbury v. Madison* at p. 177, 1803)

No other case of the judiciary in the past 30 years has affected the landscape of American campaign finance like *Citizens United v. Federal Election Commission* (hereinafter, *Citizens*) decided by the U.S. Supreme Court on January 21, 2010. Although the issues before the Court were a myriad of concerns involving federal campaign finance law, the notion that corporations (and other associations of people) could now spend unlimited sums of money to fund independent expenditures in support of or against particular candidates is why the case is referenced most consistently. In a broader context, Americans should understand not only the impact of this particular point, but also (1) the state of campaign finance law pre-*Citizens*; (2) the facts giving rise to the dispute; (3) the Court's rationale for its holding, including the thoughts of Chief Justice Roberts's concurrence and Justice Stevens's now famous dissent; and (4) the impact the decision has had in the short time since its pronouncement and what the future will hold in a post-*Citizens* campaign financing environment. This last point includes any reforms proposed, the states' rules after *Citizens* and what the future of the decision is in the U.S. Supreme Court.

Overview of U.S. Campaign Finance Laws, Pre-*Citizens United*

The major statutory framework of campaign finance regulation in the modern era was passed in 1971 in a comprehensive law known as the Federal Election

Campaign Act (FECA). The FECA's provisions are primarily codified in sections 431 through 547 of title 2, chapter 14 of the *U.S. Code* but has other provisions in other titles (such as title 26, the Internal Revenue Code, and some criminal enforcement provisions in title 18 on crimes and criminal procedure). The FECA was the first major reform legislation concerning campaign finance since the Federal Corrupt Practices Act of 1925, which strengthened disclosure requirements and increased expenditure limits (Fleishman 1972–1973, Federal Election Commission). Before that, the most comprehensive reform came from the Tillman Act in 1907, which prohibited corporations and national banks from contributing money to federal campaigns (Federal Election Commission 2012c).

Because these early laws were mostly ignored, the original version of the FECA in 1971 sought to prevent disproportionate spending in federal elections by limiting contribution levels to certain groups (e.g., individual candidates, party structures, political committees). It did so by providing a legislative framework for separate segregated funding of federal elections, most popularly known as the establishment of political action committees (or PACs). Non-natural persons, such as corporations and unions, could contribute to these PACs, but the amount these entities could contribute directly from their treasuries was limited.

The FECA has been amended numerous times in response to significant incidents concerning campaign finance, most notably in 1974 after the Watergate scandal (Wald 2003), in 1976 (implementing changes from a seminal case of the U.S. Supreme Court known as *Buckley v. Valeo*), and in 2002 after the amount of money spent in presidential and congressional campaigns escalated dramatically in the 1980s and 1990s. These three waves of amendments are explained briefly next.

In 1974, Congress amended the FECA and put strict limits on campaign contributions (Hodak 2012). These amendments sought to close loopholes left open by the original passage of the FECA in limiting contributions to all federal office candidates, both directly and through PACs and political parties. Additionally, these amendments allowed for public financing of presidential elections, with the now common "tax checkoff" box on IRS forms (Federal Election Commission 2012d). Also notable, a federal agency was created to enforce the FECA, the famous Federal Election Commission (FEC). The FEC's role would be buttressed by rules within the FECA, which required disclosure of amounts spent under the statutory scheme and strict reporting requirements of campaign spending within the FEC's time frames.

The 1976 amendments sought to legislatively respond to the Court's holding in *Buckley*. In *Buckley*, the Court stressed the difference between contributions (funds paid directly to a candidate, political party, or PAC) and expenditures (funds spent on behalf of a candidate, political party, or PAC "for the purpose of influencing any election") as laid out in the FECA and how First Amendment implications would attach to limits in each of those distinctions. Recognized by many as the first major judicial intervention in the realm of modern campaign finance law, *Buckley* held that the FECA's limits on *contributions* (then, $1,000 contributions by an individual to a single candidate; $5,000 limitation on contributions by a PAC to a single candidate; and a $25,000 limitation on total contributions by an individual during any calendar year) were constitutional (*Buckley* at p. 58, 1976). However, FECA's limits on *expenditures* violated the First Amendment's freedom of speech rights of those persons seeking to expend. The spending of money in a political context was a form of expression protected under the First Amendment. The Court said specifically the following:

> The First Amendment requires the invalidation of the Act's [FECA] independent expenditure ceiling, its limitation on a candidate's expenditures from his own personal funds, and its ceilings on overall campaign expenditures. These provisions place substantial and direct restrictions on the ability of candidates, citizens, and associations to engage in protected political expression, restrictions that the First Amendment cannot tolerate. (*Buckley* at pp. 58–59, 1976)

Notably, the *Buckley* Court did uphold, however, the FEC's reporting and disclosure system (*Buckley* at p. 61, 1976). Several other challenges before the U.S. Supreme Court took place after *Buckley,* which attempted to fit the reasoning of *Buckley* into many different campaign finance scenarios, many of which would later be relevant before the Supreme Court in *Citizens.* Some of the most notable cases where the Court struck down campaign finance regulation as violations of the First Amendment were:

- A Massachusetts state campaign finance law that limited expenditure rights of banks and business corporations for the purpose of influencing referendum proposals. *First National Bank of Boston v. Bellotti*, 435 U.S. 765 (1978)
- A provision of the Presidential Election Campaign Fund act making it illegal for independent political committees to expend more than $1,000 to further the campaign of a presidential candidate receiving public financing. *Federal Election Commission v. National Conservative Political Action Committee*, 470 U.S. 480 (1985)
- The provision of the FECA, which prohibited (at that time) the use of organizational treasury funds to fund expenditures in the pursuit of "express advocacy," when a nonprofit organization sought to publish a printed newsletter that listed political candidates that supported its views. *Federal Election Commission v. Massachusetts Citizens for Life, Inc.*, 479 U.S. 238 (1986) (hereinafter, *MCFL*). Coincidentally, the provision of the FECA under review here would be the one challenged in *Citizens United* in 2010. This section's amended version (by 2002's BCRA) would be the focal point of the controversy in *Citizens,* which ultimately accommodated the holding in *MCFL* by excluding printed materials in its definition of "electioneering communications."

In *Austin v. Michigan State Chamber of Commerce,* the Court did uphold, however, the state of Michigan's Campaign Finance Act, which prohibited corporations from using corporate treasury funds for independent expenditures in support of, or in opposition to, any candidates in elections for state office. The Court held that the state law was narrowly tailored enough to justify the compelling state interest of preventing corruption or the appearance of corruption because of the disproportionate ability of corporations (compared to individuals) to raise money in state elections (*Austin v. Michigan State Chamber of Commerce,*

494 U.S. 652 [1990].) It would be *Austin* that the Court would ultimately have to address in *Citizens*.

By 2002, "the federal election system was awash in unlimited soft money contributions to political parties and undisclosed corporation and union political expenditures" (Ryan 2008, 147). The 2002 reforms, also referred to as the Bipartisan Campaign Reform Act of 2002 (hereinafter, the BCRA[1]), or more popularly, the McCain-Feingold Act, sought to ban unregulated campaign contributions (or "soft money") in favor of the regulated, public funding known as "hard money" (Stephenson 2003). It also sought to restrict corporate or labor funding for certain election-related advertising known as issue ads or "electioneering communications" as well as place these limits in contributions to PACs who put on these types of ads (Malbin 2006, 2). Passed after almost a decade of political maneuvering during the Clinton administration in the 1990s, the BCRA's original goals in 1995 were similar to those that ultimately passed in 2002 but also included a component that would allow free television time to candidates willing to limit spending (Maisel and Brewer 2012, 145). The first substantial (and almost immediate) challenge to the BCRA was *McConnell v. Federal Election Commission,* where Senator Mitch McConnell sought, among other points, a declaration that: (1) the "soft" money prohibitions exceeded Congress's authority to regulate elections under the Constitution and (2) limits on independent expenditures to use in "electioneering communications" were unconstitutional. The Supreme Court upheld the BCRA, leaving the law largely intact (Brickner 2007, 11) even though the section on electioneering communication encompassed not only campaign speech, or "express advocacy" promoting a candidate's election or defeat, but also "issue advocacy," or speech about public issues more generally, that also mentions such a candidate. The Court concluded that there was no overbreadth concern to the extent the speech in question was the "functional equivalent" of express advocacy (*McConnell* at pp. 204–205, 206, 2003). *Citizens* would ultimately overrule the part of *McConnell's* holding relating to limits on independent expenditures and the famous "electioneering communication" (discussed in detail later in this chapter).

The case setting the stage for *Citizens* would come in 2007 where the Supreme Court would be forced to narrow the scope of what constitutes "express advocacy" in an "electioneering communication" for purposes of First Amendment scrutiny; that standard would be the baseline the justices would use in *Citizens* to ultimately strike down section 203 of the BCRA, the provision at issue in *Austin,* *McConnell* and here once more. In *Federal Election Commission v. Wisconsin Right to Life, Inc.* (hereinafter, *WRTL*), an organization wanted to run ads on television urging voters to contact U.S. senators from Wisconsin, Herb Kohl and Russell Feingold concerning the senators' position on the Senate's filibustering of federal judicial nominees. The organization was a corporation and desired to disseminate this information to voters immediately and up until the state's primary elections. The FEC asserted this would be a violation of both the BCRA's restriction (at the time) on using corporate treasury funds for electioneering communications and a violation of the time frames in which these communications could take place before an election. The Court concluded that the ads were genuine issue ads, not express advocacy or its "functional equivalent" under *McConnell,* and held that no compelling interest justified the BCRA's regulation of such ads; *as applied* here, section 203 was unconstitutional. The distinction between an *as applied* challenge and a *facial* challenge would come to light in *Citizens. McConnell's* general framework was intact, but *WRTL* revealed that the BCRA would not be beyond particularized scrutiny.

Setting the Stage for *Citizens United*

Considering money spent by the campaigns during both the nomination phase and the general election, additional independent expenditures by the parties and other groups, the total cost of the 2004 presidential contest was $1.2 billion; in 2000, that total amount was $671 million (Maisel and Brewer 2012, 145). Even after the passage of the BCRA and its provisions fully realized, congressional candidates raised $1.31 billion in the 2006 midterm elections and PACs raised an astounding $372.1 million in the same election cycle (Brickner 2007, 11). Campaign spending was continuing to climb dramatically every election cycle despite the blow that slightly chipped away at the BCRA by *WRTL.* Furthermore, candidates' ability to refuse public funding allowed spending by PACs, the party, and other channels of soft money to pour in. The proliferation of other groups protected by the tax code (such as 501(c) groups and 527 groups) in issue advocacy (made famous by the "Swift Boats for Veterans" campaign against Democrat John Kerry in the 2004 presidential race) set the stage for massive amounts of money to be spent in the 2008 race, particularly from outside forces.

Hillary Clinton had announced her intent to run for the Democratic Party's nomination for president in the election of 2008 in January 2007 (Healy 2007). The Democratic field was crowded with several contenders, including former senator John Edwards, Senators Chris Dodd and Joe Biden, Representative Dennis Kucinich, and the senator from Illinois who ultimately won the nomination and the presidency, Barack Obama. Clinton decided to announce her intent via an Internet video message on her website. It would be this medium, ironically, that would be the type that *Citizens* would seek to use and uphold as valid under the BCRA. Led by a man by the name of Floyd Brown, Citizens United sprung out of an independent campaign committee called Americans for Bush (Toobin 2012). Brown and (later president of Citizens United) David Bossie set up Citizens United as a nonprofit corporation with headquarters in Washington, D.C. (www.citizens united.org). In January 2008, it released a 90-minute documentary entitled *Hillary: The Movie.* The documentary depicted Clinton in a negative light in an attempt to dissuade Democratic primary voters from voting for her. Citizens United released *Hillary: The Movie* in theaters and DVD but sought to increase distribution by releasing the movie on-demand via streaming video over the Internet. To promote this method of release, Citizens United sought to produce "two 10-second ads and one 30-second ad for *Hillary.* Each ad include[d] a short . . . statement about Senator

Clinton, followed by the name of the movie and the movie's Website address" (*Citizens* at p. 887, 2010). The nonprofit sought to advertise the documentary using these ads on broadcast and cable television.

As a result of the 2002 BCRA amendments to the FECA, federal law prohibited express advocacy by "electioneering communications" by corporations and unions using general treasury funds. Prohibited communications were those that sought to make direct contributions to candidates or independent expenditures that expressly advocated the election or defeat of a candidate (*Citizens* at p. 887, 2010). Section 203 of BCRA defined an electioneering communication as "any broadcast, cable, or satellite communication" that referred to a "clearly identified candidate for federal office" and one that was made within 30 days of a presidential primary election or within 60

David Bossie, leader of Citizens United and producer of *Hillary: The Movie*, in his office in Washington. (AP Photo/Evan Vucci, File)

days of a general election. Furthermore, regulations in the U.S. *Code of Federal Regulations* extrapolated on the definition of "electioneering communication" by prohibiting those in presidential contests that are "publicly distributed." "Publicly distributed" was defined as reaching 50,000 people in a state where a primary election was being held. It is important to note that at the time *Citizens* was decided, corporations and unions were *not* prevented from forming separate PACs for the purposes of express advocacy. However, segregated funds (from corporation treasuries) were to be used to fund these PACs and were limited to donations only from stockholders of the corporations (or members of a union, if applicable) (*Citizens* at p. 888, 2010).

Fearing that section 203 of the BCRA would prevent the dissemination of *Hillary: The Movie*, Citizens United sued the FEC preemptively in the U.S. District Court for the District of Columbia to enjoin the application of section 203 to the documentary's release. The district court ruled that section 203 was not facially unconstitutional and also held that the disclosure and disclaimer portions of the BCRA as applied to Citizens United were also valid. Procedure in the BCRA allowed the case to go directly to the U.S. Supreme Court. The U.S. Supreme Court granted review of the case and initially heard oral arguments on the case on March 24, 2009. Through the process of oral argument, it became clear that the assistant solicitor general (the attorney arguing the case on behalf of the FEC) had broadened the narrow questions initially before the Court which simply included Citizens United's request to not have section 203 apply to their desired dissemination of *Hillary: The Movie* and the advertisements for it. The Court pressed questions involving broader questions of First Amendment protections and, in a controversial move, ordered the case for re-argument in the next term. *Citizens* was argued again on September 9, 2009, with the following *specific* question being requested by the Court: whether the Court should overrule either or both *Austin v. Michigan Chamber of Commerce* and *McConnell v. FEC* addressing the *facial* validity of section 203 of the BCRA (*Citizens United, Appellant v. Federal Election Commission*, 129 S.Ct. 2893, 2009). The specific holding of the *WRTL* case, contained to its facts, was a narrow *as applied* challenge but the legal question was about to become much broader.

The Supreme Court's Analysis in *Citizens United v. FEC*, Including Roberts's Concurrence and Stevens's Dissent

The Opinion of the Court

The Court issued its opinion on January 21, 2010, and voted 5–4. It concluded that independent expenditures, including those made by corporations, do not give rise to corruption or the appearance of corruption. Overruling *Austin* and the portion of *McConnell* that upheld the constitutionality of section 203 of the BCRA, the Court in *Citizens* effectively stated that all speakers have an important stake in political speech and that no state interest, except that of quid pro quo corruption (actual "something for something" evidence of corruption) could subvert the speaker's First Amendment free speech rights in the campaign finance arena. The next few paragraphs will focus on the Court's reasoning in reaching this decision as well as that of the concurring opinion and of Justice Steven's dissent.

On a fundamental level, the Court went back to *Buckley* and the line of cases after it to establish several important concepts in campaign finance regulation within the context of First Amendment rights. Professor Anne Tucker summarizes these points by inferring how the *Citizens* court understood the line of cases before it: (1) First Amendment–protected speech is money; (2) corporations contribute to the political marketplace of ideas; (3) there is no special threat of distortion or need to equalize individual and corporate voices; (4) corporate political speech implicates other First Amendment rights, such as freedom of association; and (5) concerns of compelled shareholder speech do not justify restricting corporate political speech (Tucker 2011, 501). Using these assumptions from its precedents (previous cases), the majority in *Citizens* could find no narrower ground to rule on the constitutionality of section 203 and held as a matter of law that independent expenditures could not be limited by law, meaning that *facially* and for all reasons, the BCRA's regulation prohibiting corporate or union treasuries from funding express advocacy ads could *never* be allowed. Although Citizens United sought a ruling that struck down only the FEC's denial of their airing of the *Hillary: The Movie* piece in the time frame prohibited by section 203, the Court went much further.

Citizens United initially argued that the piece was not an "electioneering communication" within the meaning of section 203 because it was not "publicly distributed" under that definition in the statute and CFR regulation (*Citizens* at p. 889, 2010). The Court held that the documentary was covered by the statute because the effect of on-demand streaming media would be to reach well beyond the 50,000 people threshold in the law. In fact, Citizens United admitted that it had attempted to reach a total of 34.5 million video-on-demand subscribers nationwide (*Citizens* at p. 889, 2010). Citizens United then made the argument that even if *Hillary: The Movie* was found to be an "electioneering communication," it was not one engaged in "express advocacy" as that term was defined in the controlling case of *WRTL* from 2007. *WRTL*'s test, as it interpreted section 203 of the BCRA from the *McConnell* case, was whether a communication "is the functional equivalent of express advocacy . . . [when] . . . it is susceptible of no reasonable interpretation other than as an appeal to vote for or against a specific candidate." The Court held that *Hillary: The Movie* was much more than just a "documentary film that examines certain historical events" but rather a focus on then-senator Clinton's qualifications for the office of U.S. president.

Finding that the documentary satisfied both elements of section 203, the majority in *Citizens* then classified *Hillary: The Movie* as political speech requiring the highest protections of the First Amendment. There could no "narrower ground [to resolve the case] without chilling political speech" (*Citizens* at p. 892, 2010). Many scholars on First Amendment and campaign finance law agree with this categorization. Within the context of classifying certain types of speech for the proper level of First Amendment protection versus the state's regulatory interest, Professor Richard A. Epstein writes:

> *Citizens United* is not a case involving obscenity, libel, fraud, "fighting" words, or any of the other categories of "low speech" that do not garner the same speech-protective response from the Supreme Court. *Hillary: The Movie* is not even commercial speech; even though the original plans called for the movie to be distributed on cable video-on-demand television, it is surely not some advertisement to buy or sell some particular product. (2011, 643)

This categorization is important because it presumptively protects speech, and the state (here the federal government and its restriction in section 203 of the BCRA) has the burden of proving a *compelling state interest* that is *narrowly tailored* to achieve that interest so that the regulation does not infringe on one's First

Amendment rights. The ruling in *Citizens* reveals that the only compelling state interest that could be asserted is actual (quid pro quo) corruption. Viewing section 203 as "an outright ban, backed by criminal sanctions," the majority held that the rule was tantamount to a prior restraint on political speech or a form of censorship (*Citizens* at p. 897, 2010). The PAC arrangement under section 203 was not an adequate substitute for the corporate form's entitlement to engage in political speech. "PACs are burdensome alternatives; they are expensive to administer and subject to extensive regulations" (*Citizens* at p. 897, 2010). Justice Kennedy, writing for the majority, found that out of the millions of corporations registered in the United States, only about 2,000 have attendant PACs (*Citizens* at p. 897, 2010).

In line with the general ruling almost 35 years before in *Buckley*, the Court in *Citizens* justified the unconstitutionality of expenditure limits versus constitutionally intact limits on direct contributions. The *Buckley* Court reasoned that "[t]he absence of prearrangement and coordination . . . alleviates the danger that expenditures will be given as a *quid pro quo* for improper commitments from the candidate (*Citizens* at p. 902, 2010, quoting *Buckley*, 424 U.S., at 47, 1976) (emphasis in original)." Quoting Trevor Potter, co-chair of the advisory committee to the ABA's Standing Committee on Election Law, Leslie Gordon writes over two years after *Citizens* was decided: "The government may regulate money that is corrupting and potentially corrupting, but it may not regulate wholly independent speech because, by definition [in *Citizens*], it cannot corrupt" (Gordon 2012, 20).

Corporations could not be hindered as purveyors of political speech, and as such could not be limited in how much money they could spend in independent expenditures to engage in express advocacy. While *Buckley* did not directly address the role of corporations (as opposed to individuals and people) as the source of the speech, the *Citizens* Court looked to *Bellotti* and a litany of other cases to uphold the idea that corporations can engage in First Amendment political speech: "The identity of the speaker is not decisive in determining whether speech is protected. Corporations and other associations, like individuals, contribute to the 'discussion, debate, and the dissemination of information and ideas' that the First Amendment seeks to foster" (*Citizens* at p. 900, 2010, quoting *Bellotti*, 435 U.S., at 783, 1978). *Austin v. Michigan Chamber of Commerce* created the anti-distortion principle as a compelling state interest to uphold the state law at issue in that case limiting a local chamber of commerce's general treasury funds for independent expenditures. "*Austin* found a compelling governmental interest in preventing 'the corrosive and distorting effects of immense aggregations of wealth that are accumulated with the help of the corporate form and that have little or no correlation to the public's support for the corporation's political ideas'" (*Citizens* at p. 903, 2010, quoting *Austin*, 494 U.S., at 660, 1990). Arguing that the FEC put little evidence forward alleging that Citizens United's actions would distort political speech in the campaign financing arena, the Court elected not to follow the anti-distortion principle. Moreover, finding no congruity between the reasoning in *Austin* vis-à-vis the line of cases since *Buckley*, the majority in *Citizens* overruled *Austin* and considered its holding no longer binding as law. "*Austin* interferes with the 'open marketplace' of ideas protected by the First Amendment" (*Citizens* at p. 906, 2010).

Likewise, an interest asserted in *Austin* referred to "shareholder protection" would not outweigh a corporation's right to free speech. This argument alleges that shareholders of a corporation should not be forced to support political views in their interests as shareholders when those political views are not pertinent to the objective of the corporation (i.e., usually to make a profit) and the reason for which these people became shareholders in the first place. The Court in *Citizens* did not find a place in a First Amendment analysis for this argument. "There is, furthermore, little evidence of abuse that cannot be corrected by shareholders 'through the procedures of corporate democracy'" (*Citizens* at p. 911, 2010, quoting *Bellotti*, 435 U.S., at 794, 1978). In effect, any grievances shareholders have with how the corporation chooses to spend its money should be remedied through internal procedures and corporation law, not campaign finance law. Moreover, section 203 would not properly alleviate this concern because it is not inclusive; shareholders would have this concern at any time, not just the 30- and 60-day periods addressed in the statute and not just with the type of ads covered by the regulation.

In the last section of its legal analysis, the majority in *Citizens* addressed a point that has remained controversial, the scope by which Congress or state legislatures can limit *foreign actors* as speakers in expending funds in American elections. A separate section of the BCRA prohibits *foreign nationals* from spending money in either a contribution or expenditure manner. However, the Court noted that "Section 441b [section 203 of the BCRA] is not limited to corporations or associations that were created in foreign countries or funded predominately by foreign shareholders. Section 441b therefore would be overbroad even if we assumed that the Government has a compelling interest in limiting foreign influence over our political process" (*Citizens* at p. 911, 2010, quoting *Broadrick v. Oklahoma*, 413 U.S., at p. 615, 1973). It would be this point that would drive, in part, President Barack Obama to explicitly mention the decision in *Citizens* in his 2010 State of the Union address, the first time in such a formal setting that the president would do so directly addressing justices of the Supreme Court (Liptak 2010). With six justices present, Justice Samuel Alito famously mouthed "Not True" in response to the president's concern about foreign corporations' possible future role in American elections as a result of the decision in *Citizens* (Kady 2010). Specific concerns surrounding this issue are likely to come before the Supreme Court again.

The majority in *Citizens* did uphold the disclaimer and disclosure provisions of the BCRA. Under section 311 of the BCRA, any televised electioneering communication funded by someone other than the candidate must include a disclaimer that "_____ is responsible for the content of this advertising in a clearly readable manner that lasts for at least four seconds." The statement must also clearly state that it is "not authorized by any candidate or candidate's committee; it must also display the name and address (or Web site address) of the person or group that funded the advertisement" (*Citizens* at p. 914, 2010). Also, under section 201 of the BCRA, any person who spends more than $10,000 on an "electioneering communication" within any one calendar year must file a disclosure statement with the FEC, identifying: (1) the person making the expenditure, (2) the amount, (3) the election to which it was directed, and (4) the names of certain contributors. The Court found that, even when subject to strict scrutiny, these requirements do not violate the First Amendment. "Disclaimer and disclosure requirements may burden the ability to speak, but they 'impose no ceiling on campaign-related activities'" (*Citizens* at p. 914, 2010, quoting *Buckley,* 424 U.S., at p. 64, 1976). These requirements were found valid as to both the advertisements for *Hillary: The Movie* and the documentary itself.

Chief Justice John Roberts's Concurring Opinion

Chief Justice John Roberts's concurring opinion sought to reign in the scope of the First Amendment question that the majority had addressed. In the first oral argument of the case, an attorney in the Solicitor General's office (the office charged with arguing cases before the Supreme Court when the United States is a party, here the FEC) by the name of Malcolm Stewart acquiesced to a question by Justice Samuel Alito that section 203 of the BCRA could also apply to books and other printed materials. In response, Alito stated, "That's pretty incredible. You think that if a book was published, a campaign biography that was the functional equivalent of express advocacy, that could be banned [by section 203]?" (Toobin 2012). Sensing a disconnect between Kennedy's majority opinion and the exchange at the first oral argument at *Citizens United,* Justice Roberts's concurrence (joined by Alito) sought to clarify the applicability of McCain-Feingold's section 203 to the "pervasive influence of television advertising on electoral politics" (Toobin 2012). Roberts wrote, "The First Amendment protects more than just the individual on a soapbox and the lonely pamphleteer. I write separately to address the important principles of judicial restraint and *stare decisis* implicated in this case (*Citizens* at p. 917, 2010)." In effect, he buttressed the majority's decision to overrule *Austin* and strike down section 203 in its entirety. After exhaustingly refuting the arguments made in Stevens's dissent about the scope of the Court's decision and the proper role of precedent (stare decisis), Roberts summed up the recognition of the significance of the case as follows:

> We have had two rounds of briefing in this case, two oral arguments, and 54 *amicus* briefs to help us carry out our obligation to decide the necessary constitutional questions according to law. We have also had the benefit of a comprehensive dissent that has helped ensure that the Court has considered all the relevant issues. This careful consideration convinces me that Congress violates the First Amendment when it decrees that some speakers may not engage in political speech at election time, when it matters most. (*Citizens* at pp. 924–925, 2010)

Justice John Paul Stevens's Dissent

Justice Stevens's dissent was joined by three other justices, traditionally considered the then-existing "liberal wing" of the Court: Justices Breyer, Ginsburg, and Sotomayor. Stevens wrote that the holding "threaten[ed] to undermine the integrity of elected institutions across the nation" (Gordon 2012, 20 and *Citizens* at p. 931, 2010). Although he agreed with the majority's opinion in upholding the disclosure and disclaimer requirements of the BCRA, Stevens's 90+ page dissent, the last of his long tenure on the Court, meticulously explained the flaws in the Court's reasoning as to section 203 in ruling that provision unconstitutional and sweepingly granting the rights of all persons (natural and legally created) the right to spend unlimited amounts of money in American elections.

Stevens first addressed the breadth of the Court's ruling and the distinction between an *as-applied* challenge to a statute and a *facial* challenge. Stressing that the holding did not specifically address what was before the Court, he wrote, "The Court operates with a sledge hammer rather than a scalpel when it strikes down one of Congress' most significant efforts to regulate the role that corporations and unions play in electoral politics. It compounds the offense by implicitly striking down a great many state laws as well" (*Citizens* at p. 933, 2010). This point would foreshadow the federalism balance between *Citizens* attack on a provision of the BCRA and federal laws and the eventual challenge to state laws on First Amendment grounds. He argued that the majority could have been more specific in two other ways. First, they could have indicated that the definition of "electioneering communication" in section 203 of the BCRA did not encompass video-on-demand as that medium was not pervasively available at the time of enactment of the statute, in 2002; Congress would have modified the numbers of section 203 accordingly either at initial enactment or by amendment thereafter had they sought to address the reach of video on-demand. Second, he alleged that the majority made too sweeping of a rule when it encompassed both for-profit and nonprofit corporations in its First Amendment analysis. In essence, it could have simply exempted the type of corporation that Citizens United was a 501(c)(4) organization, (under the Internal Revenue Code) because of its de minimis contributions accepted from corporations and whose message "is funded predominantly by donations from individuals who support [its] ideological message" (*Citizens* at p. 937, 2010).

In attempting to reconcile the Court's reasoning in striking down the prohibitions of section 203 but upholding the requirements of the disclosure and disclaimer sections, Stevens then turned to the PAC form allowed under the BCRA as a viable, non-cumbersome alternative for corporations that wish to engage in express advocacy through independent expenditures. "Administering a PAC entails some administrative burden, but so does complying with the disclaimer, disclosure, and reporting requirements that the Court upholds today" (*Citizens* at pp. 942–943, 2010). He argued that the individuals that make up larger corporate forms are completely within their rights to directly engage in the campaign process, including spending money. "The owners of a 'mom & pop' store can simply place ads in their own names, rather than the store's. If ideologically aligned individuals wish to make unlimited expenditures through the corporate form, they may utilize an *MCFL* organization that has policies in place to avoid becoming a conduit for business or union interests" (*Citizens* at p. 943, 2010).

Ultimately, while Stevens did agree with the majority about the importance of political speech, he expressed concerns about the majority's categorical rule that Speaker identity regulation could never hold.

> The Government routinely places special restrictions on the speech rights of students, prisoners, members of the Armed Forces, foreigners, and its own employees.

> When such restrictions are justified by a legitimate governmental interest, they do not necessarily raise constitutional problems. In contrast to the blanket rule that the majority espouses, our cases recognize that the Government's interests may be more or less compelling with respect to different classes of speakers. (*Citizens* at pp. 945–946, 2010)

Stevens pointed to existing restrictions in the area of campaigning for public office, notably state-run broadcasters that restricted independent candidates from televised debates; statutes prohibiting the distribution or display of campaign materials near polling places; and the barring of government employees from participating in or contributing to political activities. At a fundamental level, Stevens argues, the First Amendment was ratified to protect the democratic and civic engagement of individuals. Corporations do not share this same engagement desire, and their "legal loyalties necessarily exclude patriotism. . . . [T]heir obsession with dependence . . . is created when large monied interests choose to hire and please elites" (Teachout 2009). In this manner, corporations are analogized to foreign interests, prohibited from funding U.S. elections under the BCRA. Stevens argued that this was true because of the minimal number of corporations that existed at the time of the ratification of the Bill of Rights and the historical context of the debates leading up to the passage of the First Amendment.

> The Framers thus took it as a given that corporations could be comprehensively regulated in the service of the public welfare. Unlike our colleagues, they had little trouble distinguishing corporations from human beings, and when they constitutionalized the right to free speech in the First Amendment, it was the free speech of individual Americans that they had in mind. While individuals might join together to exercise their speech rights, business corporations, at least, were plainly not seen as facilitating such associational or expressive ends. . . . A corporation is an artificial being, invisible, intangible, and existing only in contemplation of law. Being the mere creature of law, it possesses only those properties which the charter of its creation confers upon it. (*Citizens* at p. 950, 2010, quoting Chief Justice John Marshall in *Trustees of Dartmouth College v. Woodward*, 17 U.S. 518, 1819 in the latter section of the above quote)

Legislative history also indicated, according to Justice Stevens, the intent to distinguish between individuals and corporations in campaign finance going back as far as the Tillman Act mentioned earlier; in that law, he noted, Congress and the American people were concerned with both the threat of actual corruption and Americans' perception of corruption due to the growing power of corporations in the late 1800s. This distinction was upheld as a compelling state interest through all Supreme Court cases referenced above until *Citizens*. Special functions of the corporate form "such as limited liability, perpetual life, and favorable treatment of the accumulation and distribution of assets . . . allow them to spend prodigious general treasury sums on campaign messages that have 'little or no correlation' with the beliefs held by actual persons" (*Citizens* at p. 956, 2010, quoting *Austin*, 494 U.S., at pp. 658–659, 660, 1973).

Stevens ended his dissent referencing the work of the lower district court of both this case and that of *McConnell* passed initially after the enactment of the BCRA, arguing that the majority holding in *Citizens* would never allow for the finding of corruption in elections until it actually occurred. As such, this would effectively never be found until the corrupting influence achieved its goal—placing a particular candidate in office with interests endeared not to that of the electorate but to another interest. Scholars reiterate this principle by referring to a distortion of outputs, the discharge of public duties (Issacharoff 2010). In sum, because of the disproportionate amount of money corporate interests can spend, "electoral outcomes are distorted as a result of concentrated corporate and private wealth," which can lead to a breakdown of the fundamental definition of democracy by "potential private capture of the powers of the state" (Issacharoff 2010). Stevens ended his dissent and his almost 35-year term as a Supreme Court Justice, with this warning:

> At bottom, the Court's opinion is thus a rejection of the common sense of the American people, who have recognized a need to prevent corporations from undermining self-government since the founding, and who have fought against the distinctive corrupting potential of corporate electioneering since the days of Theodore Roosevelt [and the Tillman Act]. It is a strange time to repudiate that common sense. While American democracy is imperfect, few outside the majority of this Court would have thought its flaws included a dearth of corporate money in politics. (*Citizens* at p. 979, 2010)

Impact of the *Citizens United* Decision on Campaign Finance—The *Speechnow.org* case and the Rise of Super PACs

Speechnow.org v. FEC

In theory, the holding in *Citizens* created a new channel of funds in U.S. elections in the name of free speech. How would it be implemented? Since direct contributions to candidates and parties were still prohibited, it was unclear how the decision in *Citizens* would impact U.S. electoral politics. This "impact" would come two months after *Citizens* in a decision by the U.S. Court of Appeals for the D.C. Circuit known as *Speechnow.org v. Federal Election Commission* (hereinafter, *Speechnow*). In *Speechnow*, a nonprofit association (and its five constituent members and potential donors) asked the FEC to issue an advisory opinion determining whether the association had to register as a PAC and whether the donations it received qualified as "contributions" under existing campaign finance laws. The association sought only to "engage in express advocacy supporting candidates for federal office who share[d] its view on First Amendment rights of free speech and freedom to assemble" (*Speechnow* at p. 689, 2010). The issue before the court was whether, in light of the Supreme Court's holding in *Citizens*, contributions *to* groups making only independent expenditures in furtherance of express advocacy could be limited. This D.C. Circuit's decision would go on to create the mechanism that has caused much controversy in the 2012 presidential election—the independent expenditure committee, or Super PAC.

The D.C. Circuit held that, "in light of the [Supreme] Court's holding as a matter of law [in *Citizens*] that independent expenditures do not corrupt or create the appearance of *quid pro quo* corruption, contributions to groups that make only independent expenditures also cannot corrupt or create the appearance of corruption" (*Speechnow* at p. 694, 2010). The appellate court went on to say:

> [G]iven this analysis from *Citizens United*, we must conclude that the government has no anti-corruption interest in limiting contributions to an independent expenditure group such as SpeechNow. This simplifies the task of weighing the First Amendment interests implicated by contributions to SpeechNow against the government's interest in limiting such contributions. (*Speechnow* at p. 695, 2010)

These mandates in light of the holding referenced earlier flowing from *Citizens* allowed unlimited contributions to these so-called Super PACs but still required disclosure to the FEC. The petition to review the holding of *Speechnow* by the U.S. Supreme Court was denied on November 1, 2010, effectively giving tacit endorsement to the analysis of the D.C. Circuit (*Keating v. Federal Election Commission*, 131 S.Ct. 553, 2010).

Super PACs

Super PACs are the "independent expenditure committees" allowed by the decision in *Speechnow*. These organizations represent "spending by individuals, groups, political committees, corporations or unions expressly advocating the election or defeat of clearly identified federal candidates" (Federal Election Commission 2012b). Super PACs have similar reporting and disclosure requirements to PACs. Both groups must file monthly or quarterly statements with the FEC. These reports must include: (1) total receipts and disbursements; (2) name, address, occupation, and employer of those who contribute more than $200 in unique or aggregate contributions per year; (3) the name and address of the recipient of disbursements exceeding $200; and (4) the purpose of the disbursement (Garrett 2011). Additionally (and not applicable to traditional PACs), Super PACs must also separately report their independent expenditures when they aggregate at least $10,000 and must report to the FEC within 48 hours; their report must also include the name of the candidate in question and whether the expenditure supported or opposed that candidate (Garrett 2011). Unlike traditional PACs, Super PACs cannot make contributions to candidate campaigns (Garrett 2011). They can only engage in independent expenditures to advocate for the election or defeat of a candidate (statements such as "vote for _____" or "don't elect _____"); they cannot be affiliated with a candidate or political party when they engage in express advocacy. It has been this point that has caused much consternation as to the Court's reasoning in *Citizens* and the ability to prove corruption by proving coordination between these groups and candidates and/or parties. Super PACs' ability to accept unlimited contributions as a result of *Speechnow* likens them to the political advocacy groups regulated by the Internal Revenue Code, namely the 527 and 501(c) organizations.

The impact of Super PACs was felt only marginally in the 2010 congressional midterm elections because of the limited time from which they were allowed after the decision in *Speechnow*. However, "in just 10 months of operation in 2010, almost 80 Super PACs emerged, spending a total of approximately $90 million— more than $60 million of which went to elect or defeat federal candidates. . . . Ten of these organizations accounted for almost 75% of all Super PAC spending" (Garrett 2011). The leader in spending was American Crossroads, spending $25.8 million in 2010. In terms of where all Super PAC monies were spent with respect to specific congressional elections, the most funds were spent to oppose Democratic candidates in the Senate, a total of $20.5 million (Garrett 2011). In contrast and just a few examples: $11 million was spent to oppose Republican candidates in the Senate, $9 million to oppose Republican candidates in the House of Representatives, $6 million to oppose Democratic candidates in the House, and $7 million to support Republican Senate candidates (Garrett 2011). The single race with the most Super PAC money spent was the Colorado senate race, with $10 million spent (Garrett 2011).

As of December 2011, almost two years after the decision in *Citizens*, Congress had not formally amended federal campaign finance laws to recognize the role of Super PACs, and despite minimal FEC advisory opinions, no formal regulations from that agency have been issued (Garrett 2011). However, the Democrats in the Senate have attempted to introduce legislation in response to the proliferation of Super PACs. Most recently, Senator Sheldon Whitehouse of Rhode Island introduced on March 21, 2012, the DISCLOSE Act (Democracy Is Strengthened by Castling Light on Spending in Elections Act) of 2012 (gpo.gov). The law would amend the FECA to provide for additional disclosure requirements for corporations, including the requirement to allow shareholders to vote on whether corporate treasury funds should be spent on campaign purposes (Strong and Carney 2012). The bill is pending in the Senate Committee on Rules and Administration and does not look like it can move to full floor action while the Democratic party maintains a bare-majority status in the Senate, not enough to prevent a 60-seat vote to stop a Republican filibuster. Senator Mitch McConnell, party in the first challenge to the BCRA, *McConnell v. FEC*, has promised that the DISCLOSE Act would not pass. Similar legislation by Democrats in the House of Representatives (introduced as recently as February 9, 2012) has been stalled as well (gpo.gov).

The proliferation of Super PACs in the 2012 campaign season was expected not only because a lack of formal regulation by either Congress or the FEC but also because, as a general rule, more money is generally in play during presidential election years than in midterm elections. Thus, the information presented next may seem disproportionately higher than the reported numbers from the 2010 elections but accommodates that the office of president was up for election in 2012. Data reported to the FEC have shown that the highest single donations to Super PACs have come from individuals, not corporations or unions. Over 780 Super PACs were registered with the FEC for the 2012 elections (Federal Election Commission 2012b). The largest single transaction amount expended by a Super PAC in the 2012 presidential election was $17.6 million by Restore Our Future, Inc. during the general election cycle, spent in opposition to the candidacy of Democrat Barack Obama, made on October 23, 2012 (Federal Election Commission 2012a).

Comedian Stephen Colbert, left, with his attorney Trevor Potter during an appearance before the Federal Election Commission to ask for a media exemption to create a political action committee on June 30, 2011, in Washington, D.C. (Photo by Mark Wilson/Getty Images)

As an example of its spending power, Restore Our Future, Inc., in its June 2012 monthly report to the FEC, listed receipts of approximately $31.3 million year-to-date and disbursements of approximately $46.5 million for the same period. In an attempt at political satire, popular comedian Stephen Colbert formed his own Super PAC called, "Americans for a Better Tomorrow, Tomorrow" and raised over $1 million by the end of January 2012 (Riley 2012). Poking fun at the complexity of federal campaign finance laws and the amount of money allowed by *Citizens* and *Speechnow*, Colbert used his humor to show the problems inherent in the current situation and how broken he believed the system to be.

The States and Campaign Finance Reform

The States—Survey of Campaign Finance Laws and Reforms, Post *Citizens United*

The states rely on three mechanisms to prevent corruption or the appearance of corruption: disclosure, contribution limits, and public financing (National Conference of State Legislatures 2011a). All states require some form of disclosure but vary in the frequency and detail of disclosure reports (National Conference of State Legislatures 2011a). Many states have moved to electronic disclosure because it is inexpensive, quick, and efficient with reports available on the state elections regulatory body's website much more quickly than in the days of paper reporting. Most states commonly place limits on contributions to candidates, PACs, and political parties. Four states (Missouri, Oregon, Utah, and Virginia) have no limits, and seven others have minimal limitations. In the remaining 39, there are limitations on contributions to candidates from individuals, political parties, PACs, corporations and unions, with a handful of state prohibiting contributions from corporations and unions outright (National Conference of State Legislatures 2011b). Spending limits (as a subset of public financing) are favored by some, but *Buckley* established that the First Amendment does not allow limitations placed on the candidate himself or herself to privately fund his or her own campaign. Spending limits that are optional are often upheld and popular in some states. Twenty-five states have public funding programs; these can either provide funds directly to individual candidates or parties or offer tax incentives to citizens who make political contributions. An offshoot of public financing of elections, known as "Clean Elections," is a type of program allowing candidates to finance their campaigns almost entirely with public funds. Once a candidate qualifies by collecting a specified number of small contributions, he or she then agrees to abide by strict campaign spending limits and is barred from receiving any additional private funds. Instead, the candidate receives a grant from the state to finance his or her campaign (National Conference of State Legislatures 2011b). New Jersey and a handful of other states have applied the Clean Elections public financing model, with varying degrees of success.

Justice Stevens warned in his *Citizens* dissent about the impact of the decision on state laws, and while the case was limited to an interpretation of federal campaign finance law, many states have responded legislatively and as mentioned later, the battle in the courts may continue. The 24 states that restricted corporate independent expenditure spending at the time *Citizens* was decided looked at "repealing or rewriting" their laws to avoid attacks under the decision in *Citizens* (National Conference of State Legislatures 2011c) in the latter part of 2010 and into 2011 and 2012. Seventeen of these states simply repealed the unconstitutional section, but some went further to apply stricter disclosure and disclaimer regulations upheld in *Citizens*. Some states have also attempted to amend their corporations' laws to give greater shareholder rights when corporations decide to make expenditures in the political arena (more about this reform is addressed later in this chapter). Even states not directly affected by the holding in *Citizens* amended their laws to either strengthen their disclosure and disclaimer rules or to augment shareholder rights when corporations make political expenditure decisions; New York and California are two examples in this area (National Conference of State Legislatures 2011c). Lastly, nine states (among them Pennsylvania and New Jersey) have passed nonbinding resolutions expressing their discontent with the *Citizens* decision.

Challenges in the Courts—Will the U.S. Supreme Court Look at Citizens Again?

Because of the connection to First Amendment free speech issues and the Supremacy Clause in the Constitution, decisions of the Supreme Court can have direct impact on state campaign finance laws. *Austin* was a challenge to a Michigan state campaign finance regulation. Most notably before *Citizens,* the Supreme Court struck down the state of Vermont's campaign finance expenditure *and* contribution limits in *Randall v. Sorrell* in 2006. The Court used its *Buckley* rationale to strike down state expenditure limits; it deemed state contribution limits unconstitutional because of their "low maximum levels" and found them too restrictive to survive First Amendment scrutiny (*Randall* at p. 237, 2006).

Fourteen months after *Citizens* was decided, the Supreme Court addressed a challenge to Arizona's campaign finance laws in *Arizona Free Enterprise Club's Freedom Club PAC v. Bennett*. A particular provision called for matching public financing for candidates running in opposition to privately funded candidates. Once those matched public funds were exhausted, even independent expenditure groups (IEGs) were limited to addressing only issues, and not express advocacy for or against particular candidates. The Court reiterated that this interest of "leveling the playing field" was not a compelling state interest that would survive First Amendment scrutiny (*Arizona Free Enterprise* at p. 2825, 2011). The Court also refuted the state's anticorruption interest in stating that, "[b]urdening a candidate's expenditure of his own funds on his own campaign does not further the State's anticorruption interest. . . . Including independent expenditures in the matching funds provision cannot be supported by any anticorruption interest" (*Arizona Free Enterprise* at p. 2826, 2011). Forestalling the debate over public funding as a general funding mechanism, the majority warned, "We do not today call into question the wisdom of public financing as a means of funding political candidacy. That is not our business. But determining whether laws governing campaign finance violate the First Amendment is very much our business" (*Arizona Free Enterprise* at p. 2828, 2011). Justice Kagan's dissent stressed the serious reform that Arizona wished to seek to prevent corruption *in* political office by regulating campaign finance and placing the interest of office holders in line with those of the people of Arizona. "On the heels of a political scandal involving the near-routine purchase of legislators' votes, Arizonans passed a law designed to sever political candidates' dependence on large contributors. They wished . . . to stop corrupt dealing" (*Arizona Free Enterprise* at p. 2845, 2011). She focused on this to highlight the difference between *Citizens* dealing with provisions of the federal BCRA and a state's wish to enact a law to avoid the appearance of corruption within its own borders.

Perhaps no other state-level case since *Citizens* has been more closely watched than *American Tradition Partnership (fka Western Tradition Partnership) v. Bullock, Attorney General* decided by the Supreme Court of Montana on December 30, 2011. In that case, three corporations challenged a state law from 1912 that prohibited corporations from making expenditures (or contributions) in conjunction with candidates for office, PACs, or political parties. The law did not prohibit the corporations from establishing a separate PAC to make these expenditures. The Montana Supreme Court indicated that while the U.S. Supreme Court did not find evidence of corruption in *Citizens*, a need for shareholder protection, or a reason to prevent potential distortions of the electoral process by disproportionately large corporate expenditures, this state court did find such evidence and could rule, even under *Citizens*, that the state's compelling interest in preventing corruption would serve to legitimize legislative action. The Montana Supreme Court expressed particular concern with plaintiffs Western Tradition Partnership (WTP) and its activities. Initially registered as a corporation in Colorado but licensed to do business in Montana and elsewhere, the court noted that WTP was "terse in its explanations of its organization, funding, activities, and intent. It claims to be a foreign corporation but it is not a business corporation. Its purpose . . . is to solicit and anonymously spend the funds of other corporations, individuals and entities to influence the outcome of Montana elections" (*Western Tradition Partnership* at p. 7, 2011). Acting merely as a "conduit for anonymous spending" and operating "in disregard for and without complying with Montana law, . . . it is difficult to determine how [WTP] might by implicated by [the statute], but given the evidence presented [at the district court level], we will assume there is a direct impact" (*Western Tradition Partnership* at p. 7, 2011).

The Montana Supreme Court reversed the decision of the lower court and upheld the constitutionality of the 1912 Montana law indicating that *Citizens* was limited to a set of facts involving federal law and the BCRA, while the circumstances of the Montana law and its anticorruption objectives were different from that of *Citizens*. "While *Citizens United* was decided under its facts or lack of facts, it applied the long-standing rule that restrictions upon speech are not per se unlawful, but rather may be upheld if the government demonstrates a sufficiently strong interest" (*Western Tradition Partnership* at p. 6, 2011, quoting *Citizens*, 130 S.Ct., at 898, 2010). Because of the state's history of corruption in politics and the reasons for the passage of the 1912 law, coupled with the evidence taken at the lower court by depositions and affidavits, the Montana Supreme Court found evidence of corruption. It alluded to the unique size, economy, and history of the state as being a special factor in this analysis:

> Clearly the impact of unlimited corporate donations creates a dominating impact on the political process and inevitably minimizes the impact of individual citizens. As to candidates for political office, § 13–35–227(1), MCA, is designed to further the compelling interest of the people of Montana in strong voter participation in the process. While corporations have first amendment rights in political speech, they do not have the vote. (*Western Tradition Partnership* at p. 12, 2011)

The court found that the ease with which corporations could file as a PAC in Montana did not make that requirement by the statute an undue burden as did the FEC PAC filing requirements reviewed in *Citizens*.

> WTP can still speak through its own political committee/PAC as hundreds of organizations in Montana do on an ongoing basis. Unlike the Federal law PACs considered in *Citizens United*, under Montana law political committees are easy to establish and easy to use to make independent expenditures for political speech. . . . [C]orporate PACs can make unlimited independent expenditures on behalf of candidates. The difference then is that under Montana law the PAC has to comply with Montana's disclosure and reporting laws. (*Western Tradition Partnership* at p. 13, 2011)

Two justices of the Montana Supreme Court dissented, finding that the 1912 statute should be found unconstitutional. The dissenters stressed the alternative of working with the disclosure requirements that *Citizens* upheld to save the statute.

Citizens United holds unequivocally that "[n]o sufficient governmental interest justifies limits on the political speech of nonprofit or for-profit corporations". . . . In light of *Citizens United*'s clear directive that the State cannot prohibit corporate expenditures, our review and construction of the challenged statute should focus on preserving disclosure requirements as applied to such expenditures in order to protect the overriding interest in preventing corruption. (*Western Tradition Partnership* at p. 14, 2011)

The dissenting justices also foreshadowed the future of the case in saying, "Respectfully, I cannot agree that this 'Montana is unique' rationale is consistent with *Citizens United*. And I seriously doubt this rationale is going to prevail in the Supreme Court when this case is appealed, as it almost certainly will be" (*Western Tradition Partnership* at pp. 17–18, 2011). While not agreeing with the holding in *Citizens*, Justice Nelson stressed Montana's obligation to respect a Supreme Court ruling:

Admittedly, I have never had to write a more frustrating dissent. I agree, at least in principle, with much of the Court's discussion and with the arguments of the Attorney General. More to the point, I thoroughly disagree with the Supreme Court's decision in *Citizens United*. I agree, rather, with the eloquent and, in my view, better-reasoned dissent of Justice Stevens. As a result, I find myself in the distasteful position of having to defend the applicability of a controlling precedent with which I profoundly disagree (*Western Tradition Partnership* at p. 18, 2011). . . . Therefore, and with all due respect to my colleagues, I believe this Court is simply wrong in its refusal to affirm the District Court. Like it or not, *Citizens United* is the law of the land as regards corporate political speech. There is no "Montana exception." (*Western Tradition Partnership* at p. 19, 2011)

The future of the Montana case before the U.S. Supreme Court is addressed below under "Potential Judicial Review."

The Future for Campaign Finance Regulation

Proposed Legislative Reforms

In addition to bills like the DISCLOSE Act, scholars in the field and policy actors in government have proposed other ways to curb the potential for unlimited spending introduced by *Citizens* and *Speechnow*. (It is important to note, however, that the rather strict reporting, disclosure, and disclaimer laws upheld in both cases are argued by some to be an adequate balance, in and of themselves, to the government's interest in preventing corruption in American campaign spending.)

Some have advocated for reform outside the traditional legislative and executive regulatory campaign finance model, to look to either "corporate law or ex post regulation such as lobbying reform or even legislative recusal" (Kang 2012). One reform advocates for increased shareholder roles in corporations if those corporations choose to spend funds from corporate treasuries on electioneering and other political expenditures. The Shareholder Protection Act of 2011 would apply this check to corporations that seek to go public; the bill was introduced in the House in July 2011 by Massachusetts Democrat Michael Capuano but stalled in the Capital Markets and Government Sponsored Enterprises Subcommittee. Corporations that are not public would be subject to state laws restricting the activities of corporate entities, though even those could be subject to First Amendment challenges (Kang 2012). Moreover, others argue that because of limited shareholder involvement in the spending activity of most American corporations, such an approach would have minimal effect; company management and directors in corporations would still make the spending decisions, even those involving political and electoral spending.

Another approach is to regulate money in the political process through lobbying reform (Kang 2012). With the goal of eliminating even the appearance of corruption, lobbying law strongly monitors the amount of money that lobbyists can contribute to the campaigns of the future office holders they will seek to influence, and lobbyists are required to disclose those amounts to both houses of Congress. However, it is unclear how current law could be modified to combat the perception (or the reality) that some lawmakers are "owned" by lobbyists. For example, amendments to the FECA imposed by the Honest Leadership and Open Government Act of 2007 already require lobbyists to report "bundling," the practice of collecting multiple contributions from clients or other sources in order to deliver a large combined sum to a candidate or candidate's committee.

Former special prosecutor Archibald Cox, Mrs. Cox, Senator Hugh Scott, R-PA, and Senator Edward Kennedy, D-MA, from left to right, entering the Supreme Court in Washington on November 10, 1975, to hear an argument on the Federal Election Campaign Act of 1974. (AP Photo)

A third approach for reform proposes the involvement of mass media to regulate the spending. The Federal Communications Commission (FCC) enforces rules concerning broadcast television, including the Equal Time Rule (in 47 U.S.C. § 315), which attempts to ensure that all candidates get equal access and exposure to voters in this medium. Because of the rapid advance of technology in television, including the expansion of satellite and on-demand avenues for transmitting political messages to voters, some argue that the FCC could expand the Equal Time Rule to cable, Internet, and other "electioneering communication" channels to counter the spending concerns spawned by *Citizens* (Kendrick 1992; Podlas 2009).

Finally, in both the House and the Senate, there have been proposals for an amendment to the U.S. Constitution to overturn the decision in *Citizens*. Since the decision in that case was reached on constitutional grounds, a constitutional amendment would be the only vehicle by which Congress could overturn the work of a co-equal branch (the federal judiciary). One such example, introduced by Senator Max Baucus (D-Montana) in January of 2012, would give Congress the power to regulate, by statute, the direct contribution *and* independent expenditures of corporations and "entities organized and operated for profit." The same amendment would give states co-equal powers of regulation of such entities within their borders (gpo.gov). However, amendments to the U.S. Constitution are extremely difficult to bring to fruition, as the two-step process requires passage by a two-thirds vote of both houses of Congress and then ratification by three-fourths of the states.

Potential Judicial Review

On February 17, 2012, the U.S. Supreme Court stayed the judgment of the Montana Supreme Court in *Western Tradition Partnership* until they could decide whether to review the case. In an unconventional move for an application for a stay, Justice Ginsburg, although respecting precedent and the stay, advocated to revisit *Citizens* by stating:

> Montana's experience, and experience elsewhere since this Court's decision in *Citizens United v. Federal Election Commission* make it exceedingly difficult to maintain that independent expenditures by corporations "do not give rise to corruption or the appearance of corruption." A petition for certiorari will give the Court an opportunity to consider whether, in light of the huge sums currently deployed to buy candidates' allegiance, *Citizens United* should continue to hold sway. (*American Tradition Partnership v. Bullock* at pp. 1307–1308, 2012a)

In a speech at the University of Arkansas in June 2012, Justice Stevens (who wrote the dissent in *Citizens*) said, "The Court must then explain its abandonment of, or at least qualify reliance upon, the proposition that the identity of the speaker is an impermissible basis for regulating campaign speech. . . . It will be necessary to explain why the First Amendment provides greater protection for some nonvoters than that of other nonvoters" (Mears 2012). On June 25, 2012, the Supreme Court summarily rejected the petition for review in *American Tradition Partnership* reversing the judgment of the Montana Supreme Court and effectively ruling the

Montana statute prohibiting corporations unconstitutional as not in line with *Citizens*. As to the question of whether the decision in *Citizens* would apply to the state statute, the Court indicated that "there can be no serious doubt that it does. . . . Montana's arguments in support of the judgment below either were already rejected in *Citizens United*, or fail to meaningfully distinguish that case" (*American Tradition Partnership, Inc. v. Bullock, Attorney General of Montana*, 132 S.Ct. 2490, 2491 2012b). The summary disposition shows the conservative majority's affirmation of the holding of *Citizens United* and the conviction with which they (Roberts, Scalia, Thomas, Alito, and Kennedy) believe that the First Amendment protects all persons—those natural (human beings) and those juridical (legal entities created by state statute). The dissent by the Court's liberal wing (Breyer, Ginsburg, Sotomayor, and Kagan) stressed the overbroad concerns of the *Citizens United* holding and its relationship to the states. Breyer, writing for the dissent, stated, "[E]ven if I were to accept *Citizens United*, this Court's legal conclusion should not bar the Montana Supreme Court's finding, made on the record before it, that independent expenditures by corporations did in fact lead to corruption or the appearance of corruption in Montana" (*American Tradition Partnership* at p. 2491, 2012b).

In the Supreme Court term beginning in October of 2013, the justices heard a case brought by an Alabama resident, Shaun McCutcheon, which challenges the two-year aggregate limits of the BCRA on campaign contributions. McCutcheon and other plaintiffs wanted to contribute more money to the Republican National Committee and other Republican committees than is allowed by the BCRA's two-year limit. The allegation, like in *Citizens* and *Western Tradition Partnership*, is based on the First Amendment's free speech interest. What makes this case significant is it could be the first substantial challenge in the "contribution" realm not the "expenditure" realm as that distinction was made in *Buckley* to federal campaign finance laws. The D.C. district court upheld the limit as serving a "cognizable government interest" (in preventing corruption) and the limit was reasonable and the U.S. Supreme Court ruled, on April 2, 2014, that the aggregate limits of the BCRA on contributions violates free speech. The ruling was 5–4.

Conclusion

What, then, is likely to change the future state of campaign finance law? Will it be a Supreme Court ruling more definitive than *Citizens*? Will it be an amendment to the Constitution? It could take something more intangible: broad acceptance of the idea that the electorate can make an informed decision based on the merits and issue stances of a particular candidate, without being swayed by the vast amounts of money being spent for or against particular candidates. Some policy actors, scholars, and citizens subscribe to the "hydraulic theory," which suggests that no law, regulation, court decision, or other reform can ever make a meaningful change because "money, like water, will almost instantly find its way undiluted into the cracks, no matter how the law changes" (Malbin 2006, 96).

According to the Center for Responsive Politics, Super PACs reported total receipts of approximately $828 million and total independent expenditures of

$609 million in the 2012 election cycle. If the protection against corruption is the independent nature of these funds (i.e., the candidate not coordinating the raising or spending of these funds), the average voter will have to decide whether these amounts do or do not affect candidates' responsiveness to the electorate. Civic engagement may be the best hope for those who seek further restrictions on the role of money in politics, given the lack of prosecution by either the FEC or state authorities of many cases of alleged abuse and increasing popular discontent with the work of the Supreme Court (favorability rate of 52% in April 2012, the lowest in years). In American democracy, the public has the ultimate right to weigh in on the nature of electoral fairness and freedom of political speech.

Note

1. The acronyms "BCRA" and "FECA" may be used interchangeably from this point forward in the context of a discussion on the general applicability of federal campaign finance laws. Note that "section 203 of the BCRA" challenged in *McConnell, WRTL,* and *Citizens United* is also considered the relevant section of the FECA, since the BCRA was simply a package of amendments to the FECA, albeit many, many amendments.

References

American Tradition Partnership v. Bullock. 132 S.Ct. 1307 (Supreme Court of the United States, 2012a).

American Tradition Partnership v. Bullock. 132 S.Ct. 2490 (Supreme Court of the United States, 2012b).

Arizona Free Enterprise Club's Freedom Club PAC v. Bennett. 131 S.Ct. 2806 (Supreme Court of the United States, 2011).

Austin v. Michigan State Chamber of Commerce. 494 U.S. 652 (Supreme Court of the United States, 1990).

Bipartisan Campaign Finance Reform Act (McCain-Feingold Act) of 2002, Pub. L. No. 107–155, 116 Stat. 81.

Brickner, Benjamin, with Naomi Mueller. (2007). *Clean Elections: Public Financing in Six States.* New Brunswick, NJ: Rutgers University Eagleton Institute of Politics.

Buckley v. Valeo. 424 U.S. 1 (Supreme Court of the United States, 1976).

Center for Responsive Politics. (2012). "2012 Outside Spending, by Super PACs." Accessed June 30, 2012. http://www.opensecrets.org/outsidespending/summ.php?cycle= 2012&chrt=V&type=S.

Citizens United v. Federal Election Commission. 130 S.Ct. 876 (Supreme Court of the United States, 2010).

Epstein, Richard A. (2011). "*Citizens United v. FEC*: The Constitutional Right That Big Corporations Should Have But Do Not Want." *Harvard Journal of Law and Public Policy* 34, no. 2: 639–661.

Federal Election Commission. (2012a). "2012 Independent Expenditure." Accessed June 21, 2012. http://www.fec.gov/data/IndependentExpenditure.do?format=html.

Federal Election Commission. (2012b). "2012 Independent Expenditure Filers." Accessed June 21, 2012. http://www.fec.gov/press/press2011/ie_type.shtml.

Federal Election Commission. (2012c). "Appendix 4: The Federal Election Campaign Laws: A Short History." Accessed June 18, 2012. http://www.fec.gov/info/appfour .htm.

Federal Election Commission. (2012d). "Presidential Election Campaign Fund (PECF)." Accessed June 18, 2012. http://www.fec.gov/press/bkgnd/fund.shtml.

Federal Election Commission v. National Conservative Political Action Committee. 470 U.S. 480 (Supreme Court of the United States, 1985).

Federal Election Commission v. Wisconsin Right to Life, Inc. 551 U.S. 449 (Supreme Court of the United States, 2007).

First National Bank of Boston v. Bellotti. 435 U.S. 765 (Supreme Court of the United States, 1978).

Fleishman, Joel L. (1972–1973). "Freedom of Speech and Equality of Political Opportunity: The Constitutionality of the Federal Election Campaign Act of 1971." *North Carolina Law Review* 51: 389.

Garrett, R. Sam. (2011, Dec. 2). "Overview and Issues for Congress." Washington, DC: Congressional Research Service.

Gordon, Leslie A. (2012, May). "Citizens Dis-United: Justices May Take Another Look at Controversial Campaign Finance Case." Accessed June 20, 2012. http://www.aba journal.com/magazine/article/citizens_dis-united_justices_may_take_another_look_at_ campaign_finance_case/.

Healy, Patrick. (2007, Jan. 7). "Clinton's Announcement Makes Waves in '08 Field." *New York Times.* Accessed July 31, 2013. http://www.nytimes.com/2007/01/20/us /politics/20cnd-clinton.html?pagewanted=all&_r=0.

Hodak, George. (2012, Jan.). "Precedents: *Buckley v. Valeo* Decided." Accessed June 20, 2012. http://www.abajournal.com/magazine/article/january_30_1976_buckley_v._valeo_ decided/.

Honest Leadership and Open Government Act ("HLOGA") of 2007, Pub. L. No. 110–81, 121 Stat. 735.

Issacharoff, Samuel. (2010). "On Political Corruption." *Harvard Law Review* 124, no. 1: 118–142.

Kady II, Martin. (2010, Jan. 27). "Justice Alito Mouths 'Not True.'" *Politico.* Accessed July 31, 2013. http://www.politico.com/blogs/politicolive/0110/Justice_Alitos_You_lie_ moment.html.

Kang, Michael. (2012). "The Campaign Finance Debate after *Citizens United.*" *Georgia State University Law Review* 27, no. 4: 1161–1167.

Keating v. Federal Election Commission. 131 S.Ct. 553 (Supreme Court of the United States, 2010).

Kendrick, Christopher. (1992). "The Case for Re-Regulating of Campaign Broadcasting." *Southwestern University Law Review* 21: 185.

Liptak, Adam. (2010, Jan. 28). "Supreme Court Gets a Rare Rebuke, in Front of a Nation. "*New York Times.* Accessed July 31, 2013. http://www.nytimes.com/2010/01/29/us /politics/29scotus.html.

Maisel, L. Sandy, and Mark D. Brewer. (2012). *Parties and Elections in America.* Lanham, MD: Rowman & Littlefield Publishers, Inc.

Malbin, Michael J. (2006). *The Election after Reform: Money, Politics, and the Bipartisan Campaign Reform Act.* Lanham, MD: Rowman & Littlefield Publishers, Inc.

Marbury v. Madison. 5 U.S. 147 (Supreme Court of the United States, 1803).

McConnell v. Federal Election Commission. 540 U.S. 93 (Supreme Court of the United States, 2003).

McCutcheon v. Federal Election Commission. 133 S.Ct. 1242 (Supreme Court of the United States, 2013).

McCutcheon v. Federal Election Commission. 572 U.S. ____ (Supreme Court of the United States, 2014).

Mears, Bill. (2012, May 31). "Former Justice Stevens Criticizes Court over Campaign Spending Rulings." *CNN.* Accessed June 26, 2012. http://www.cnn.com/2012/05/30 /politics/stevens-campaign-spending.

National Conference of State Legislatures. (2011a, Oct. 3). "Campaign Finance Reform: An Overview." Accessed June 22, 2012. http://www.ncsl.org/legislatures-elections /elections/campaign-finance-an-overview.aspx.

National Conference of State Legislatures. (2011b, Oct. 3). "Contributions Limits: An Overview." Accessed June 22, 2012. http://www.ncsl.org/legislatures-elections/elections/campaign-contribution-limits-overview.aspx.

National Conference of State Legislatures. (2011c, Jan. 4). "Life after *Citizens United*." Accessed June 22, 2012. http://www.ncsl.org/legislatures-elections/elections/citizens-united-and-the-states.aspx.

Podlas, Kimberlianne. (2009). "'I'm a Politician, But I Don't Play One On TV': Applying the 'Equal Time' Rule (Equally) to Actors-Turned-Candidates." *Fordham Intellectual Property, Media and Entertainment Law Journal* 20, no. 1: 165–224.

Randall v. Sorrell. 548 U.S. 230 (Supreme Court of the United States, 2006).

Riley, Charles. (2012, Jan. 31). "Colbert Super PAC Rakes in $1 Million." *CNNMoney*. Accessed June 27, 2012. http://money.cnn.com/2012/01/31/news/economy/colbert_super_PAC_filing/index.htm.

Ryan, Paul. (2008). "The Law of Lobbying: *Wisconsin Right to Life* and the Resurrection of *Furgatch*." *Stanford Law and Policy Review* 19: 130–163.

Speechnow.org v. Federal Election Commission. 599 F.3d 686 (United States Court of Appeals for the District of Columbia Circuit, 2010).

Stephenson, Evan. (2003). "Game Theory and the Passage of McCain-Feingold: Why the Democrats Willingly and Rationally Disadvantaged Themselves." *Journal of Law and Politics* 19: 425–470.

Teachout, Zephyr. (2009). "The Anti-Corruption Principle." *Cornell Law Review* 94: 341–413.

Toobin, Jeffrey. (2012, May 21). "Annals of Law—Money Unlimited: How Chief Justice John Roberts Orchestrated the *Citizens United* Decision." *The New Yorker*. Accessed July 31, 2013. http://www.newyorker.com/reporting/2012/05/21/120521fa_fact_toobin.

Tucker, Anne. (2011). "Flawed Assumptions: A Corporate Law Analysis of Free Speech and Corporate Personhood in *Citizens United*." *Case Western Reserve Law Review* 61, no. 2: 497–550.

United States House of Representatives. (2012). 112th Congress, 1st Session. *H.R. 2517, To Amend the Securities Exchange Act of 1934 to Require Shareholder Authorization before a Public Company May Make Certain Political Expenditures, and for Other Purposes*. Accessed June 21, 2012. http://www.gpo.gov/fdsys/pkg/BILLS-112hr2517ih/pdf/BILLS-112hr2517ih.pdf.

United States House of Representatives. (2012). 112th Congress, 2nd Session. *H.R. 4010, To Amend the Federal Election Campaign Act of 1971 to Provide for Additional Disclosure Requirements for Corporations, Labor Organizations, and Other Entities, and for Other Purposes*. Accessed June 21, 2012. http://www.gpo.gov/fdsys/pkg/BILLS-112hr4010ih/pdf/BILLS-112hr4010ih.pdf.

United States Senate. (2012). 112th Congress, 2nd Session. *S. 2219, To Amend the Federal Election Campaign Act of 1971 to Provide for Additional Disclosure Requirements for Corporations, Labor Organizations, Super PACs and Other Entities, and for Other Purposes*. Accessed June 21, 2012. http://www.gpo.gov/fdsys/pkg/BILLS-112s2219is/pdf/BILLS-112s2219is.pdf.

Wald, James C. (2003). "Constitutional Grounds for Controlling Soft Money." *Southern California Interdisciplinary Law Journal* 12: 319–350.

Western Tradition Partnership v. Attorney General. 271 P.3d 1 (Supreme Court of Montana, 2011).

Watchdogs and Guidedogs: Journalism and Political Influence in the New Media Era

Michael Phillips-Anderson and Marina Vujnović

It has been argued, over and over again, that the digital age and the Internet have changed the profession of journalism in profound ways—some we may not recognize for years to come. The main focus of this chapter is on one change that is already apparent and troubling: the shift in the role of journalists from "watchdogs" to "guidedogs." We believe that this change threatens the function of journalists as mediators between the public and institutions of power.

Interestingly, the definition of a journalist as a professional can stir much more controversy and debate than the definition of journalism as a practice. So who is a journalist in the digital age? Let's take a look at the following definition:

> The journalist in the postmodern digital era can be defined as the individual who gathers information with the aim of distributing it to the public. What counts as journalistic activity, therefore, is a function of the content of that activity, and not of the journalist's training or the media organization in which the journalist operates. (Wiesslitz and Ashuri 2011, 1040)

At the core of this definition, as we see it, is a view of journalism as a profession that does not necessarily require training. This paradigm has been advanced since the advent of World Wide Web communication. For example, Curran (2003) argues that virtually anyone can enter the realm of online journalism with nothing more than minimal skills, a computer, and access to Internet.

But even if we accept this paradigm as is, the question of who does journalism remains. For example, Singer et al. (2011) found that journalism on the web is still overwhelmingly the work of traditional journalists and traditional media organizations. In fact, mainstream media simply extend their coverage to online platforms and often perform gatekeeping practices similar or identical to those they provide on traditional news platforms. The transition to online platforms has not been an easy one, as we will show in our discussion of the Clinton-Lewinsky scandal. However, the overwhelming agreement on the core function of journalism—to provide citizens with information about public affairs so they can be responsible participants in the democratic process—still remains regardless of how one views the work of journalists.

However, economic and technological factors are increasingly posing a challenge to this core function. For example, even though more media outlets are now available, ownership of media organizations is arguably more heavily centralized than ever before in the history of media communication (Delli Carpini 2004). In that equation, what happens to the watchdog function of journalism? Watchdog journalism often refers to investigative journalism, and means that journalists train a skeptical and questioning eye on the institutions of power and investigate potential wrongdoings in the interest of the public. But today, the leading media corporations are among those institutions of power. Can professional journalists be depended on to investigate their employers? In other words, will a watchdog bite its owner?

Some researchers conclude that the responsibility for maintaining journalism as part of the democratic process is now shared between journalists and publics or audiences (Bardoel and Deuze 2001). The core of this argument is that given the overwhelming amount of information that circulates on a daily basis, journalists not only lack time and sometimes knowledge of what is going on in the world but also the resources to gather all that information, verify it, and distribute it to the public. Thus the role of a journalist becomes that of a guidedog, someone who guides users through overwhelming amount of information. This change from the watchdog function to the guidedog function not only impacts what type of news is reported but also results in a shift from reportage to commentary/opinion.

There is no consensus about what these developments may ultimately mean for the philosophical and ethical standards of professional journalists. Some observers have coined the term "moral journalism" to capture the traditional practice of putting public interests first, but their observations focus more on the newsgathering process than on the profession itself. For example, Wiesslitz and Ashuri (2011, 1036) define moral journalists as "professional agents who mediate their words through the media technologies available to them." Similarly, Delli Carpini (2004) argues for the professional journalistic role of mediation between the public and media. One thing is clear, though. Whether or not journalists are best fit to sort out information for the public, they are no longer the primary or sole gatherers of information. Journalism, read broadly, and the work of professional journalists is being continually redefined, and reporting of straight facts is losing ground to commentary and opinion. As we will later argue, this focus on commentary and opinion is worrisome. So-called expert opinion in the news has become the chief way to report, especially on the 24-hour cable networks. Say there is a news story about a presidential announcement. Typically, cable news shows will feature two partisan speakers to explain why the announcement was good or bad or how it will affect the next election cycle. What this kind of journalism misses is the investigation into the accuracy or objective consequences of the announcement. It also reinforces the perception that there can only be two ways to look at an issue, ignoring the voices of those who might not fall into the Democratic or Republican camps.

We begin this chapter with an analysis of the media as a forum for lobbying strategies used by different political, economic, and social institutions of power. This sets the stage for discussion of four cases that show how lobbying and political influence function across a range of new media platforms.

Lobbying and Media

Blurring lines between political commentary, public relations, and journalism was at the center of a public debate in January 2005, when *USA Today* exposed the financial dealings of Armstrong Williams, a conservative journalist who frequently promoted the controversial No Child Left Behind Act (NCLB). Williams presented himself as an unbiased journalist on his own nationally syndicated television show. He never revealed to his audience that he was paid $240, 000 in return for the NCLB promotion; the deal was part of a $1 million fee paid by the U.S. Department of Education to the Ketchum Inc. public relations firm. In addition, Williams failed to disclose that he had arranged for U.S. Education Secretary Rod Paige to promote NCLB throughout 2004 on both his syndicated radio and TV programs. Williams was also CEO of his own public relations company, Graham Williams Group (GWG).

Why was this considered a major case in terms of confronting the changing face of journalism? Aren't journalists supposed to argue for causes they believe in? Some would call Williams's work advocacy journalism, or defend his right to argue for a particular perspective, especially if it has social value. But the problem was that Williams's financial incentives made it nearly impossible to decipher whether he was acting in the interest of his clients or in the public interest. It raised questions of credibility, and even honesty.

When the story broke, White House press secretary Scott McCllelan denied any illegal activity. But because he would not address the question of whether other journalists were being paid through similar arrangements, the watchdog group Citizens for Responsibility and Ethics in Washington requested copies of contracts between the federal government and more than 20 other public relations companies. In September 2005, the Government Accountability Office ended the debate with its decision that the payments to Williams by the Department of Education were illegal because of his failure to disclose the conflict.

Is this a matter of propaganda, lobbying, public relations, or journalism? Or is it all the above? If mixed together, it leaves us with a badly tasting cocktail. Williams's case shined a spotlight on three important issues:

(1) Blurring lines between journalism and public relations, especially in cross media platforms that are now more readily available than ever before
(2) Potential masking of lobbying efforts and/or the business of promotion as opinion, expert sourcing, or even objective reporting
(3) What constitutes a breach of journalistic ethics

Hidden from the eyes of the public is how the media may be used to benefit individuals or companies. For example, in 2003 *The Nation* magazine revealed the fact that retired general Barry McCaffrey and NBC's military analyst promoted military contactors on different cable networks without disclosing that they were being paid. Despite public consternation, this practice did not stop: in 2008, *The New York Times* exposed many former military officials using media to lobby for military contractors. New media were added to the mix in 2009, when bloggers exposed

Richard Wolffe, a guest host for Keith Olbermann's *Countdown*, in a Williams-like conflict: Wolffe worked for a large public relations company "specializing in strategies for managing corporate reputation" (Jones 2010, 12).

The blurring of the line between journalists and commentators, as well as the lax disclosure of conflicts of interest, poses a significant problem for the public. How widespread are these problems? According to Jones (2010, 12), author of *The Nation* expose, 10 years after the Williams controversy at least 75 public relations representatives, registered lobbyists, and corporate representatives were appearing on all major cable news networks "to promote their financial and corporate interests . . . with no disclosure of the corporate interests that paid them."

What is the role of the media, cable networks, and journalism in all this? Cable networks are corporations engaged in lobbying themselves. They don't only look away from ethical standards of professional journalism when it comes to lobbying; they lobby themselves. For example, media companies have heavily lobbied for business-friendly changes to FCC regulations. Media "use more lobbyists and spends more money than securities and investment firms or unions to influence federal decision-making," asserts one observer (McChesney and Nichols 2003, 16). From this perspective, corporations, interest groups, media, and government are all in the business of maintaining the political status quo—with no concern for the ethics of journalism or the interests of the public.

In a world where opinions are abundant, truth-seeking and objective reporting are on the decline, and consolidated media corporations have little incentive to compete, what has come to define news is a work of what Pfister (2010, 63) calls "opinion leaders." The information imparted by these individuals tends to be in sync with the well-established views of their colleagues. The Internet is put to use for the purpose of finding more information to support those opinions and not to challenge them. It is true that many members of the public participate enthusiastically in the delivery of today's opinion-driven news shows. But this may produce what Dean (2009, 2) calls "communicative capitalism," in which digital media create a sense of efficacy that traditionally lay within the realm of politics. Instead of taking political action, people simply substitute online participation. There is danger to democracy if this behavior leads to lack of actual participation in the political process, such as voting.

Some of the weakening of traditional journalistic standards can be traced to government policies, particularly the Telecommunications Act of 1996, which liberalized media ownership and loosened the restrictions on lobbying by media corporations. But more access and more choice don't necessarily mean better or more objective information. To the contrary, the 1996 policy changes greatly strengthened the connections between established media institutions and powerful politicians—increasing the incentive for media executives to be helpful rather than critical. As pointed out by Starr (2004, 30), only the media, because of First Amendment protections and campaign-finance laws, are free to promote candidates as they see fit without any legal limitations. This is a particularly serious concern with regard to broadcast journalism, which still delivers most information to the largest number of Americans. Broadcast journalists are often seen at industry conventions "mingling" and discussing policy issues with government officials, industry lobbyists, and advertisers (Layton 2004, 27). These cozy relationships are often undisclosed to the public. The same journalists who mingle over champagne and caviar with government regulators and corporate moguls then "cover" those events under the guise of objective journalism, exclaiming: Here's the news!

In view of these developments, the decline of investigative reporting is unsurprising. A 2007 article in *American Journalism* titled "Lying to Get the Truth" pointed out that even a mainstream newspaper like *The Washington Post*, with its renowned Watergate history, has significantly cut back on "aggressive methods of reporting" (Lisheron 2007). In 1996, researchers for the Center for Public Integrity and the *Columbia Journalism Review* found that

Vice President Al Gore looks on as President Clinton uses an electronic pen to sign the Telecommunications Reform Act on February 8, 1996, at the Library of Congress in Washington, D.C. (AP Photo/Doug Mills)

the 50 largest media organizations spent $111.3 million to lobby Congress and the White House. This figure grew by over 20 percent in the next four years (Lewis 2000, 20). Today, a smaller number of big players in the media are spending more money on lobbying than ever before (close to half a billion dollars in 2012). (A potential counterweight to this trend is the ease with which interest groups now use online forums to lobby mainstream journalists for coverage they would not otherwise get. This democratizing element may help to keep media organizations, and individual journalists, in touch with the public.)

Next, we turn to discussions of particular cases that illustrate complex points of intersection between new and traditional media. We demonstrate some of the effects on politics, society, and journalism. First, we look at the first big story of new media era.

Bill Clinton, Monica Lewinsky, and Matt Drudge (1998)

The first major political story of the Internet era was the Clinton-Lewinsky scandal. It first appeared not in a newspaper or on television, but on a website called *The Drudge Report*. Matt Drudge's original post on January 19, 1998, challenged both political and journalistic norms. He asserted that *Newsweek* was sitting on its own reporter's story about Clinton's affair with an intern. Michael Isakoff had spent a year investigating the story, acquiring taped conversations between former Clinton White House intern Monica Lewinsky and her friend Linda Tripp in which Lewinsky acknowledged the affair. The *Newsweek* editors faced their publication deadline on January 17 still unsure if the story was accurate, wondering if Lewinsky was credible or if they had been fed misinformation. Knowing that the consequences of such a story, true or false, would be huge, they decided to wait for additional confirmation of the facts. Two days later, Matt Drudge broke the story. Two days after that, traditional media finally picked up the trail.

The Drudge Report began as an e-mail newsletter, distributed by subscription for $10 per year. These were the early days of online news; in 1999 only half of Americans had even been online. At the time of the Clinton-Lewinsky scandal, online journalism was clearly not the main news source for most Americans. Many major newspapers maintained a policy of publishing stories online only after they had appeared in the print version of the paper. The idea was that people would still have to buy the newspaper or wait until later to read the story online. Today's expectation that nearly all news stories appear online before print is largely the results of changes in editorial policy during this time.

How did new journalistic ventures like *The Drudge Report* change norms of coverage? At the time, news organizations were still trying to figure out if there were journalistic differences between print news, television news, and online news. According to CNN's Scott Woelfel, "There was an attitude of, 'I don't know if we could put this in the paper, but we could put it on the Web site'" (quoted in Lasica 2003). Journalism has always faced a tension between speed and accuracy. Does it make sense to sit on a story if another news organization is going to print it first, or if it is not possible to get further verification for your claims? Reporters typically want a story that is fully confirmed with no errors, but in many cases they would also like to be either the first one publishing a scoop or, at the very least, not be left behind. Online coverage tipped the balance toward speed. This led to the publication of rumor, which even if labeled as such can affect the public's perception of an issue and the media's coverage of it.

Did Drudge's report represent a political agenda against President Clinton or against mainstream news organizations? Was it a new form of journalism, one that applied different criteria for determining the newsworthiness of a story? Was it significant that Drudge did not have gatekeepers like the editors at *Newsweek*? While there are no definitive answers to these questions, we know that independent online journalists tend to take a different approach than more traditional, institutionally based journalists. For all the talk about political biases in the press, one of the strongest biases is in favor of maintaining access to power. That is not to say that traditional journalists will not run stories that are critical of those in power, but their concern for keeping their access can lead them to sit on stories, not cover some subjects, or give the political figures time to respond. Early in the Clinton-Lewinsky scandal, most Americans were "highly critical of the media's fact checking, its objectivity and the amount of punditry associated with the story" (Pew Center 1998). A practitioner of new media journalism might not be held back because of those concerns. That can have positive and negative consequences for politicians and the public. People want to know that the news they encounter is reliable, but they also want to know what is really happening, especially when those in power do not want them to know.

The journalistic investigation into the Clinton-Lewinsky affair did not start out online, but by the time it was over the Internet had come to dominate how the story was covered. The online coverage changed over the course of the story and was more closely aligned with traditional American journalistic norms. One observer commented: "By the time the Starr report was released eight months later, the tables had turned: The Internet largely dictated how the story played out, and online news organizations responded with respectful, restrained, serious coverage. And by then the role of individual 'cybermongers' like Drudge seemed to have faded" (Lasica 2003). Just as the Clinton-Lewinsky scandal marked an important moment in political history, it also ushered in a new era of journalism. The goals, norms, and ethics of journalism challenged by the scandal's coverage continue to evolve as the people and venues in journalistic practice expand.

CBS News, Dan Rather, and Memogate (2004)

Unprecedented issues of new journalism, crowdsourcing, new technologies, and agenda setting took center stage in 2004, during a controversy variously called "Memogate," "Rathergate," or the Killian documents affair. At stake was the outcome of the presidential election and the reputation of a leading media figure. When the dust settled, George W. Bush was reelected to the presidency, several CBS news employees lost their jobs, and Dan Rather resigned from the *CBS Evening News*.

There had long been questions about George W. Bush's military service, but no hard evidence had been found. Bush committed to serve in the Texas Air National Guard from 1968 until 1974, but the only known

CBS Anchor Dan Rather at a news conference at CBS studios in New York. (STAN HONDA/AFP/Getty Images)

records indicated that his service concluded in May 1972. The Associated Press filed a Freedom of Information Act lawsuit in June 2004 to obtain all documents related to Bush's military service. It was in this climate of questioning Bush's service that the network news program, *60 Minutes*, aired a story on September 8, 2004. Dan Rather reported about documents that supposedly came from the files of Colonel Jerry Killian and suggested that Bush received preferential treatment even though he did not fulfill his National Guard commitments. In the report, Rather stated that *60 Minutes* enlisted a "handwriting analyst and document expert who believes the material is authentic," although it would turn out these experts warned CBS that the documents might have been forgeries. Lieutenant Colonel Bill Burkett, a Texas Army National Guard veteran who supplied the documents to CBS News, claimed to have destroyed the originals after faxing them to the network. Fairly quickly, typography experts and amateur investigators claimed that the documents were forgeries. Interestingly, the White House's first media response was not to deny the authenticity of the documents or their content, but to dismiss the story as a partisan political attack.

The path of questioning the authenticity of the documents went from Internet forums and blogs to the mainstream media and is a clear example of crowd-sourcing, that is, online collaborative problem solving. While some instances of crowdsourcing involve a problem specifically posted for the crowd to solve, the Memogate example developed more spontaneously as large numbers of interested amateurs and professionals questioned the authenticity of the documents. Within a few hours of the broadcast, a poster called "Buckhead" on the conservative website Free Republic commented that "every single one of these memos . . . is in a proportionally spaced font, probably Palatino or Times New Roman. In 1972 people used typewriters for this sort of thing, and typewriters used monospaced fonts . . . I am saying these documents are forgeries, run through a copier for 15 generations to make them look old. This should be pursued aggressively" (Buckhead 2004). A few weeks later, Buckhead was revealed to be the screen name of Harry McDougald, a politically active Republican and attorney. Nothing in the post indicated a source for the claims or evidence concerning McDougald's credibility.

Before 8:00 A.M. the next morning, Scott Johnson (2004), writing on the conservative political blog *Power Line*, offered a story inspired by McDougald's post. In a detailed analysis of the authenticity of the documents, Johnson corrected some of the claims in Buckhead's post using comments from *Power Line* readers. Major newspapers, including *The New York Times*, *Washington Post*, and *USA Today*, ran stories that reported the questions surrounding the authenticity of the documents. Dan Rather defended his original reporting in a September 10 broadcast and claimed that the critics were "partisan political operatives." On September 15, Rather interviewed Marian Carr Knox, Colonel Killian's former secretary, who claimed that while she did not type the documents and that they appeared to be forgeries, they did represent Killian's thoughts about Bush.

On Monday, September 20, CBS reported that Burkett admitted lying about the documents. Rather said "If I knew then what I know now, I would not have gone ahead with the story as it was aired, and I certainly would not have used the documents in question." He then apologized for CBS's handling of the story and announced that CBS would launch an investigation. In November 2004, Dan Rather announced that he would retire as anchor of the *CBS Evening News* the following March, a seat he had held since 1981 when he took over for Walter Cronkite. CBS eventually fired four executives and producers for their mishandling of the story.

Despite the clear influence of amateur investigators in this case, Jonathan Klein (2004), a former CBS news executive in charge of *60 Minutes* said, "You couldn't have a starker contrast between the multiple layers of checks and balances [at *60 Minutes*] and a guy sitting in his living room in his pajamas writing." It is indisputable that such amateur reporters tend to be untrained in journalistic practices, and are often politically motivated. Because of their personal involvement, they are often willing to devote time and attention to details of a story which the traditional media are unable or unwilling to invest. Still, there must be interaction between amateur and traditional media for the wider public to benefit. The traditional media are still the essential agenda setter and gatekeeper for most viewers and readers. The products of bloggers and amateur reporters may cover stories ignored by the mainstream media, but unless they are picked up by a major news source, most people will not see the information—or will have no reason to trust it.

The Debut of the *Huffington Post* (2005)

The Huffington Post, which bills itself as "The Internet Newspaper," represented a bridge between early Internet news websites, blogs, and traditional news operations. Today it carries original columns of news and opinion as well as wire service and cross-posted content. As a news aggregator, *The Huffington Post* collects stories posted on other websites that may be of interest to its readers. It is one of a growing number of politically themed news sites. Another leading example of a political news aggregator is RealClearPolitics.com, while sites with mostly original reporting include the online versions of major newspapers and Politico.com. Unlike Google News, where the story selection is automated via an algorithm, *The Huffington Post* uses human editors to select those stories that will be featured. The financing for the site is ad driven, rather than a pay for subscription model.

The website was founded in 2005 by Arianna Huffington, Jonah Peretti, Kenneth Lerer, and Andrew Breitbart. Huffington was a conservative political commentator in the early 1990s before switching to more liberal views and running in the 2003 California gubernatorial recall election. Paretti was a co-founder of Buzz-Feed, and Lerer is its chairman. Breibart, a conservative political commentator, had worked for *The Washington Times* and *The Drudge Report*. In 2011, AOL bought *The Huffington Post* for $315 million. In addition to the main site, *The Huffington Post* has several local sites covering major U.S. cities and multiple international and foreign language editions. As of June 2012, *The Huffington Post* was the 25th most frequently visited U.S. website and the third most visited news site on the web, trailing Yahoo! News and CNN Interactive and finding a larger audience than the BBC News or *New York Times* websites. It is also the first solely digital publication to win a Pulitzer Prize.

Beyond the main group of columnists, the site hosts the work of more than 9,000 bloggers, including politicians, academics, and celebrities (e.g., U.S. secretary of labor Hilda Solis, George Lakoff, and Alec Baldwin). Several prominent journalists moved from traditional news outlets to *The Huffington Post,* including Howard Fineman, formerly of *Newsweek.* In addition to its sections about business, entertainment, and culture, *The Huffington Post* has extensive political coverage. Along with headlines and reaction to current political news, there is the "HuffPost Fundrace," an online tool to track campaign contributions by name, location, or employer, and "Off the Bus," reporting on the 2012 presidential campaign by citizen (e.g., amateur) journalists.

Other websites frequently allow *The Huffington Post* to cross-post their content (what used to be called reprinting in the physical publishing world). The benefit for the originating websites and authors is that the cross-posting may give them greater exposure while *The Huffington Post* is able to generate content without paying writers or editors. There have been strikes, boycotts, and lawsuits surrounding this practice due to the concern that writers are forced to work for free if they want this kind of exposure. Readers also face a possibly difficult consequence from such frequent cross-posting: it can be difficult to identify the agenda behind any particular article, or to judge its credibility. Has the author been paid by *The Huffington Post* for the contribution? Is the article a cross-post from another media organization that is financing the work or a press release or promotional piece? Some of these questions are rooted in our notions of professionalism. Generally we think of professionals as people who were paid to perform their services while amateurs do it merely for their love of the activity. *The Huffington Post* model blurs, or even eliminates, such distinctions.

Websites like *The Huffington Post* can give the appearance of hosting an open, freewheeling conversation between writers and readers, who can comment on stories just as they do on most web versions of print newspapers. But *Huffington Post* commenters are not free to post any content they wish. The site sometimes moderates comments before displaying them and warns commenters that "if your comments consistently or intentionally make this community a less civil and enjoyable place to be, you and your comments will be excluded from it" (2012). *The Huffington Post* links with social networking sites to enable readers to see what people in their networks are reading and to share stories of interest. In addition, it has taken steps to identify commenter characteristics, awarding badges to commenters for being widely connected, sharing a large number of stories, flagging abusive comments, and "consistently contributing insightful, informative, and engaging commentary" (2012). Readers can follow their favorite commenters just as they might follow the regular columnists. In some ways, this gives the commenters standing comparable to the professional writers and encourages a kind of citizen journalism, albeit one ultimately controlled by *The Huffington Post.*

WikiLeaks and Government Secrets (2007)

What are the political implications of a media group that challenges existing laws concerning the classification of government and corporate materials by publishing such information on the web? How should traditional media cover the online disclosure of information that their own editorial policies might have prohibited them from publishing in the first place? These questions are being wrestled with by politicians and traditional news organizations primarily because of the group known as WikiLeaks.

Founded in 2007, WikiLeaks describes itself as a "not-for-profit media organization. Our goal is to bring important news and information to the public. We provide an innovative, secure and anonymous way for sources to leak information to our journalists" (2012). The group's objective is to publish primary source documents, often classified government or secret corporate information, for the public and the media to examine. Its editorial model uses anonymous sources, the vetting of documents by reporters, and analysis of those documents in news stories. The principal value WikiLeaks articulates is transparency of information, believing that it will lead to less corruption and better functioning of governments and corporations.

Most of the people who work for WikiLeaks maintain their anonymity. The most high-profile member of WikiLeaks is creator Julian Assange, who acts as the editor-in-chief. A few other people work full time on the site, while hundreds participate occasionally, and usually, anonymously. WikiLeaks is supported through private donations and volunteer work of reporters and lawyers. Following several widely covered disclosures, the group has experienced difficulties in acquiring donations due to interference from financial institutions; its writers allege the existence of an organized "financial blockade."

Despite the name, WikiLeaks is not a "wiki" like Wikipedia. A wiki is a website where users can alter or add to the content, although there may be some moderation by editors or by the website community. While the original version of the website allowed users to edit the posts, WikiLeaks no longer allows users to post directly to the site. The name stayed, though the functionality of the platform changed. The website often publishes its own documents and stories, but has also released leaked documents in collaboration with traditional media organizations, including *The Guardian*, *The New York Times*, *Al Jazeera*, and *Le Monde*.

WikiLeaks has covered a number of politically significant stories. For example, it has released U.S. military airstrike footage and classified documents from the wars in Iraq and Afghanistan. In April 2010, WikiLeaks disclosed a video from an American helicopter that showed the killing of Iraqis, some armed and some carrying cameras mistaken for weapons. The video was allegedly supplied to WikiLeaks by U.S. Army Private Bradley Manning. In November 2010, WikiLeaks released secret U.S. Department of State diplomatic cables, also allegedly leaked by Manning. The cache of more than 250,000 cables included U.S. assessments of foreign governments, covering more than 40 years of State Department secrets. The disclosure was made in collaboration with traditional news organizations with all sides agreeing to publish the cables only with significant redaction. By September of 2011, unredacted copies of the cables became available online. U.S. secretary of state Hillary Clinton said, "This disclosure is not just an attack on America's foreign policy interests. It is an attack on the international community, the alliances and partnerships, the conversations and negotiations that safeguard global security and advance economic prosperity" (*PBS Newshour* 2010).

The disclosure and easy dissemination of classified materials can have a tremendous impact on politics. From the viewpoint of WikiLeaks and its supporters, open access to information helps to stop abuse and exploitation of power. Institutional forces, such as governments and corporations, are more likely to see disclosure as a threat to their missions of protecting their citizens or their bottom line. Either way, the type of journalism practiced by WikiLeaks raises significant legal questions.

There was a time when individual countries found it easy to regulate speech and the press. Because online journalism crosses national borders, it also crosses national laws. The WikiLeaks website is available throughout the world and has servers in multiple countries, but is primarily hosted in Sweden, which does not allow the government to question the press concerning anonymous sources. Some sources may have chosen to submit documents to WikiLeaks because of uncertainty of whistle-blower protections in their home countries. U.S. law is ambiguous, but many First Amendment experts believe that, based on several Supreme Court cases, anyone who gives classified information to the press could be subject to prosecution. Nonetheless, the press has the freedom to report about the disclosure without penalty.

One such case is a clear precedent for the issues raised by WikiLeaks—and also demonstrates the significant political consequences of disclosure. In 1971, Daniel Ellsberg leaked what came to be known as the "Pentagon Papers," a U.S. Department of Defense history of the Vietnam War. The documents showed that the war was going much less well than either the Johnson or Nixon administrations had admitted to the public. Ellsberg, a former

President Lyndon B. Johnson talking to troops at Cam Ranh Bay, South Vietnam, during the Vietnam War. (AP Photo)

Founder of the WikiLeaks website, Julian Assange, explaining a website during a press conference in London in 2010. (AP Photo/Lennart Preiss)

Defense Department employee, had turned against the war and given the report to *The New York Times*. Public access to the report was secured through two Supreme Court cases, one which supported the right of *The New York Times* to publish the materials and another which upheld Senator Mike Gravel's entering of the report into the *Congressional Record*. Even with these precedents in place, the U.S. government, among other national governments, has examined the options for shutting down WikiLeaks, prosecuting its participants, and placing financial hurdles in its way.

Since 2011 a substantial portion of the stories on WikiLeaks have been about the organization itself, particularly the Bradley Manning case, founder Julian Assange, and the "financial blockade" of their organization. Bradley Manning was arrested in May 2010 for allegedly providing WikiLeaks with military videos and documents related to the war in Iraq and the release of diplomatic cables. The controversial Julian Assange has received awards from Amnesty International and was the Reader's Choice for *Time* magazine's Person of the Year in 2010. He has also been accused of sexual assault in Sweden and has challenged his extradition from the United Kingdom. The U.S. Justice Department launched a criminal investigation concerning his leaking of the State Department cables.

While the many controversies associated with WikiLeaks may be distracting its leadership, there is little doubt that the practices it pioneered will expand to other sites. The use of the Internet to anonymously disclose secret information is likely to have long-term effects on corruption, diplomacy, and politics.

Journalists as Fact Checkers

Politicians always lie. Or do they? How are we to know? Researching the accuracy of political claims may never have been the first priority of journalism, but it has long been nearly equal in importance to straight reportage. In addition to knowing what politicians say, the public needs to know if what they say is accurate. This has given rise to a formalized journalistic endeavor known as "fact checking."

There are two main types of political fact-checking websites: those that investigate statements by politicians and those that investigate media coverage of political news. Among the sites that fact check political discourse, some are supported by universities, while others are run by both commercial and nonprofit media. An example is FactCheck.org, part of the Annenberg Public Policy Center at the University of Pennsylvania, which claims to be "a nonpartisan, nonprofit 'consumer advocate' for voters that aims to reduce the level of deception and confusion in U.S. politics" (*FactCheck.org* 2012).

Some individual news outlets also have fact-checking operations. Notable examples include "PolitiFact" (2012) at the *Tampa Bay Times* and "The Fact Checker" (2012) at *The Washington Post*. These websites use varying scales to indicate the truthfulness of a statement. The measurements are designed to be engaging and easy for the reader to understand. PolitiFact uses a "Truth-o-Meter" with rankings from "True" to "Pants-on-Fire," while *The Washington Post* awards one to four "Pinocchios" depending upon the severity of the inaccuracy. These scales give the impression of scientific measurement, but there is no clear standard that differentiates the requirements for the levels.

There are also organizations that follow media coverage of politics, usually with the purpose of exposing partisan bias with which they disagree. On the left, Media Matters (http://mediamatters.org/) identifies itself as a "progressive research and information center dedicated to comprehensively monitoring, analyzing, and correcting conservative misinformation in the U.S. media" (Media Matters for America 2012). On the right, NewsBusters (http://newsbusters.org/) claims to be "the leader in documenting, exposing and neutralizing liberal media bias" (*NewsBusters.org* 2012). These sites serve largely to reinforce the opinions already held by their readers.

The writers and editors of fact-checking sites select statements to evaluate based on their following of the news and on reader suggestions. These sites do not facilitate or encourage citizen journalism per se, but rather provide citizens a route to seek clarification from sources they consider credible. Numerous forms of political communication are ripe for evaluation, including speeches, e-mails, TV and radio appearances, direct mail, and advertisements. The Internet has made it much easier to check the accuracy of a politician's statement against primary sources, media reports, and scholarly evidence.

Glenn Kessler, the fact checker at *The Washington Post*, argues that fact checking is not a replacement of journalism but rather "a supplement . . . when I was a political reporter, I was often frustrated that I would be covering the day-to-day statements of the candidates and never really had an opportunity to step back and really examine what the truth was behind that statement" (quoted in NPR 2012). In terms of objectivity, many of the stories produced for fact-checking websites could be classified as falling somewhere between reporting and commentary.

What is difficult about the fact-checking enterprise is that most statements made by politicians are not simply true or false. They are usually interpretations of events designed to highlight their own agenda, what we might call spin. It is also difficult to determine if someone made a mistake or intentionally tried to distort or deceive. There have long been efforts by some journalists to check the facts supplied by politicians, but the rise of online journalism has led to a proliferation of websites and media projects with the sole function of identifying the accuracy of political discourse. It is important to note that lying, omitting details, and mischaracterizing a situation are moral and ethical issues, not (usually) illegal acts. There are no laws that mandate the accuracy of political speech unlike, for example, limitations on some claims about commercial products. So while a soda company cannot claim that its beverages cure cancer, politicians are free to say they will cure cancer only if we elect them.

What effect has fact checking had on political discourse? Politicians will some-times use reports from fact-checking websites to support their own arguments. The most notable example was part of the 2004 vice presidential debate between Dick Cheney and John Edwards. Cheney attempted to defend his record as CEO of Halliburton on the basis of FactCheck.org's analysis. It is worth noting that he got the details wrong, including the name of the website and the claim that FactCheck.org had rebutted Edwards's charges about his corporate past. From a political com-munication standpoint, however, such errors may not matter; there were far more viewers of the vice presidential debate than visitors to FactCheck.org's website to read its original story or its follow-up to Cheney's claims. Given that most readers of fact-checking websites are likely to be more attentive to politics than the average Internet surfer, they may only seek confirmation of views they already hold. But there is some evidence that politicians have responded to evaluations by changing language posted on websites or altering details of an argument. Politicians and political organizations may also use a fact checker's evaluation as evidence of the untrustworthiness of their opponents.

One concern is whether or not anyone checks the fact checkers. There are citi-zen journalists who comment on these websites to identify mistakes. But check-ing itself can be seen as part of the political discourse rather than as a neutral process. Some high-profile fact-checking organizations display their own political biases, selecting one group for greater scrutiny than another (Hemingway 2011). Also, there is no clear delineation of the kinds of statements fact checkers should evaluate. It seems fairly straightforward to scrutinize a particular piece of evi-dence (like a dollar figure in a federal budget or a claim to be accurately quot-ing a third party); but fact checkers are on shakier ground when they attempt to evaluate someone's opinion. Journalist Dan Kennedy (2011) argues that fact checkers need "increasing quantities of fuel to keep the fires burning. And there just isn't enough. The fact-checkers are shifting from judging facts to indulging in opinion, but they're not necessarily doing it because they want to. They're doing it because politicians don't flat-out lie as frequently as we might suppose." Fact checking inevitably displays a selection bias; editors know that stories about truthful statements make less interesting reading than assertions about politically motivated dishonesty. Fact checkers might give the impression that politicians lie much more frequently than they actually do, suggesting that the public should view this new journalistic product no less critically than any other.

Conclusion

We began this chapter by looking at the definition of journalists, and argued that perhaps the biggest change in the digital age has been in the re-definition of who journalists are and what journalists do (rather than what journalism is). We also contended that the professional journalism paradigm has been seriously challenged by the amateurs and ordinary citizens who have become the newsgatherers while professional journalists have turned toward tasks like sorting information, mediating, gatekeeping, and drawing meaning from the news. In the context of this paradigmatic change, we explored larger issues of lobbying and political influence in American society.

Our analysis suggests that media organizations are major players in the world of lobbying and political influence. In fact, the media play a dual role—while professional journalists are influenced by lobbying groups, they may also be lobbyists themselves. We believe that media institutions are among the largest lobbying machines currently in existence in America, reflecting the recent trends of media corporatization, consolidation, and politization. These changes have also enabled, or at least accelerated, the move of professional journalism away from strict reportage to social and political commentary—even news-focused humor.

Simultaneously, the stark polarization of media between left and the right has left some audiences discontented and distrustful. Many have taken advantage of new online outlets to express their own voices and draw attention to topics ignored by mainstream journalists. In the process, they have challenged and helped to reinvent the watchdog role of professional journalists.

A final question remains: To the degree that today's journalists still keep a check on the government and other institutions of power, who keeps the media in check? Where we find a robust new culture of Internet fact checking and citizen "watchdogging," we also find that nonprofessional journalists and fact-checking organizations lack real political influence. There are unresolved conflicts among ill- versus well-intentioned fact checkers, journalists versus public relations practitioners, and citizens versus professional journalists, all sharing the new world of abundant information but often missing the truth, intentionally or not. In particular, we view with caution the many new pathways for inserting corporate speech and politically motivated discourse into everyday life, social and personal relations, education and culture, often under the guise of disinterested journalism.

But we remain optimistic that the online culture of "watchdogging" will ultimately advance American democracy by emphasizing the importance of transparency and creating a world where it is increasingly difficult to tell lies. Who will benefit? Everyone. This argument does not work solely in the public interest. It is our belief that the recent challenges to professional journalism are healthy and constructive. To regain and sustain credibility, journalists will need to return to their core role of keeping powerful institutions honest—including media organizations themselves.

References

Barodel, Jo, and Mark Deuze. (2001). "'Network Journalism': Converging Competencies of Old and New Media Professionals." *Australian Journalism Review* 23, no. 2: 91–103.

Buckhead. (2004). "Documents Suggest Special Treatment for Bush in Guard [Post 47]." *Free Republic*. Accessed June 11, 2012. http://www.freerepublic.com/focus/f-news/1210662 /posts.

Curran, James. (2003). "Global Journalism: A Case Study of the Internet." In Couldry Nick and Curran James, eds. *Contesting Media Power: Alternative Media in a Networked World*. Lanham, MD: Rowman & Littlefield, pp. 227–241.

Dean, Jodi. (2009). *Democracy and Other Neoliberal Fantasies: Communicative Capitalism and Left Politics*. Durham, NC: Duke University Press.

Delli Carpini, Michael. (2004). "The Tasks in Creating a New Journalism." *Nieman Reports* X (Winter): 61.

"The Fact Checker." (2012). *The Washington Post*. Accessed June 12, 2012. http://www .washingtonpost.com/blogs/fact-checker.

FactCheck.org. (2012). "About Us." Accessed June 28, 2012. http://factcheck.org/about/.

Hemingway, Mark. (2011). "Lies, Damned Lies, and 'Fact Checking.'" *The Weekly Standard*. Accessed June 11, 2012. http://www.weeklystandard.com/articles/lies-damned-lies-and-fact-checking_611854.html?page=3.

The Huffington Post. (2012). "Frequently Asked Questions." Accessed June 12, 2012. http:// www.huffingtonpost.com/p/frequently-asked-question.html.

Jones, Sebastian. (2010, March). "The Media-Lobbying Complex." *The Nation*: 12–16.

Johnson, Scott. (2004, September 9). "The 61st Minute." *Power Line*. Accessed June 11, 2012. http://www.powerlineblog.com/archives/2004/09/007699.php.

Kennedy, Dan. (2011, December 13). "PolitiFact and the Limits of Fact-Checking." *The Huffington Post*. Accessed June 11, 2012. http://www.huffingtonpost.com/dan-kennedy /politifact-and-the-limits_b_1144876.html.

Klein, Jonathan. (2004, September 10). "The O'Reilly Factor." *Fox News*.

Lasica, J.D. (2003). "Internet's Role in the Clinton-Lewinsky Scandal." *Journalism.org*. Accessed June 25, 2012. http://www.journalism.org/node/1788.

Layton, Charles. (2004). "Lobbying Juggernaut." *American Journalism Review* 26, no. 5: 26–35.

Lewis, Charles. (2000). "Media Money: How Corporate Spending Blocked Political Ad Reform and Other Stories of Influence." *Columbia Journalism Review* 39, no 3: 20–27.

Lisheron, Mark. (2007). "Lying to Get the Truth." *American Journalism Review* 29, no 5: 28–35.

McCheseney, Robert. W., and John Nichols. (2003, February 24). "Media Democracy's Moment." *The Nation* 276, no. 7: 16–20.

Media Matters for America. (2012). "About Us." Accessed June 28, 2012. http://mediamat ters.org/p/about_us/.

NewsBusters.org. (2012). "About NewsBusters.org." Accessed June 28, 2012. http://news busters.org/about-newsbusters-org.

NPR. (2012, January 10). "Political Fact-Checking under Fire." *Talk of the Nation.* Accessed July 26, 2013. http://www.npr.org/2012/01/10/144974110/political-fact-checking-under-fire.

PBS NewsHour. (2010, November 29). "Third Massive WikiLeaks Disclosure Creates Ripple Worldwide." Accessed June 25, 2012. http://www.pbs.org/newshour/bb/government_programs/july-dec10/wikileaks1_11-29.html.

Pew Research Center for the People & the Press. (1998). "Popular Policies and Unpopular Press Lift Clinton Ratings." Accessed June 15, 2012.] http://www.people-press.org/1998/02/06/popular-policies-and-unpopular-press-lift-clinton-ratings/.

Pfister, Damien Smith. (2010). "Introduction to Special Issue: Public Argument/Digital Media." *Argumentation and Advocacy* 47, no 2: 63–66.

PolitiFact. (2012). "About PolitiFact." Accessed June 12, 2012. http://www.politifact.com/about/.

Singer, Jane B., David Domingo, Ari Heinonen, Alfred Hermida, Steve Paulussen, Thorsten Quandt, Zvi Reich, and Marina Vujnovic. (2011). *Participatory Journalism: Guarding Gates at Online Newspapers.* Malden, MA: Wiley and Blackwell.

Starr, Paul. (2004). "Check and Balance." *The American Prospect* 15, no. 7: 30.

Wiesslitz, Carmit, and Tamar Ashuri. (2011). "Moral Journalists: The Emergence of New Intermediaries of News in an Age of Digital Media." *Journalism* 12, no. 8: 1035–1051.

WikiLeaks. (2012). "About." Accessed June 13, 2012. http://wikileaks.org/About.html.

21st-Century Influence and the Presidency: Social Media, Campaigns, and Transitions

Heath Brown and Anne Whitesell

Introduction

For decades, scholars, political commentators, and the public have dithered over whether interest groups embody the best of U.S. politics through pluralism or the worst through unequal representation and preferences for the wealthy. David Truman (1951) emphasized the pluralistic tradition in American politics that would benignly generate groups on all sides of a policy issue. But Schattschneider (1960) and others later found fault with the rosy picture of the pluralists and opined that the community of interest groups was biased in favor of the advantaged. Scholars ever since have debated the issue.

Changing federal regulations on interest groups and the rise of social media technology since the late 1990s promise to complicate these long-standing debates. This chapter ponders the following questions: Have U.S. Supreme Court decisions invited too much money into political campaigns? Do interest groups that support candidates get rewarded with a "seat at the table" during the policy planning phase of governance? Does technology equalize political opportunities or exacerbate existing political inequalities? The answer to these questions can be found through an investigation of the intersection of social media, political campaigns, and presidential transitions. This chapter probes how policymakers use social media to influence the public and how the public—sometimes represented by interest groups—uses social media to influence the political process in the 21st century.

Interest Groups and Presidential Campaigning

It has become an accepted part of politics today that interest groups participate in election campaigns, but this is a relatively new phenomenon. One reason for this is that membership-based interest groups, those that rely upon dues-paying individuals or organizations to fund operations, have faced a thorny dilemma when it comes to campaigns: how to support favored candidates without offending certain members. This is a particular problem for large groups with a geographically or ideologically diverse membership such as a national trade association or labor union. Endorsing specific policies is relatively easy for an organization, but endorsing a specific candidate who may hold a variety of contradictory beliefs may be more difficult. The National Education Association (NEA), for example, did not endorse a presidential candidate until 1976, cognizant of the fact that the partisan affiliations of NEA members were equally split between the Republican and Democrat parties and independents (Brown 2012). Many other groups have a base of members that is similarly split along partisan and ideological lines. Even if they can reach consensus on specific issues which the group will pursue, Walker (1991) showed in 1980 that less than one quarter (22.9%) of interest groups used "electioneering" as a political tactic. It is often easier and safer for an interest group to simply wait until the campaign is over and then seek to influence the winner.

Since the 1970s, the number of interest groups has been on the rise. This is particularly true of nonmembership groups, sometimes called single-issue groups or citizen advocacy groups, which coalesce around a common idea rather than a trade or vocation, and which are funded through donations, endowments, and foundation grants (Skocpal 2007). Without having to worry about satisfying an ideologically diverse membership, many of these new groups see aggressive campaign work as a tactical asset to meeting their policy interests. But since nearly all of these groups are legally organized as 501(c) 3 nonprofits with IRS restrictions on just how political they can be, interest groups of all types have increasingly turned to creating political action committees (PACs) to financially support candidates. PACs operate in tandem with a larger interest group, but raise money separately and can spend money with fewer limits. There were nearly 4,500 PACs operating in 2009, a four-fold increase since the 1970s, and the number continues to rise (Rozell, Wilcox, and Madland 2006; Census 2012). The interest group PAC allows donors to legally funnel money to support candidates above the limits set on individual donations. The PAC can then donate to different parties and to candidates who have been allies on key policy issues in the past or who promise to do so if elected. But PACs have been highly regulated since the 1970s decision of *Buckley v. Valeo*, which ruled on Congress's creation of the Federal Election Commission (FEC) and many other federal regulations on campaign finance. The Supreme Court enshrined a campaign finance system of limitations on how much groups could raise (no more than $5,000 per member) and spend (no more than $5,000 per campaign); the justices also approved requirements for federal campaign reporting to the FEC.

In the most recent calendar year (2011), interest group PACs representing the top five business sectors alone spent nearly a billion dollars on the candidates. Interest group PACs often split their donations between Republicans and Democrats, frequently favoring an incumbent, regardless of party affiliation. For example, over the last two decades the National Association of Realtors, the membership interest group representing the real estate industry, has given $41 million to candidates: 50 percent to Republicans and 48 percent to Democrats (based on data from the Center for Responsive Politics, opensecrets.org, May 2012). The Credit Union National Association split its $20 million 51 percent Republican 49 percent Democrat. Other interest groups such as the International Association of Firefighters and the National Auto Dealers Association have favored candidates from a single party, Democrats and Republicans, respectively.

Supreme Court and Super PACs

And then came *Citizens United*, the landmark Supreme Court decision that over-turned a century of legal precedent related to the First Amendment, money, and politics. A series of interrelated judicial decisions in 2010, in particular *Speech-Now.org v. Federal Election Commission*, legalized unlimited and largely unregulated amounts of donations to new organizations, called independent expenditure-only committees or Super PACs. Super PACs cannot donate directly to campaigns, but can spend as much as they wish on political advertisements that support or oppose candidates. These Super PACs introduce a new and revolutionary dimension into the discussion of interest groups and campaigns.

While it is too early to fully evaluate the activities of Super PACs, news reports already provide evidence of their size and of the direction of their tactics. During the campaign for the Republican nomination for president in 2012, Super PACs were formed to support each of the major candidates. For example, based on data provided by the website http://opensecrets.org, Winning Our Future raised $16 million (primarily from the casino mogul Sheldon Adelson and his wife) to support former Speaker of the House of Representatives Newt Gingrich. And Restore Our Future, another Super PAC, generated over $50 million to back former governor of Massachusetts Mitt Romney. Super PACs have focused most of their resources on television advertising, the most direct way to reach a wide range of potential voters, but also a very expensive tactic.

U.S. senator Sheldon Whitehouse (D-RI) during a news conference about disclosure of Super PAC donors on Capitol Hill on February 1, 2012, in Washington, D.C. (Pete Marovich/Getty Images)

In some ways, the rise of Super PACs may dislodge interest groups from the central role they previously played in financing outside campaign influence. Most Super PACs are supported by just a handful of individual donors who in the past would have been prevented from spending so much money on each campaign. Campaigns may now feel beholden to these individual donors who can provide as much financial support as even a large interest group. But many of these same donors can also give to certain organizations which, following a 2007 ruling by the FEC, do not have to report their donor names to any federal agency provided the money is not given with the specific instructions to use it for election activities. As long as nonprofit organizations labeled as 501(c)4 do not have lobbying and electioneering as their *primary purpose*, they have wide latitude to participate in elections and the public has no way to know who is providing them with their money. This begs the question for students and scholars: will these changes in law and regulations exacerbate the concerns of those worried about money in politics, or is it simply the manifestation of the same inequities that exist in our larger society?

Interest Groups and Presidential Transitions

While interest groups, PACs, and Super PACs dominate voter mobilization, campaign finance, and issue advertising, it is think tanks that control presidential transition planning. Campaigns typically focus on a small number of highly salient issues such as foreign affairs, major social welfare programs like health care or education, or personality and character, but actual presidential governance demands attention to hundreds of issues of which the public is rarely aware. For this reason, think tanks or research organizations, staffed with dozens of policy analysts, budget specialists, and economists, are well positioned to help guide candidates and ultimately the new president. The DC-based Brookings Institution was the first in 1960 to play this role, sidling up to both presidential candidates, Richard Nixon and John F. Kennedy, with an array of technocrats and policy experts who had planned out the necessary steps the new president would need to take upon election—they even offered free office space and use of their library. In a largely non-ideological fashion, Brookings opined on the manner in which a transition should be executed, which policy areas were most critical, and which federal positions needed to be filled first. Kennedy's victory signaled the ascendancy of Brookings as the voice of rational, nonpartisan government planning.

Brookings played this role for a generation, with Democrats and Republicans alike, until conservatives grew tired of what they viewed as the left-leaning outlook of Brookings, and empowered the newly formed Heritage Foundation to plan for the Reagan transition. Heritage mounted a massive effort to prepare for the transition, organizing dozens of sympathetic scholars, interest group officials, and think tank researchers to author *Mandate for Leadership*, a best-selling articulation of how then-Governor Ronald Reagan could transition to power. Heritage was clear: it aimed to provide Reagan's presidential transition team with advice based on conservative principles and beliefs, not simply the practical suggestions typically offered by Brookings. Heritage was so successful and influential that 36 of its

Heritage Foundation president Edwin J. Feulner Jr. (center) speaking at a podium with U.S. president Ronald W. Reagan (second left) and others at a Heritage Foundation function. (Photo by Diana Walker/Time Life Pictures/Getty Images)

associates were appointed to the Reagan administration, second only to another think tank, the Hoover Institute, which had 55 officials chosen (Abelson 2006).

Heritage's efforts during the 1980 transition had a lasting influence on Washington politics and subsequent transitions. The presidential transition period has increasingly been seen as the first, and arguably most effective, point in the presidency to foment change. By starting early, long before election day, an eager interest group, advocacy organization, or think tank can shape the presidency through ideas, people, and policy.

This trend was never clearer than in 2008. The Center for American Progress (CAP), a 501(c) 3 nonprofit and think tank, with an affiliated politically oriented wing called CAP Action Fund, had worked as a Democratic government-in-exile for much of the Bush administration. Headed by former president Bill Clinton's Chief of Staff John Podesta, CAP was peripherally involved in the campaign, but at the center of the transition. Podesta was chosen to lead the Obama pre-election presidential transition planning during the summer of 2008 and CAP, as Heritage had in 1980s, began to author a comprehensive set of recommendations called *Change for America*. Dozens of contributors to *Change for America* were chosen to serve on presidential transition teams, and several were then hired to staff the White House and other key federal positions. Most importantly, many of the very ideas CAP advocated for, such as the creation of an Office on Social Entrepreneurship and changes in environmental policy, were soon established by executive order and overseen by those affiliated with CAP, such as Special

Advisor Van Jones for Green Jobs, Senior Advisor Michele Jolin, and energy czar Carol Browner.

The slow drift from the role played by Brookings to that of CAP has been met with little opposition. The federal regulations on think tank activities, either those rules administered by the FEC for campaign activities or by the Internal Revenue Service for tax-status and lobbying, are largely silent on the pre-election and post-election transition period. While lobbyists were forbidden by President-Elect Obama to donate to his transition planning efforts, think tank officials rarely register as lobbyists, and were thus immune from these restrictions. Those interested in the presidency must ask: Will think tanks continue this evolution to become so synonymous with interest groups that no organized group in Washington can claim a non-ideological or nonpartisan role in the policy process? Or will a new type of organization emerge that reclaims the mantle of rationality, science-based decision making, and impartiality?

Influencing Policymakers and Social Media

Whether during the campaign or the transition, public communication is one of the key tactics used by groups to influence policy. The purchase of political advertisements on radio or television has been the conventional approach interest groups use. These ads are highly regulated by the Federal Communication Commission and are very expensive. Newer forms of communication, such as social media, that are largely unregulated and relatively cheap have emerged.

Social media differ from other forms of communication in that a network of users generates it. Traditional television, radio, and print media rely on journalists and editors to gather and distribute information to the public. With social media, however, the public can express opinions and disseminate information independent of traditional media sources, whether through commenting on Facebook pages, posting videos, or tweeting about current events (Auer 2011). This trend started even before social media came to dominate online communication, with the advent of electronic bulletin boards and weblogs or blogs. As journalists and political commentators became regular blog readers, the scope of traditional media coverage expanded to include what was being discussed online (Woodley 2008). With the power to generate and circulate content, social media users became participants in the policymaking process, a role that was previously limited to politicians, commentators, celebrities, and public administrators (Auer 2011). Not only could social media users publicize their complaints about policy and those responsible for creating it, they could also make recommendations for new policy to better address their concerns (Auer 2011).

The use of social media to expand the conversation about public policy issues can be considered a type of civic engagement. Civic engagement moves "an individual away from disinterest, distraction, ignorance and apathy towards education, understanding, motivation, and action" (Obar, Zube, and Lampe 2011, 4). In addition to talking about private matters online, Facebook and Twitter users are talking about public matters. Such online discussion among friends may encourage those who had previously been disengaged to pay more attention to policy issues. Emerging research from Obar et al. (2011) shows that many interest group representatives believe that social media will facilitate greater civic engagement. Social media users can post links to articles and videos to provide those unaware of current affairs with more information. With this increased awareness of policy issues, social media may also be used in turn to promote collective action, which is achieved through numerous activities, ranging from voting to joining special interest groups and actively campaigning for policy change. The common thread among these activities, however, is that collective action brings people together in an effort to achieve political or social change (Obar et al. 2011). Organized interests have begun using social media as a method of promoting civic engagement and collection action. Established groups, such as the Christian right, have embraced the use of social media as a strategy to gain access to policymakers and influence the public agenda. More recently, social media have provided a platform for citizens to raise concerns over specific policy changes, such as Internet piracy laws.

The Christian Right

Faith-based groups such as the Christian (or religious) right possess a unique set of characteristics that give them an advantage in the type of civic engagement and collective action that leads to political mobilization; combined with using technology, these groups have the opportunity to organize followers and become a powerful voice in setting the public agenda. Among many religious groups, there are strong, charismatic leaders who can use their influence to further political and social goals (Boerl, Frazier-Crawford, and Perkins 2011). One such leader who used his religious position for political ends was Pat Robertson. Robertson, an ordained Baptist minister, was introduced to the national audience with his talk show *700 Club*, and launched a presidential campaign in 1988 (Wilcox and Robinson 2010). Although unsuccessful, Robertson's campaign engaged Christian conservatives and changed the makeup of state and local Republican Party committees (Wilcox and Robinson 2010).

In addition to encouraging Christian conservatives to engage in politics by turning out to vote and becoming members of local party committees, the Christian right raised awareness of public policy issues. James Dobson and the Christian group he founded, Focus on the Family, influenced public debate on same-sex marriage, health care reform, and other social issues (Wilcox and Robinson 2010). Dobson is familiar with the advantages of social media in disseminating information; in 2010, he used Facebook to announce that he was leaving Focus on the Family to start a radio program with his son. In the same Facebook post, Dobson asked his supporters to raise $2 million for the program (Goldstein 2010).

In addition to charismatic leaders, the followers of these groups have a built-in strong collective identity in their shared faith (Boerl et al. 2011). Although the movement includes members of all faiths, the vast majority are white evangelical Christians (Wilcox and Robinson 2010). In essence, one of the main challenges in political mobilization—assembling a community of individuals with common beliefs—has already been overcome. Members of the religious right know generally where they, and the other members of the movement, stand on many issues, and they can be expected to vote for many of the same candidates. The shared Christian beliefs cannot be taken for granted; in fact, over the years several factions have arisen within the movement. For example, Evangelical Environmental Network (EEN) is composed of Christian conservatives concerned with environmental issues, such as protection of endangered species, that have traditionally not been addressed by the Christian right. The Internet was integral in bringing together this small section of the larger movement (Boerl et al. 2011). The EEN has been criticized by other parts of the movement for its support of Environmental Protection Agency regulations, and controversy continues over the role of humans in climate change (Geman 2012). Another faction of the Christian right that has benefited from the Internet is Emergent Christianity. Emergent Christianity is not defined by a uniform set of beliefs, and is a loosely structured movement within the Christian right. The lack of central authority reflects a general trend of decentralization among Internet movements (Ryan and Switzer 2009). The emerging church is also using online tools, such as social networks and podcasts, to reach out to a younger audience (Boerl et al. 2011).

Lastly, because these groups are brought together in organized churches, many of the logistical challenges interest groups face, such as fund-raising, are already addressed (Boerl et al. 2011). Congregation members often see one another face to face at least weekly at church services, and can spread the message they hear while at services to those outside of the church (Wilcox and Robinson 2010). The dissemination of information is not limited to the networks of congregation members. Through the years, the religious right has been able to use media and technology to broadcast its message to a much wider audience. The rise of televangelism in the 1960s, for example, showed the influence of Christian fundamentalists nationally. Between the late 1960s and the mid-1980s, televangelism viewers increased from about 5 million to nearly 25 million (Boerl et al. 2011, 70). Jerry Falwell's *Old Time Gospel Hour* was broadcast on more than 300 television stations throughout the country (Wilcox and Robinson 2010, 43). Moving into the Internet age, conservative Christian groups began utilizing e-mails to alert their followers of important policy developments. Supporters of the Family Research Council, for example, can receive state-specific action alerts (Wilcox and Robinson 2010). Focus on the Family e-mails roughly 4 million monthly newsletters, in addition to nearly 6 million e-mails to its subscribers (Wilcox and Robinson 2010, 78). The number of people exposed to the beliefs and positions of the religious right multiples when it is spread through social media, in which one topic spread by enough people can become a "trending topic" in a city, region, or even worldwide.

Social Media and Policy Change: SOPA and PIPA

Online social networks provide a forum for like-minded individuals to discuss current government policies and raise awareness of overlooked issues that they feel should be placed on the public agenda. Citizens can use social media to post their grievances, sign online petitions, and organize physical meetings. Does this type of discussion and mobilization result in substantive policy change? In at least one case, the answer appears to be yes.

In late 2011, both the House of Representatives and Senate brought to the floor legislation that sought to decrease illegal downloading of music, TV shows, and movies, and increase interest user privacy (Wortham 2012). The House bill, the Stop Online Piracy Act (SOPA), was co-sponsored by over 20 representatives, including members of both parties. Similarly, the Senate's PROTECT IP Act (PIPA) had a rare degree of bipartisan support and more than 40 co-sponsors. In addition, the bills were supported by various major industries, such as movie studios and record labels, and influential interest groups, such as the U.S. Chamber of Commerce (Oremus 2011). Passage of the bills appeared inevitable.

But Internet companies began protesting the legislation, believing the language of the bills could threaten the existence of such widely used sites as YouTube, Flickr, and Wikipedia. Within days of this development, politicians began speaking out against the legislation, with leaders such as Nancy Pelosi suggesting the need to revise the legislation, all while using the Twitter hash tag #DontBreakTheInternet (Oremus 2011). Over 80,000 social media users called their legislators to complain about the legislation after being called to action by Tumblr (Wortham 2012). Companies joined together to sponsor an "American Censorship Day"; Wikipedia participated by shutting down and providing encyclopedia entries only on the legislation in question. The Google logo on its home page was covered in black for the day, and more than 4.5 million visitors signed an online petition against the legislation. Within 24 hours, politicians were withdrawing their support for the bills, and House Speaker John Boehner admitted that the future of the bill was in question (Tsukayama and Halzack 2012). While the mobilization of social media users around the legislation was not the sole cause of its abandonment, the course of events suggests that online communication has become an importance source of political mobilization and increased civic participation. As citizens increasingly use social media to talk about public policy issues, policymakers are taking notice.

Influencing the Public and Social Media

Social media also permit those in power—elected officials and policymakers—and those seeking office to interact directly with voters and other constituents. Ever since print newspapers ran the competing claims of Federalists and anti-Federalists, communication technologies have aided political propagandizing, but digitization has increased the speed, directness, and precision of these interactions. Shogan (2010) tracked the increasing usage of information technologies in Congress from e-mail to Twitter to YouTube. Many members of Congress and their staffs eagerly incorporated these new technologies into their operations, but others resisted such rapid change while institutional rules, such as those against using laptops on the floor of Congress, delayed universal usage. President Obama challenged notions of the traditional White House press briefing by holding a "virtual presser" through Google+ in January 2012. Rather than face dogged questions from the likes of famously tough White House correspondent Helen Thomas, the president fielded questions submitted through video clips on YouTube and in an online chat room.

The speed with which the Internet has been integrated into campaigns means that research is just barely catching up to it. Evidence from the 2000 presidential election showed that less than 5 percent of survey respondents used the Internet to donate money or volunteer for a campaign (Dulio and O'Brien 2004). Just eight years later, the Internet emerged as a primary mechanism used by both major campaigns to mobilize campaign volunteers and donors. In 2008, the campaign for then-senator Barack Obama used e-mail and the Internet to aid its fund-raising endeavors. Rather than rely on in-person fund-raising events or standard mail, the campaign used electronic fund-raising to solicit donations from millions of individuals who had signed up at various websites supportive of the candidate. Electronic fund-raising is both inexpensive and incredibly effective. The strategy was so successful in 2008 that the Obama campaign was able to surpass previous fund-raising by presidential candidates, nearing $500 million, just from its online efforts, thereby permitting the candidate to forgo the limits associated with federal financing. The campaign claimed that the average donation was less than $80 and that they received over 6 million donations from 3 million supporters (Vargas 2008).

Social media were also integrated into the 2008–2009 presidential transition. In an effort to reinforce campaign themes of transparency and open government, the Obama transition team required any group or individual requesting a meeting to discuss policy or personnel to post their advisory letter to a public website. Hundreds of letters were uploaded and available for comment and discussion through the "Seat at the Table" policy at http://www.change.gov. The public and social nature of this medium may have encouraged greater discussion of new policy recommendations than in the past when groups would meet with the transition team in near secret. However, the Obama transition team had to place limits on just how transparent they would be with the "Seat at the Table" policy. They reported online which groups they met with, but not if the meeting had a single representative from the interest group. They also published online nearly all of those letters submitted by groups, but redacted those that addressed specific personnel recommendations. These exceptions make sense in retrospect, but cause some scholars, such as Cary Coglianese (2009) of the University of Pennsylvania, to question whether the Obama administration's promise of total transparency raised unrealistic expectations for the public.

In 2012, social media continued to grow in importance for those in office, but it also became less transparent. It was reported that the president's re-election team paid several companies—including a $11.4 million contract with General Dynamics—to do extensive data mining of potential voters, donors, and supporters using many of the most common social media outlets. The project was called Dreamcatcher and used complex codes to search the personal Facebook and Twitter accounts of individuals for voting and donation patterns (Issenberg 2012). They then allegedly used what was learned from those searches to "micro"–target e-mail messages to individuals based on race, religion, and other characteristics gleaned from the web. According to Beckett and Larson (2012), the technology can target a different e-mail at the husband and wife of a married couple. They reported an example, where a couple received two different e-mails from the Obama campaign, each e-mail soliciting a campaign donation, but one—sent to the

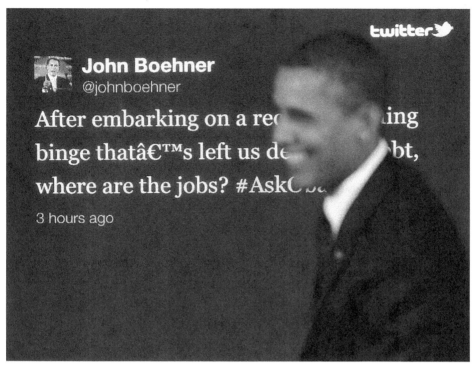

U.S. president Barack Obama answering a question from House Speaker John Boehner during a Twitter Town Hall meeting at the White House in Washington, D.C., in 2010. (© Zhang Jun/ Xinhua Press/Corbis)

husband—included reference to a "new, super-easy" way to donate online and the other—sent to the wife—included an anecdote about a 61-year-old grandmother. One e-mail asked for $20 and the other for $25. Such subtle variations may be based on different vulnerabilities and weaknesses that trigger different responses in different potential donors or voters. Students and scholars may ask: Are there privacy concerns that should limit political campaigns from mining information shared on publicly available social media networks? Should candidates pledge to respect the privacy of constituents, or should they be free to use whatever data are available to them to win election?

Conclusion

It is difficult to disentangle the relationships between money, technological change, and politics. Technology has made money less important and more important at the same time. Social media have been used to influence policymakers and the governmental agenda, while policymakers have increasingly relied on it to change public opinion, garner support, and win votes. Making sense of these interconnected social phenomena is particularly difficult at this point in history. We sit in the middle of the storm, unable to predict with certainty its ultimate size or the future direction it will take. However, this chapter has drawn attention to some important facets of political influence in the 21st century. First, regulatory change at the national level will likely increase the amount of money in politics in the near future. Whether increases in money will have a direct policy impact remains to be seen.

Second, interest groups are extensively using social media to influence policy and politics. The information technology revolution over the past 20 years and the advent of social media platforms such as Facebook, Twitter, and YouTube offer opportunities for new groups to enter into the policymaking process. On the other hand, certain technologies—such as those data collection tools employed by presidential candidates—remain very expensive and are effectively out of reach for organizations without significant resources. It is still unclear whether social media will further democratize U.S. policymaking or simply mirror the same structures already in place.

Finally, interest groups are just one type of outside influence on the policy process. The 21st century may increasingly see the rise of hybrid organizations, which combine elements of a traditional membership-based group, a foundation-supported, single-issue-based group, and a research-oriented think tank. The presidential transition phase of the policy process offers a perspective on how these new types of groups might seek to influence an incoming administration without ever spending a dollar on a campaign donation.

But what is on the horizon? Will a future Supreme Court reinterpret the constitutionality of campaign regulations? Will ever-changing technologies replace the current array of social media platforms and establish new political communication pathways? These questions may remain unresolved, and continue to stimulate debates about the nature of U.S. democracy for many years to come.

References

Abelson, Donald E. (2006). *A Capitol Idea: Thinks Tanks and US Foreign Policy*. Montreal: McGill-Queen's University Press.

Auer, Matthew R. (2011). "The Policy Sciences of Social Media." *The Policy Studies Journal* 39, no. 4: 709–736.

Beckett, Lois and Jeff Larson. (2012). "Reverse-engineering Obama's Message." *Pro Publica* Accessed April 13, 2014. http://www.propublica.org/article/reverse-engineering-obamas-message-machine.

Boerl, Christopher, Wayne Frazier-Crawford, and Chris Perkins. (2011). "The Political Pluralisation of American Evangelicals: How Old Media Built a Movement, and Why the Internet Is Poised to Change It." *International Journal for the Study of the Christian Church* 11, no. 1: 66–78.

Brown, Heath. (2012). *Lobbying the New President: Interests in Transition*. New York: Routledge.

Census, United States. (2012). "Table 422, Compendia." *Statistical Abstract*. Accessed April 13, 2014. https://www.census.gov/compendia/statab/2012/tables/12s0422.pdf.

Coglianese, Cary. (2009). "The Transparency President? The Obama Administration and Open Government." *Governance* 22, no. 4: 522–544.

Geman, Ben. (2012, Feb. 8). "Religious Right Bashes Green Evangelicals for Supporting EPA Rules." *The Hill*. Accessed November 25, 2012. http://thehill.com/blogs/e2-wire/e2-wire/209465-pro-life-leaders-bash-green-evangelicals-over-epa-rule.

Goodstein, Laurie. (2010, Jan. 16). "Radio Show for Focus on the Family Founder." *The New York Times*. Accessed November 25, 2012. http://www.nytimes.com/2010/01/17/business/media/17dobson.html?_r=1.

Issenberg, Sasha. (2012, Jan. 13). "Project Dreamcatcher." *Slate*. Accessed November 25, 2012. http://www.slate.com/articles/news_and_politics/victory_lab/2012/01/project_dreamcatcher_how_cutting_edge_text_analytics_can_help_the_obama_campaign_determine_voters_hopes_and_fears_.html.

Obar, Jonathan A., Paul Zube, and Clifford Lampe. (2011). "Advocacy 2.0: An Analysis of How Advocacy Groups in the United States Perceive and Use Social Media as Tools for Facilitating Civic Engagement and Collective Action." Accessed November 25, 2012. http://ssrn.com/abstract=1956352.

O'Brien, Erin and David Dulio. (2004). "Campaigning with the Internet: The View from the Bottom." In Jim Thurber and Candice Nelson eds. *Campaigns and Elections American Style,* 2nd ed. Boulder, CO: Westview Press, pp. 173–194.

Oremus, Will. (2011, Nov. 30). "The Rise of the Geek Lobby: Can Google, Facebook, Tech Wonks, and Web Activists Kill the Stop Online Piracy Act?" *Slate*. Accessed November 25, 2012. http://www.slate.com/articles/technology/technocracy/2011/11/stop_online_piracy_act_can_the_geek_lobby_stop_hollywood_from_wrecking_the_internet_.html.

Rozell, Mark. J., Clyde Wilcox, and David Madland. (2006). *Interest Groups in American Campaigns: The New Face of Electioneering.* 2nd ed. Washington, DC: CQ Press.

Ryan, Michael, and Les Switzer. (2009). *God in the Corridors of Power: Christian Conservatives, the Media, and Politics in America.* Santa Barbara, CA: ABC-CLIO.

Schattschneider, E. E. (1960). *The Semi-Sovereign People.* New York: Holt, Rinehart, and Winston.

Shogan, Collen. (2010). "Blackberries, Tweets, and YouTube: Technology and the Future of Communicating with Congress." *PS* 43, no. 2: 231–233.

Skocpol, Theda. (2007). "Government Activism and the Reorganization of Civic Democracy." In Paul Pierson and Theda Skocpol, eds. *The Transformation of American Politics: Activist Government and the Rise of Conservatism.* Princeton, NJ: Princeton University Press:. 39–67.

Truman, David. (1951). *The Governmental Process: Political Interests and Public Opinion.* New York: Alfred A. Knopf.

Tsukayama, Hayley, and Sarah Halzack. (2012, Jan. 19). "Internet Blackouts Appear to Have Desired Effect." *The Washington Post*. Accessed November 25, 2012. http://www.washingtonpost.com/business/technology/senators-drop-support-of-piracy-bill-after-protests/2012/01/18/gIQA848M9P_story.html.

Vargas, Jose A. (2008). "Obama Raised Half a Billion Online." *The Washington Post*. Accessed April 13, 2014. http://voices.washingtonpost.com/44/2008/11/obama-raised-half-a-billion-on.html.

Walker, Jack. (1991). *Mobilizing Interest Groups in America: Patrons, Professionals, and Social Movements.* Ann Arbor, MI: University of Michigan Press.

Wilcox, Clyde, and Carin Robinson. (2010). *Onward Christian Soldiers?: The Religious Right in American Politics.* 4th ed. Boulder, CO: Westview Press.

Woodly, Deva. (2008). "New Competencies in Democratic Communication?: Blogs, Agenda Setting and Political Participation." *Public Choice* 134: 109–123.

Wortham, Jenna. (2012, Jan. 20). "Public Outcry over Antipiracy Bills Began as Grass-Roots Grumbling: Many Voices on the Web, Amplified by Social Media." *The New York Times*: B1.

State Party Political Action Committees: Maintaining Political Relevance amid Campaign Finance Reforms

Michael J. Brogan

Introduction

State-level party political action committees (PACs) serve as the fund-raising arm for state political parties. In the campaign world, these organizations are referred to as "money groups" (Perrow 1970; Eismeier and Pollack 1985). They are extensions of various party caucus groups and/or serve as adjunct organizations of the major political parties (Knoke and Wood 1981). Depending upon whether the state party is in the majority (or minority) in the state legislature, state-party PACs are likely to determine which candidates to fund based either on an incumbent-protection strategy or as part of an attempt to add seats (Thompson, Cassie, and Jewell 1994). State party organizations also account for the largest percentage of funding to state legislative candidates when compared to other funding sources (Gierynski and Breaux 1998). The effectiveness of state-level party PACs has allowed the major political parties to increase their financial role in state campaigns (Kettler and Hamm 2011).

At the federal level, the Bipartisan Campaign Reform Act of 2002 had a significant impact on campaign contribution patterns of state party PACs. The act banned soft money contributions—that is, funds not subject to federal contribution limits—resulting in a direct effect on state party PACs. A major provision of the act is to require state party PACs to fund any federal activities with "hard money" contributions—meaning those funds subject to federal contribution limits (Francia, Wesley, and Wilcox 2013). The requirement caused a significant decrease in total contributions collected by the major state political parties. Prior to the implementation of the act, the national party PACs and their state counterparts engaged in a process in which "hard" campaign finance contributions from the former were transferred to the latter in exchange for soft money contributions. Whether this provision effectively ended the existence of soft money in the campaign process is unclear. On one hand, the law effectively reduced, or in some jurisdictions eliminated, the transfer of "soft money" to state party operations from the national parties. However, the law may have simply transferred this funding source from parties to independent expenditure groups acting outside of existing party structures (La Raja 2008; Malbin 2008).

As a result of the federal law, it appears that state party PACs have shifted their focus from the national parties as their primary source of contributions to individual donors and to state-level committees (primarily candidate committees and ideological groups). This has diminished the role and influence of the national parties on state parties (Kolodny and Dwyre 2003). State party PACs are trying to offset the loss from national party funding as a result of BCRA while maintaining their own political viability in the electoral process. Regardless of the impact of federal campaign finance reforms, state party PACs remain the lynchpin in supporting candidates financially and technically by connecting with voters, as well as continuing to oppose rival party candidates (Morehouse and Jewell 2003).

The second significant reform to impact state party PACs has been the implementation of public campaign funding in 24 states of qualifying candidates in legislative (16) and/or statewide contests (8). In addition to either partial or full public funding of candidates, 10 states offer public subsidies of qualifying political parties, in legislative and gubernatorial elections (NCSL 2010). Proponents of the reform have touted its ability to "level the playing field" between candidates, reduce the influence of moneyed interests in politics, and make elections more competitive, while opponents argue that public campaign funding is a form of candidate welfare, disengages candidates from the public by eliminating the process of political fund-raising, and does not increase electoral competition because of other structural factors, such as incumbency and partisan composition of the electorate (Brogan and Mendilow 2012).

This chapter argues that the impact of BCRA and public funding schemes on state party PACs has forced a shift of fund-raising strategy. In states with public campaign financing, state party PACs were more dependent upon "super donors" (individuals in the 95th percentile of financial contributions during a given election cycle). "Soft money" contributions to party PACs from wealthy individual donors are more likely to be strongly allied with the major parties, thus providing them with an additional incentive to donate to these groups (Apollino and La Raja 2004). As a consequence, public funding programs have not reduced the role of moneyed interests in politics but rather, through a smaller pool of donors, concentrated the influence of these interests over state political parties that offer public campaign financing.

Moreover, the impact of BCRA and public campaign funding reforms have not only caused state political parties to adapt to these regulations, but more fundamentally have provided legal mechanisms that have empowered their role in the campaign process. As a consequence, state party PACs' adaptability to campaign finance reforms ensures that these organizations remain influential in the campaign process. Their leverage in public campaign funding systems is their ability to engage donors through separate fund-raising activities in order to enhance the electoral prospects of their parties' candidates. Donors who wish to be free from the contribution and spending limits of public funding schemes can direct funds to state party PACs in order to attack the opposition at the state and district levels, as well as to signal other independent expenditure groups about their overall electoral strategy. State party PACs, therefore, have an amplifying effect on the electoral environment in the states: they fund candidates' campaigns, provide campaign services to candidates (e.g., polling, consulting, staffing), engage in party-building initiatives throughout the states, and tackle outreach efforts to voters (Jewell and Morehouse 2001; Kettler and Hamm 2011). To accomplish these tasks, state party PACs serve as an effective conduit of donor money that can be used outside of public financing. Thus candidates have become more dependent upon party leaders as a result of public campaign finance reform (Francia, Hernson, Frendreis, and Gitelson 2006).

This chapter provides a brief overview of the impact of federal- and state-level campaign finance reforms on fund-raising efforts by state party PACs. It also presents empirical evidence on how state party PACs have adapted to various changes in campaign finance laws at both the state and national levels. The final section of the chapter discusses the implications of the changes in state party PAC fund-raising activity for the durability of state political parties, how they have maintained their political relevance, and what we may expect in the future in terms of strategic behavior among party leaders.

Evaluating the Evidence: An Overview of Fund-Raising Activities by State Party PACs in Light of Campaign Finance Reform

Overall, there has been an 85 percent increase (in 2010 dollars) in total contributions to candidates and committees from 2000 to 2010. During this same period there was a 13.8 percent decrease in contributions to state party PACs. Most of this drop can be attributed to BCRA, which led to a significant decline in national party donations to state parties. Yet when comparing 2004 (the first major election cycle after BCRA) to 2010, state party PACs saw an increase of 33 percent in total contributions. State party PACs were able to offset the loss of funding from the national parties from other funding sources. These changes are discussed in more detail later.

Before identifying the shift in the fund-raising strategy of state party PACs sources, it is important to note who funds these organizations. The money comes from individual donors, either directly or indirectly through other PACs (Gierzynski and Breaux 1998). From 2000 to 2010, state party PACs raised an average of 76 percent of their total funding from other political committees and approximately 24 percent from individual donations. At the federal level, donations to national party PACs come predominantly from other PACs, unions, and corporate donations (Ansolabehere, de Figuerido, and Synder 2003).

Table 1 summarizes the 10-year average (adjusted to 2010 dollars) of the top 10 committees that funded the Republican and Democratic state party PACs from 2000 to 2010.

The findings summarized in Table 1 indicate a shift in state party PAC contribution patterns before and after BCRA. In total, party committees accounted for 60 percent of the Republican state party PAC totals in 2000 and 64 percent of the Democratic state party PAC contributions. These funds came primarily from the national parties. In 2000, 36 percent of total contributions from party committees to the Republican state party PACs came from the National Republican Party, and 40 percent of contributions to Democratic state party PACs came from the Democratic National Party. On a proportional basis, 3 percent of total party committee funding in 2010 came from the Democratic National Party and roughly 1 percent from the Republican National Committee.

Table 1. Average Committee Contributions to Republican State Party PACs (2000–2010)

Rank	Committee Type	Percent 2000	Percent 2010	Ten-Year Average
1	Party Committees	60	8	$63,669,039
2	Candidate Committees	8	22	$42,182,026
3	Real Estate	2	4	$9,689,780
4	Conservative Policy Organization	0	13	$8,589,026
5	Insurance	2	5	$7,798,834
6	Lawyers/Law Firms	2	2	$4,755,502
7	Health Professionals	1	2	$4,341,143
8	Casinos/Gambling	1	1	$4,144,920
9	Telecom Services	1	2	$4,109,945
10	Hospitals/Nursing Homes	1	2	$3,655,776

Average Committee Contributions to Democratic State Party PACs (2000–2010)

Rank	Committee Type	Percent 2000	Percent 2010	Ten-Year Average
1	Party Committees	64	12	$77,469,080
2	Candidate Committees	9	24	$51,013,396
3	Public Sector Unions	4	13	$22,156,578
4	Lawyers/Law Firms	4	5	$13,275,346
5	Liberal Policy Organizations	1	7	$9,989,235
6	Building Trade Unions	1	6	$8,324,117
7	Miscellaneous Unions	1	4	$5,866,827
8	Real Estate	1	2	$4,373,353
9	Insurance	1	2	$3,665,500
10	Transportation Unions	1	1	$3,543,167

Notes

1 Committees that have been coded as "UNKNOWN" are not included.

2 Adjusted to 2010 dollars based on CPI.

3 Percentages are based on total contributions received by each state party PAC in 2000 and 2010.

Source: National Institute on Money in State Politics (www.followthemoney.org).

To compensate for the loss of national party money, state party PACs have increased contributions from candidate committees. From this source of funding, less than 10 percent of total contributions in 2000 came from candidate committees. These contributions rose from 8 percent in 2000 to 22 percent in 2010 for Republican state party PACs and from 9 percent in 2000 to 24 percent in 2010 for Democratic state party PACs. This trend follows a similar pattern for national party PACs. As a consequence, there has been a need by the party leadership to "lean more heavily on rank and file members" to generate funds not only for their campaigns but also for party PACs (La Raja 2008, 5).

In addition, state party PACs have shifted their fund-raising strategies away from the national parties toward more ideological organizations. Both liberal and conservative organizations have stepped up their contributions to state party PACs. Contributions from liberal groups to Democratic state party PACs rose from 1 percent in 2000 to 7 percent in 2010. Conservative groups' donations to Republican state party PACs jumped from less than 1 percent in 2000 to 13 percent in 2010.

The Growing Importance of "Super Donors"

One particularly significant shift in fund-raising activity among the Democratic and Republican state party PACs after BCRA is the reliance on individual donations from "super donors." Typically the individuals who donate to political party PACs fall into a few categories: those who do so for ideological reasons ("ideologues"), out of political interests ("investors"), or based on feelings of personal identification with elected officials ("intimates") (Francia, Green, Hernson, Powell, and Wilcox 2003). In 2000, the percentage of total receipts from "super donors" was 10 percent; that increased to 14 percent in 2010 for Republican state party PACs. For Democratic state party PACs, there was an increase from 7 percent in 2000 to 10 percent in 2010.

Approximately 24 percent of total donations to state party PACs come from individual donations. Among this source of funding, 81 percent of total funding comes from "super donors." Figure 1 plots the percentage of total individual contributions to the Democratic and Republican state party PACs from 2000 to 2010. On average, Republican state party PACs have raised $1.50 from "super donors" for every dollar raised from "super donors" by Democratic state party PACs from 2000 to 2010.

The effect of "super donors" on state party PACs has at least two other important dimensions. First, roughly 5 percent of donors who gave to state party PACs donated approximately 80 percent of all contributions to these organizations from 2000 to 2010. Of this group, the 10-year average (in 2010 dollars) contribution to Democratic state party PACs is $12,680 and for Republican state party PACs, $17,526.

Second, "super donors" behave as "monetary surrogates" (Mansbridge 2003, 523). Gimpel, Lee, and Pearson-Markowitz (2008) argue that the reason these individuals donate to party PACs in states where they do not live—and thus cannot vote—is because it provides a more "consequential and rewarding" experience than simply voting for a given candidate within their district (374). In other words, these donors are seeking to expand their political influence beyond their own state residence.

There are abundant opportunities for "super donors" to give to campaigns and committees at the state level. Since the states vary in their campaign finance laws

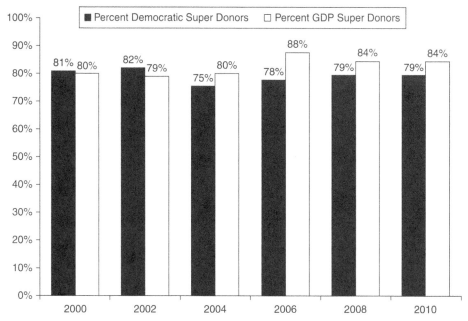

Figure 1. Percentage of Total Individual Contributions to Democratic and Republican Party PACs from "Super Donors" (2000–2010)

Source: National Institute on Money in State Politics (www.followthemoney.org).

regarding individual contribution limits to PACs, as well as whether individual donors can fund PACs across state lines, this provides individual donors with a variety of outlets. Though "super donors" may not be geographically located in a particular state, they do, nevertheless, have substantial impact on campaign outcomes in states in which they do not permanently reside. Figure 2 summarizes average out-of-state contributions to both major state party PACs from 2000 to 2010. Overall, Republican state party PACs received an average of $6,513 from out-of-state "super donors," while Democratic state party PACs collected an average of $8,913. For Democratic state party PACs, the top three states were Oregon $23,807, Washington $19,903, and Missouri $19,060. The top three states to receive out-of-state contributions for the GOP state party PACs were California ($78,249), New Mexico ($18,666), and Texas ($14,866).

The Impact of State Campaign Finance Laws on State Party PAC Contributions

A final area of interest is the impact of state campaign finance laws on contributions. Hogan, Hamm, and Wrzenski (2006) found that states with greater restrictions on contributions (by individuals, unions, and corporations) had smaller donations to candidates from interest groups. Moreover, Hogan (2000) found that, though contribution limits do significantly affect state-level campaign spending, the overall impact of these restrictions is modest.

On the whole, campaign finance regulations differ by state. Fifty-four percent of the states do not have individual contribution limits to state party PACs and the

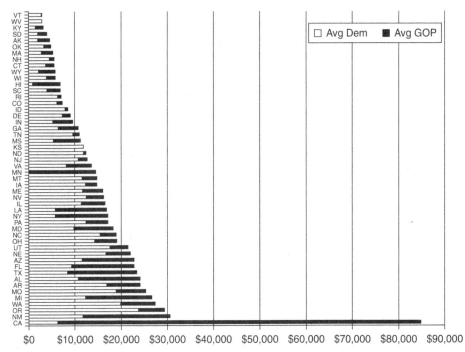

Figure 2. Average Out-of-State Contributions to Republican and Democratic State Party PACs from "Super Donors" (2000–2010)

Source: National Institute on Money in State Politics (www.followthemoney.org).

same percentage of states do not have restrictions on PAC-to-PAC contributions or contributions from national parties to state party PACs. Figure 3 graphs the impact of campaign finance laws on state party PAC contributions. Other things being equal, in terms of contribution amounts, states that have weaker campaign finance regulations (ranging from 1 to 4 on the horizontal axis of Figure 3) can expect an average of $8.3 million in contributions while in states with stricter laws (ranging from 14 to 17 using the same scale on Figure 3) state party PACs would likely receive an average of $1.8 million The national average in state party PAC contributions is roughly $5 million which is illustrated in the graph as the dotted line across each category. Overall, the effects plotted in Figure 3 of campaign finance laws suggest that—after accounting for state-level differences, electoral effects, and differences in state political institutions—total state party PAC funding is directly, and negatively, impacted by campaign finance laws.

Public Funding of State-Level Candidates, Political Parties, and the Role of "Super Donors" in State-Level Party PAC Contributions

Proponents of public campaign financing schemes contend that freeing candidates from their fund-raising obligations enables them to spend more time on other campaign efforts (Francia and Hernson 2003). However, while publicly subsidized candidates are less likely to seek campaign contributions from wealthy donors, this does

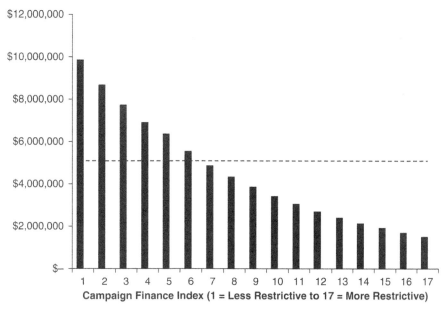

Figure 3. Predicted Average State Party PAC Funding by State-Level Campaign Finance Index
Source: National Institute on Money in State Politics (www.followthemoney.org).

not mean they can run their campaigns on the cheap. Where candidates are restrained by public funding laws, the political parties have filled the fund-raising "void." State party PACs serve as a conduit for contributions from well-financed individuals to aid candidates indirectly in their electioneering efforts (Brogan and Mendilow 2012).

In terms of fund-raising contribution patterns, "super donors" are likely to donate to state party PACs more than 40 times what normal donors would contribute, other things being equal. In dollars, this would be approximately $12,222 per "super donor." In states that have public campaign funding, state party PACs receive an additional $1,840 in funding from "super donors" compared to all other donors.

The impact of this effect is plotted in Figure 4, which compares the differences between "super donors" and all other donors who made contributions to state party PACs in states that have public campaign funding and in those that do not. A likely reason is the increased importance of the political parties in helping candidates who accept public funding to get elected through separate fund-raising activities to attack the opposition, provide professional campaign consulting and services to candidates, voter outreach, and party building (Brogan and Mendilow 2012). As a consequence, state party PACs have evolved in this system as a pivotal actor in helping their party either achieve or maintain majority status in the states.

The Future for State Party PACs

The state political parties have embraced two major strategies in adapting to campaign finance reform at the federal and state levels. These strategies stem from the parties' durability in being able to connect citizens to government (Dahl 1983).

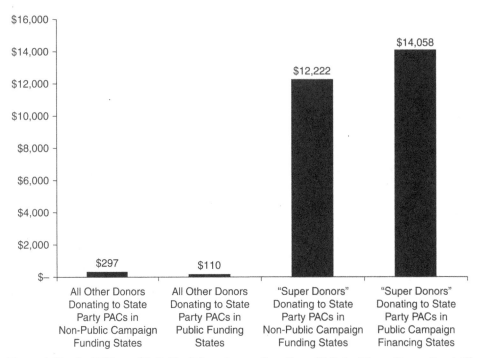

Figure 4. Marginal Effects of Individual Donations to State Party PACs by "Super Donors" and All Other Donors in States with Public Campaign Funding versus States without Public Campaign Funding

Source: National Institute on Money in State Politics (www.followthemoney.org).

First, state party PACs now rely more on contributions from candidate committees and from ideological organizations after BCRA. The reduction in hard money contributions from the national political parties has been offset by an increased diversification of funding sources by state party PACs, which has increased their relevance among a broader array of interests and also demonstrated their resilience within the political environment. By 2010, state party PACs had received a 33 percent increase in total receipts since 2004 (the election following BCRA). The rise in contributions points to a continued trend of increased fund-raising even as regulators make efforts to restrict campaign expenditures and donations.

Individual donors have also been an effective source of campaign funds for state party PACs. In particular, state parties have focused on cultivating contributions from "super donors." The reliance by the parties on "super donors" indicates that political influence is concentrated among a select group of individuals. In states with public financing, these donors are even more important in their ability to fund state party PACs. Furthermore, out-of-state donations from wealthy donors have also given state parties increased electoral influence across state boundaries.

But the biggest adaptation of state party PACs to BCRA and public financing has been the expansion of their role as a conduit for campaign contributions from candidates, ideological groups, and "super donors." While BCRA and public financing have led to some changes in their fund-raising tactics, there is no conclusive evidence that the political system has been radically transformed. Instead, campaign reform schemes have simply reinforced the status quo. State party leaders have been very successful in adapting to these changes. This means that state political parties have not only maintained their political relevance amid federal and state campaign reforms but have also actually become more influential in the electoral process.

State party leaders can be expected to further expand their fund-raising activity in response to recent court decisions. Specifically, *SpeechNow.org v. Federal Election Commission* led to the creation of Super PACs, while *Citizens United v. Federal Election Commission* opened the floodgates to virtually unlimited corporate money in electioneering. State party PACs are likely to become more crucial as indirect facilitators of new groups and donors who are independent of traditional party structures. They may also use the media to send tactical signals to independent groups. Because of the state party PACs' adaptability, resilience, and durability, campaign finance reform efforts have not stopped them; instead, they have changed their contours and widened their reach.

The primary litmus test for a functioning democracy is a vibrant and competitive party system—one in which political parties can raise sufficient funds to compete at the polls. While noble in intent, efforts to curb the influence of special interests in the political process do come at a cost to democracy.

Campaign finance rules are designed by individuals who hold political power, and typically wish to maintain it. Even when the intention of reforms is to avoid fraud or corruption by the parties, the changes can have an unintended effect on the relationship between citizens and government. Campaign finance reform can serve as a veiled attempt by politicians to attempt to restrict advocacy on specific issues they would rather not discuss, curtail opposing views that critique their performance in office, and more fundamentally maintain the status quo.

The rise of independent expenditure groups in the states is an unintended consequence of well-meaning reforms, which have transformed campaigning by creating new avenues for attack ads while minimizing any accountability for these messages (La Raja 2008). The problem caused by these groups is their lack of transparency and accountability to voters, who lose their ability to either reward or punish the organizations' actions during a given campaign. At least when parties or candidates engage in a particular behavior, voters are able to link an action to an actor, and respond directly with their votes. Future efforts to restrict party funding need to effectively balance the public interest (e.g., disclosure, transparency, and accountability) with the ability of political parties to freely function in the democratic system (e.g., through issue advocacy, broad and specific representation of diverse interests, and the ability to link citizens to government). Unfortunately, reformers have no "silver bullet."

References

Ansolabehere, Stephen, John M. de Figuerido, and James M. Synder, Jr. (2003). "Why Is There So Little Money in U.S. Politics?" *Journal of Economic Perspectives* 17, no. 1:105–130.

Apollino, D. E., and Raymond J. La Raja. (2004). "Who Gave Soft Money? The Effect of Interest Group Resources on Political Contributions." *Journal of Politics* 66, no. 4: 1134–1154.

Brogan, Michael J., and Jonathan Mendilow. (2012). "The Telescoping Effects of Public Campaign Funding: Evaluating the Impact of Clean Elections in Arizona, Maine, and New Jersey." *Politics & Policy* 40, no. 3: 490–515.

Dahl, Robert. (1983). *Dilemmas of Pluralist Democracy: Autonomy vs. Control*. New Haven, CT: Yale University Press.

Eismeier, Theodore J., and Philip H. Pollock, III. (1985). "An Organizational Analysis of Political Action Committees." *Political Behavior* 7, no. 2: 192–216.

Francia, Peter L., and Paul S. Herrnson. (2003). "The Impact of Public Finance Laws on Fundraising in State Legislative Elections." *American Politics Research* 31, no. 5: 520–539.

Francia, Peter L., John C. Green, Paul S. Hernson, Lynda W. Powell, and Clyde Wilcox. (2003). *The Financiers of Congressional Elections: Investors, Ideologues, and Intimates*. New York: Columbia University Press.

Francia, Peter L., Paul S. Herrnson, John P. Frendreis, and Alan R. Gitelson. (2006). "The Battle for the Legislature: Party Campaigning in State House and State Senate Elections." In *The State of the Parties: The Changing Role of Contemporary American Parties*. Lanham, MD: Rowman & Littlefield Publishers, Inc., pp. 171–189.

Francia, Peter L., Wesley Joe, and Clyde Wilcox. (2013). "Campaign Finance Reform in the Post– Citizens United Era." In *Campaigns on the Cutting Edge*, 2nd ed. Washington, DC: CQ Press., pp. 157–176.

Gierzynski, Anthony, and David A. Breux. (1998). "The Financing Role of Parties." In Joel A. Thompson and Gary F. Moncrief, eds. *Campaign Finance in State Legislative Elections*. Washington, DC: Congressional Quarterly Inc., pp. 185–205.

Gimpel, James G., Frances E. Lee, and Shanna Pearson-Merkowitz. (2008). "The Check Is in the Mail: Interdistrict Funding Flows in Congressional Elections." *American Journal of Political Science* 52, no. 2: 373–394.

Jewell, Malcolm, and Sarah M. Morehouse. (2001). *Political Parties and Elections in American States. 4th ed.* Washington, D.C.: CQ Press.

Kettler, Jaclyn, and Keith E. Hamm. (2011.) "The Evolving Role of Party Committees in State Legislative Campaigns during the 21st Century: A Preliminary Assessment Paper presented at 11th Annual State Politics and Policy Conference Dartmouth College, Hanover NH, June 4–5, 2011.

Klodoney, Robin, and David A. Dulio. (2003). "Political Party and Adaptation in US Congressional Campaigns: Why Political Parties Use Coordinated Expenditures to Hire Political Consultants" *Party Politics* 9, no. 6: 729–746.

Knoke, David, and James R. Wood. (1981). *Organized for Action*. New Brunswick, NJ: Rutgers University Press.

Kousser, Thad, and Raymond J. LaRja. 2002. "The Effect of Campaign Finance Laws on Electoral Competition: Evidence From the States." *Policy Analysis* 426: 1–10.

La Raja, Raymond. (2008). *Small Change: Money, Political Parties, and Campaign Finance Reform*. Ann Arbor: University of Michigan Press.

Malbin, Michael J. (2008). "Rethinking the Campaign Finance Agenda." *The Forum* 6, no. 1: 1–16.

Mansbridge, Jane. (2003). "Rethinking Representation" *American Political Science Review* 97, no.4: 515–528.

Morehouse, Sarah M., and Malcolm E. Jewell. (2003). "State Parties: Independent Partners in the Money Relationship." In *The State of the Parties: The Changing Role of Contemporary American Parties*. Lanham MD: Rowman & Littlefield, pp. 151–168.

National Conference of State Legislatures (NCSL). (2010, Jan. 6). "Public Financing of Campaigns: An Overview." Accessed July 27, 2013. *www.ncsl.org/legislatures-elections /elections/public-financing-of-campaigns-overview.aspx#footnote_A*.

Perrow, Charles. (1970). "Members as Resources in Voluntary Associations." In Walter R. Rosengren, ed. *Organizations and Clients*. Columbus, OH: Charles E. Merrill, pp. 93–116.

Thompson, Joel A., William Cassie, and Malcolm E. Jewell. (1994). "A Sacred Cow or Just a Lot of Bull? Party and PAC Money in State Legislative Elections." *Political Research Quarterly* 47, no. 1: 223–237.

Section C
Corruption

The Roots of Corruption

Amy Handlin

When an incident of public corruption gets prolonged national attention, it usually involves one or more federal officials, agencies, and/or lobbyists. For example, the Jack Abramoff lobbying scandal in 2006 ensnared then-House Majority Leader Tom DeLay, as well as several other key congressmen and officials in the Bush administration. In a highly publicized 2009 case, former representative William Jefferson was convicted of bribery after investigators found $90,000 stashed in his freezer. Former Illinois governor Rod Blagojevich, sentenced to 14 years in jail in 2011, became notorious partly because he tried to auction off President Obama's vacated U.S. Senate seat. But corruption need not touch Washington to corrode public trust. Unfortunately, it does considerable damage in state and local governments, where most politicians begin their careers and citizens develop basic perceptions and expectations.

Few state or local governments are actually rife with corruption. But there are enough crooked officeholders to undermine public confidence, especially in a small community where even a single indictment looms large. The downfall of one trusted leader, like a judge or sheriff, is enough to sap civic pride, especially at a time when every errant local politician attracts round-the-clock blogosphere buzz. According to the Foundation for Ethics in Public Service, founded in 2009 to help root out these crimes, the steadiest stream of corruption allegations involves local sheriffs, economic development boards, and court personnel (Foundation for Ethics in Public Service 2011).

In 2005, nearly 90 percent of those polled by the Associated Press described public corruption as a serious problem (Associated Press 2005). Two years later, only 10 percent of respondents to a Pew survey believed the country was "making progress" against corruption, while almost half said it was getting worse (Cillizza 2007). In 2010, another survey revealed that 70 percent of U.S. voters believed their representatives were willing to sell votes for cash or campaign contributions (*USA Today* Editorial 2010). Moreover, the public's cynicism feeds on itself. As one political scientist describes this phenomenon:

> Revelations of scandal, or the belief that wrongdoing is common even if it never comes to light, can upset one's general image of the way politics works, or who wins and loses and how, and of one's own ability to influence government. While idealized

pictures of American politics have never fully corresponded with reality, they can still be matters of great emotional investment. This is not to say that everyone starts out with these ideals in mind, only to suffer some loss of political innocence later. But for those who hold at least a few of these perceptions, corruption can strike a heavy blow. (Johnston 1986)

What causes the slide of powerful people into ignominy, from Capitol Hill to town hall? Reacting to a spate of corruption in 2006, a *New York Times* analyst observed: "Arrogance gave way to recklessness, which in turn opened the door to criminality" (Eichenwald 2006). Tellingly, however, this observation wasn't about government: it described Enron, the business behemoth that collapsed in iniquity. Clearly, the hubris that poisoned corporate culture can seep into the public sector too.

Structural and Political Roots

More specifically, there are long-standing structural and political forces helping to breed corruption. Chief among them is the extreme fragmentation of government. U.S. taxpayers support approximately 88,000 public jurisdictions. States are carved into hundreds, sometimes thousands of tiny administrative slivers, each with its own governing body and taxing authority—and minimal, if any, oversight. These may include cities, counties, towns, school districts, and a vast array of entities responsible for specialized services like irrigation, firefighting, or public housing. For example, there are 6,835 governmental units in Illinois; 5,070 in Pennsylvania; 4,700 in Texas; and 4,607 in California. In practice, this means that legions of officials have unchecked access to billions in public funds. Politicians in some states routinely hold multiple government offices, creating public fiefdoms where no one dares to question the boss. When so many individuals have an independent power base funded on the taxpayer's dime, the odds are overwhelming that a few will give in to avarice.

Some scholars tie recent upswings in corruption to increasingly intrusive national and local government regulation. Every new rule, they argue, creates an opportunity for officials to bend or break it in return for payoffs. As the bureaucracy grows, so does the number of potential thieves. "If you want to cut corruption cut government," advises economist Gary Becker (Becker and Becker 1997).

Many communities have weak or nonexistent ethics laws; for example, officials may be allowed to give government jobs to members of their families, accept valuable gifts from vendors, or continue to serve in public office after being indicted for corruption in that office. Additionally, lax enforcement can pose a problem even where rules are tough. For example, compliance with Georgia's strict statutes is supposedly monitored by an agency that has no investigators (*Ledger Enquirer* Editorial 2011).

Where it is legal, the practice known as "double dipping"—holding more than one public position simultaneously—is particularly corrosive. In New Jersey, some

Former HealthSouth CEO Richard Scrushy, left, and his wife, Leslie, leaving federal court after the first day of the sentencing phase of his federal corruption trial in Montgomery, Alabama, in 2007. (AP Photo/Rob Carr)

local officials have held over a dozen posts each. The problem occurs because the holder is obligated to serve different masters, all with their own, often conflicting, interests. Amid the tangle of responsibilities and expectations, a double dipper often ends up serving no one but himself or herself. One such official, former New Jersey state senator Wayne Bryant was one of the most powerful members of the legislature before his conviction for bribery and fraud. In return for steering millions in public funds to favored individuals and institutions, he allegedly received a no-show job to pad his taxpayer-paid pension—on top of three other government positions. His defense? "'You may not like it,' [Bryant's attorney] Carl Poplar said of the multiple job holdings, 'but it's not illegal and it's not uncommon'" (Rothman 2008).

Another factor is the complexity and cost of today's local government. In early America, even the greediest official had little to steal. Public institutions were scarce, and expenditures were modest. But today's venal small town mayor—let alone a big city alderman or state lawmaker—has access to millions in cash and public property. As expenditures continue to mushroom, on everything from parcels of land to management consultants, so do enticements to thievery. There is always some unscrupulous operator ready to offer a five-figure bribe in return for a seven-figure government contract. It can also be tempting to "borrow" cars, computers, or other public resources.

Public scrutiny deters abuses of power. Conversely, officials are more likely to cut ethical corners when no one is looking. Unfortunately, there is a vicious cycle:

Former New Jersey senator Wayne Bryant, center, walking with his wife Cheryl Spicer and his lawyer Carl Poplar as they leave federal court following Bryant's sentencing in Trenton, New Jersey. Bryant was sentenced to four years in prison for bribery and fraud after being convicted of being paid for a job that required no work at a state university in exchange for securing state funding for it. (AP Photo/Mel Evans, file)

when corruption causes citizens to turn away from government, their inattention encourages more corruption.

Procedural transparency, too, is inimical to thievery. But government spending practices can be murky and misleading. The best known of these questionable methods is "earmarking," used by members of Congress to direct taxpayer money to pet projects without debates or votes. Earmarking came under heavy fire after former representative Duke Cunningham was convicted in 2005 of taking bribes in return for these appropriations, but legislators debated for years before restricting the popular and long-entrenched practice.

Similar types of under-the-radar discretionary spending are available to officials in some cities and states. Members of the New York City Council, for example, showered millions on favored organizations and institutions—until the public learned that members routinely allocated funds to phony groups, with names like "Coalition of Informed Individuals." The fakery was a convenient way to disguise the magnitude and purpose of the actual disbursements (Rivera and Buettner 2008). In 2010, Los Angeles County supervisors doled out over $3 million each (Zavis 2011). Every council member in Louisville, Kentucky, can steer

$100,000–$175,000 annually to his or her choice of building projects: Over a four-year period, the members distributed 3,400 of these "Neighborhood Development Fund" grants (Klepal 2011; Wolfson 2011).

State legislators may insert so-called member projects in their budgets, the practical equivalent of earmarks. Among the local projects funded without debate in the 2008–2009 Texas budget were a zoo and a skate park (Castro 2007), while Florida legislators quietly approved such 2011 expenditures as $15 million to build a "public safety institute" and $500,000 to improve a horse park (Caputo 2011). In New Mexico, two state senators sponsored a $65,000 allocation to a sculpture garden developer who eventually vanished (Jennings 2011). In New York, former Senate Majority Leader Joseph Bruno got a two-year prison sentence (later overturned) after funneling big state grants to his partner in a horse breeding business (Confessore and Hakim 2009).

Finally, politicians can make matters worse by looking the other way. Notwithstanding the rock stars of public corruption like Jefferson, Abramoff, or Blagojevich, most offenders are low-level, small-time crooks. Even when they are not, it is easier to dismiss them as aberrations than to acknowledge the flaws in a system that facilitated their crimes. For instance, after Connecticut governor John Rowland pleaded guilty to mail and tax fraud, ending months of scandal that tarnished local officials around his state, House Speaker John Amann allowed that government was "wounded." But he was also quick to repeat what can become a mantra in political circles: "Most people [in government] have their hearts in the right place—to serve the public" (Baldor 2004).

Amann's point is well taken. But when lawmakers disregard corruption, they miss an opportunity to head off future misdeeds—and bolster public confidence—with stronger laws, training, and oversight.

Corruption occurs in many forms. Here are three major variations:

1. Bribery: An official is paid, usually in cash, to deliver a vote, job or other official action. For example, former Governor Rowland steered business to government contractors in return for free renovations of his summer cottage.
2. Extortion: The converse of bribery, extortion is the threat to withhold an official action unless the extorter is paid. A health inspector might threaten to report code violations unless a salon owner produces a "gratuity."
3. Discrimination in administration of law or application of the rules: Common examples are ticket-fixing or granting a license without documentation, usually in return for some kickback or favor. Federal investigators caught 26 employees of the Arizona Department of Motor Vehicles issuing fake driver's licenses and identity cards. (O'Brien 2005)

Slippery Slopes

Few government officials are born crooks. They do not enter public service eager to abuse the people's trust.

Former Connecticut governor John G. Rowland and his wife, Patty, talking to reporters outside U.S. District Court in New Haven, Connecticut, in 2004. Rowland pleaded guilty to a single count of conspiracy to steal honest services. (AP Photo/Bob Child)

But in the course of doing their jobs, many officials find themselves at the edge of a slippery slope: an ethically ambiguous or challenging decision point. Taking a dishonest turn at that juncture leads to increasingly dubious behaviors. Say a building inspector spots a defect in a structure being sold by his friend, a local developer. If he reports the violation, it will kill the sale. So he deliberately overlooks it, justifying the decision to himself as a harmless, one-time favor.

The problem is that one favor facilitates another. Deceit is like any other learned behavior: the inspector finds it easier every time he does it. As he develops a reputation for being "helpful," he is sought out by favor-seekers. It is only a matter of time until he is offered cash in return for coming through. In fact, an extensive federal bribery probe of Chicago's Building and Zoning Departments snared dozens of just such "helpful" officials. Over more than a decade, these investigators falsified reports, altered computer data, and coached developers in how to circumvent city codes. In return, they received envelopes stuffed with money—in amounts pegged to the seriousness of the violations they had agreed to overlook (Coen 2009).

Of course, whether or not an official starts to slip toward iniquity depends on many factors, not least his or her own moral compass. Honest decision making is more than just obeying the law: even the strongest code of ethics cannot anticipate every choice between right and wrong. Being ethical means doing what is in sync with one's own values and standards, and with the expectations of the community. It also means striving to avoid harm to others, defined narrowly (family and friends) or broadly (the citizens). Two prominent ethicists describe ethics in public life as "not about selfishness, greed, scumbags; not merely compliance to the law; not finger-pointing . . . [but about making] difficult choices that create positive precedents and outcomes, and perhaps, even, make this a better place to live in" (Freeman and Werhane 2007).

However, there are certain pernicious influences in politics and public life with the potential to push a morally unsteady official over the edge. Among the most widely recognized are conflicts of interest; gifts; nepotism and cronyism; political patronage; use of confidential information; and campaign contributions and practices.

Conflicts of Interest

An official has a conflict of interest whenever his or her loyalties are divided: in other words, he or she has a personal stake in a public decision. Casting a vote can make him or her rich. Supporting a project can win him or her a job. Approving a contract can reward a political ally—or punish a foe. These situations crop up regularly in local government, where many decision makers serve only part time and earn a living in the private sector. They naturally have business contacts, relationships, and investments that do not always line up with the public interest. For instance, Mayor Jones has a conflict of interest if his auto dealership seeks to supply the town's police cars. Board of Education chairman Smith has a conflict if he owns land that the school district is considering for purchase.

Conflicts of interest are also the most common type of ethical dilemma faced by state lawmakers. According to the National Conference of State Legislatures, "conflicts of interest typically arise when a legislator or staff member has the potential to receive a personal benefit based on his or her public position. Often, the personal benefit is a financial one (Conflicts of Interest)."

Money need not change hands to create a conflict of interest. Consider these three scenarios:

1. A state Supreme Court justice intervenes with the prosecutor, police, and court officials to influence a case involving his son. In each interaction, the justice goes out of his way to make sure he is recognized, pointedly handing out business cards to anyone who does not know his title.
2. A city council staff member pressures a valet parking attendant to take responsibility for damage to his car. There is no proof the attendant caused the damage. When the parking firm's managers appear, the staffer warns them that their permits "have to come through my desk in my office."
3. Legislators with control of a university's state funding are treated to special tickets for its most sought-after football games. The tickets are largely unavailable to ordinary fans. They are also distributed to the mayor and many other local government officials—including the county engineer responsible for constructing and maintaining roads in the vicinity of the stadium.

Each of these examples is real. In the first situation, the New Jersey judge was censured for "misusing his office to advance a personal interest" (Toutant 2007). In the second, the Boston City Council staff member was fined $1,000; the Massachusetts ethics commission commented: "Using one's official position to influence the resolution of a private dispute can only undermine confidence in government" (Finucane 2008). In the case of the Ohio State University football tickets, no action was taken: the practice was questioned by government watchdog groups but defended by the college—and by the lucky recipients. (However, one lawmaker was forced to resign his seat after revelations that he sold his tickets on eBay for $13,000 [I-Team: OSU Football-Who Gets Special Prices? 2008]).

Some political scientists argue that divided loyalties are inevitable in citizen legislatures. They believe the cure—limiting lawmaking bodies at every level to full-time, career politicians—would be worse than the disease. They may be right. But theories aside, there is no question that conflicts of interest can lead to duplicity, secrecy, double-dealing—or worse.

Gifts

Few businesspeople would look askance at a box of candy from an employee, a bouquet of flowers from a customer, or a bottle of wine from a vendor. In the private sector, such tokens of appreciation are routine, even expected as a matter of courtesy. Why, then, should anyone think that a mayor can be bought for a lunch?

The problem is not the free sandwich. It is, again, the slippery slope. A suspicious, cynical public has reason to worry that today's innocent trinket can pave the way for tomorrow's bribe. For a crook, it is only a small step from accepting trifles to demanding tributes. Even an honest official can be tempted to twist arms, however gently, to help someone who has showered him or her with presents. Unfortunately, a trivial exchange can morph into an extravaganza of avarice.

For example, former Mayor Sheila Dixon of Baltimore, Maryland, allowed a prominent developer to treat her to a mink coat, a Persian lamb jacket, costly beauty products, and lavish trips. She shook down another for gift cards, claiming they would be distributed to needy families. Instead, Dixon used Best Buy gift cards to buy herself CDs, DVDs, a camcorder, a PlayStation 2, and an Xbox. She also stole Toys R Us gift cards intended for poor children. A grand jury indicted Dixon on 12 counts involving theft, fraud, perjury, and official misconduct. Upon her conviction for embezzling the $500 gift cards, one juror commented: "The denomination doesn't matter. It's a trust issue" (Bykowicz and Linskey 2009).

Nepotism and Cronyism

What's wrong with an alderman steering a contract to his old college chum? Why is Mayor Smith on a slippery slope if she hires her brother, an experienced lawyer, to represent the town?

Public officials who defend nepotism (preference for relatives) and cronyism (preference for friends) typically assert that these practices do no harm. In fact, they claim, taxpayers get better service from people with a personal motive to make government leaders look good.

Sometimes, that can be true. But it is beside the point. The presence of nepotism and cronyism means the absence of standards and safeguards. When these practices run rampant, there are no objective measures of performance. Private relationships take priority over public needs.

Worse, any type of favoritism creates a cynical workplace culture with no incentive for ordinary employees to improve. "Occasionally it was a joke when we saw a job announcement come out and we would say, 'I wonder who they want promoted now?'" said a worker at California's nepotism-riddled Unemployment Insurance Appeals Board (Ortiz 2008).

More broadly, nepotism and cronyism fly in the face of two bedrock American values: fairness and equal opportunity. Both are central to integrity, and the perception of integrity in government. As stated in New York City's public procurement rules:

> The underlying purposes of these Rules . . . are to ensure the fair and equitable treatment of all persons; to ensure appropriate public access; and to foster equal employment opportunities. . . . To this end, public employees and elected officials having responsibility for contracting at all levels shall encourage competition, prevent favoritism, and obtain the best value in the interest of the City and the taxpayers. (New York City Procurement Policy Board Rules)

Some argue that occasional favoritism is acceptable, even desirable. For instance, why not hire a councilman's uncle to work for the town if he happens to be available sooner than other applicants? But occasional impartiality is not a mark of good government—it is just another slippery slope. At any given time, an unscrupulous official can find staggering numbers of employable relatives and friends. When a manager for the Los Angeles Housing Authority steered contracts worth half a million dollars to his brothers (Roderick 2007), for instance, it was hard to believe that no other firms were ready to handle the work. There can be no guarantee that merit will count unless it is built into basic hiring and purchasing rules, like these:

- Requiring competitive bids for products and services.
- Publicly advertising jobs and hiring criteria.
- Requiring officials to recuse themselves from votes that could benefit a relative.
- Documenting reasons for and against hiring and procurement decisions.
- Authorizing regular, independent audits of hiring and procurement decisions.
- Making audits readily accessible to the public.

Nepotism and cronyism are corrosive even when public expenditures are not involved. In an increasingly common twist, unethical public officials look to take care of their friends not with government paychecks, but by pressuring private employers to hire them. This can be justifiable if the official knows a job applicant and has a legitimate basis for recommending him. Some codes of ethics explicitly permit it: for example, New Jersey allows legislators to help a job seeker as long as there is no promise or exchange of anything of value in return for the favor. But what about more subtle uses of influence? Is it improper to write a reference on official letterhead, thus suggesting that the applicant has some government imprimatur? What if the official calls a potential employer of his sister, casually mentioning city contracts that could materialize in return for his "help"? Clearly, it is at least a nascent form of corruption when a public office becomes a recommendation mill.

The story of the "Friends and Family Plan" in Miami-Dade County, Florida, illustrates how nepotism and cronyism can cause tangible harm to ordinary citizens:

> In 2002, officials in Miami-Dade County, Florida faced a vexing problem. The rapidly growing, increasingly traffic-congested metropolitan area was in dire need of mass transportation upgrades that the government couldn't afford.
>
> In pursuit of a new revenue source, then-Mayor Alex Penelas embarked on an ambitious campaign to win public approval for a half-cent sales tax dedicated to mass transit. It would not be an easy sell—voters had repeatedly rejected tax proposals in the past. But Penelas got high-powered help from the Transport Workers Union, whose members advocated enthusiastically for the so-called People's Transportation Plan.
>
> The transit tax passed in November 2002. But it did not usher in the promised golden era of cutting-edge transportation for all. Instead, the tax proceeds fueled a hiring spree for a favored few: relatives, friends and supporters of Penelas, various county commissioners, top county staff and other local officials. Many of the hires were made indirectly, through a murky arrangement with temporary personnel agencies that discouraged public scrutiny. Background checks were skipped or ignored: At least four of the well-connected new employees turned out to have shady pasts or criminal records. During an earlier corruption scandal, one had taken over $50,000 in kickbacks.
>
> To make matters worse, the managers also cut a backroom deal with the Transport Workers Union, never disclosed to the public or submitted to commissioners for a vote. The agreement reclassified hundreds of jobs so as to speed promotions and deliver big raises—less than a week after the 2002 election.
>
> Over the next six years, details of what was dubbed the "Friends and Family Plan" leaked out as it became apparent that mass transit improvements would fall far short of Penelas' promise. The transit agency's payroll budget ballooned—there were 1400 new employees, and the number of six-figure salaries more than tripled. But in 2008, Miami Metrorail had fewer trains than in 2002. Bus routes were cut back, and there was not enough money to replace aging vehicles. (Lebowitz 2008)

As one rider lamented, "We had temporary 24-hour bus routes. They disappeared. We had a temporary increase in bus routes. Most of them are cut. But I've seen plenty of people with jobs. They took care of themselves" (Lebowitz and Barry 2008).

Political Patronage

The practice of rewarding partisan loyalists with jobs or contracts is seen as a means of party-building—at least among those who believe that political support is for sale. This slippery slope is, however, on the decline in most of the country.

In the pre–World War II heyday of patronage, the financial muscle of party machines in New York, Chicago, Baltimore, and other large cities enabled them to bankroll virtually all local campaigns. When machine-backed candidates won public office, they paid their debt to the party by hiring the rank and file—and by turning a blind eye to bribery, racketeering, embezzlement, and myriad other forms of corruption.

But in the mid-20th century, civil service reforms made it difficult to continue rewarding party adherents with government jobs. Also, the spread of mass media and of modern campaign techniques freed candidates from dependence on the machines. In 1990, the U.S. Supreme Court delivered a further blow: in the landmark case known as *Rutan v. Republican Party of Illinois*, the justices declared unconstitutional "promotion, transfer, recall, and hiring decisions based on party affiliation and support," declaring them "an impermissible infringement on public employees' First Amendment rights" (*Rutan v. Republican Party of Illinois, 1990*). (The Court recognized, however, that partisan loyalty may be relevant to some jobs, and that political affiliation may be taken into account if it serves the public interest.)

Where patronage lives on, it is now balanced by at least some degree of merit-based decision making. While party machines still exist, they are held in check by legal scrutiny, public suspicion—and a new generation of civic activists for whom politics is its own reward.

Use of Confidential Information

In November 2011, a CBS News program exposed what was described as insider trading on Capitol Hill—members of Congress trading stocks based on nonpublic information disclosed to them during committee hearings and debates. The concerns were not new; in fact, similar criticisms had been leveled during the Credit Mobilier scandal of the 1870s, when legislators were accused of selling discounted railroad stocks. But key leaders of the House of Representatives were now touched by the controversy, including the powerful chairman of the House Financial Services Committee. Amid a public outcry, Congress hastily passed the STOCK Act ("Stop Trading on Congressional Knowledge") in February 2012. The legislation subjected members to federal antifraud laws, banning them from acting on or disclosing confidential information about any publicly traded company.

But government officials at all levels routinely handle confidential documents, from medical reports to credit records. They make daily decisions based on data never provided to the public. While members of Congress have allegedly enriched themselves by insider stock trading, local officials have profited by using confidential information in other, equally unethical ways.

Suppose that as part of an urban revitalization program, several city agencies will soon be renting office space downtown. But the plan has not been made public. If

A BADLY USED BIRD.

*Brother Jonathan (to his bird of freedom).—*Wal, I swow, you're having a pretty durned bad time of it, ain't you, Baldy! What with Mormons, Indians, Credit Mobilier, and general dishonesty, it is a wonder you are not dead. Nothing but your remarkably strong Constitution has saved you.

"A Badly Used Bird." Brother Jonathan looks at U.S. Eagle wounded by Mormons, Indians, Credit Mobilier, and general dishonesty, saying nothing but "your re-markably strong Constitution has saved you." Published in Wild Oats, 1873. (Library of Congress)

a municipal official with knowledge of this information were to tip off his friend, a commercial real estate broker, he would be in violation of the public trust. He might even expect a kickback in return for the tip.

Inside information about property valuations and land use plans can be particularly valuable. In Parsippany, New Jersey, a planning board official was convicted of trading tips and favors in return for at least $36,000 in secret payoffs. According to the indictment, the information enabled a developer to pay a bargain-basement price for a tract that skyrocketed in value when it was approved as the site for 360 homes and condominiums (Frank 2008).

Campaign Contributions

The cost of a modern political campaign would shock the candidates of yesteryear, who could not have imagined spending hundreds of thousands, even millions of dollars, to run for a state or federal office—and only marginally less to be competitive in a major city or county election. One reason is that contests at every level are increasingly media-driven; another is a steady drop-off in volunteers, forcing candidates to hire staff. The burgeoning industry called "political consulting" has created demand for pricey, high-tech services like micro-targeting research. Whatever the causes, today's campaigns are akin to military arms races, focused on the acquisition of ever-bigger and more powerful weaponry. But unlike the army, candidates cannot stockpile arms unless they succeed in amassing private donations.

Like any other torrent of cash, political fund-raising creates temptations to steal, hide, or divert resources; or, more specifically, to sell promises of action or access. There have been enough abuses to erode public trust in the integrity of the electoral process. In states with an elected judiciary, outsize donations to judicial candidates create the impression that verdicts are for sale. In response, every level of government now regulates how, from whom, and in what amounts politicians are allowed to raise money. With variations from state to state, there are caps, disclosure requirements, timing restrictions, and other rules.

Unfortunately, not even the strictest campaign finance regulations have come close to eliminating the trading of votes, jobs, or contracts in return for donations, known as "pay to play." While these agreements are illegal, prosecutors rarely succeed in proving a quid pro quo. So the practice is widely acknowledged to exist around the country as a system of informal, wink-and-nod exchanges, undocumented, and readily camouflaged.

Pay-to-play exists in near-infinite variety. Some schemes are fairly primitive: for example, the former sheriff of Buncombe County, North Carolina, was convicted of extorting cash from video poker companies in return for allowing them to operate illegally. According to the indictment, he kept some of the money in the trunk of a car to keep it handy for his own gambling habit (Associated Press 2008).

Other pay-to-players are more sophisticated. Former Alabama governor Don Eugene Siegelman was convicted of bribery, fraud, and obstruction of justice after taking $500,000 from a leading state businessman in exchange for a seat on the regulatory board governing the donor's business. Siegelman later attempted to mislead the FBI by setting up a sham bank transaction to conceal his payoffs (*U.S. v. Siegelman and Scrushy*, 2006). In New Mexico, the state pension fund lost $90 million after investing with a firm run by large contributors to Governor Bill Richardson. According to a whistle-blower lawsuit filed against the firm, "The defendants sold the state of New Mexico a worthless combination of liars' loans, lethal leverage and toxic waste. The pressure to invest in [the firm] was motivated by illegal and improper inducements—kickbacks or bribes in the form of campaign contributions" (Braun 2007).

Former Illinois governor Rod Blagojevich was a pay-to-play master long before he had a U.S. Senate seat to sell. Over eight years in office, he amassed $58 million largely from "favor seekers rewarded with state contracts, appointments and regulatory breaks" (*New York Times* Editorial 2008a). In one instance, his price was $100,000 to sign legislation favorable to the horse-racing industry. In another, he sought $50,000 in return for a state allocation to Chicago's Children's Memorial Hospital. The amount $650,000 appeared to buy an appointment to the Illinois Gaming Board (Maag 2008).

As the *Washington Post* commented: "It's easy to look at Mr. Blagojevich's downfall . . . and ask: What's the matter with Illinois? But it's not just Illinois. The seamy story should prompt a reexamination at every level of government about whether enough has been done to preclude similar scandals" (*Washington Post* Editorial 2008).

Certain fund-raising vehicles are also dubious, like cash. In some states, political candidates are prohibited from taking any cash contributions. Elsewhere, it may be allowed in small amounts, or as long as there is proper documentation. But these donations are notoriously hard to track and verify. Fairly or not, cash is generally tainted by the fact that it is, literally, the currency of corruption.

Another type of donation is an outright form of trickery, a way of getting around contribution limits. Let's say you support Candidate X but haven't made a donation. Another supporter, who has already given X as much as he is allowed, offers to reimburse you for writing a check to the campaign on his behalf. "It's a win-win for both of us," he assures you. "I'll be able to do more for my friend, and you won't

Former Illinois governor Rod Blagojevich, right, walks with his attorney as he arrives at the Federal Correctional Institution Englewood in Littleton, Colorado, on March 15, 2012, where he began serving his 14-year sentence for corruption. (AP Photo/Ed Andrieski)

be out the money." If you agree, you could be subject to federal investigation as a "conduit"—a person who deliberately hides the source of a political contribution. It wouldn't matter whether you knew of the scheme, or even if you were aware of the law. Your transgression could land you in prison for up to five years.

Campaign Practices

In some ways, unethical behavior is so endemic to the political system that newcomers can be corrupted just by trying to get in. Here are four practices with a history of causing trouble.

1. Signature-Gathering

The first step in running for office is to get on the ballot. Depending on where they live and what office they seek, candidates need to file various forms such as a declaration of candidacy and a campaign registration statement. In most cases, they are also required to obtain signatures on a nominating petition. Signature-gathering is a time-honored democratic tradition with both practical value and symbolic significance. It enables the candidate to test the waters in a productive way, gathering concrete evidence of support from would-be constituents.

The number of required signatures may be identical for anyone seeking a particular office, no matter where the candidate lives or the size of the district he seeks to represent. Sometimes this standard requirement is small: for instance, all county sheriff candidates must get 50 signatures in Ohio, or 100 in New Jersey. But there is enormous variation. In Pennsylvania, for example, 1,000 signatures are required on a nominating petition for any county office.

Signature requirements can also be based on a formula that reflects some characteristic of the district, like population or voter registration. Florida is among the states with such a formula: candidates for any county office need enough signatures to represent 1 percent of the total number of registered voters in the county. This isn't daunting in a small county like Hendry, where the 1 percent rule amounts to only 157 signatures. But it is a major undertaking in Miami-Dade County, where county candidates must obtain nearly 11,000 names.

Petition circulation is heavily regulated in most states. Typically, the rules spell out precisely who is allowed to be a circulator or a signer, and what information is required to accompany every signature. Few details are overlooked; it is common to regulate even when a petition can be left unattended (almost never).

But despite states' best attempts at oversight, the process can be easily subverted. There are plenty of signature-gathering "experts" looking to take advantage of inexperienced or unethical candidates. Instead of a means to give voice to ordinary voters, petitions can become a profit-oriented mockery of those voters.

In 2006, for example, the Oregon media exposed a black market of petition circulators trading cash for signatures on the street. So many signature-gathering agents and subagents had been hired that it was difficult to hold anyone responsible (Moore 2006). In 2008, a Pittsburgh political consultant pled guilty to packing petitions with phony names and signatures of dead people (Associated Press 2008). The common practice of public workers collecting signatures for the reelection campaigns of incumbent officials—their bosses—raises serious concerns about coercion and payback.

2. *Targeting Voters*

"Targeting" is the practice of identifying voters whose party affiliation and/or voting history make them likely supporters of a particular candidate—or not. It is critical to the efficient use of campaign resources. For example, expensive mailings can be limited to fairly small numbers of promising prospects. Issue advocacy materials can be directed just to people concerned about those issues. Get-out-the-vote phone calls can focus on those who reliably go the polls. The candidate can divide his time between trying to win over undecided voters, and building the enthusiasm of people who already support him.

But pinpointing unsupportive voters can also lead to risky behaviors—at the extreme, to crimes of voter suppression or intimidation. In 2006, the former New England Regional Director of the Republican National Committee went to jail for scheming to disrupt telephone service to Democratic party offices and a firefighters' ride-to-the-polls program (*US v. Tobin*, 2006). In 2007, Democrats in upstate New York allegedly directed Republican voters to incorrect polling places (*New York Times* Editorial 2008b). In communities with high concentrations of legal immigrants and naturalized citizens, it is not unusual for warnings to be spread by campaign operatives—often by untraceable word of mouth—that these voters could face deportation if they go the polls.

3. *Campaign Hiring*

Though campaign staff work behind the scenes and are paid with private funds, it is fair for opponents and the media to scrutinize who they are and how they attempt to influence the public. A candidate's hiring decisions, and what he or she expects of his or her staff, are reflections of his or her values and indicators of how he or she would perform in public office.

For example, nepotism in campaign hiring is common. Occasional attempts to stop it have fallen flat; a ban proposed in the 2008 Louisiana legislature was defeated unanimously. While restrictions apply in certain publicly funded races, most candidates are free to pay salaries to members of their families—or even to themselves.

Whatever their merits in terms of credentials or experience, it is reasonable to suspect that a candidate who puts his relatives on the payroll would, if elected, be looking to get them hired by the government. Moreover, campaign salaries paid to family members can raise eyebrows: New York City Councilman Larry Seabrook, for instance, paid nearly $50,000 to his brother, the manager of a halfway house (Rivera, Buettner, and Rashbaum 2008).

A candidate who puts campaign funds into his own pocket raises obvious questions about how he might seek extra cash once in public office. According to Common

Cause, the nonprofit government watchdog group: "The question always is: Is there value for the money, or is this just another way to divert campaign funds for personal use?" (Rivera et al. 2008).

Even thornier is the problem of hiring public employees. They can be uniquely valuable to a campaign, because they understand policy issues and have a stake in better government. But they are generally prohibited from engaging in political activity on public time or with public resources, including computers and telephones. So they can be hired by a candidate only to work after hours, on weekends or during vacations.

In practice, the time and resource restrictions are hard to enforce. Wink-and-nod violations are common. Many candidates take risks with public employees on their staffs, knowing that little of the wrongdoing is ever uncovered. But some is: Former Pennsylvania legislator Mike Veon got caught directing over $1 million in taxpayer-funded bonuses to statehouse employees for doing political work, often on state time (Davies 2008). In campaigns as in other organizations, casual disregard for one law encourages a cavalier attitude toward other laws—a typical starting point for corruption.

4. *Shady Tactics*

Publicly, no one endorses campaign tactics based on deception or misrepresentation. There is no guide to political dirty tricks. But in the absence of meaningful regulation, the temptations are strong to engage in dubious activities. Tactics like push polls and cyber-deception may not run afoul of the law, but they breed disrespect for honesty, fairness, and the integrity of the democratic process.

A political poll is a legitimate research tool. A push poll is a fraudulent form of telemarketing, designed to dish dirt on a candidate under the guise of research. Unlike genuine voter surveys, push polls are typically very short (only one or two questions) and extremely negative toward a candidate or issue. The caller avoids naming the source of the call and will not explain how the information is being used or by whom. She asks questions like: Do you support Tom White even though he has been accused of extortion?

Even when there is a shred of truth to such a slur, the push poll is a deliberate attempt to distort and sensationalize it. For instance, Tom White may indeed have been accused of lawbreaking, but the criminal complaint could have been fabricated and filed by his opponent. The official position of the American Association for Public Opinion Research on this tactic is unequivocal:

Political advocacy calls made under the guise of a survey abuse the public's trust. They gain the attention of respondents under false pretenses by taking advantage of the good will people have toward legitimate research. They go beyond the ethical boundaries of political polling by bombarding voters with distorted or even false statements in an effort to manufacture negative attitudes. The hostility created in this way affects legitimate surveys by reducing the public's willingness to cooperate with future survey requests (AAPOR)

Cyber-deception describes a range of shady techniques invented by a new generation of political tricksters. Five examples include the following:

1. Bulk campaign e-mails: usually containing lies or unfounded accusations that appear to originate from credible sources like newspapers, government agencies, or civic groups.
2. "Phishing": attempts to furtively obtain voters' personal data.

3. "Pharming": hacking into domain servers so as to redirect traffic from real campaign websites to phony ones.
4. "Typo-squatting": buying domain names with slight misspellings of a candidate's name, so as to misdirect or misinform the candidate's supporters—even to steal campaign donations.
5. Anonymous or fake-name blog posts: The future probably holds worse, like spyware designed to track voters' surfing habits and make them easier prey. Ever-cheaper and hard to trace, such cyber-deceptions are clearly the future of dirty politics. Nothing can stop them—except ethics.

Of course, some politicians and officials rob, cheat, and lie to the public just because they can. For example, an Illinois treasury employee opened a bank account under a false name in order to steal $250,000 from the state budget (Zelinski, 2009). But there are bad actors in every sphere of human activity. While they can never be eliminated, they can be isolated—and caught.

References

AAPOR Statement on Push Polls. Accessed July 27, 2013. www.aapor.org.

Amann, House Speaker J., as quoted in Baldor, L. (2004). "U.S. Targets Government Corruption." *Boston Globe*. Accessed December 25, 2012. http://www.boston.com.

Associated Press. (2005). "AP Poll: Lawmaker Standing Falls." *NBC News*. Accessed November 27, 2012. http://www.msnbc.msn.com/id/10387184/ns/politics/t/ap-poll-lawmaker-standing-falls-among-public/.

Associated Press. (2008). "Man Pleads Guilty to Forging Names on Ballot Petitions." *Newark Examiner*. Accessed December 2, 2012. www.examiner.com.

Becker, G., and G. N. Becker. (1997). *The Economics of Life*. New York: McGraw Hill.

Braun, M. (2007). "Pay-to-Play Cost New Mexico $90 Million, Lawsuit Says." *Bloomberg Press*. Accessed Jan. 20, 2012. www.bloomberg.com.

Bykowicz, J., and A. Linskey. (2009). "Baltimore Mayor Convicted of One Count of Fraud." *Baltimore Sun*. Accessed December 2, 2012. http://www.baltimoresun.com.

Caputo, Marc. (2011). "Florida Legislature's Budget Ax Spares Many Hometown Projects." *Miami Herald/St. Petersburg Times*. Accessed April 22, 2012. http://www.miamiherald.com.

Castro, A. (2007). "Much of Pork Spending in State Budget Going to Craddick Supporters." Accessed June 9, 2012. http://www.lubockonline.com.

Cillizza, C. (2007). "Parsing the Polls: How Much Does Corruption Count?" *The Washington Post*. Accessed November 27, 2012. http://voices.washingtonpost.com/thefix/parsing-the-polls/parsing-the-polls-corruption-c-1.html.

Coen, J. (2009). "Chicago Zoning Inspector Pleads Guilty to Taking Bribes." *Tribune Business News*. Accessed November 3, 2012. http://www.chicago.tribune.com.

Confessore, Nicholas, and Danny Hakim. (2009). "Bruno, Former State Leader, Guilty Of Corruption." *New York Times*. Accessed December 8, 2012. http://www.nytimes.com.

Davies, Dave. (2008). "Scandal in the Statehouse: 12 Democrats Face Corruption Charges." *Philadelphia Daily News*. Accessed December 2, 2012. www.philly.com.

Eichenwald, K. (2006, May 26). "Verdict on an Era." *New York Times*: C1, 6.

Finucane, M. (2008). "Council Aide Fined in Ethics Case." *Boston Globe*: B3.

"Foundation for Ethics in Public Service." *Report Public Corruption*. Accessed November 27, 2012. http://www.reportpubliccorruption.org/public-officals-corruption.html.

Frank, Al. (2008). "Prominent Builder Faces Bribery Trial." *Star Ledger*: 18.

Freeman, E., and P. Werhane. (2007). "Presentation to the Emerging Leaders Program of the State Legislative Leaders Foundation." University of Virginia.

"I-Team: OSU Football—Who Gets Special Prices?" (2008). *KY Post.* Accessed November 7, 2012. http://www.KYPost.com.

Jennings, Trip. (2011). "Martinez Latest to Target Pork Spending." *The New Mexican.* Accessed April 21, 2012. http://www.santafenewmexican.com.

Johnston, M. (1986). "Right and Wrong in American Politics: Popular Conceptions of Corruption." In A. Heidenheimer, M. Johnston, and V. LeVine, eds. *Political Corruption: A Handbook.* New Brunswick, NJ: Transaction Publishers, pp. 743–760.

Klepal, Dan. (2011). "Despite Efforts, Discretionary Spending Continues to Flourish in Louisville." *Courier-Journal.* Accessed April 9, 2012. http:// www.courier-journal.com.

Lebowitz, L. (2008). "Transit Hires Included the Well-Connected." *Miami Herald.* Accessed December 21, 2012. http://www.miamiherald.com.

Lebowitz, L., and R. Barry. (2008). "Gravy Train." *Miami Herald.* Accessed December 21, 2012. http://www.miamiherald.com.

Ledger Enquirer Editorial. (2011). "So Georgia Has Tough Ethics Laws . . . So What?" Accessed June 17, 2011. www.ledger-enquirer.com.

Maag, C. (2008). "Illinois Impeachment Panel Hears of Fund-Raising." *New York Times*: A14.

Moore, Scott. (2006). "Illegal Signature Gathering Continues." *The Portland Mercury.* Accessed Dec. 2, 2012. www.portlandmercury.com.

National Conference of State Legislatures Website. "Conflicts of Interest." http://www.ncsl.org.

New York City Procurement Policy Board Rules, Section 1–03. Accessed July 27, 2013. http://www.nyc.gov.

New York Times Editorial. (2008). "Governor Blagojevich's Bombast." *New York Times*: 7.

New York Times Editorial. (2008). "The Case for Election Reform." *New York Times*: A18.

O'Brien, D. (2005). "Cracking Down on Public Corruption." *Federal Bureau of Investigation Headline Archives.* Accessed June 20, 2012. http://www.fbi.gov.

Ortiz, J. (2008). "State Worker: Nepotism Poisons the Workplace." *Sacramento Bee.* Accessed November 27, 2012. http://www.sacramentobee.com.

Rivera, R., and R. Buettner. (2008). "Speaker Says Council Allotted Millions to Fake Groups and Spent It Elsewhere." *New York Times*: C9.

Rivera, Ray, R., Buettner, and W. Rashbaum. (2008). "In Council Campaigns, Relatives on the Payroll." *New York Times*: A1.

Roderick, K. (2007). "Corruption in the Housing Authority." *Los Angeles Times.* Accessed July 29, 2012. http://wwwlaobserved.com.

Rothman, C. (2008). "Once-Powerful Lawmaker's Corruption Trial Begins." *Star Ledger.* Accessed September 16, 2012. http:// www.starledger.com.

Rutan v. Republican Party of Illinois. 1990. 497U.S.62: 497.

Toutant, C. (2007). "N.J. Ethics Panel Finds Judge Abused Office by Interceding in Son's Dispute, Urges Censure." *New Jersey Law Journal.* Accessed July 13, 2012. http://www.law.com.

USA Today Editorial. (2010, Aug. 19). "Verdict in Blagojevich Trial Is No Exoneration." *USA Today*: 8A.

"US v. Siegelman and Scrushy." (2006). Report to Congress on the Activities and Operations of the Public Integrity Section of the US Dept. of Justice.

"US v. Tobin." (2006). Report to Congress on the Activities and Operations of the Public Integrity Section of the US Dept. of Justice.

Washington Post Editorial. (2008). "Lead Us Not. . . ." *Washington Post.* Accessed Dec. 2, 2012. www.washingtonpost.com.

Wolfson, Andrew. (2011). "Louisville Metro Council Members Hand Out $7.1 Million in Grants over 4 Years." *Courier-Journal.* Accessed April 9, 2012. http:// www.courier-journal.com.

Zavis, Alexandra. (2011). "LA County Supervisors Approve Guidelines on Discretionary Funds, Drop Proposal for Greater Oversight." *Los Angeles Times*. Accessed April 5, 2012. http://www.latimes.com.

Zelinski, A. (2009). "Crooked Politicians Costing Illinois $300M in 'Corruption Tax:' Professor." *Huffington Post*. Accessed March 30, 2012. http://www.huffingtonpost.com.

The Corruption Tax

Amy Handlin

There is no such thing as "trivial" public corruption. Whatever its form and scope, it is a serious drain on the economy wherever and whenever it occurs. Indirectly, communities pay a price in political and civic disengagement. More directly, businesses and residents shoulder a hefty "corruption tax."

How It Is Levied

The corruption tax is "levied" in at least five ways.

Overpriced, Shoddy Goods and Services

When government contracts are awarded to businesses in return for bribes or kickbacks, not only are honest competitors shut out, but expenses are typically padded to cover the illicit payouts. Moreover, a company that gets contracts through crooked deal-making has little incentive to deliver quality service—or any service. A federal investigation into Chicago's "Hired Truck" program, for example, found that firms bribed officials in return for hauling contracts but actually performed little or no work (Zelinski 2009). Boston's corruption-ridden "Big Dig" downtown roadway project made history not just for its record-breaking $14 billion price tag, but also for substandard materials, structural flaws, cost overruns, fraudulent billing and lax oversight that culminated in the death of a 38-year-old motorist (Saltzman 2009).

Wasteful Expenditures

To reward their allies—and sometimes, to punish their enemies—corrupt officials look for opportunities to create no-show jobs, give out unnecessary or overpriced contracts, hire unqualified cronies, and hike public salaries. They rarely hesitate to incur public costs for private benefit. For instance, former Pennsylvania legislator Mike Veon used state employees to drive two motorcycles to South Dakota so the bikes would be ready when he and his wife flew there for a vacation (Duclos 2008). A lucrative contract with Chicago's Department of Aviation was steered to a firm whose executives were golf buddies of the assistant commissioner and employers of his son (City of Chicago IGO 2010). Former New Jersey state senator and budget committee chair Wayne Bryant got a no-show job paying $35,000 per year at the University of Medicine and Dentistry in return for supporting increases

A car crushed by ceiling panels that fell in the Big Dig Tunnel in Boston on July 10, 2006, killing a passenger. The report by the board found problems with the bolt-and-epoxy system used to hold the 4,600-pound concrete ceiling slabs. The investigation showed 20 anchors pulled out from the tunnel roof. (AP Photo/ Massachusetts State Police via National Transportation Safety Board)

in the school's funding (Anastasia 2011). The FBI began investigating the government of Cuyahoga County, Ohio—an influential political base with more voters than nine states—in part because of questionable hires made by the elected county auditor. According to local media reports, "Ninety-three of 283 employees in [the auditor's] office are politically connected. . . . One was a former strip club manager with political connections who had [the auditor's] endorsement as 'a people person'" (Sheeran 2008).

Damage to Economic Vitality

Corruption may drive existing businesses out of a community, leaving a bigger tax burden on those who remain and causing other kinds of damage, like unemployment, to the community. Political arm-twisting can discourage firms from bidding on public contracts or developing expertise in serving local needs. Even a whiff of official impropriety can be a deal-breaker for companies looking for a place to locate or expand. The simple reality for an honest local proprietor is that he or she needs a level-playing field in order to compete. As summarized by one economic development expert: "There is an issue with trust in the political system, being able to rely on a certain set of rules. . . . Corruption creates tremendous uncertainty, and uncertainty is bad for business" (Hughlett and Wong 2008). According to the U.S. attorney for eastern Louisiana—who indicted 213 state and local officials and their private accomplices over seven years—rampant corruption in New Orleans had facilitated a "brain drain" and a decline in the city population, to 450,000 from over 600,000, long before Hurricane Katrina (Carey 2008).

Even the U.S. Committee on Economic Development, an association of America's corporate leaders, has taken up the issue of public corruption as a top concern. In 2005, USCED issued this warning: "A vibrant economy and well functioning business system will not remain viable in an environment of real or perceived corruption, which will corrode confidence in government and business" (Committee on Economic Development 2005).

Costs of Investigation and Prosecution

It is not unusual for a high-profile corruption case to drag on for a decade or more, with taxpayers footing the bill. For example, the investigation of former Illinois governor George Ryan—eventually convicted for fraud and racketeering—took 13 years. Such pursuits are not only expensive, but they also suck up other legal and judicial resources already insufficient to fight violent crime and social ills.

Indeed, faith in the judicial system itself can be undermined by corruption. For example, New York's process for choosing judges has long been the subject of lawsuits and reformers' dismay. Rife with threats, swaps, influence-peddling, and arm twisting, it was further tarnished when Brooklyn Democratic party ex-chairman Clarence Thomas was convicted of extorting over $20,000 from an aspiring judicial candidate in return for the boss's support (Ginsberg 2007).

Cynicism toward the Democratic Process

Campaign practices like deception, illicit fund-raising, and voter intimidation undermine citizens' trust in the integrity of elections. When a jaded public gives up on honest government, the result is a lack of interest and involvement in local elections, as evidenced by low voter turnouts. Despite hot contests for several city commission seats in Florida's chicanery-riddled Broward County, for example, over 90 percent of voters in the 2010 election stayed home. No one doubted the reason. Noting the "languid spell" cast over the local races, a journalist observed: "The few voters who showed up to cast a ballot attributed the pervasive voter apathy to recent reports of government corruption in South Florida." One resident commented simply: "People have lost interest . . . [They] are fed up with corruption in local government" (Gollan 2010).

Scholars, too, have noted that trust in government matters. In particular, it influences people's perceptions of the legitimacy of public institutions and their willingness to accept policy decisions. "While outcomes and inclusiveness of decision-making processes are of concern," comments one political scientist, "equally important are procedural aspects of how individuals perceive the fairness of the process" (Fedi, Mannarini, and Maton 2009).

While the corruption tax cannot be quantified with precision, estimates are eyepopping. At the federal level, the Government Accountability Office has calculated that the amount siphoned off by theft and fraud is at least 10 percent of expenditures on all federal government programs—tens of billions of dollars. In Chicago, the cost of corruption has been pegged at around $300 million (Zelinski 2009). In New Jersey, an estimated price tag of $1 billion has never been documented but is considered realistic. "It's not that a billion dollars in cash actually changes hands each year," says a former head of the Prudential Business Ethics Center at Rutgers University. "But if you believe that corruption distorts incentives so the right decisions are not being made, then a large number like that makes sense" (Daks 2009).

In summary, the FBI provides the following explanation of why public corruption is its top criminal investigative priority:

> Public corruption is a breach of trust by federal, state or local officials—often with the help of private sector accomplices. Corrupt public officials undermine our country's national security, our overall safety, the public trust, and confidence in the U.S. government, wasting billions of dollars along the way. This corruption can tarnish virtually every aspect of society. For example, a border official might take a bribe, knowingly or unknowingly letting in a truck containing weapons of mass destruction. Or corrupt state legislators could cast deciding votes on a bill providing funding or other benefits to a company for the wrong reasons. Or at the local level, a building inspector might be paid to overlook some bad wiring, which could cause a deadly fire down the road. (FBI 2010)

Three Faces of the Corruption Tax

Ultimately, the effects of the corruption tax on a particular community depend on the nature of the crime and other factors like the personality and power of the perpetrator. There are as many different impacts as different crooks. When corruption touches the U.S. Congress or the White House, as in the 2006 Abramoff scandal, there is an obvious blow to public trust in the highest echelons of government. But lower-profile cases—by far the most common—might play out in other ways that cause more targeted and tangible harm.

In any case, public corruption is never a victimless crime. Sometimes, its impact is strong enough to permanently alter a municipality, county, or state. The following are three examples.

Marlboro, New Jersey, Mayor Matt Scannapieco

In 1990, Marlboro was a quiet rural community of 20,000, with a farming heritage and an all-American image. Fifteen years later, the population had doubled and every public facility was bursting at the seams. Local taxes had skyrocketed as the government struggled to cope with sprawl, congestion, environmental degradation, and overcrowded schools. Worse, Marlboro had become synonymous with corruption.

The man at the center of the town's transformation served as mayor from 1992 through 2003. He was an inveterate, gregarious booster of his community—especially among developers eying its hundreds of acres of open land. One of Scannapieco's priorities was to pack influential land use boards with his supporters—who made sure his developer friends got a royal welcome when they proposed projects that were oversized, overpriced, and underscrutinized.

By 1997, the mayor was cashing in on these friendships. He intervened directly to get approvals for at least a half dozen high-cost, high-profit subdivisions, often at higher densities than normally allowed. In return, he pocketed $245,000. His allies were busy working their own big-builder relationships: A planning board member took bribes for pushing to rezone a 150-acre property, while the chairman of a municipal utilities authority engaged in extortion and tax evasion. Thanks in large part to the officials' foul play, 3,388 new homes were built in the 33-square-mile town between 1995 and 2005, far more than anyone had ever anticipated or prepared for.

Eventually, the FBI was tipped off about the ring of crooked developers and the officials who did their bidding for a decade. When Scannapieco and his cronies pled guilty in 2005, it put an end to their crimes—but not to Marlboro's problems. As the new mayor, Robert Kleinberg, bitterly observed: "We're going to be paying for the corrupt acts of the former officials for a long time to come . . . [their convictions don't] unbuild the homes, uncrowd the schools or decongest the road" (Smothers 2005).

In an unprecedented attempt to recoup some of the town's resources, Kleinberg filed suit against Scannapieco and his accomplices under the Racketeer Influenced and Corrupt Organizations Act (RICO). But RICO was designed to fight organized crime, not corrupt politicians; the case was dismissed in 2008. A judge ruled that Marlboro had no proof of specific, quantifiable injury—only a defrauded citizenry, a depleted budget, and a ruined reputation.

Birmingham, Alabama, Mayor Larry Langford

After its steel industry collapsed in the 1970s, Birmingham clawed its way back to economic vitality. By the late 1990s, it hummed with growth and optimism. As the county seat of booming Jefferson County, Birmingham had become a regional center for banking, health care, and higher education. No one imagined that just a few years later, the county would be in such dire fiscal peril that it would be forced to contemplate asking the court for protection from creditors—in other words, filing for bankruptcy.

At the center of the collapse was Mayor Larry Langford, a colorful politician who never hesitated to think big. During his years in various local offices, he pushed to construct an amusement park, a domed football stadium, a trolley network, a Pentagon-style municipal building, and a canal to bring cruise ships into Birmingham—from 250 miles away. In 2008, he proposed a bid to host the 2020 Olympics.

But behind the scenes, Langford's real priority was sewers: more precisely, the complex financing deals undertaken by Jefferson County to pay off $3.2 billion in debt. The county had borrowed heavily—many said irresponsibly—for a massive sewer project with costs that spiraled out of control and sparked a host of shady borrowing schemes. Among the wheeler-dealers were two of Langford's friends, a local banker and a lobbyist.

The three conspired to pay the mayor hundreds of thousands of dollars, in cash and other valuables, for his help in steering county bond business to favored

Birmingham mayor Larry Langford, left, speaks to reporters at the federal building with his wife Melva Langford for jury selection in his trial in 2009, in Tuscaloosa, Alabama. A federal jury convicted Birmingham mayor Langford on all charges of accepting bribes in exchange for funneling $7.1 million in bond business to a prominent investment banker. (AP Photo/ Butch Dill)

firms. The booty included a Rolex watch, designer clothes, audio equipment, and a $50,000 personal loan—arranged for Langford by his banker friend and paid off for him when he defaulted. For their part, his partners raked in hefty fees and payoffs. Meanwhile, Jefferson County descended into fiscal chaos.

But Langford's flamboyant behavior attracted suspicion. In 2007, he was investigated by the Securities and Exchange Commission, which ultimately sued him for taking $156,000 in bribes. In 2008, he and his accomplices were arrested by the FBI on over a hundred charges of bribery, conspiracy, fraud, money laundering, and tax evasion. Convicted in 2009 on 60 counts, Langford was sentenced to 15 years in jail and fined over $100,000. His cronies also received lengthy prison sentences. As *The Birmingham News* editorialized: "No wonder Jefferson County and Alabama are sick to their stomachs about corruption in government" (*Birmingham News* 2008).

But Langford's conviction didn't end the financial debacle that he helped to create. In November 2011, Jefferson County filed for the biggest local government bankruptcy in American history, affecting an unknown number of individual investors as well as financial institutions (Walsh 2011). Before the filing, one analyst stated bluntly: "Jefferson County is the scariest situation in the market today" (Burnsed 2009).

Massachusetts State Senator Dianne Wilkerson

In the late 1970s, a wave of public corruption in Massachusetts led to the formation of the Ward Commission, charged to find reasons for the breakdown and make recommendations for reform. Its final report concluded: "We have learned that corruption is a way of life in Massachusetts." Published in 1980, the Ward findings prompted a wave of ethics laws that went further than most supporters had hoped and were hailed as some of the best in the country.

Apparently, however, the early reformers did not anticipate all the modern opportunities for perfidy. Nearly three decades later, there was a new generation of scoundrels at the statehouse. A standout among them was Senator Dianne Wilkerson, chair of the powerful Joint Committee on State Administration and Regulatory Oversight.

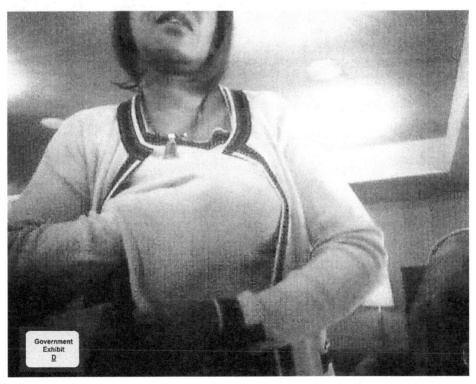

Massachusetts state senator Dianne Wilkerson, D-Boston, allegedly stuffing bribe money under her sweater at the bar at No. 9 Park restaurant in Boston. Wilkerson was arrested on October 28, 2008, by the FBI on public corruption charges. (AP Photo/U.S. Attorney's Office, File)

A high-profile though controversial fixture on the Boston scene, Wilkerson was the first African American woman to win a seat in the Massachusetts Senate. There had been previous run-ins with the law—she was convicted of failing to file federal tax returns and fined for violating state campaign finance and disclosure regulations. But until the very end, the loyalty of her constituents remained unshaken. Endorsed by the political establishment and buoyed by her prowess at the polls, she apparently felt unassailable. By 2007, she was actively welcoming the attentions of unscrupulous favor-seekers.

In an 18-month investigation, undercover FBI agents posing as businessmen caught Wilkerson taking bribes—up to $10,000 at a time—in return for development permits, liquor licenses, and legislation. Some of the more lurid exchanges were recorded on surveillance videotapes; one showed Wilkerson stuffing $100 bills into her undergarments. Here are a few highlights of the 32-page FBI indictment:

> A meeting at posh [Boston restaurant] No. 9 Park, where Wilkerson allegedly tucked 10 $100 bills into her bra; a two-day gambling spree at Foxwoods Casino after allegedly accepting a $1000 kickback at [a local cafe] . . . At one point, she allegedly laughed after an undercover agent posing as a developer handed her $10,000 and said, "That's a lot of money." She boasted that she was "arm-twisting" and "knee-cracking" city and state officials. (Levenson and Saltzman 2008)

Inadvertently, Wilkerson rendered a public service. After being indicted on more than 30 counts of bribery and corruption—despite her claim that she had received only tokens of appreciation from grateful constituents—she became a symbol of all the shortcomings in state ethics laws that had been ignored since the Ward Commission. Governor Deval Patrick formed a 12-member task force to recommend changes, but lawmakers continued to resist reform. Ultimately, Patrick threatened to veto a sales tax increase sought by the legislature unless it was accompanied by tightened ethics regulation.

In July 2009, Patrick signed an ethics bill hailed as "the most significant reform in a generation" (*Boston Globe* 2009). Among other changes, it doubled the penalties for bribery and banned legislators from accepting valuable gifts—provisions that will be remembered as legacies of Dianne Wilkerson.

References

Anastasia, George. (2011, August 25). "Third Circuit Panel Denies Wayne Bryant's Appeal." *Philadelphia Inquirer*. Accessed Feb. 10, 2011. www.philly.com.

Birmingham News Editorial. (2008, Dec. 4). *Birmingham News*. Accessed Jan. 11, 2010. http://www.bhamnews.com.

Boston Globe Editorial. (2009, June 26). "A Season of Reform." *Boston Globe*. Accessed March 2, 2010. http:// www.boston.com.

Burnsed, B. (2009, Nov. 8). "Bond Debacle Sinks Jefferson County." *Business Week*. Accessed March 7, 2010. http://www.businessweek.com.

Carey, N. (2008, August 14). "Fighting Corruption Is Hard Going in New Orleans." *Boston Globe*. Accessed March 18, 2010. http:// www.boston.com.

City of Chicago Inspector General's Office. (2010, Oct.). *Quarterly Report*. Accessed March 14, 2010. http:// www.chicagoinspectorgeneral.org.

Committee on Economic Development. (2005). "Building on Reform: A Business Proposal to Strengthen Election Finance." Accessed Feb. 10, 2010. http://www.ced.org.

Daks, M. (2009, Aug. 3). "Cost of Corruption: $1B." *NJBIZ*. Accessed March 21, 2010. http://www.njbiz.com

Duclos, S. (2008, July 11). "12 Pennsylvania Democrats Indicted in 'BonusGate.'" *Digital Journal*. Accessed March 15, 2010. http://www.digitaljournal.com.

Federal Bureau of Investigation. (2010). "Public Corruption: Why It's Our #1 Criminal Priority." Accessed March 18, 2010. http://www.fbi.gov/news/stories/2010/march/corruption_032610.

Fedi, Angela, T. Mannarini, and K. Maton. (2009). "Empowering Community Settings and Community Mobilization." *Community Development: Journal of the Community Development Society* 40, no. 3: 265.

Ginsberg, A. (2007, Feb. 24). "3-time Loser Norman Guilty." *New York Post*. Accessed Feb. 2, 2010. http://www.nypost.com.

Gollan, J. (2010, March 10). "Shechter, Castillo Keep Seats in Pines." *Sunsentinel*. Accessed March 20, 2010. http://www.sunsentinel.com.

Hughlett, M., and W. Wong. (2008, Dec. 14). "The Cost of Corruption: Image of Dishonesty Can Hurt a State's Economic Vitality." *Chicago Tribune*. Accessed Jan. 12, 2010. http://www.chicagotribune.com.

Levenson, Michael, and J. Saltzman. (2008, Oct. 29). "Bribery Defendant Wilkerson Senator Allegedly Took Cash for Help in Liquor License, Development." *Boston Globe*. Accessed Feb. 10, 2010. http//www.boston.com.

Saltzman, Jonathan. (2009, May 8). "Big Dig Contractor Modern Continental Pleads Guilty." *Boston Globe*. Accessed Feb. 1, 2010. http://www.boston.com.

Sheeran, Thomas. (2008, Aug. 17). "Corruption Probe in Ohio Rattles Political Terrain." *Coshocton Tribune*. Accessed April 3, 2010. http://www.coshoctontribune.com.

Smothers, R. (2005, July 11). "Officials Pleaded Guilty, But Town Was Changed Forever." *New York Times*. Accessed June 3, 2010. http://wwwnytimes.com.

Walsh, Mary W. (2011, Dec. 24). "Bankruptcy Filing Raises Doubts about a Bond Repayment Pledge." *New York Times*: B1.

Zelinski, A. (2009, March 30). "Crooked Politicians Costing Illinois $300M in 'Corruption Tax': Professor." *Huffington Post*. Accessed April 21, 2010. http://www.huffingtonpost.com.

Ethics in Government and Governments in Ethics

Gwendolyn Yvonne Alexis

Introduction

> Civil Government therefore, availing itself only of its own powers, is extremely defective; and unless it can derive assistance from some superior power, whose laws extend to the temper and disposition of the human heart, and before whom no offense is secret, wretched indeed would be the state of man under a civil condition of any form.
>
> —*Justice Theophilus Parsons* in Barnes vs. Falmouth Parish (1810)

This dictum from *Barnes*, an 1810 Massachusetts Supreme Court case, makes an important point about the limitations of law in controlling human behavior. While legislation imposing fines, penalties, and/or criminal sanctions may be an effective deterrent to engaging in acts specifically enumerated as barred, there will always remain a whole range of undesirable activities that are not yet covered by law. This is because lawmaking is a reactive process. Laws are often enacted in response to a scandal in which harm is inflicted upon the greater society by an event disclosing previously unimagined levels of human depravity, greed, or callous pursuit of self-interest. Therefore, there will always be behaviors that fall into a gray area of unethical, but not yet illegal conduct. A case in point: in this age of nonstop technological advances, lawmakers are continually challenged to broaden pre-digital age definitions of copyright infringement and "theft of intellectual property" to encompass the latest peer-to-peer file-sharing activity of the eminently creative, tech-savvy Millennial generation.

Hence, in the opening quote of this chapter, Justice Parsons makes a valid point about the perils of unbridled human volition—wretched, indeed, is the society dependent upon law alone to steer its populace toward ethical behavior. In 1810, religion was relied upon to provide the populace with a firm sense of right and wrong that allowed for few moral-free zones. Because of this, regular church attendance was mandatory under threat of fine or imprisonment. In fact, the *Barnes* case involved the constitutionality of a mandatory church tax that was used to support a "teacher of morality" (a pastor) in each parish in Massachusetts.

However, the Fourteenth Amendment cleared up the muddy water that existed at the time of the *Barnes* case when states like Massachusetts assumed that the First Amendment strictures against interference with the religious lives of the populace applied only to the central government (Amar 1998). The Fourteenth Amendment specifically prohibited states from demeaning any rights or privileges secured to the citizenry under the U.S. Constitution, including the First Amendment right to freedom of (and freedom from) religion. Nonetheless, states in their *parens patri?* role as protector of the public welfare have a great interest in supporting those institutions that provide moral uplift to the citizenry. (This is the reason charitable organizations are granted tax exemptions.) Of course, improving the moral tenor of society is not merely a top-down proposition; and recently states have given considerable attention to improving the moral tone at the top. This is exemplified by the ethics reform legislation being generated by state legislatures around the nation. Florida's Code of Ethics for Public Officers and Employees is typical of the ethics reform initiatives taking place at the state level. The restorative goals of ethics reform initiatives are clearly evident in a statement made by the Florida Commission on Ethics:

> Foremost among the goals of the Code [of Ethics] is to promote the public interest and maintain the respect of the people for this government. (2012, 5)

Unfortunately, the frantic pace at which legislatures are enacting laws to create commissions, boards, and committees to provide ethical oversight in state government has resulted in a somewhat haphazard, shotgun approach in which the targets of ethics reform in state government may be lobbyists, legislators, public officials, members of the judiciary, or all state employees above a certain civil service rank. To illustrate, Washington State has created three ethics oversight bodies: the Washington State Legislative Ethics Board, the Washington Public Disclosure Commission, and the Washington State Executive Ethics Board. Legislation in Illinois and Kentucky supplements their regular state ethics commissions with specialty commissions dealing exclusively with executive branch ethics. New Jersey legislation has created both the New Jersey Election Law Enforcement Commission and a state ethics commission. And, Indiana has a general ethics commission plus another ethics body that deals exclusively with the registration of lobbyists—the Indiana Lobby Registration Commission.

The focus of this chapter is New York's ethics reform legislation, the Public Integrity Reform Act of 2011 ("PIRA"), which was signed into law by Governor Cuomo on August 15, 2011. Despite its newness, PIRA is an ideal subject for studying how state governments use law in an attempt to restore public respect for government. This is because PIRA represents a composite of the various legislative approaches that states are using for ethics reform. PIRA applies to both the executive and legislative branches of government and also to lobbyists. Although PIRA does contain some stand-alone substantive provisions, the bulk of the law consists of making amendments to the following New York statutes:

- Election Law
- Public Officers Law
- Executive Law

- Legislative Law
- Retirement and Social Security Law
- Criminal Procedure Law

This chapter is divided into three parts. Part I outlines the aspirations of legislation intended to effect moral uplift; these aspirations are based on the goals of the Sarbanes-Oxley Act of 2002 ("SARBOX"), a federal statute credited with achieving this result in the corporate world. Part II discusses various components of the outline in more detail. Part III analyzes how well PIRA fits the SARBOX model for successful ethics reform legislation.

Part I: A Federal Response to Moral Decay—SARBOX

> Over the last 10 years, key elements of the Act [SARBOX] have been replicated around the world, perhaps the purest form of flattery. Today, on the heels of the global financial crisis, many jurisdictions are looking anew at policy improvements similar to those instituted by [the Act]. (Turley and Howe 2012)

The U.S. Congress enacted SARBOX to bring about a moral renaissance in the corporate governance of publicly traded corporations ("PTCs") at a time when the investing public no longer trusted PTCs or the financial information contained in their periodic filings with the U.S. Securities and Exchange Commission (SEC). Confidence in U.S. securities markets had reached an all-time low by the time SARBOX became law in 2002; the gravity of the situation is reflected in the preamble to SARBOX: "An Act to protect investors by improving the accuracy and reliability of corporate disclosures made pursuant to the securities laws, and for other purposes." Making transparency and corporate accountability the linchpins of massive corporate reform, Congress crafted a law designed to be as proactive in installing a system of internal corporate controls as it was reactive to the corporate accounting scandals that led to its enactment.

Today, over a decade after SARBOX went into effect, it is clear that the moral tenor within corporations has improved substantially since the days of Enron and progeny (Alexis 2009). The following outline classifies by objectives the four successful provisions of SARBOX:

1. Enhance organizational transparency
   a. Implement "therapeutic" disclosure
   b. Facilitate whistle-blowing
2. Enhance accountability
   a. Provide regulatory oversight
3. Minimize conflicts of interest
   a. Limit revolving door situations
4. Enhance internal ethics control mechanisms

As an outline for organizational change, SARBOX provides an ideal model for the public sector.

Part II: Four Ways That SARBOX Provisions Contribute to the Goal of Moral Uplift

Enhance Organizational Transparency through "Therapeutic Disclosure" and Whistle-Blowing

PTCs are required to file periodic reports with the SEC under the Securities Exchange Act of 1934 (Exchange Act). While these are mainly financial reports filed on a quarterly and annual basis, special reports have to be filed on a real-time basis (including website postings) whenever significant events occur between regular reporting cycles where the potential exists to materially impact company earnings. The filing of a major class action lawsuit against a PTC is such an event as such lawsuits have the potential to impair brand equity or goodwill (Alexis 2007a). The Exchange Act was significantly amended by SARBOX in order to (1) strengthen the disclosure requirements and (2) provide for enhanced fines and criminal sanctions for failure to make required disclosures—whether such failure is caused by willful misstatements or intentional omission of material facts. Additionally, corporate transparency has been enhanced by SARBOX whistle-blowing protections and its whistle-blowing mandate for internal "gatekeepers" such as attorneys and accountants. Thus SARBOX provides an excellent example of how *external* control measures (laws, regulations, and sanctions) can be used to enhance *internal* control mechanisms (Alexis 2007b). In short, it is proactive legislation.

Therapeutic Disclosure. SARBOX §403 shortens the time allowed for directors, officers, and shareholders holding more than 10 percent of the shares of a PTC (collectively referred to as "insiders") to disclose in filings with the SEC any trading on inside information. Whereas prior to SARBOX, insiders had 10 days after the close of the calendar month in which the transaction took place to file the Form 4 disclosure document with the SEC, Section 403 shortened the period to 2 business days after the insider transaction occurs (SEC 2004).

SARBOX §406 mandates disclosure of whether or not a PTC has in existence a Code of Ethics for its chief financial officer (CFO). In adopting a rule to implement the Section 406 mandate, the SEC extended the requirement to include disclosing whether or not a Code of Ethics exists for the chief executive officer (CEO) as well. This de facto requirement for a PTC to have in place a Code of Ethics for its senior executives has been described as "therapeutic" disclosure:

> The relevant concept here is so-called "therapeutic disclosure." In other words, the Act uses disclosure requirements to effect changes in substantive behavior. For example, the corporation must disclose whether it has adopted a code of ethics for its financial officers. (Bainbridge 2003, 29)

SARBOX §409 provides for Form 8-K disclosures (current reports on material changes in PTC's financial condition or operations) to be made on a "real-time" basis, which has been interpreted by the SEC to require filing a Form 8-K within four days of the occurrence of the event triggering a need for a Form 8-K. The disclosures required by these three sections of SARBOX have greatly enhanced corporate transparency.

Mandatory disclosure of trading on inside information is equally important in the public sector. Government officials and legislators have positions that make them privy to nonpublic information on a regular basis. In this vein, at the federal level, it is notable that on April 4, 2012, President Obama signed legislation prohibiting members and employees of the U.S. Congress from trading on nonpublic information. The legislation, Stop Trading on Congressional Knowledge (STOCK) Act, requires electronic filing of financial disclosure forms, which are to be made available to the public. The STOCK Act also applies to officers and employees in the executive and judicial branches of federal government.

Whistle-Blowing. SARBOX §301 requires that the Audit Committee of the Board of Directors establish internal procedures for anonymous whistle-blowing. SARBOX §307 mandates whistle-blowing by in-house attorneys who become aware of wrongdoing within a PTC lest they lose their right to practice before the SEC; this sanction has serious career implications for attorneys given that all attorneys who are employees of a PTC are deemed to be "practicing before the Securities and Exchange Commission." In fact, as discussed next, SARBOX conscripts both attorneys and accountants as in-house watchdogs in a purposeful attempt to prevent these SARBOX-dubbed "securities professionals" from becoming in-house aiders and abettors of fraud. Moreover, for the whistle-blowing attorney, Section 307 provides that if the wrongdoing is not rectified after he or she has reported same to the board Audit Committee, then he or she must blow the whistle to outside authorities (such as the U.S. Attorney's Office or the SEC).

Section 806 protects employees of PTCs who blow the whistle from retaliatory actions by an employer by providing the whistle-blower with the right to file a lawsuit against the retaliating employer with the Secretary of Labor, as well as the right to file a civil lawsuit for compensatory damages. Section 1107 provides for imposition of a fine and/or imprisonment of up to 10 years for retaliating against a whistle-blower.

Laws facilitating whistle-blowing and mandating full disclosure are symbiotic. Encouraging whistle-blowers to come forward significantly increases the transparency of an organization; moreover, it promulgates an internal system of checks and balances to create and reinforce high ethical standards. Thus the four sections of SARBOX dealing with whistle-blowing represent proactive legislation, not just a reactive or punitive response to corruption. In short, incentives and protections for whistle-blowing should be included in all state legislation aimed at ethics reform. One way to accomplish this is for states to have a stand-alone whistle-blowing statute to complement their ethics laws. This is what Florida has done:

IX. Whistle-Blower's Act

In 1986, the [Florida] Legislature enacted a "Whistle-blower's Act" to protect employees of agencies and government contractors from adverse personnel actions in retaliation for disclosing information in a sworn complaint alleging certain types of improper activities. Since then, the Legislature has revised this law to afford greater protection to these employees.

While this language is contained within the Code of Ethics, the Commission has no jurisdiction or authority to proceed against persons who violate this Act. Therefore, a person who has disclosed information alleging improper conduct governed by this law and who may suffer adverse consequences as a result should contact one or more of the following: the Office of the Chief Inspector General in the Executive Office of the Governor; the Department of Legal Affairs; the Florida Commission on Human Relations; or a private attorney. (§ 112.3187—112.31895, Fla. Stat.)

Enhance Accountability by Providing Regulatory Oversight

SARBOX enhances accountability by subjecting management executives and professionals in PTCs to greater oversight and holding them individually responsible for organizational wrongdoing that occurs on their watch. In other words, these upper echelon individuals become gatekeepers (Alexis 2009). Section 3(a) of SARBOX gives the SEC authority to promulgate new rules and regulations as necessary to further the public interest; violation of any of these rules and regulations may be punishable by substantial fines and imprisonment. SARBOX §101 establishes the Public Company Accounting Oversight Board (PCABO, pronounced *peek-a-boo*) to oversee audits of PTCs, thus introducing regulation of public accountants (who were previously answerable only to the licensing authority in the states where they practiced). Section 302 requires a PTC's CEO and CFO to sign company financial reports, to establish and maintain internal controls, and to attest to the fact that corporate financial reports are not misleading.

All three sections (§§3[a], 101, and 302) are proactive; making more individuals accountable for organizational wrongdoing, strengthens internal checks and balances and can be expected to lower the incidence of wrongdoing. Obviously, the public sector could benefit from similar requirements.

Minimize Conflicts of Interest by Limiting Revolving Door Situations

SARBOX has three sections dealing with conflicts of interest. Section 301(A) specifies that each member of a PTC's Audit Committee shall be an independent (outside) director. Section 206 is aimed at the so-called revolving door, and prohibits public accounting firms from performing audits for a PTC if any of the PTC's higher echelon officers were previously employed by the public accounting firm "and participated in any capacity in the audit" of the PTC within a one-year period prior to the proposed audit. Section 402 prohibits a PTC from making personal loans to its executives.

In government, the problem of the revolving door between the public and private sectors is so common that scholars have coined the term "regulatory capture" to describe its harmful results:

The concern here is one of "regulatory capture," where regulators end up serving industry instead of the public. Former industry representatives can certainly make

good regulators because they have an intimate understanding of the regulated industry, the issues involved, the regulations themselves, and industry business practices.
But they can also bring with them a mindset carried over from their time as corpo-
rate representatives, favoring industry profits over citizen health, safety, and welfare.
As for movement in the other direction, there is very little good to be said about it.
Generally, corporations pay former regulators for their knowledge of how to navigate
the regulatory process most efficiently and, even more, for their agency contacts.
(Zivian 2012)

Laws decreasing the frequency of conflict of interest situations are decidedly proactive and enhance the kind of internal controls that prospectively ward off ethical
breaches (Alexis and Pressman 2010).

Enhance Internal Ethics Control Mechanisms

Three sections of SARBOX epitomize the use of legislation to enhance internal
control mechanisms. Section 305 raises the fitness standard for those who would
serve as officers and directors of PTCs; and Section 1105 gives the SEC authority
to prohibit persons who have violated the securities laws from serving as officers or
directors of PTCs. Section 805(a)(5) admonishes the U.S. Sentencing Commission
to strengthen the sentencing guidelines utilized by federal judges to impose sanctions on organizations for criminal wrongdoing. This SARBOX directive led the
U.S. Sentencing Commission to create a Model Compliance and Ethics Program,
with an anonymous whistle-blowing system made an integral part of the program.
The model is set forth in the U.S. Sentencing Guidelines (§8B2.1). For PTCs, adopting the model in full became essential since SARBOX prohibits national securities
exchanges from listing companies that do not have anonymous whistle-blowing
systems in place (Section 301[A]).

Section 8B2.1 of the U.S. Sentencing Guidelines further provides that the PTC's
board of directors is the "governing authority"—the place where the buck stops.
This clear delineation of board responsibility provides a strong incentive for the
corporate board to have a Compliance and Ethics Program in place to take advantage of the "safe harbor" offered by Guideline §8B2.1; namely, that an organization
that diligently implements an ethics program in accordance with the guideline (and
which provides ethics training for its employees) will not be held vicariously liable
for subsequent wrongdoing by employees acting in clear violation of established
policy. Rare (or more accurately, nonexistent) is the board who would pass up this
opportunity to escape liability. Such a board would run the risk of board members
being held individually liable should disgruntled shareholders file suit on behalf
of the corporation (Alexis 2007b). Moreover, vicarious liability sanctions can be as
severe as mandatory delisting of a PTC's stock by the national securities exchanges.

Part III: Ethics Reform Legislation and SARBOX

Despite the 2007 enactment of legislation . . . to "reform" New York State's ethics laws, as
a result of several scandals involving New York State officials and legislators, ethics reform

was a dominant theme of Andrew Cuomo's 2010 campaign for Governor. During his first six months in office, Governor Cuomo made ethics reform a legislative priority, using the bully pulpit across the State to convince the Legislature to enact his proposal. (Glaser, Oppenheimer, and Pearlman 2011)

Like SARBOX, the New York ethics reform legislation is a product of recent scandals revealing the seemingly boundless capacity of powerful people to use their positions for personal gain. In the short period between the enactment of New York's 2007 ethics reform legislation and the January 1, 2011, start of Andrew Cuomo's term as governor, three sitting members of the New York State Legislature were indicted. Eliot Spitzer—who had been admonished for his role in "Troopergate"—was forced to resign his 13-month governorship because of a prostitution scandal. (Aides in Spitzer's administration ordered New York State police to keep tabs on the Senate Majority Leader's travel in the hope of catching Spitzer's Republican rival misusing state aircraft privileges.) Spitzer's replacement, David Paterson, limped to the end of his short tenure as governor-by-succession haunted by accusations of witness tampering, soliciting free Yankees tickets, and perjury (for which the Commission on Public Integrity fined him $62,125 just as he was leaving office in December 2010).

Thus it was not surprising when restoring confidence in government became Cuomo's top priority. Like many state governors faced with shriveling public trust, Governor Cuomo made ethics reform a signature goal. A serious overhaul of government ethics must extend to everyone on the state payroll, not just those at the top; in the minds of state residents, the public servants who deliver day-to-day services represent the face of officialdom. Hence an ethics refurbishing must occur in both the legislative and executive branches of government. Since PIRA applies to both the executive and legislative branches of government, it provides an appropriate canvas for applying the SARBOX design. Next, the four sections of the

New York State governor Eliot Spitzer making a statement to reporters during a news conference in 2008 in New York where he apologized to his family and the public after a report that he was involved in a prostitution ring. (AP Photo/Mary Altaffer)

SARBOX-based outline are used as topic headings to organize the discussion and assessment of PIRA.

First, it is important to draw a distinction between legislation that merely imposes sanctions (reactive law) and legislation intended to influence behavior prospectively, either by deterring corruption directly or by enhancing internal controls so as to decrease the opportunities for unethical conduct (proactive law). The provisions of PIRA dealing with sanctions will be discussed only where they serve as deterrents.

Enhance Organizational Transparency

Disclosure is the centerpiece of PIRA. The statute sets forth an onerous 25-page "Financial Disclosure Statement" that must be completed annually by every state-wide elected official, state officer, member of the legislature, political party chairman, and every candidate for statewide elected office or for the legislature. These Financial Disclosure Statements are to be filed with the PIRA-created Joint Commission on Public Ethics (JCOPE), which will post the statements on the Internet. This is akin to the *therapeutic* disclosure under SARBOX in that advance knowledge of the need to disclose all financial transactions and business relationships should deter state officials from operating in gray areas. In fact, one of PIRA's most ambitious transparency tools required that, effective January 1, 2013, the Office of General Services (OGS) launch a new online database, dubbed "Project Sunlight." This project requires state agencies, boards, commissions, the State University of New York (SUNY), City University of New York (CUNY), and all other public authorities having at least one governor-appointed member to supply OGS with a list of individuals, firms, and other entities that have appeared before them as a representative or advocate for a client or customer. OGS will make these lists available to the public through its Project Sunlight database.

PIRA's mandatory financial disclosure provisions also cover lobbyists and their clients, who must report any relationship in which compensation in excess of $1,000 annually is paid directly or indirectly to state officials in exchange for "goods, services or anything of value" (PIRA, Part A, § 8). Of course, any relationship disclosed on a lobbyist's disclosure statement should also show up on the Financial Disclosure Statement of the state official involved, thereby providing a system of checks and balances.

Transparency in state government is the end goal of the disclosure provisions of PIRA. This entails more than just aggregating Financial Disclosure Statements from legislators and public officials. Indeed, it is to this end that Project Sunlight requires a vast array of governmental bodies to compile lists of individuals, firms, and other entities that appear before them, as representatives or advocates, to advance the interests of their respective clients or customers.

Since JCOPE is itself a governmental body, it has the same ethical obligation as other governmental bodies to be transparent. But PIRA misses the issue of who regulates the regulator, as indicated in the following quote:

(b) Notwithstanding the provisions of article seven of the public officers law [Open Meetings Law], *no meeting or proceeding . . . of the commission shall be open to the public,* except if expressly provided otherwise by the commission [JCOPE] or as is required by article one-A of the legislative law. (PIRA, Part A, § 6; emphasis added)

Where legislation specifically exempts a regulator from complying with New York's open meetings law, there is little chance for the public to hold the regulator accountable. The obvious intent of the law is that, except for executive sessions, "every meeting of a public body shall be open to the general public" (Public Officers Law, Art. 7, §103[a]).

Hence, PIRA falls far short of the SARBOX standard in terms of enhancing transparency. Indeed, PIRA misses an opportunity both to make JCOPE's operations transparent and to render its individual members jointly and severally accountable to the public. During its first year of operations, JCOPE was roundly criticized for its tendency to exclude the public from its meetings by declaring an "executive session." Although legal, this dubious tactic attracts, rather than diverts, public attention:

> The public portion of the meeting today lasted roughly 26 minutes and then entered closed-door executive session. JCOPE has been criticized for operating with little to no transparency since its formation earlier this year. (Reisman 2012)

Of course, this is the opposite of transparency in government and calls into question the ethics of the "ethics police." Rather than pursuing the objectives of PIRA to make state government more transparent, the would-be ethics reformers are taking cover under the letter of the law while ignoring its spirit.

An additional shortcoming of PIRA is that the law does not contain whistle-blowing incentives or protections. This is particularly troubling in light of JCOPE's skimpy investigatory staff, a problem that will be discussed in more detail later in this chapter.

Enhance Accountability

It's true, CPI [Commission on Public Integrity] had no authority to investigate the legislature, but despite that, we did much to change the culture of legislature with our power to investigate and impose penalties on quite a few lobbyists that gave them gifts. That had a significant impact on changing the culture there, and I think most people agree that there should be a more independent body to oversee the legislature.

—*Barry Ginsberg, former director of CPI (Hoe 2011)*

Under PIRA, the Commission on Public Integrity (CPI) was replaced by JCOPE, which—unlike CPI—does have authority to oversee and investigate the conduct of the legislature (along with the executive branch and lobbyists). However, JCOPE's authority to oversee the legislature means nothing without sufficient manpower to either oversee or conduct investigations of the legislature. There are 212 members of the New York legislature; but JCOPE is working with a staff of approximately

40 persons. With this limited staff, it is to oversee "tens of thousands of State offic-ers and employees, legislative members and employees, and registered lobbyists and clients located throughout the State" (2013 Annual Report). JCOPE maintains offices in Albany, Manhattan, and Buffalo so the staff of 40 is spread pretty thin. Indeed, the Information Services Section that was included in its inaugural Organi-zation Chart (see Figure 1) based upon a budget of $3,781,000 for the 2012/2013 fiscal year—a budget 2.5 percent lower than the 2011 budget of its predecessor agency, CPI— does not appear in a revised Organization Chart set forth in the 2013 Annual Report.

Without sufficient staff to make legislators view JCOPE as a serious watchdog agency, the presence of other checks and balances becomes increasingly impor-tant. Here again, an anonymous whistle-blowing system would serve JCOPE well in that it would at least convey the sense that "someone is watching," especially if there were monetary incentives for blowing the whistle such as those that exist in federal laws like the False Claims Act, which provides for the whistle-blower to receive a portion of any monies recovered by the government from the wrongdoer.

The deficit in manpower will also limit JCOPE's ability to review the Financial Disclosure Statements being filed by all 212 members of the legislature, public offi-cials in the executive branch, and lobbyists. JCOPE's organization chart (Figure 1) shows that the "Audit and Review" section has a staff of 14, with 5 working as "com-pliance auditors," 7 working as "filing specialists," and 2 working as "confidential assistants." This imbalance means that despite disclosure being a centerpiece of PIRA, the "Audit and Review" section will function as record keepers rather than as auditors who detect irregularities in filed Financial Disclosure Statements. Alas, this is generally the experience of regulatory bodies collecting huge amounts of financial disclosure data:

> The financial disclosure process comes closest to being labeled "window dressing," in that disclosure forms are not scrutinized with the rigor that is characteristic of other commission activities. Ethics administrators admit there are probably many omis-sions on financial disclosure forms that go undetected. (Smith 2003, 288)

Additionally, JCOPE's propensity to hide behind the "executive session" exemp-tion to the Open Meetings Law significantly undercuts its accountability to the public. Indeed, such a modus operandi lends a Star Chamber quality to JCOPE's proceedings.

PIRA increases the civil penalty for failing to file or for filing a false Financial Disclosure Statement (a fine of up to $40,000); and also provides for referral to the "appropriate prosecutor" who may bring a criminal proceeding against the violator for commission of a Class A misdemeanor. Additionally, for public offi-cials entering the state payroll after PIRA's effective date of August 15, 2011, being convicted of a felony or pleading guilty to commission of a felony could result in the forfeiture of their state pension. It is possible that the severity of these

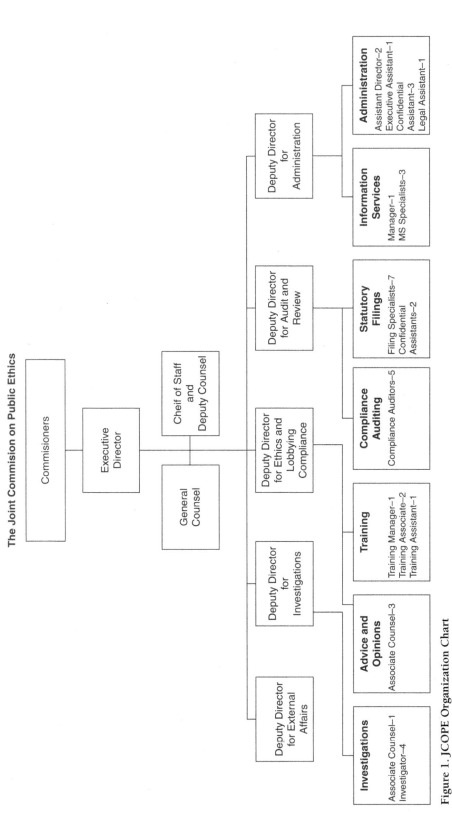

The Joint Commision on Public Ethics

Commisioners

Executive Director

General Counsel

Cheif of Staff and Deputy Counsel

Deputy Director for External Affairs

Deputy Director for Investigations

Deputy Director for Ethics and Lobbying Compliance

Deputy Director for Audit and Review

Deputy Director for Administration

Investigations
Associate Counsel–1
Investigator–4

Advice and Opinions
Associate Counsel–3

Training
Training Manager–1
Training Associate–2
Training Assistant–1

Compliance Auditing
Compliance Auditors–5

Statutory Filings
Filing Specialists–7
Confidential Assistants–2

Information Services
Manager–1
MS Specialists–3

Administration
Assistant Director–2
Executive Assistant–1
Confidential Assistant–3
Legal Assistant–1

Figure 1. JCOPE Organization Chart

sanctions will incentivize people to comply with the law and file timely reports of their financial transactions and business relationships. Nevertheless, it should be kept in mind that Enron was current on all of its filings with the SEC; alas, more is needed than merely motivating pro forma compliance with the law. Legislation that only serves to punish past acts (i.e., reactive legislation) will fail to achieve the desired behavior modification, namely, making public officials more circumspect about accepting gifts, entering into questionable business liaisons, ignoring conflicts of interest, and so forth.

It is too early to predict whether the stiffer sanctions are functioning proactively as a deterrent to wrongdoing. JCOPE has not been in business long enough to make a realistic comparison of the caseload experience of CPI with that of JCOPE. As of July 27, 2012, all pending Enforcement Actions listed on the JCOPE website had been opened by its predecessor, CPI. However, based on JCOPE's limited manpower, it is unlikely that it will be able to institute a sufficient number of enforcement actions to make public officials fear punishment for filing *false* Financial Disclosure Statements. Hence, timely filings will likely be made even with misstatements or omissions—in the well-founded belief that only a failure to file will attract the attention of the regulators. Such is the fate of regulatory agencies at both the state and federal levels. They achieve only pro forma compliance with their rules and regulations because their perpetual shortage of manpower and their budgetary limitations are well known by those subject to their regulation. To remedy this, regulatory agencies such as the SEC and the IRS file a number of high-profile lawsuits each year to attract widespread publicity and let would-be violators know that there is a chance (although remote) of having criminal sanctions applied in their case. Here again, PIRA misses out on an important opportunity to make potential wrongdoers lose sleep over possible detection of their misdeeds; an anonymous whistle-blowing hotline could help rectify the situation.

Minimize Conflicts of Interest

The Financial Disclosure Statements mandated under PIRA are a critical step in bringing conflicts of interest to light. Financial Disclosure Statements filed by legislators are reviewed by the Legislative Ethics Commission (LEC); and LEC, alone, has authority to impose penalties upon members of, or candidates for, the legislature for violation of the Public Officers Law. PIRA provides that LEC is to establish rules relating to "possible conflicts between private interests and official duties of present members of the legislature and legislative employees" (N.Y. Legislative Law, § 80[k]). Likewise, JCOPE is charged with establishing rules and regulations to prevent conflicts of interest with respect to public officials working in the executive branch and in state agencies. Both LEC and JCOPE are to make annual assessments of the degree of compliance with the rules and regulations that they have promulgated. Consistent with a Model Ethics Law propounded by Common Cause, JCOPE is to conduct periodic random reviews of filed Financial Disclosure Statements.

PIRA contains a number of definitions that help alert people to situations where conflicts of interest are likely to occur. For example, PIRA amends the Election

Law to add a definition of "political communication"; amends the Public Officers Law to add a definition of "compensation"; and amends the Legislative Law to add definitions of "reportable business relationship," "lobbying," and "gifts." Additionally, PIRA provides for both LEC and JCOPE to issue advisory opinions, which may head off some potential conflicts. Also worth noting, though these provisions existed before PIRA, is that the New York Public Officers Law contains adequate provisions to slow down the revolving door between government and the private sector for executive branch employees.

Enhance Internal Ethics Control Mechanisms

Using a purely external control mechanism (an ethics commission) is not enough to ensure ethical government. Conversely, using only an internal control or check is equally inadequate. Recognizing a balance between both approaches reaffirms the importance of structural mechanisms to facilitate ethics, but it reinforces the individual's role in preserving ethics in government. (Smith 2003, 294)

PIRA has a number of provisions creating internal control mechanisms that "facilitate ethics." As was previously noted, both JCOPE and LEC are authorized to issue advisory opinions. These advisory opinions will serve to interpret the laws and regulations administered by JCOPE. In particular, the advisory opinions will help sharpen the ethics sensibilities of public officials subject to the ethics laws administered by JCOPE (see Figure 2). Likewise, PIRA directs JCOPE and LEC to promulgate conflict of interest guidelines that should have a prospective deterrent effect.

One of the main vehicles for enhancement of internal controls comes by way of PIRA mandates for ethics training to be provided by JCOPE for all individuals

---

Public Officers Law §73
Restrictions on the activities of current and former state officers and employees

Public Officers Law §73-a
Financial disclosure

Public Officers Law §74
Code of Ethics

Executive Law §94
Joint Commission on Public Ethics; Functions, Powers and Duties

Civil Service Law §107
Prohibition against certain political activities; improper influence

Legislative Law §80
Legislative Ethics Commission; Functions, Powers and Duties

Figure 2. Ethics Laws Administered by JCOPE

subject to the financial disclosure requirements. This training is a key vehicle for enhancing internal controls. It has three formats: (1) a comprehensive ethics training course, (2) an online ethics orientation for persons newly subject to the financial disclosure requirements, and (3) ethics seminars—required every three years—to update the comprehensive course (N.Y. Executive Law §94[10]). However, JCOPE's staffing problems and budgetary limitations have hindered its ability to offer all three of the ethics training programs so far. A visit to the *Training & Educational Services* link on JCOPE's website on July 30, 2012, revealed the following post:

> **Please note: The Commission is not providing instructor-led training at this time.** We will keep all requests we receive on file and follow-up as staffing permits. Online training remains available, as indicated below. (New York State Joint Commission on Public Ethics 2012)

Conclusion

This chapter has argued that legislation can be used to raise the bar for ethical behavior when it enhances internal controls in a way that deters wrongdoing and encourages ethically mindful choices. Using SARBOX, a seminal law that has worked a moral renaissance within corporate America, a set of aspirational goals were developed as benchmarks for assessing New York's Public Integrity Reform Act (PIRA). Unfortunately, PIRA falls short; in particular, it suffers from the absence of both whistle-blowing incentives and protections.

Given that the state's newly created Joint Commission on Public Ethics (JCOPE) has a very small staff to carry out its task of overseeing both the executive and legislative branches of state government, whistle-blowing incentives—as well as any information that can be gleaned from whistle-blowers—are sorely needed. Otherwise, it is highly unlikely that JCOPE will be any more successful than its predecessor, the Commission on Public Integrity (CPI), in improving the ethical tenor of a government consistently plagued by scandals. An additional troubling fact is that PIRA exempts JCOPE from the Open Meetings Law (as well as from the Freedom of Information Act); this means its proceedings will be shrouded in a cloak of secrecy. Accountability is created and reinforced by transparency—not by meetings held behind closed doors.

References

Alexis, Gwendolyn Yvonne. (2007a). "Coming Home to Roost: Offshore Operations from an In-House Perspective." In John Hooker, John F. Hulpke, and Peter Madsen, eds. *Controversies in International Corporate Responsibility.* Charlottesville, VA: Philosophy Documentation Center, pp. 55–67.

Alexis, Gwendolyn Yvonne. (2007b). "From Lapdog to Watchdog: The Post-SARBOX Corporate Board." *New York State Bar Association Journal* 79, no. 3 (March/April): 22–25.

Alexis, Gwendolyn Yvonne. (2009). "Legislative Excess or Regulatory Brilliance? Corporate Governance after SARBOX." In Julian Friedland, ed. *Doing Well and Good: The*

Human Face of the New Capitalism. Charlotte, NC: Information Age Publishing, pp. 215–236.

Alexis, Gwendolyn Yvonne, and Steven Pressman. (2010). "After Shame; Before Corporate Moral Obligation (CMO): Ethical Lag and the Credit Crisis." *International Journal of Management Concepts and Philosophy* 4, nos. ¾: 244–266.

Amar, Akhil Reed. (1998). *The Bill of Rights: Creation and Construction.* New Haven, CT: Yale University Press.

Bainbridge, Stephen M. (2003). "The Creeping Federalization of Corporate Law." *Regulation* (Spring): 26–31.

Florida Commission on Ethics. (2012). *Guide to the Sunshine Amendment and the Code of Ethics for Public Officers and Employees.* Accessed Jan. 31, 2013. http://www.ethics.state.fl.us/publications/2012%20Guide%20Booklet_Internet.pdf.

Glaser, Mark F., Joshua L. Oppenheimer, and Jeffrey H. Pearlman. (2011). "Public Integrity in 2011 and Beyond: Another Reform Act Comes to New York." New York. Greenberg Traurig Law Firm. July 1, 2011. Accessed July 30, 2012. http://www.gtlaw.com/portalresource/albcle3.

Hoe, Pei Shan. (2011). "Parting Words from the State Ethics Watchdog. (Interview with Barry Ginsberg, Departing Executive Director, CPI)." *The New York World.* November 22, 2011. Accessed July 24, 2012. http://www.thenewyorkworld.com/2011/11/22/parting-words-from-the-state-ethics-watchdog/.

JCOPE. (2013). *2013 Annual Report—New York State Joint Commission on Publc Ethics.* ("2013 Annual Report"). Accessed April 15, 2014 http://www.jcope.ny.gov/pubs/POL/2013%20JCOPE%20Annual%20Report.pdf.

New York State Joint Commission on Public Ethics. (2012). Accessed July 30, 2012. http://www.jcope.ny.gov/enforcement/ ("JCOPE").

NEW YORK STATUTES: Criminal Procedure Law, Section 220.51; Executive Law Section 94; Legislative Law Sections 1 and 80.

Public Integrity Reform Act (L. 2011, Ch. 399).

Public Officers Law, Sections 73; 73-a; and Article 7, §103(a) "Open Meetings and Executive Sessions."

Reisman, Nick. (2012). "Cameras Told to Leave Public Portion of JCOPE Meeting." *YNN Capital Tonight.* May 31, 2012. Accessed July 30, 2012. http://capitaltonightny.ynn.com/category/ethics/.

Securities and Exchange Commission. (2002). "Proposed Rule Disclosure Required by Sections 404, 406, and 407 of the Sarbanes-Oxley Act of 2002." Securities Act Release No. 33-8138; Exchange Act Release No. 34-46701; IC-25775; File No. S7-40-02, 2002. Accessed July 30, 2012. http://www.sec.gov/rules/proposed/33-8138.htm.

Securities and Exchange Commission. (2004). "Additional Form 8-K Disclosure Requirements and Acceleration of Filing Date," Securities Act Release No. 33–8400, Exchange Act Release No. 34-49424, File No. S7-22-02.

Smith, Robert W. (2003). "Enforcement or Ethical Capacity: Considering the Role of State Ethics Commissions at the Millennium." *Public Admininistration Review* 63, no. 3 (May/June 2003).

Thomas Barnes v. The Inhabitants of the First Parish in Falmouth, 6 Mass. 401(Massachusetts Supreme Court, 1810).

Turley, James S., and Steve Howe. (2012). "Executive Summary. *The Sarbanes-Oxley Act at 10: Enhancing the Reliability of Financial Reporting and Audit Quality.*" Ernst & Young, LLP. Accessed Jan. 31, 2013. http://www.ey.com/US/en/Issues/Governance-and-reporting/SOX-2.

U.S. Codes and Statutes:
Exchange Act of 1934, 15 U.S.C. 78m
Sarbanes-Oxley Act of 2002 . Pub. L. 107–204, 116 Stat. 745 ("SARBOX")
Stock Act of 2012, Pub. L. 112–105, 126 Stat. 292

U.S. Constitution
  First Amendment
  Fourteenth Amendment
U.S. Sentencing Guidelines Manual. 2004. Section 8B2.1.
Zivian, Anna. (2012). "Earth Matters: When Business & Government Mix." *Environment (as reported in Telluride Inside)*, May 18, 2012. Accessed July 28, 2012. http://www.telluride inside.com/2012/05/earth-matters-when-business-government-mix.html.

The Cause and Impact of Congressional Ethics Reforms*

Joseph Patten

Introduction

Congressional job approval rates were at an all-time low in 2012, with only 10 percent of Americans voicing approval of Congress and 90 percent expressive disapproval (Gallup, August 14, 2012). Recent polls also reveal that half of the public considers most members of Congress to be corrupt. This is not exactly what James Madison had in mind when he integrated the theories of Locke and Montesquieu into the design of our representative government. The public distrust of Congress comes on the heels of a steady accumulation of corruption cases over the past 40 years. These cases include the Abramoff Scandal, the investigation of William Jefferson (D-LA), the Duke Cunningham (R-CA) bribery case, James Traficant's (D-OH) expulsion, the House Banking Scandal, the Keating Five Scandal, the Abscam Scandal, and Koreagate to name but a few. In the broadest sense this study will examine how recently enacted ethics reforms can help to improve the public perception of our *Broken Branch* of government (Mann and Ornstein 2006).

This chapter delves into the complexities of congressional corruption by examining four cases: the Abscam scandal, the Keating Five scandal, the Duke Cunningham scandal, and the Jack Abramoff scandal. These cases were chosen because each represents a distinct form of congressional corruption and because each has shaped the ethical landscape of Congress. These cases also underscore dissimilarities in the level of enforcement of distinct forms of congressional corruption. They also bring to light the extent to which Congress has been reactive rather than proactive in regulating the ethical behavior of members. They also helped pave the way for the Honest Leadership and Open Government Act of 2007, and the creation of the Office of Congressional Ethics in 2008. It is the contention of this study that both have been successful in helping to advance ethical standards in Congress.

Overview of Congressional Ethics

The delegates at the Constitutional Convention empowered Congress with the authority to impeach and remove from office executive officers and federal

---

*Note: Some passages of this chapter were previously published in *Politics & Policy* 35, no 2 (June 2007).

judges. The Framers borrowed the concept of impeachment from the British in order to curb abuses of power in the executive and judicial branches of government. But who checks abuses of power in Congress? The Framers authorized Congress to establish and impose its *own* ethical standards. Article I, Section 5 of the Constitution states "each house shall be the judge of the elections, returns and qualifications of its own members" and may "punish its members for disorderly behavior, and, with the concurrence of two thirds, expel a member." Congressional sanctions of unprincipled members come in one of three forms:

1. A written reprimand from the Ethics Committee.
2. A censure, where members are publicly rebuked on the floor of Congress.
3. Congressional expulsion. (*Congressional Quarterly* 1992)

Only two members of Congress have been expelled over the last 140 years—Rep. Traficant (D-OH) in 2002 and Rep. Myers (D-PA) in 1980. The uncommonness of expulsions caused many to question whether asking Congress to impose its own ethical standards was equivalent to asking the fox to guard the proverbial henhouse.

In fairness, political corruption in Congress has been difficult to discern, not to mention prove, in part because there can be a fine line between successful legislative behavior and unethical conduct. Members of Congress are now spending a significant amount of time raising campaign funds and assisting constituents in casework, leaving less time for policy enactment and oversight responsibilities. The ethical boundaries surrounding these activities are vaguely defined, while the necessity of mastering these political skills is critical to the success of modern legislators (Tolchin and Tolchin 2001). Cases of political corruption are sometimes shadowy because there is frequently no bright line as to when a legislator's conduct in constituent case work and fund-raising takes them through the beaded curtain of corruption. Members of Congress, after all, have conflicting responsibilities between advancing the public's interest while advocating for the private interests of constituents, which can sometimes be mutually exclusive goals (Cain, Ferejohn, and Fiorina 1987).

Some also suggest that modern ethical reforms, such as institutional sunshine laws and tougher campaign finance disclosure rules, might simply reveal indiscretions that went largely unnoticed in gone-by eras (Herrick 2003). Nonetheless, it is the contention of this study that ethics reforms were long overdue because Congress had been reluctant to establish and enforce ethical standards on members, perhaps because of a common interest in permitting activities that facilitate the reelection goal. A brief synopsis of the Abscam scandal, the Duke Cunningham scandal, the Keating Five scandal, and the Abramoff scandal sheds light on Congress's reluctance to punish ethical transgressions and a comparison can be drawn as to how ethical standards have improved as a result of the Honest Leadership and Open Government Act in 2007 and the creation of the Office of Congressional Ethics in 2008.

The Study

This study distinguishes between varieties of corruption by fashioning a congressional corruption matrix that differentiates between two overarching dimensions of political corruption. The first element builds on Thompson's (1995) research and measures the scope of political corruption by discriminating between individual and institutional forms. Was the unethical act committed in isolation of other members (i.e., individual corruption), or was there collusion among members of Congress (i.e., institutional corruption) in carrying out the duplicitous act? The second dimension of congressional corruption distinguishes between the member's motivations for engaging in the unethical and/or illegal act. Was the member motivated by the appeal of a personal gift (i.e., private gain corruption), or was the member motivated by the pursuit of campaign contributions and/or career ambitions (i.e., career-advancing corruption)?

These two dimensions are then collapsed into four types of political corruption: (1) Private Gain-Institutional corruption (The Abscam scandal), (2) Private Gain-Individual corruption (the Duke Cunningham scandal), (3) Career Advancing-Institutional corruption (the Keating Five scandal), and (4) Career Advancing-Individual corruption (the Jack Abramoff scandal). The Abscam scandal is classified as a "private gain-institutional" form of corruption because members were motivated by the allure of cash bribes and because of member collusion in the case. The Duke Cunningham case is classified as a "private gain-individual" form of corruption because Cunningham acted alone in accepting $2.4 million in bribes from two defense contractors. The Keating Five scandal is categorized as a "career advancing-institutional" form of corruption because five senators conspired to intervene with federal regulators on behalf of Charles Keating, who in turn organized political fund-raisers on behalf of the senators. The Abramoff scandal is the most difficult case to categorize because here corruption was motivated by goals of career advancement and personal self-enrichment. It was classified as a "career-advancing individual" form of corruption because most of the corrupting influents either enhanced reelection concerns (e.g., campaign contributions) or augmented power within Congress (e.g., K Street Project) (Table 1).

This corruption matrix is of great consequence because it underscores distinctions in the level of enforcement of dissimilar forms of congressional corruption. This typology moves beyond the narrow and widespread conception of political corruption as merely constituting the illegal transgressions of public officials induced by the allure of personal self-enrichment. Enforcement of personal

Table 1.

Corruption Matrix	Institutional Corruption	Individual Corruption
Personal Gain	Abscam Scandal	Duke Cunningham Scandal
Career Advancement	Keating Five Scandal	Jack Abramoff Scandal

gain forms of congressional corruption is guided by well-established legal brib-ery standards, and these are characteristically enforced robustly by external law enforcement agencies.

This matrix gives prominence to the increasingly mordant, yet until recently, largely unregulated form of career-advancing corruption. Career-advancing forms of congressional corruption highlights how ethical conflicts can emerge in the course of fund-raising and in the delivery of constituent casework, the standard fare in the daily activities of members of congress. This form of congressional cor-ruption is particularly corrosive because it fuels public cynicism that congressional decisions primarily serve the private interests of the well-heeled members of soci-ety, rather than the public interest. This is particularly troublesome because when citizens are distrustful of public behavior, they become cynical about their own ability to influence public decision making, thereby cultivating political alienation and threatening the very foundation of American democracy itself (Warren 2004). This study will examine how Congress has been historically unsuccessful in regu-lating ethical behavior and how checks against career-advancing forms of corrup-tion have improved since recent ethics reforms in Congress.

Personal Gain-Institutional Corruption

Abscam is the name given to a sting operation of the Federal Bureau of Investiga-tion (FBI) that netted seven members of Congress, including one U.S. senator and six members of the House of Representatives in 1980. The term "Abscam" refers to Abdul Enterprises Ltd. a fictitious company used by the FBI to lure members of Congress into accepting bribes. The news that members of Congress were vide-otaped accepting bribes from FBI agents posing as Arab businessmen raised serious questions about both the integrity of the legislative process and FBI investigative tactics. U.S. representatives Richard Kelly (R-FL), Michael Myers (D-PA), Ray-mond Lederer (D-PA), and Frank Thompson (D-NJ) were all videotaped accepting money in exchange for supporting private immigration legislation. Congressman John Jenrette (D-SC) and John Murphy (D-NY) were convicted of accepting bribes through middlemen (Green 1997). Harrison Williams (D-NJ), the only U.S. sena-tor convicted in the investigation, was videotaped agreeing to use his influence to obtain government contracts for a nonexistent titanium processing plant in exchange for a concealed financial stake in the fictitious company.

All seven legislators were sentenced to serve between 18 months to three years in prison. Congressman Kelly (R-FL) later had his conviction overturned on an entrapment defense, despite videotaped evidence of him accepting $25,000 from agents. Congressmen Jenrette (D-SC), Kelly (R-FL), Murphy (D-NY), and Thomp-son (D-NJ) were all defeated in reelection bids, while Congressman Lederer and Senator Williams (D-NJ) resigned from office. Congressman Myers (D-PA) was expelled from the House of Representatives on October 2, 1980, marking the first time a member had been expelled since the U.S. Civil War era.

The Abscam scandal is categorized as a "private gain" form of corruption because members were motivated by the allure of large sums of money intended for per-sonal use. It is also categorized as a form of institutional corruption because of the

Senator Harrison Williams, D-NJ, with FBI agent Richard Farhardt who was posing as an Arab sheik called Yassir Habib as a part of the ABSCAM Sting Operation. The FBI charged that Williams engaged in bribery and conspiracy when Williams allegedly promised to introduce legislation favorable to the phony sheik. (AP Photo)

level of congressional collusion in the case. Frank Thompson (D-NJ), for instance, personally recruited Staten Island Congressman John Murphy (D-NY) into the fold.

The sting found its way to Congress's doorstep via an unrelated enquiry. The investigation originated in Long Island, New York, in 1978 as a relatively routine investigation aimed at recovering stolen art and fraudulent security certificates (Noonan 1984). The FBI recruited Melvin Weinberg, a recently arrested confidence man, to assist in the venture. Weinberg posed as the chairman of Abdul Enterprises, the FBI front company created to attract thieves looking to sell stolen art or fraudulent security certificates. The FBI even deposited $1 million into a bank account under the name of Abdullah Enterprises to establish credibility and to cover operating costs.

FBI agents established a relationship with a professional forger, who eventually recommended that the "sheiks" open a gaming casino in Atlantic City, New Jersey. The agents were then assured that Camden, New Jersey, Mayor Angelo Errichetti could arrange for a gaming license in exchange for a financial kickback. Errichetti was also a New Jersey state senator and was generally regarded as the most powerful political figure in southern New Jersey. Mayor Errichetti's involvement in the investigation ultimately steered the FBI to other public officials, including the seven members of Congress (Green 1997).

Myers and Lederer were the first members of Congress to act on behalf of the FBI agents. They agreed to sponsor a private relief bill granting U.S. residency to Abdul Rahman and Yassir Habib, who were actually FBI agents. Frank Thompson

(D-NJ), one of the most powerful Democratic figures in Washington at the time, was then recruited to participate in the scandal. Thompson was videotaped accepting a briefcase holding $45,000 in exchange for sponsoring another private immigration bill. The Abscam scandal remains one of the most embarrassing chapters in the history of the U.S. Congress.

Personal Gain-Individual Corruption: The Duke Cunningham Scandal

Randall "Duke" Cunningham was sentenced to eight years and four months in prison after pleading guilty to one count of bribery and one count of tax evasion in November of 2005. The scope of legislative malfeasance in the Cunningham case is unparalleled in the sordid history of congressional corruption. Cunningham was convicted of accepting $2.4 million in bribes from two defense contractors in exchange for securing $240 million worth of government contracts. What is most astounding is the degree to which the illegal activity unfolded in plain view. The investigation was initiated after newspaper reporters wondered how Congressman Cunningham was able to afford a mansion, yacht, and a Rolls Royce on a congressional salary.

Cunningham had a distinguished career as a naval fighter pilot and openly boasted in campaigns that many of his flying maneuvers were depicted by Tom Cruise in the 1986 film *Top Gun*. His proficiencies in military affairs landed him a prestigious committee assignment on the Defense Appropriation Subcommittee, which provides oversight on military funding allotments. This committee assignment made him a natural target of defense industry lobbyists. Cunningham accepted bribes from two defense contractors named Brent Wilkes and Mitchell Wade. Cunningham intervened with the Pentagon in order to secure government contracts to convert government documents into digital form for Wilkes and Wade. The most notable example is a $9.7 million contract to scan "engineering drawings from the 1870s and images of boats from the 1910s" in the Panama Canal Zone even though Pentagon procurement officers requested the funds be used for more pressing needs at the U.S. Army's Missile Command (Calbreath and Kammer 2005). The Assistant Undersecretary of Defense Louis Kratz later disclosed he never encountered anything close to the level of political pressure exerted by Cunningham to go forward on the superfluous project (Babcock 2005). It was later revealed that Cunningham even prepared a "bribe memo" on congressional stationary that detailed how much he expected to be paid for each government contract earmarked to one of the two defense contractors. The Cunningham scandal is classified as personal-gain forms of corruption because it involved a clear violation of existing bribery standards.

Corruption motivated by career advancement, on the other hand, is vaguely defined and rarely enforced. The bribery standard has never been applied to campaign contributions and fund-raising activities. The Keating Five case, in fact, represents the first time members of Congress were sanctioned for going too far in advancing the interests of private citizens. The Keating Five case highlights how ethical conflicts can emerge in the course of raising campaign revenue and in the delivery of constituent services.

Career-Advancing Institutional Corruption: The Keating Five Scandal

The Keating Five scandal made headlines during the 2008 presidential election because of Senator John McCain's (R-AZ) involvement in the controversy years before. Parallels have also been made between this scandal and the 2008 bailout of America's financial industry. The Keating Five scandal was linked directly to the Savings and Loan debacle of the late 1980s. The name itself is derived from Charles H. Keating Jr., a Phoenix construction company owner and anti-pornography advocate, who went on to become the poster child for the corrupt practices that resulted in the $300 billion taxpayer bailout of mismanaged banks. This case represents the most expensive political scandal in American history. The saga behind the Keating Five scandal began when Keating made an application to purchase the Lincoln Savings and Loan in Irvine, California. Lincoln had a strong reputation for sound fiscal administration and boasted the lowest delinquent mortgage rates in California while demonstrating a commitment to mortgage-deprived areas (DeLeon 1993). The Savings and Loan industry was substantially deregulated during the Reagan era in the 1980s. Keating early on played a leading role in lobbying against regulations that barred thrifts from making commercial investments. He also raised regulatory eyebrows by investing Lincoln's federally insured funds into risky commercial investments, including the purchase of "junk" bonds from controversial financier Michael Milken.

The plot thickened when the San Francisco branch of the Federal Home Loan Bank (FHLB) initiated a standard audit of Keating's Lincoln Savings. It was in this context that Keating solicited assistance from his friends in the U.S. Senate. He was rightfully concerned that auditors might recommend seizing Lincoln for irregular lending practices of federally insured funds. Keating first contacted Senator Dennis DeConcini (D-AZ), his strongest ally in Washington. An infamous meeting was then arranged between Senators DeConcini (D-AZ), Alan Cranston (D-CA), John Glenn (D-OH), John McCain (R-AZ), Donald Riegle (D-MI), later known as the Keating Five, and federal bank regulators.

The meeting with the federal bank regulators lasted a little over two hours. The senators interrogated the regulators with great vigor on Keating's behalf. One of the federal regulators William Black later commented on how he felt intimidated in the meeting and remarked "you really did have one-twentieth of the Senate in one room, called by one guy, who was the biggest crook in the S&L debacle (Muller 1999 1). The tables were quickly turned, however, when the bank examiners defiantly stated they were about to issue a criminal referral against Keating for violating lending laws at Lincoln. The senators were visibly shaken by the news, and the meeting ended shortly thereafter.

Did the senators violate federal law or Senate ethics here? It was not clear. The Senate Ethics Committee investigated the matter for 14 months, which included 26 days of televised hearings on C-Span. Over 25 million Americans turned in to hear the committee's verdict. No member of Congress throughout history had to this point been reprimanded for intervening on behalf of a constituent. The findings of the Ethics Committee did little in the way of clarifying the matter. The committee ultimately determined that four of the senators, namely DeConcini, McCain,

Senators John Glenn (D-OH), left, Dennis DeConcini (D-AZ), and John McCain (R-AZ), right, arrive at the Senate Ethics committee hearing room in 1990 on Capitol Hill. Five senators would face charges that they took part in alleged influence peddling to help former savings and loan owner Charles H. Keating Jr. (AP Photo/John Duricka)

Riegle, and Glenn were guilty of expressing poor judgment for interfering with a federal audit, but concluded that punishments were not in order for the four because it would be "setting the standard after the fact" (Elving 1991, 3). Senator Alan Cranston received the harshest treatment and was censured by the Senate because he approached bank regulators six more times after learning that the Board was issuing a criminal referral against Keating. Cranston also received almost $1 million from Keating over a two-year period, with the money going primarily to voter registration groups directed by Cranston's son.

The case highlights the tendency of the Ethics Committee to "individualize" institutional corruption in an effort to "exonerate" the institution (Thompson 1993). Conversely, accused members typically justify misconduct by "institutionalizing" their behavior, discounting the importance of accusations by claiming other members engage in similar activities. Senator Cranston, for instance, in his defiant censure speech in front of 95 senators stated that "my behavior did not violate established norms. . . . Here, but for the grace of God stand you" (Kuntz 1991).

Career–Advancing Individual Corruption: The Abramoff Scandal

Jack Abramoff was the leading Washington lobbyist for seven Native American tribes with casino interests. He and his colleagues collected $82 million from the tribes over a four-year period and used these funds to sway Washington power brokers. The Indian Gambling Regulatory Act of 1988 permits tribes to launch gambling operations on reservations in states with legalized gambling. At the time there were more than 400 Native American casinos spread throughout 26 states (Lowry 2006). The politically inexperienced tribes were allured by Abramoff's claims of political access to White House Advisor Karl Rove and Representative Tom DeLay (R-TX). The Coushatta Tribe of Louisiana paid Abramoff $32 million to squelch rival tribal plans to build gaming industries contiguous to Coushatta casinos, amounting to $38,000 for each of the 837 Coushatta tribal members (Schmidt 2005, 1). Tribal members were later flabbergasted upon learning of Abramoff's effrontery in referring to them as "monkeys," "troglodytes," and "idiots" in an e-mail to his partner Michael Scanlon. Abramoff and Scanlon, a former press secretary for Representative Tom DeLay (R-TX), devised a "gimme five" scheme whereby Abramoff referred trial business to Scanlon's Public Relations firm in return for a 50-percent kickback of funds. Scanlon later pled guilty in federal court for devising this machinate and for conspiring to bribe public officials. The investigation primarily targeted two members of Congress, including Representative Robert Ney (R-OH) and Representative Tom DeLay (R-TX), although several other members had been implicated.

Former House Majority Leader Tom DeLay waiting for his sentencing decision at the Travis Co. Courthouse in Austin, Texas, in 2011 following his November 24 conviction on charges of money laundering and conspiracy to commit money laundering in a scheme to illegally funnel corporate money to Texas candidates in 2002. (AP Photo/Jack Plunkett)

The Abramoff scandal found its way to Congress by way of a murder investigation in Florida. In September of 2005 homicide detectives arrested three suspects for the gangland-style murder of Konstantinos "Gus" Boulis, a multimillionaire Greek immigrant who made his fortunes in the restaurant, real estate, and casino industries.

Boulis moved to Miami in 1998 where he ventured into the casino boat industry, purchasing Sun Cruz Casino Boats in 1994 (Continetti 2005, 11). In 1998, Boulis was required to sell the fleet after being indicted for violating U.S. shipping laws. His attorney discussed Boulis's legal predicament with Abramoff, his colleague in a Washington law firm. Abramoff then recruited his college friend Adam Kidan to join him in purchasing Sun Cruz. Short of funds, Abramoff and Kidan entered into a secret and unlawful agreement with Boulis whereby Boulis agreed to overlook a $20 million down payment in exchange for retaining a 10-percent share of the fleet. On January 3, 2006, Abramoff pleaded guilty to wiring fraudulent documents to bank lenders that deceived them into thinking that a $23 million down payment had been wired to Boulis. The investigation linked to Congress when it was discovered that Congressman Robert Ney (R-OH) intervened on Abramoff's behalf during volatile moments in the Sun Cruz negotiations. Abramoff sought to intimidate Boulis by leveraging his congressional connections during one of the negotiating stalemates. Congressman Ney inserted comments into the *Congressional Record* that referred to Boulis as a "bad apple" and accused Sun Cruz of "making illegal bets" and "not paying out their customers properly" (Ney 2000, 53). Abramoff, his wife, and Kidan each contributed $1,000 to Ney's campaign closely following this intervention. The following year Abramoff, Kidan, and three Sun Cruz officials each contributed $1,000 to Ney's campaign, and Abramoff made a separate $2,500 contribution to his political action committee after Ney once again inserted language into the *Congressional Record*, this time praising the new stewardship of Sun Cruz. Federal authorities grew interested as to why a congressman from Ohio took such an active interest in a casino boat transaction in Florida that culminated in the murder of the seller.

Ney was listed as "Representative #1" in the Abramoff indictment. As chair of the Committee on House Administration, Ney held sway over key perks such as assigning congressional office space and allocating government contracts, earning him the nickname the "Mayor of Capitol Hill." In 2002 Ney authorized a government contract to an Israeli telecommunications company to install cell phone antennas in the House. It was later revealed that Abramoff was paid $280,000 to lobby on the company's behalf (Grimaldi and Schmidt 2005, 1).

Ney was also implicated in the "Tigua Tribe" debacle. At the behest of the rival Coushatta tribe, Abramoff and Scanlon successfully lobbied for the revocation of the Tigua tribe's gaming license in El Paso, Texas. Abramoff even secretly paid the former Christian Coalition head Ralph Reed over $2 million to lead religious conservatives in the effort (Hearn 2004). After arranging the revocation of Tigua's gaming license, Abramoff persuaded tribal members that he could "rectify the gross indignity perpetrated by the Texas state authorities" and had already secured congressional support to assist in the recuperation of the license (Schmidt 2005). Ney inserted an amendment to reopen the Texas casino in the Help America Vote Act after receiving a $32,000 contribution from the tribe. It was a poor investment as Senator Dodd (D-CT) later stripped the amendment from the final draft of the bill. Other tribes financed a St. Andrews golf trip in Scotland that included Abramoff, Ney, Ralph Reed, and David H. Safavian, a White House procurement officer in President George W. Bush's administration, who was later arrested in connection with the Abramoff investigation (Smith and Schmidt 2005). Ney has since pleaded guilty to corruption charges and was sentenced to 27 months in prison.

Former House Majority Leader Tom DeLay (R-TX) once referred to Abramoff as one of his "closest and dearest friends" and accepted trips to Scotland and Saipan in the Northern Mariana Islands that were arranged and paid for by Abramoff's clients. Abramoff played a crucial role in DeLay's "K Street Project." K Street is the street address to over 30,000 Washington lobbyists (Knowlton 2006, 1). The K Street Project was a DeLay initiative that sought Republican dominance over the Washington lobbying industry. DeLay, nicknamed the "Hammer" by House colleagues, forcefully instructed lobbying firms to hire more Republican lobbyists and to terminate relationships with Democratic lobbyists. DeLay, for instance, was instrumental in removing a $1.5 billion tax relief provision for the Motion Picture Association of America (MPAA) after MPAA named Dan Glickman, a former secretary of agriculture in the Clinton , to head the organization (Drew 2006). DeLay also pressured the lobbying industry to hire Republican staffers and congressional family members. He also compelled lobbyists to serve as "outside whips," instructing them to persuade rank-and-file Republicans to support the legislative agenda of House leaders (Drew 2006). Lobbyists were also expected to raise large sums of campaign revenue in return for access to congressional leaders.

Abramoff came to personify the indecorous ethos of the K Street Project through his association with the Alexander Strategy Group lobbying firm. The firm was founded by DeLay's former chief of staff Ed Buckham and employed Tony Rudy, who previously served as both a DeLay staffer and an Abramoff employee. Buckham opened this firm in 1998 with an initial contract DeLay secured from the Enron Corporation. The firm lured clients by openly promoting that it "could deliver access to DeLay" (Kornblutt and Justice 2006, 1). Alexander Strategy Group and Abramoff shared clients and worked hand in hand in steering government contracts to clients. The firm folded after the Abramoff indictment and DeLay has long since relinquished his House leadership role and his congressional seat.

How Are Personal Gain and Career-Advancing Forms of Corruption Dissimilar?

The combined effect of the Abscam scandal, the Keating Five scandal, the Duke Cunningham scandal, and the Abramoff scandal played a large role in inspiring the passage of the Honest Leadership and Open Government Act and the creation of the Office of Congressional Ethics. The Abscam and Cunningham scandals are classified as personal gain forms of corruption because each involved a clear violation of existing bribery standards. Ethical reform in Congress is unlikely to deter legislators who are willing to flaunt federal law. These two cases culminated with the imprisonment of eight members of Congress. Congress typically intervenes in private gain forms of corruption after the facts have been investigated by law enforcement authorities. Here, Congress has historically abdicated its constitutional responsibility to regulate congressional behavior to law enforcement. Private gain forms of corruption are guided by bribery laws that are clearly defined and relatively simple to follow. Title 18 of the U.S. criminal code makes it a federal crime for members of Congress to "solicitor or receive a bribe for the performance of an official act." Prosecutors thus have the burden of establishing a *quid pro quo*, where political favors or funds are given in exchange for a particular act, a standard easily met in the Abscam and Cunningham cases. Seven of the eight members involved in these two scandals had resigned or were defeated in reelection bids before the Ethics Committee even concluded its investigation.

Conversely, corruption motivated by career advancement is vaguely defined and has been rarely enforced prior to the creation of the Office of Congressional Ethics. The bribery standard has never been applied to campaign contributions. The Keating Five case, in fact, represents the first time that members of Congress were sanctioned for going too far in advancing the interests of private citizens. Career-advancing corruption is more insidious and thus is more corrosive to our system of government because prior to the creation of the Office of Congressional Ethics it had been permitted to flourish. The Keating Five and Abramoff cases highlight how if left unchecked influential and well-heeled groups are able to procure services from members as they simultaneously contribute to campaigns, organize fund-raising venues, sponsor travel junkets, and hire staff and/ or family members. Robert S. Bennett, the Special Counsel of the Keating Five enquiry, proposed rigorous ethical standards against career-advancing forms of corruption in his final report. He recommended institutional rules against legislators receiving campaign contributions from individuals or groups attempting to procure services, and regulations against engaging in conduct that appears to be improper to a reasonable, nonpartisan, fully informed person. Prior to the creation of the passage of the Honest Leadership and Open Government Act and the creation of the Office of Congressional Ethics, Congress never acted on any of these recommendations.

However, the aftermath of the Abramoff indictment prompted a national outcry for lobbying reform. The K Street Project transformed the relationship between lobbyists and lawmakers in fundamental ways. The number of Washington lobbyists doubled to 34,750 from 2000 to 2005. The industry generated over $3 billion a year in revenue from clients seeking to influence our government, more than the $2.5 billion worth of campaign contributions expected to be generated in the 2012 election cycle (Birnbaum 2006, 1). The Abramoff scandal also highlighted problems stemming from the "revolving door," the tendency of members and staffers to launch well-paid lobbying careers after serving on Capitol Hill (Public Citizen 2005). For instance, during the Abramoff era former Congressman Tauzin (R-LA) left his seat to earn over $2 million a year as a lobbyist (Stearns 2004). Prior to Ethics Reforms, half of the 198 departing members of Congress from 1998 through 2005 went on to register as Washington lobbyists (Public Citizen 2005).

Congress has also been very slow to regulate against unethical behavior in the lobbying industry. The Lobbying Disclosure Act of 1995 simply required lobbyists to register with Congress and to disclose approximate expenditures (Tennebaum 1999). This act does not require lobbyists to disclose fund-raising activities or the names of those they lobby. The act has been widely criticized for both its vagueness and its weak enforcements mechanism. During the Abramoff era, for instance, 7,000 firms lobbying Congress failed "to file one or more disclosure forms required by law," yet only three were fined (Knott 2005).

The Abramoff case also highlighted the proclivity of members to curry favor by "earmarking" projects to clients. Jack Abramoff referred to the House Appropriations Committee as a "favor factory" for its willingness to furtively earmark projects during the final stage of the legislative process in exchange for campaign contributions (*Christian Science Monitor* 2006). The number of earmarks skyrocketed during the Abramoff era. The amount of federal-earmarked funds tripled during this time over a 10-year period to $67 billion (Levey 2007). Allowing members to unilaterally and anonymously appropriate federal funds produced a natural setting for corruption to flourish. Duke Cunningham also mastered the art of earmarking projects in his relationship with defense contractors. This practice also exacerbates the federal deficits and can threaten national security. Cunningham, for instance, bragged of his prowess in earmarking funds from the "black" budget to defense contractors.

Congress has been reactive rather than proactive in regulating career-advancing forms of corruption because of a common interest in tolerating unethical behavior that facilitates the reelection goal. Public ethics was front and center in American politics after the Abramoff scandal because of a widely held view that Congress had abdicated its constitutional authority to regulate the behavior of members. This was troublesome because career-advancing forms of corruption fosters public cynicism that congressional decisions merely serve to reflect the private interests of donors rather than the public good. When members of the public become mistrustful of governmental action, they become pessimistic about their own ability to influence decisions and grow estranged from civic life. This is most problematic because democratic theory rests on the foundation that active citizenship is required in order to inform representative government. The Framers recognized the importance of a politically vibrant citizenry in establishing a social contract between Congress and the public, deeming it inextricably linked to human development itself.

Ethics Reforms in the Modern Era

The good news is that these congressional scandals have led to significant ethics reforms in Congress by way of the Honest Leadership and Open Government Act of 2007 and the creation of the Office of Congressional Ethics in 2008. The Honest Leadership and Open Government Act was signed into law by President George W. Bush on September 14, 2007. This act amended some of the perceived weaknesses on the Lobbying Disclosure Act of 1995 by: (1) addressing the "revolving door" issue, (2) bringing greater transparency to the earmarking process, (3) strengthening lobbying disclosure requirements, and (4) placing greater restrictions on lobbyist-sponsored junkets (Straus 2008).

The "revolving door" between Congress and the lobbying industry has raised concerns about both the motivations of those serving in Congress and the integrity of our legislative process. Left unchecked, some might enter public service for the purpose of leveraging their political connections into a financial windfall by joining a lobbying firm after leaving Congress, thereby attracting undesirable public servants. It could also fuel public cynicism about whether government primarily pursues the public's interest or the private interests of its members. One recent study found that congressional staffers turned lobbyists experience a 24 percent drop in revenue once their former boss (i.e., member of Congress) leaves office, thus underlining the extent to which lobbying salaries are commensurate with political connections to members (Blanes et al. 2012). Another study examined the 50 most successful Washington lobbyists and found that 13 are former members of Congress, 21 are former congressional staffers, and three are family members of members of Congress. Only 13 of the 50 lack a direct tie to a member of Congress (Blanes et al. 2012).

To address these concerns the Honest Leadership and Open Government Act sought to close the "revolving door" between senators and the lobbying industry by extending the "cooling-off" period between congressional service and the lobbying industry from one year to two, while maintaining the one-year cooling-off period for House members. In addition, senior senate staffers now fall under the cooling-off period, and must wait one year before lobbying any congressional office, expanding the previous one-year ban against lobbying their former senate office. The act also prohibits former House staffers from lobbying their former office or congressional committee for one year after leaving Capitol Hill.

The act also addressed "earmark reform" by including a provision that the Senate follow a House rule requiring the online publishing of all earmark requests 48 hours prior to the vote. The measure also stipulates that earmarks must now include the name of the member requesting the earmark, the name of the entity receiving the earmarked funds, and an explanation as to how the funds will be used. In 2010, Congress placed much tougher restrictions against earmarks that also appear to be working. These earmark reforms have caused a considerable drop in both the number of congressional earmarks and the amount of public funds now earmarked. One study found that the numbers of earmarks dipped from 9,129 in 2010 to only 152 in 2012. The same study found that the $16.5 billion earmarked in 2010 dropped to $3.3 billion in 2012 (CNN Politics Fund 2012).

One of the most significant features of the Honest Leadership and Open Government Act stems from the sordid behavior found in the Abramoff scandal. One of the reasons Jack Abramoff wielded such influence on Capitol Hill was because he was very effective in raising large sums of money for members of Congress at private fund-raisers in his DC restaurant. And all of this happened without any paper trail linking the member of Congress to Abramoff because lobbyists were not required to disclose these types of activities. This act changed that by requiring members of Congress to report lobbyist involvement with bundled contributions exceeding $15,000. The act also requires lobbyist to file quarterly disclosure forms and stiffened penalties for violating disclosure requirements from $50,000 to $200,000 (Common Cause 2012).

Lastly, the act places greater restrictions on the relationship between members of Congress and lobbyists. Again, in reaction to Abramoff funding private trips for members of Congress, the act prohibits members of Congress from participating in political junkets and prohibits lobbyists from furnishing members of Congress with gifts. The act also prohibits members from flying free on private aircraft furnished by lobbyists, requiring that members now pay fair market value for transportation. These four provisions have helped to transform in positive ways the relationship between members of congress and lobbyists.

Office of Congressional Ethics

The creation of the Office of Congressional Ethics (OCE) in 2008 is even more significant than the Honest Leadership and Open Government Act in bringing about monumental changes in congressional ethical standards. Throughout history one of the inherent challenges facing congressional ethics has been that members of Congress have been asked to regulate their own behavior. While there were major disagreements at the Constitutional Convention, the Framers did share one basic conviction: that power in one branch of government must be used to counterbalance power in the other branches of government. James Madison extended on these concerns in Federalist Paper No. 51, when he asserted that "ambition must be made to counteract ambition" and that "if men were angels, no government would be necessary. If angels were to govern men, neither external or internal controls on government would be necessary." The Framers were thus deeply concerned that some leaders might place their private interests over the public interest, which is why they incorporated some ethical oversight powers in our system of checks and balances. By making each branch of government independent, and by structuring the government so that each branch is checked by another, one branch of government is prevented from becoming dominant and/or unresponsive to the public. Perhaps the chief problem has been that the Framers did not extend the principle of checks and balances on the matter of congressional ethics. While the legislative branch checks the executive and judicial branches with impeachment powers, neither the executive nor judicial branches were constitutionally empowered to check congressional behavior.

Throughout history advocates for stronger ethical standards in Congress have asked for an external check on congressional behavior. Legislation calling for an Independent Office of Public Integrity frequently never made it out of committee. However, that all changed after the Abramoff scandal, when half of the American public perceived members of Congress as corrupt. Then speaker of the House Nancy Pelosi (D-CA) promised legislation that would "drain the swamp" in Washington and pave the way for a Congress deserving of the public's trust. And the symbol of congressional ethics reform was the newly created Office of Congressional Ethics.

The Office of Congressional Ethics was officially created on March 11, 2008, with the enactment of H.Res. 895. It was created to help the House Committee on Ethics investigate grievances against members of the House, and serves as a quasi-Grand Jury to the House Committee. The purpose of the OCE is to "supplement but not supplant" the function of the House Committee on Ethics (Straus 2011, 2). The OCE consists of six members serving four-year terms. Because it is structured as a nonpartisan committee, three of the members are selected by the speaker of the House and three of the members are selected by the House Minority Leader. Members are directly appointed to the committee, and there is no confirmation process. The original chair of the committee, Leo Wise, stepped down in 2010. Peter Goss, a former member of Congress (R-FL) and the former director of the Central Intelligence Agency (CIA) during the Bush administration, serves in the role as of this writing.

The primary purpose of the OCE is to investigate potential unethical and/or criminal behavior in congress. Prior to conducting a full investigation, two of the six members, at least one appointed by the speaker and one appointed by the minority leader, must submit that there is a "reasonable basis to believe the allegation based on all the information then known to the board" (Straus 2011, 18). If the OCE finds probable cause, it has 45 days to further investigate the matter. The OCE then submits a report to the House Committee on Ethics that recommends either a further investigation or a dismissal of charges because of a lack of evidence. The report to the House Ethics Committee should include a: (1) "finding of fact"; (2) "description of relevant information that was not obtained and witnesses not interviewed"; and (3) "recommendations for the issuance of subpoenas"; and (4) "citations of relevant law, rule, regulation, or standard of conduct relevant to the investigation" (Straus 2011, 20). In compliance with Article 1, Section 5 of the Constitution, it is ultimately up to the House of Representatives as to whether to "punish members for disorderly Behaviour, and, with the Concurrence of two thirds, expel a member."

While unpopular with some members of Congress, the OCE has thus far made a significant impact on regulating the behavior of members. As of 2012, it has reviewed 58 cases, and has found enough incriminating evidence to recommend further investigation in 32 of them, and has recommended the dismissal of 26 cases (*New York Times* 2012). Some members of Congress complain that the OCE is too aggressive in investigating members, and some have threatened to cut the OCE's budget. But the OCE has already established that it is a much more effective investigative body than its House counterpart.

In 2010, the OCE issued a report to Congress that it believed there was credible evidence that Congressman Charles Rangel (D-NY) might have violated House rules by accepting payment from Citigroup and other corporations to attend a conference in the Caribbean. This revelation ultimately forced Congressman Rangel to give up his chairmanship of the powerful House Ways and Means Committee. A few months later, the OCE requested a further examination of Congresswoman Maxine Waters (D-CA) for requesting that representatives from the National Bankers Association meet with officials from OneUnited Bank for the purpose of providing assistance to the bank. Congresswoman Waters's husband was a board member and stock holder of the bank and the bank received a $12 million federal bailout (Office of Congressional Ethics 2011). The House Ethics Committee, in a controversial ruling, voted to exonerate Congresswoman Waters in 2012. In 2011, the OCE found evidence that Congressman Don Young (R-AK) may have accepted campaign contributions to his "legal expense fund" in excess of the $5,000 permitted per calendar year (Office of Congressional Ethics 2011). The House Ethics Committee later ruled in favor of Congressman Young. In 2012, the OCE requested the House Ethics Committee further investigate whether Congressman Rob Andrews (D-NJ) improperly used campaign funds to pay for his daughter's graduation party, and personal trips to California and Scotland. Congressman Roberts later resigned from Congress in February of 2014.

The major point is ethical standards are enhanced even when OCE investigations do not lead to criminal referrals or House sanctions. The historical problem with political corruption in Congress has been that the House has not seriously investigated political corruption. The OCE has already transformed the ethical landscape in Congress because there is now an external watchdog armed with investigative powers watching them. Even if cases are later dismissed by the largely ineffectual House Committee on Ethics, there is now at least some transparency and accountability in the process in that constituents and/or candidates in subsequent elections can bring improper behavior into the light. Plus, members are now much more likely to avoid career-advancing forms of corruption to avoid the embarrassment of a public investigation.

Conclusion

The purpose of this chapter is to highlight that members of Congress have conflicting responsibilities to advance the public interest while advocating for the private interests of constituents. It provides a congressional corruption matrix that distinguishes between personal gain and career-advancing forms of corruption. Personal gain forms of corruption are strictly enforced and guided by federal bribery standards, as demonstrated in the Abscam scandal and the Duke Cunningham scandal. Career-advancing forms of corruption are vaguely defined and have been infrequently enforced, as evidenced in the Keating Five scandal and the Abramoff scandal. This is troublesome because career-advancing forms of corruption foster the public cynicism that congressional decisions serve the private interests of political elites rather than serving the public's interest.

In 1964, the Senate created the Senate Select Committee on Ethics to establish and enforce ethical standards in the Senate. Three years later, the House crafted the Committee on Standards of Official Conduct, which in 2012 was renamed the Committee on Ethics to do the same. These committees have tortured histories because of the awkwardness created by asking members to investigate the behavior of working colleagues and/or personal friends. In Federalist Paper No. 10, James Madison stated that "no man is allowed to be a judge in his own case, because his interest would certainly bias his judgment, and, not improbably, corrupt his integrity. With equal, nay with greater reason, a body of men are unfit to be both judge and parties at the same time."

It is for these reasons that Congress was wise to enact the Honest Leadership and Open Government Act of 2007 and to create the Office of Congressional Ethics in 2008. While Congress still suffers from low public approval ratings, there is reason for optimism that ethical reforms can help elevate public trust in our legislative branch.

References

Babcock, Charles R. (2005, Nov. 3). "Contractor Linked to Bribery Case Worked Together." *The Washington Post*: A-2.

Birnbaum, Jeffrey H. (2006, March 30). "Senate Passes Lobbying Bill." *The Washington Post*: A01.

Blanes, Vidal, Mirko Jordi Draca, and Christian Fons-Rosen. (2012). "Revolving Door Lobbyists." American Economic Review, 102 (7): 3731-48.

Cain, Bruce, John Ferejohn, and Morris Fiorina. (1987). *The Personal Vote: Constituent Service and Electoral Independence*. Cambridge, MA: Harvard University Press.

Calbreath, Dean, and Jerry Kammer. (2005, Dec. 4). "Contractor Knew How to Grease Wheels." *San Diego Union Tribune*. ego.com/news/politics/Cunningham/20051204-9999-1n4adcs.html.

Christian Science Monitor Editorial. (2006). "House GOP and the Favor Factory." Accessed July 31, 2013. http://www.nybooks.com/articles/19092.

CNN Politics Fund. Accessed July 31, 2013. http://articles.cnn.com/2012-04-17/politics /politics_congress-earmarks-report_1_earmarks-congressional-pigs-book-citizens-against-government-waste?-s=pm:politics.

Common Cause. (2012). "Ethics in Government." Accessed July 31, 2013. http://www .commoncause.org/site/pp.asp?c=biIOIZNJKjK0F&b=8217569.

Congressional Quarterly. (1992). *Congressional Ethics: History, Facts, and Controversy*. Washington, DC: Congressional Quarterly.

Continetti, Matthew. (2005). "Money, Mobsters, Murder: The Sordid Tale of a GOP Lobbyist's Casino Deal Gone Bad." *The Weekly Standard* 11, no. 11. Accessed July 31, 2013. http://www.weeklystandard.com/Content/Public/Srticles/000/000/006/37cyikk.asp.

DeLeon, Peter. (1993). *Thinking about Political Corruption*. Armonk, NY: M.E. Sharpe.

Drew Elizabeth. (2006, Feb. 1). "House GOP and the Favor Factory." *Christian Science Monitor*. Accessed July 31, 2013. http://www.csmonitor.com/2006/0201/p08s01-comv .html?s=widep.

Elving, Ronald D. (1991, March 2). "Senators Cleared by Panel Await Political Judgment." *Congressional Quarterly Weekly Report*.

Gallup Poll. (2012, Aug. 14). Accessed July 31, 2013. www.gallup.com/poll/156662 /Congress-Approval-Ties-Time-Low.aspx.

Green, Gary S. (1997). *Occupational Crime*. Chicago: Nelson-Hall Publishing.

Grimaldi, James, and Susan Schmidt. (2005, Oct. 18). "Lawmakers Abramoff Ties Investigated." *The Washington Post*: 1.

Hearn, Josephine. (2004). "Rep Ney Says He Was Duped by Abramoff." *The Hill*. Accessed July 31, 2013. http://thehill.com/leading-the-news/rep.ney-says-he-was-duped-by-Abramoff-2004-11-18.html.

Herrick, Rebekah. (2003). *Fashioning the More Ethical Representative: The Impact of Ethics Reforms in the U.S. House of Representatives*. Westport, CT: Praeger Publishers.

Knott, Alex. (2005). *Industry of Influence Nets More Than $10 Billion*. Special Report. Center for Public Integrity. Accessed July 31, 2013. http://www.public integrity.org/lobby /report.aspx?aid+675.

Knowlton, Brian. (2006, Jan. 11). "Lobbyist Scandal Has a K Street Home." *International Herald Tribune*: 1.

Kornblutt, Anne E., and Glen Justice. (2006, Jan. 8). "Officials Focus on a 2nd Firm Tied to DeLay." *The New York Times:* 1.

Kuntz, Phil. (1991, Nov. 23). "Cranston Case Ends on Floor with a Murky Plea Bargain." *Congressional Quarterly Weekly Report.*

Levey, Noam N. (2007, Jan. 4). "Bush, Democrats Joust over Earmarks." *Los Angeles Times:* 1.

Lowry, Rich. (2006). "Indian Givers: The Tribal Casino Scandal." National Review Online. Accessed July 31, 2013. http://www.nationalreview.com/articles/216504/indian-givers /rich-lowry.

Mann, Thomas E., and Norman J. Ornstein. (2006). *The Broken Branch: How Congress Is Failing America and How to Get it Back on Track.* New York. Oxford University Press.

Muller, Bill. (1999, Oct. 3). "The Keating Five." *The Arizona Republic:* 1.

New York Times Editorial. (2012, Sept. 21). "Congress's Unpopular Watchdog." *New York Times.* http://www.nytimes.com/2012/09/22/opinion/congress-unpopular-watchdog. html.

Ney, Robert. (2000). "Comments Inserted in the Congressional Record." *Congressional Record: Proceeding and Debates of the 106th Congress* 146, no. 53.

Noonan, John T. (1984). *Bribes.* New York: Macmillan Publishing Company.

Office of Congressional Ethics Webpage. Accessed July 31, 2013. http://oce.house .gov/2011/12/december-20-2011---oce-referral-regarding-rep-waters.html.

Public Citizen. (2005). "Members of Congress Increasingly Use Revolving Door to Launch Lucrative Lobbying Careers." Accessed July 31, 2013. http://www.citizen.org/pressroom /release/.cfm?ID=1999.

Schmidt, Susan. (2005, March 13). "Casino Bid Prompted High Stakes Lobbying." *The Washington Post:* 1.

Smith, Jeffrey R., and Susan Schmidt. (2005, Sept. 20). "Bush Official Arrested in Corruption Probe." *The Washington Post:* 1.

Stearns, Matthew. (2004). "Departing Lawmakers Cash in Years of Service for Big Bucks." Accessed July 31, 2013. http://www.commondreams.org/headlines04/1222-01.htm.

Straus, Jacob R. (2008). Honest Leadership and Open Government Act of 2007: The Role of the Clerk of the House and Secretary of the Senate. Congressional Research Service. Order Code RL34377.

Straus, Jacob R. (2011, Jan. 26). "House Office of Congressional Ethics: History, Authority, and Procedures." *Congressional Research Service.* R40760, p.20.

Tennebaum, Jeffrey S. (1999). "Lobbying Disclosure Act of 1995: A Summary and Overview for Associations." Accessed July 31, 2013. http://www.venable.com/publications .cfm?action=view&publication_id=478&publication_type_id=2.

Thompson, Dennis F. (1993). "Mediated Corruption: The Case of the Keating Five." *American Political Science Review* 87, no. 2: 369–381.

Thompson, Dennis F. (1995). *Ethics in Congress: From Individual to Institutional Corruption.* Washington, DC: Brookings Institution.

Tolchin, Susan J., and Martin Tolchin. (2001). *Glass Houses: Congressional Ethics and the Politics of Venom.* Boulder, CO: Westview Press.

Warren, Mark E. (2004). "What Does Corruption Mean in a Democracy?" *American Journal of Political Science* 48, no. 2: 328–43.

40731

REF
324
DIR

Dirty deals? : an
encyclopedia of
lobbying, political
influence, and

$317.57